GIN,
JESUS,
AND
JIM CROW

MAKING THE MODERN SOUTH

David Goldfield, Series Editor

Gin, Jesus, & Jim Crow

Prohibition and
the Transformation
of Racial and
Religious Politics
in the South

Brendan J. J. Payne

LOUISIANA STATE
UNIVERSITY PRESS
BATON ROUGE

Published by Louisiana State University Press
lsupress.org

DESIGNER: Andrew Shurtz
TYPEFACES: Benton Modern, Sorbonne

Portions of chapters 1, 2, and 3 first appeared in "Defending Black
Suffrage: Poll Taxes, Preachers, and Anti-Prohibition in Texas,
1887–1916," *Journal of Southern History* 83 (Nov. 2017): 815–52.
Portions of chapter 5 first appeared in "Southern White Protestant
Men, Church-State Relations, and Prohibition in Texas, 1865–1920,"
Social History of Alcohol and Drugs 29 (Winter 2015): 92–111.

Cataloging-in-Publication Data are available
from the Library of Congress.

ISBN 978-0-8071-7148-6 (cloth: alk. paper) |
ISBN 978-0-8071-7770-9 (pdf) |
ISBN 978-0-8071-7769-3 (epub)

To all who endured
in the prohibition struggle
unequal treatment under law,
the denial of civil rights,
and the loss of liberty;
and
to all who persisted
in the righteous struggle
for social justice, civil rights,
and true Christian liberty
in an imperfect world.

Contents

Preface

WHEN WRITING ON ANY TOPIC, a brief explanation of the author's personal background relevant to the subject is a courtesy to the curious or suspicious reader. As this book primarily concerns race, prohibition, and religion, I will address each in turn.

First, regarding race: my ancestors hailed from Sweden, Germany, France, and Britain. Simply put, I am "white." Too often, white scholars like me have—intentionally or accidentally—neglected voices of people of color in the historical record and so have given a less than accurate impression of the past. Part of the solution is welcoming more scholars of color, who tend to ask questions that are essential to correcting historical narratives. Along many others, I applaud the expanding body of scholarship of people of color throughout the academy and bemoan the inequalities that still exist in higher education, particularly in the lack of diversity of full professorships and other leadership positions. I also see it as my duty to produce anti-racist scholarship, to correct the inaccuracies of our understandings of the past, and to recognize that Black lives matter in the past just as much as in the present.

Second, on prohibition: this book covers prohibitionist "drys" and anti-prohibition "wets," and I must confess personal sympathy for the wets. That said, I refrain from imbibing alcohol for several reasons. The Baptist institution in South Carolina where I teach has a rule against employees drinking. Also, abstaining is good for my health, my wallet, and friends who struggle with alcohol addiction. My "dry-wet" background gives me some sympathy for drys as well. I have also come to recognize the historic evils of the alcohol industry, from political corruption to social harm, and to realize that drys of all races were sincerely attempting to reform society by combating genuine threats to a healthy society. That said, this book does not pull any punches about the racial prejudices of white prohibitionists, particularly in the US South. While I do not intend to dismiss southern white drys' genuine concerns about alcohol or to reduce them to mere racism, the intimate connection between prohibition and Jim Crow demands greater scholarly attention. Accordingly, this book centers on that ominous aspect of prohibition in the South, not on drys' often-legitimate fears about the alcohol traffic, which many scholars have written about for decades.[1]

Finally, regarding religion: I was raised by white evangelical parents and have since attended an array of Christian churches—mainline Presbyterian, independent Reformed, African Methodist Episcopal—before settling into the Anglican tradition. As such, I consider myself an "insider" to Christianity and personally appreciate the profound impact that religion in many forms can have on people's lives, for better and for worse. While other religious voices on prohibition also existed in the time and place covered—particularly Jewish, Muslim, and Native American—this book focuses on Christianity because of its predominance among Black and white southerners of the time, and because every book must admit its limits.[2]

Acknowledgments

IT IS MEET AND RIGHT to give thanks to all who made this book possible. To personally acknowledge all who have supported me in this endeavor would exceed limitations of space and time, but it is my joy to thank a few of them by name.

Pride of place goes to my mentors. Barry Hankins oversaw an early version of the manuscript and first drew my attention to Baylor's history PhD program with his delightful book *Jesus and Gin*, which also inspired this book's title (along with Kristin Kobes Du Mez's *Jesus and John Wayne*). Garth Rosell first inspired me to seek a doctorate in history and prompted me to study prohibition and religion through an independent study. Along with Garth, thanks also to Gwenfair Adams and David Hempton, whose letters of recommendation got me into Baylor's PhD program.

Studying at Baylor was a privilege and a delight that laid the foundation for this work. Work on a research paper for Kim Kellison's class on the US South in 2012 focused my doctoral research. Many other professors there, including Beth Allison Barr, David Gawrych, Barry Hankins, Philip Jenkins, Thomas Kidd, Michael Parrish, James SoRelle, Joan Supplee, Joe Stubenrauch, Julie Sweet, and Andrea Turpin, also broadened my perspective and took a genuine interest in my welfare not only as a scholar, but as a person. My fellow graduate students, including but not limited to Scott Anderson, Prisca Bird, Ryan Butler, Alyssa Gerhardt Craven, Tim Grundmeier, Paul Gutacker, Jacob Heiserman, Joel Illif, Adina and Sam Kelley, Elise Leal, Ben Leavitt, Matt Millsap, Jonathan Riddle, Nick Pruitt, Paul Putz, Lynneth Miller Renberg, David Roach, and Brady Winslow, shared with me an even deeper sense of comradery, along with countless sources, insights, and evenings that immeasurably enriched my research and my time in Waco, Texas. Sic 'em Bears!

Colleagues at my current academic home, North Greenville University, have been an inspiration and encouragement to me in this project, particularly my dean, H. Paul Thompson, whose interest in our shared niche field of race, religion, and prohibition led to a job and a close friendship. Professors Feliccia Smith and Paul Yandle, along with other faculty and many students, remind me by word and deed that scholarship must always be in the pursuit of justice. Thanks to student workers Leslie Meyers and Micah Stevens, who helped with research and editing.

The research for this book would not have been possible without financial and archival support. Baylor University's Graduate School and History Department not only covered the costs of my tuition but also aided travel for research and academic conferences. Baylor's Presidential Scholarship and Guittard Fellowship further helped me focus on my studies. The Danforth Center for Religion and Politics at Washington University in St. Louis funded my trip to their 2014 Beyond the Culture Wars Conference, whose participants offered valuable feedback on my then-nascent research. Thanks to numerous people at Baylor University's Texas Collection for the Burney Parker Research Fellowship and at Southern Methodist University's Bridwell Library for the Visiting Scholar Fellowship and Scholar in Residence accommodations, which greatly enriched my research. The Southern Baptist Historical Library and Archives made possible my research in Nashville with their Lynn E. May Jr. Study Grant, and their staff were also exceedingly helpful, particularly thendirector Bill Sumners and current director and archivist Taffey Hall. Thanks to Johnana Clark, Shirley Bowie, and Luther Oelke at the Region 4–South Archives of the Evangelical Lutheran Church of America in Seguin, Texas. Particularly during the 2020 pandemic, the Chronicling America newspaper archives sponsored by the Library of Congress and the National Endowment for the Humanities were invaluable. Other online sources such as the Hathi Trust and Archive.org were likewise helpful throughout the process to examine countless digitized sources at leisure. My gratitude goes to all those librarians and archivists whose names I have forgotten yet whose aid led to wonderful discoveries.

This book owes much to feedback I received when presenting portions of it at conferences and in journals. Discussions on several panels at the American Society of Church History, the Alcohol and Drugs Historical Society, and the Conference on Faith and History pushed me to develop these ideas further. Some key findings in this book were presented for the first time in an article in the *Journal of Southern History* in November 2017, which likewise helped me rethink and restructure my argument. Michael Parrish, one of my professors at Baylor, gave invaluable help with getting this work published. Thank you.

Faith and family powered me through this project. In traditional Christian fashion, I thank God—Father, Son, and Holy Spirit—for giving me insight, stamina, and energy to complete this work and for reminding me that even within Divinity there is diverse community, which has inspired me to seek out a plurality of perspectives in my research and to heed marginalized voices. I thank my parents, Nancy and Philip, who taught me that there need be no contradiction between strong faith, sound scholarship, and self-giving love. And who else but Catherine—best of wives and best of women—could be such an unstinting supporter, faithful friend, and exacting editor, all while managing an editing business and writing fantasy novels. Her input has improved the manuscript and my life in countless ways.

Finally, a disclaimer. The views presented in this book may not represent the views of everyone who contributed to this project, including my place of employment. Many have enriched this text with their conversations, suggestions, and insights. What faults remain are fully mine.

GIN,
JESUS,
AND
JIM CROW

Introduction

ON JULY 9, 1912, a Baptist minister wrote a letter in which he rebuked the Texas Brewers Association. In that era, pastors often denounced the alcohol traffic for spawning crime, economic waste, political corruption, women's degradation, moral degeneration, and countless ailments. Brewers were, in a word, evil. For decades before and after that 1912 letter, the United States endured a culture war over prohibition—the legal ban on the manufacture, transportation, and sale of alcohol. The drama played out in churches, legislatures, courthouses, alleyways, prisons, and voting booths. Prohibitionist "drys" battled anti-prohibition "wets," legitimized political preaching, and, from January 1920 to December 1933, banned the alcohol traffic throughout the United States. The nation's most powerful dry organization, the Anti-Saloon League (ASL), was organized by a Congregational minister and used the motto: "The Church in Action Against the Saloon." God, it seemed, was on the side of the drys.

But that July 1912 letter told a very different story. For one thing, its author was John B. Rayner, a political organizer who had been the most famous African American in the Populist Party. For another, he did not object to the brewers' business. Indeed, he had spent much of the past seven years campaigning against prohibition. He just wanted to be paid.

The payment he demanded was not unearned or unreasonable; it was back pay for his invaluable political services over the past seven years that had helped keep the brewers' business legal. Rayner claimed to have tipped the balance in twenty "local option" contests—votes to ban or legalize alcohol in towns, cities, or counties—and mobilized thousands of Black farmers, whose votes had averted statewide prohibition in 1911. In an earlier letter, he claimed to have mobilized tens of thousands of Black voters. He used "Machiavellian diplomacy" in African American "religious, educational and business gatherings," employing know-how from his days as a Populist Party boss. In short, he was a "protagonist" against prohibition who did more for anti-prohibition "than all the other [African Americans] combined." Rayner claimed not to have profited personally from this but rather sold or mortgaged his best properties for the cause, while brewers prospered.[1]

What would compel a Christian minister to endure such suffering for an industry so disreputable that most Protestant churches advocated its abolition? Rayner claimed that he did it because "the liberty of man is in danger."[2] For many believers, then as now, Christian liberty meant more than abstract forgiveness of sins and hope for the hereafter; it meant freedom in the here and now. Christian wets used the language of Christian liberty to preach against prohibition, and this took on a special significance in the Black church. At that time, African Americans were losing civil liberties far more pressing than the freedom to drink. Under Jim Crow, millions of Black Americans across the South lost their right to vote. Restrictive voting laws such as poll taxes had virtually eliminated African American influence over statewide elected office in the region by 1902. Nonetheless, many Black citizens across the South could still vote—if they could afford poll taxes. African Americans whose faith compelled them to vote found supporters in the alcohol lobby: a wealthy, white-owned industry willing to do anything to secure votes. It seemed a match made in heaven.

This is not just a story of John Rayner or of African American Christians working with brewers. It is not even just a history of anti-prohibition in the South. Rather, this book offers a religious and racial history of prohibition's rise and fall in the US South from 1885 to 1935. Race (particularly white and Black) and religion (particularly Christianity) are two areas in which prohibition wrought profound changes to the cultural landscape of the South and the whole nation. While some aspects of the connections between prohibition, race, and religion have received scholarly attention, other aspects have remained understudied. The book gives as much distinct emphasis to prohibition's relationship to Christianity as to its relationship to race, and it focuses as much on the anti-prohibition movement as on prohibitionists.

Approach and Sources

While the book moves between emphases on race and religion for the sake of analytical clarity, it sees the two as parts of a seamless cultural whole. As Kristin Kobes Du Mez argues in *Jesus and John Wayne*, a supposedly theological category such as "'conservative evangelical' is as much about culture as it is about theology"—and the culture she focuses on concerns constructions of gender, politics, and race.[3] While Du Mez's book focuses on white evangelicals since 1945, her statement also resonates with "lived religion" approaches to ethno-religious communities from New England Puritans to present-day charismatics.[4] Viewing prohibition through the twin lenses of race and religion enables in-depth attention to how stray strands of theology and minority figures ordinarily overlooked in prohibition studies might cast the overall picture in a new light.

This study arrives at these findings by heeding quieter or unheard voices and by noting absences of language just as much as their presence. African American and more traditionalist churches have received less attention on prohibition (and other culture-war issues) than white evangelicals, yet some searching reveals that the former groups played major roles in the contest. Though most wets did not scream their religious credentials as loudly as most drys did, close analysis of theological and ritual details reveals convictions that informed the wet stance of millions of southern voters. Indeed, the toning down of religious and racial rhetoric in the 1930s was itself a major development in the prohibition debate, signaling a significant break from past activism. Approaching religious practice as always potentially interacting with politics and cultural issues such as race, even when religious rhetoric is not obviously linked to activism, helps uncover the subtle—and therefore understudied—connections between faith and politics.[5]

This study employs a wide array of primary sources, including election data, secular and religious newspapers, denominational minutes, speeches, correspondence, and contemporary publications. Archives from Texas to Tennessee and abundant digitized sources were invaluable for this research. It is unfortunate that, even in the best archives, African American denominational sources are generally less complete than comparable white sources, but enough sources have survived to give a decent impression of the debates over prohibition in Black churches. Speeches from white evangelical wets and surviving correspondence from brewers (thanks to the vigorous investigations of Texas's attorney general, B. F. Looney) provided priceless insights as well. This book's main contribution, however, is not so much uncovering new sources as viewing widely available evidence through the twin lenses of religion and race. In both areas, prohibition and anti-prohibition reshaped the order of southern society and politics.

(Anti-)Prohibition and Race

Viewing prohibition through the lens of race clarifies larger political trends in the South, particularly around the term "Gin Crow." Gin Crow is peculiar phrase which, as far as this author knows, is unique to this book, and it asserts that prohibition in the US South was closely linked to Jim Crow, an array of measures that aimed to secure white supremacy through racial segregation and the suppression of Black votes. The links between prohibition and Jim Crow that constitute Gin Crow can be divided into four broad categories: chronology, white dry support, Black resistance, and racial enforcement. First, chronologically, statewide prohibition existed in the South only during Jim Crow (except in Mississippi, which remained nominally dry into the 1960s).

Second, white drys transitioned their tactics from openly seeking interracial coalitions in the 1880s to seeking victory through suppressing Black votes and converting white votes. White drys believed it was the only reliable path to prohibition in the region. As Ann-Marie Szymanski observed, "disfranchisement of blacks principally enhanced the opportunities for dry success by eliminating one of the leading rationales for Democratic unity in the South": namely, white-only control of political power.[6] Howard Rabinowitz and Richard Hamm likewise contend that African Americans' tendency to vote against prohibition, especially in close elections, was a major argument for their disfranchisement, which in turn helped prohibition succeed in the South.[7] Some of the most prominent drys in the South—including "Father of American Prohibition" Richmond Pearson Hobson, prohibition "martyr" Edward Ward Carmack, Methodist Bishop James Cannon, and Ku Klux Klan Grand Wizard Hiram Wesley Evans—were also notorious white supremacists who deployed racist rhetoric to advance their dry cause. In short, white drys supported Jim Crow, which in turn enabled prohibition's success.

Discussions of race, religion, and alcohol in the South cannot be separated from discussions of gender. As Joe Coker argues, racial hierarchy, honor, and gender roles were essential components in prohibition's rise in the South.[8] One obvious example of those three value sets coming together for prohibition was the specter of a drunken Black man attacking a white woman. This racist trope, the worn excuse for lynchings and all manner of white-supremacist violence, was also a piece of white dry propaganda in the South. If alcohol in the hands of Black men symbolized a vital threat to the racial and gendered order, then abolishing that threat by law became an imperative. In fact, some drys urged prohibition so that lynchings could be avoided: without demon rum, docility would replace danger, and all would be well. The exaggerated fear of disorderly Black men assaulting white women loomed large in the imagination of honor-bound white southerners and played no small role in prohibition's rise in the region. By their rhetoric and actions, prominent white drys advanced and upheld the racial hierarchy of Jim Crow.

Third, due to this dynamic, African American participation in local and statewide prohibition elections in the 1900s and 1910s effectively became a form of resistance to Jim Crow. Though Jim Crow laws depressed Black voter turnout immediately, thousands of African Americans continued to decide prohibition elections at the local and state levels into the 1910s in defiance of laws that attempted to erase their political influence. Admittedly, Black resistance to Gin Crow was circumscribed. Jim Crow laws had disfranchised most—though not all—African Americans by the first decade of the twentieth century, and white Democrats exercised a stranglehold on statewide offices and state legislatures throughout the region. African American voters responded by overwhelmingly backing the brewers, who were desperate enough to do anything, even undermining Jim Crow, to stay in business. White supremacists in the wet coalition unwittingly helped to prop up interracial politics by protecting the alcohol lobby, which was the most powerful white industry to mobilize Black voters and to subvert Jim Crow poll taxes. To oppose Gin Crow (southern prohibition) in the 1910s was to oppose Jim Crow, and that opposition was stronger and went longer than scholars have previously thought possible.[9]

Scholars have not realized how much Black votes mattered in prohibition contests in the 1910s. African Americans decided countless local option elections and even several statewide elections across the South as late as 1910 (Florida), 1911 (Texas), and 1912 (Arkansas). Sociologist Ann-Marie Szymanski claims that African Americans' impact on prohibition elections in the South is difficult to verify, since drys lost those statewide referenda "despite the diminished voting power of southern blacks."[10] However, that same evidence could also suggest that wets won in those states precisely because African Americans continued to vote despite restrictive voting laws. Wets won those election precisely because of Black voters, not despite their absence.

Perhaps scholars have overlooked African American voters of the 1910s because prohibition had so thoroughly devastated Black voting by 1920. Just as disfranchising Black voters helped dry up the South, so also the imposition of prohibition, by removing the political protection of the alcohol lobby, finally silenced mass Black voting across the South. Statewide prohibition across the South in the mid-to-late 1910s accomplished what Jim Crow laws on their own failed to do: end meaningful and mass voting for Black southerners.

Fourth, during prohibition's regime, racial minorities were disproportionately arrested and punished for violations of drug laws. White drys were concerned not only with containing Black votes but also with controlling Black bodies. Aaron Griffith has observed that, "Throughout the nation's history, race has been a crucial backdrop for American thinking and policymaking on criminal justice," and this is no less true on prohibition enforcement.[11] As Michelle Alexander has demonstrated, mass incarceration has been and continues to be one of the major drivers of systemic racial inequality. Lisa McGirr likewise argues that, just as racial minorities face higher arrest rates, higher conviction rates, and more time served than whites in the latter-day War on Drugs, so it was a century ago in the War on Alcohol. Then as now, unequal enforcement of drug laws provided a useful tool for whites to control Black souls. If opposition to the War on Drugs today constitutes opposition to the "New Jim Crow," opposition to prohibition then constituted opposition to the old Jim Crow.[12]

In short, prohibition's timing, implementation, resistance, and enforcement made it an integral part of Jim Crow, such that those who resisted prohibition in the South were effectively defying Gin Crow, whether or not they did so intentionally. Even when white wet Christians did not explicitly oppose Jim Crow, their anti-prohibition activism in the 1900s and 1910s effectively prolonged African American suffrage and thus delayed complete racial disfranchisement in the region.

The racial story of Gin Crow does not stop in 1920, however, but continued until its repeal in the 1930s. As Barry Hankins correctly notes, African Americans "played almost no part" in prohibition contests in the 1920s because they "were not allowed to participate" in what had become a "white culture war."[13] However, white drys continued to invoke racial fears against the wet presidential candidate in 1928, once again linking Gin Crow to white supremacism. Then in 1932, white southerners worried less about the Democratic presidential nominee's wet stance than white unity, especially after the Republican White House had transgressed white southern racial and gender lines by treating an African American congressman's wife as an equal to white women. The relative absence of racial language during the repeal debates of the 1930s compared with the prohibition debates of the 1910s demonstrates how much prohibition had affected and been affected by racial politics in the South over just a few years.

The rise of white women in southern politics from the 1910s to the 1930s corresponded to the political decline of African Americans. The language of cleaning up politics though prohibition and (white) women's suffrage together took on explicitly racial dimensions in the South. Particularly after drys suffered narrow losses in statewide elections across the South in the 1910s, white drys increasingly complained that Black (and in Texas, Mexican) men could vote against prohibition while white women could not vote for it. The wet coalition in the 1930s South had virtually no African Americans, but it grew to include prominent white women, including state legislators and a governor. The move of respectable white women into wet ranks signaled another shift: women's support gave wets the moral high ground previously held by drys, in part because white women did not feel they needed prohibition anymore to protect them from Black men. While Jim Crow remained for decades more, Gin Crow died in part because it was no longer needed to maintain the racial order.

(Anti-)Prohibition and Christianity

Prohibition also reshaped southern Christianity in four major ways. First, before dry agitation gained supremacy in the early twentieth century, most southerners stood with millennia of Christian tradition, which had blessed moderate consumption of fermented drinks at home and in the sacred act of communion. Many Christian southerners loudly objected to prohibition as an alien innovation in theology and polity. To justify their political reform, drys first reshaped communion, denominations, and Bible interpretation to fit with their common-sense objections to alcohol, then deployed a combination of righteous indignation, racial invective, and modern organization to implement their political vision. Many scholars have noted that prohibition was politically progressive, but few have observed how deeply it transgressed the theological orthodoxies of the South.[14] The political revolution of prohibition was necessarily preceded by a religious one.

Second, religion played a major role on both sides in the culture war before prohibition's zenith, and this book pays particular attention to the neglected role of Christian rhetoric for wets. Joseph Locke and other scholars have noted how drys mainstreamed political preaching in the South and so created the Bible Belt, but none have paid comparable attention to how wets also deployed boldly religious rhetoric.[15] The contest over prohibition in the South included multiple Christian identities and theologies competing for social dominance. Christian wets ranged from Episcopalian bishops and Catholic priests to Black Baptist ministers and lay white Southern Methodists. Some wets claimed that prohibition was irreconcilable with traditional Christian teachings on morality, liberty, moderate alcohol use, and communion wine. Before drys could argue against alcohol in general, they had to abolish ritual communion wine in their churches, demonstrating how their political views led them to dispense with or modernize ancient Christian rites. Even some white evangelicals, usually lay politicians, objected to prohibition on carefully reasoned Christian tradition and the Bible, revealing a divide between pulpit and pew even in supposedly bone-dry denominations. The South's religious-political scene, at least before 1920, was rich in complexity. A South that largely condemned dry ministers' political preaching in the 1880s had by the 1920s embraced it, and prohibition had opened the door to Christianity playing explicitly on *both* sides of culture wars. As some drys wryly noted, wets may have objected to political preaching when drys did it, but they did not mind political preaching when it was on *their* side.[16]

Third, the prohibition movement in the South started off as somewhat religiously ecumenical but ended up fueling anti-Catholic bigotry. While some northern Republicans labeled Democrats the party of "rum, Romanism, and rebellion" in 1884, southern drys from the 1880s to the 1910s attempted to win over Catholics, and a few prominent Catholics such as Archbishop John Ireland supported prohibition. When prohibition became the law in the late 1910s, however, the religious calculus shifted. The only US governor ever elected under the Prohibition Party banner, Sidney Johnston Catts of Florida, rode into office in 1917 on a wave of anti-Catholic bigotry. The second iteration of the Ku Klux Klan embodied racial and religious prejudice in the 1910s and 1920s, and as Lisa McGirr has noted, prohibition "enabled the Klan's rise to power."[17] The presidential election of 1928 raised anti-Catholicism to a fever pitch as the Democratic nominee, Al Smith, was a wet Catholic. Prominent southern Protestants from the progressive Southern Methodist James Cannon in Virginia to the Fundamentalist Baptist J. Frank Norris in Texas led an insurrection against the Democratic Party's nominee and shattered the "Solid South" with a seamless blend of dry and anti-Catholic rhetoric.

Fourth, the effort to repeal prohibition in the South in the 1930s signaled a retreat from the vigorous political preaching of the 1910s and 1920s toward more secular rhetoric. Just as racial language cooled from the election of 1928, so also did stridently religious language, or at least such language was mostly on the losing side. The election of 1928 had bitterly divided the South's solidly Democratic white electorate with political preaching, yet the elections of 1930 and 1932 reunified white Protestant Democrats and punished politicians who had strayed from the party fold. The Democratic presidential nominee in 1932 was another wet New Yorker, but this time he was safely Protestant.

Unity around this Protestant candidate ironically weakened the sway of white Baptist and Methodist political preachers who insisted that prohibition was the single issue to unite all Christian voters.

Preachers may have lost political sway in the Great Depression as many sought salvation through the ecumenical New Deal, but women's political clout had never been stronger. Many southern women led the charge for repeal with less distinctively Christian rhetoric than the Woman's Christian Temperance Union (WCTU). While prohibition's marginalization of nonwhites in the South persisted for decades after repeal, some non-Protestants, particularly white Catholics, politically rose in the region after the nadir of 1928, with some Catholic women serving prominent roles in repeal organizations.

Some scholars have interpreted the repeal of prohibition as the death knell for white Protestant cultural ascendency in the United States, yet in the South it was more of a tactical retreat that foreshadowed a later return.[18] By pushing the religious narrative past the usual cutoff date of 1920, when prohibition seemed victorious, this trend becomes clear. While political preaching by clergy and laity alike would rise again in the South, ranging from anti–New Deal conservative evangelicals to African Americans in the civil rights movement, its moment would have to wait.[19]

Organization

The book proceeds more or less chronologically. Each chapter touches on both race and religion, though some focus more on one or the other. Part I, "Bourbon Rule," considers the difficulty of prohibition taking root in the South in the nineteenth century. Most southerners, white and Black alike, embraced a moderate stance on alcohol based on traditional Christian theology and practice, from interpretations of Bible passages to communion wine, so drys were fighting against the cultural and religious current. Chapter 2 explores the interracial politics of prohibition campaigns of the 1880s in North Carolina, Georgia, Tennessee, and Texas. While white fears and Black doubts undermined attempts at multiracial dry coalitions, the fact that such attempts occurred at all demonstrates the fluidity of race relations in the pre–Jim Crow period.

Part 2, "Gin Crow," considers the rise and fall of statewide and federal prohibition in the region in light of race and religion. Southern white backlash to the apparent failure of interracial politics in the 1880s—along with reaction to the multiracial populist movement—led white drys to favor Jim Crow laws and suppress Black votes. Prohibition in the South, which had once been associated with multiracial coalitions, became intertwined with white-supremacist laws and law enforcement.

Yet many Black and white Christians resisted this new dry order in the 1900s and 1910s. Clergy and laity alike deployed traditional Christian arguments about temperance, the Bible, and liberty against prohibition. African Americans, using networks that included Black churches, allied with brewers to speak out, organize, and cast decisive votes against local option and statewide prohibition referenda from one end of the South to the other. After prohibition triumphed on the state and national levels, enforcement of prohibition disproportionately targeted racial and ethnic minorities, legitimated political preaching by white culture warriors, and emboldened white-supremacist and anti-Catholic politics from the second Ku Klux Klan to the anti–Al Smith movement in 1928.

The final chapter details how the repeal of prohibition in the South was "lily-white": white women played decisive roles in repeal, but African Americans were not empowered by the demise of Gin Crow in the 1930s as they had been by resistance to its rise in the 1910s. Also, the repeal effort appealed far less explicitly to race or religion than either wets or drys had in the days before statewide and federal prohibition, indicating broader ebbs and flows in the region's relationship between race, religion, and politics. A brief epilogue sketches subsequent development in alcohol regulation, religiously infused politics, and the re-empowerment of racial and religious minorities across the South.

Terms

More clarification of terms is in order. Prohibition is distinct from yet produced by the temperance movement founded in the 1820s. Some temperance advocates avoided only distilled drinks and used lighter fermented drinks, while others believed only capital-T Total abstinence from alcohol (teetotalism) would do. Another divide formed between those who focused on moral suasion and those who promoted legal bans on alcohol (prohibition). Though prohibitionists often conflated their cause with "temperance," others also clung to that title. Some historians use capitalized "Prohibition" to refer to federal prohibition through the Eighteenth Amendment, enforced from 1920 to 1933. Since state and local prohibition laws existed long before and—especially in the South—long after federal prohibition, this book prefers lowercase "prohibition," meaning any law at the local, state, or federal level forbidding the sale of all alcoholic beverages with few exceptions (such as medical and sacramental purposes).

A related issue is how to label those for and against prohibition. From the nineteenth century to the 1910s, anti-prohibitionists were often called "antis" and prohibitionists "prohis," though by the 1920s they were usually labeled "dry" and "wet." This text will prefer the simpler and more natural language of "dry" for prohibitionists and "wet" for anti-prohibitionists, while acknowledging its anachronistic nature for earlier chapters.

Like "prohibition," "the South" is a fuzzy term with multiple possible definitions.[20] This book chiefly uses "the South" to refer to the eleven formerly Confederate states: Alabama, Arkansas, Florida, Georgia, Louisiana, Mississippi, North Carolina, South Carolina, Tennessee, Texas, and Virginia. There are several reasons for this. First, this narrative mostly takes place after the Civil War and Reconstruction, which forged a distinctive southern history and identity. However, when briefly referencing the antebellum period, a broader definition of the South is used, including slave states such as Kentucky and Maryland.

Also, the former Confederacy shares a distinctive regional arc for prohibition. After resisting statewide dry laws longer than any other region in the country, statewide prohibition persisted there longer than the rest of the nation. While a few northern states went dry before or in the decades following the Civil War, no formerly Confederate state went dry until Georgia in 1908. Yet by 1918, every formerly Confederate state except Louisiana had banned alcohol on the state level.[21] Having gone dry, the South was more reluctant to get wet again than other regions. When national prohibition was repealed by December 1933, statewide prohibition was still on the books for most southern states for several more years.[22] Mississippi did not end statewide prohibition until the 1960s, decades longer than any other state. Even today, a few locales are still dry in the South. Blue laws limiting any sale of alcohol at certain times persist from Texas to the Carolinas.

Another reason to define the South as the former Confederacy is demographic: this book highlights African Americans, so it makes sense to focus on the states where most of them lived prior to and during the Great Migration. This reality prompts further explanation of racial terms.

Regarding race, this book follows an emerging trend among reporters and scholars to use capitalized "Black" rather than lowercase "black" to refer to Americans of African descent, while continuing the convention of using lowercase "white" for Americans of primarily European descent. Several such vocabular transitions have occurred in the past century, as a survey of scholarly titles over time quickly reveals. "Negro" was a common term until the 1970s, when changing norms replaced the term with "black" and "African American." As the latter terms still have widespread currency, this text uses "Black" (as an adjective) interchangeably with "African American" in the US context. Following similar scholarly developments, the text uses "Amerindian" to refer to indigenous Americans but retains the traditional "Latino" to refer to people of Latin American descent (because that follows standard usage in contemporary Spanish, whereas the now-fashionable "Latinx" is unpronounce-able in Spanish). For all such terms, the author acknowledges that their usage is debated and may well become outdated soon. When quoting others, older spellings and usages are preserved.

To appreciate the extent to which prohibition brought seismic shifts to race and religion in the South, one first must go back to the days of Bourbon rule, when most southerners, Black and white alike, regarded alcohol as a gift of God.

I
Bourbon Rule

THE SOUTH BEFORE PROHIBITION

THE CLASS OF PEOPLE who came to power in the South after Reconstruction until the early twentieth century were commonly called "Bourbons." Their name was a reference to the French and Spanish royal family that had fallen from power decades earlier, indicating their old-fashioned conservatism. The name "Bourbon" also had connections to the Marquis de Lafayette, who was descended from that line, thus linking the American Bourbons to the early independence period and Lafayette's friend Thomas Jefferson. In some states, such as Jefferson's home state of Virginia, the ruling party preferred to call itself "Conservative" rather than "Democrat" for some years after Reconstruction. These Bourbons saw themselves as the defenders of the South's traditions against the radical reforms of Republican Reconstruction. And one of those traditions the Bourbons defended was the production, sale, and consumption of alcoholic beverages, including the native southern drink, bourbon.

First crafted in Virginia (later eastern Kentucky) in the late-eighteenth century, bourbon whiskey is corn-based and aged in charred oak casks, giving it a distinctive taste and reddish color.[1] The drink likely took its name from its birthplace, Virginia's capacious Bourbon County, which was subsequently broken up into over a dozen counties after Kentucky became a state in 1792. Part of that region became Kentucky's Bourbon County, which hosted many

bourbon distilleries as early as 1785, further cementing the connection between the name and the drink. The product grew in quality and popularity
over the years, and the name "bourbon" became widespread by the 1840s to
distinguish it from other forms of whiskey. European distillers and vintners
in 1960 gave American bourbon a special status reserved for other national
beverages such as Scotch whiskey and French cognac. Congress declared
bourbon a "distinctive product of the United States" in 1964 and clarified that,
among other rules, true bourbon must be crafted in the United States. The
Kentucky Bourbon Trail, officially established in 1999, attracts over a million
visitors annually to enjoy this national treasure in its natural habitat.[2]

This happy overlap between the conservative Bourbon Democrats and
the South's distinctive drink did not begin or end with a naming coincidence.
Opposition to alcohol prohibition in the South in the late-nineteenth century
was conservative in every sense of the word because prohibition threatened
the existing social, political, and theological order. Theologically, traditionalist
Christians opposed prohibition for its challenge to older ideas about temperance, the Bible, communion wine, and liberty. Politically and socially, some
prohibitionists proposed radical changes from giving women the right to vote
to promoting potent multiracial political coalitions for statewide elections in
the 1880s, just a few short years after Bourbons had tried to eliminate African
Americans as a force in southern politics. While the South in the early twentieth century would become a dry citadel, in the late-nineteenth century it was,
in every sense, under Bourbon rule.

1
Old-Time Religion
CHRISTIAN TRADITION AGAINST PROHIBITION

WHILE NO HISTORIAN KNOWS for certain the first distiller of bourbon, a leading candidate was a Baptist minister, Elijah Craig.[1] Converted to the Baptist faith in 1764 and ordained in 1771, Craig suffered imprisonment at least twice for preaching against the established church of Virginia. He moved to Kentucky in 1785 or 1786 and gained a reputation as a greater preacher than his brothers Joseph and Lewis, who were also Baptist pioneers there. Elijah's preaching voice was "like the loud sound of a sweet trumpet" that "commonly brought many tears from the hearers" and converted many. He was also an entrepreneur: he built Kentucky's first sawmill, made rope, fulled cloth, and founded a bourbon distillery around 1789. He was known for church controversies and spent most of his money chasing after new business ventures, leaving his family poor when he died in May 1808. Yet the *Kentucky Gazette* eulogized him: "If virtue consists in being useful to our fellow citizens, perhaps there were few more virtuous men than Mr. Craig."[2] At least in the early nineteenth century, distilling bourbon was a mark of virtue for a Baptist minister.

Elijah Craig's story illustrates how some pious southerners in the nineteenth century saw no need to choose between liquor and the Lord. Even strict Baptists tolerated crafting, selling, and drinking high-proof distilled beverages, to say nothing of fermented beverages such as wine and beer with less alcoholic content. Permissive attitudes to intoxicating drinks persisted amid early nineteenth-century revivals, commonly called the Second Great Awakening, and most southerners carried these views with them to the late nineteenth century. This permissive attitude toward alcohol stretched back much further than the colonial era; it continued a millennia-long Judeo-Christian tradition of appreciation for both common and consecrated drinks.

Traditional Christian attitudes towards alcoholic beverages tended to oppose prohibition in four areas. While classical Christian views of temperance meant moderate use, prohibitionists' insistence on total abstinence from alcohol more closely followed Islamic teaching. Passages of the Bible also supported moderate alcohol use, particularly regarding wine. The celebration of Christian communion had always involved sacred wine until the nineteenth-century innovation of grape juice. And early American views on Christian liberty, particularly in the South, emphasized limited government and anticlerical politics.

Church structure mattered in these debates. Top-down Methodists tended to be more united, better organized, and earlier supporters of prohibition than bottom-up Baptists. Theology also mattered. "High church" groups such as Catholics, Episcopalians, and Lutherans tended to defer to traditional readings favoring wine in communion and at home, while relatively "low church" denominations such as Baptists, Methodists, and Presbyterians were more likely to defy ancient tradition and embrace theological novelties such as prohibition.

The American transformation from traditional views on temperance, the Bible, communion, and liberty to the modern innovation of prohibition was facilitated by a remarkable shift in how American Christians derived their spiritual authority from a common-sense, republican, individualist reading of the Bible. As changing circumstances and modern science revealed new threats from alcohol abuse, many American Christians used Scripture to defend a totalistic rejection of alcoholic drinks. They argued for alcohol abstinence on the grounds of experience, expediency, and proper application of general Christian principles, though even some prohibitionists admitted that the Bible did not forbid drinking as such. Other Christians deployed the Bible to defend a more traditional view that alcohol was not evil but was a gift of God.

Christian Temperance

Wets claimed that totalistic opposition to alcohol, whether through teetotalism or prohibition, undermined traditional Christian teaching that moderate use promoted morality better than total abstinence. "Temperance" had throughout Christian history been understood not as abstinence from alcohol but as the moderate use of pleasure. Only in modern times did temperance take on a connection with alcohol. Following Aristotle's notion of finding virtue between two extremes, ancient and medieval theologians developed articulations of Christian virtue that rested between the extreme vices of excess and deficiency. For such theologians and philosophers, temperance lay between the excess of self-indulgence, which was common and dangerous, and the deficiency of shunning pleasure, which was so rare in Aristotle's time that he invented a name for it: "insensibility." The great medieval Catholic theologian Thomas Aquinas explicitly tackled the issue of whether shunning pleasure could be considered a vice and concluded that abstinence could be praiseworthy or necessary in certain circumstances for the sake of physical or spiritual health, but even so pleasure ought not to be shunned altogether.[3] Translating the virtue to alcohol use, self-indulgence meant drunkenness, insensibility meant abstinence, and temperance meant moderate drinking.

Given this long-standing understanding of temperance, prohibition would have seemed absurd to Americans before the nineteenth century. Even the exacting Pilgrims and Puritans of seventeenth-century New England had no problem with fermented spirits; the Mayflower was well-stocked with them. The Puritan Francis Higginson sailed for Massachusetts Bay in 1629 with forty-five casks of beer and twenty gallons of brandy for his Puritan relatives and community, and Jonathan Edwards's father enjoyed an ordination party in 1698 provisioned with four quarts of rum and eight quarts of wine. Increase Mather preached that "wine is from God" but "the drunkard is from the Devil." Historian Mark Noll notes that some scholars think Increase's son Cotton Mather coined the phrase, but if so, he was echoing Increase's words from 1673: "Drink is in itself a creature from God, and to be received with thankfulness."[4] Early Americans followed classical Christian theology to argue that alcoholic beverages were God-given, so insisting upon complete abstinence was not virtue but vice.

If early Puritans in colonial New England could and did distinguish alcohol's good and evil uses, the denizens of the US South had even fewer qualms about alcohol. Even by the accounts of Ernest Cherrington, a prolific researcher for the Anti-Saloon League, colonial Americans had "no condemnation of intoxicating liquors as such," and even though use of alcoholic drinks "increased by leaps and bounds," the "moral and religious forces" of the day had "no attitude of hostility to intoxicants," but only against drunkenness.[5] Indeed, liquors "in themselves were considered wholesome and necessary," and when taken in "moderation . . . were considered helpful and stimulating."[6]

This classical notion of temperance enjoyed widespread acceptance by American Christians until the early nineteenth century, when alcoholism in the United States reached epidemic proportions. Advances in distilling technology, the profitability of converting grain crops into alcoholic beverages, the replacement of milder beverages like beer and cider with stronger drinks like whiskey, and social acceptance of heavier drinking was turning the United States after the Revolution into the "Alcohol Republic," as historian W. J. Rorabaugh put it. By 1830, an average American over fifteen years old drank eighty-eight bottles of whiskey annually, nearly three times the average today. Drinking became synonymous with drunkenness. These excesses prompted reformers like Lyman Beecher to form in 1826 the American Temperance Society (ATS) and to spearhead a national temperance movement against the destructive influences of alcohol. Temperance advocates initially preferred moral suasion to combat the evils of demon rum. The Virginia ATS chapter in 1827, for example, denounced the "intemperate use of spirituous liquors" but did not call for total abstinence, much less for prohibition.[7] Prohibitionists, however, insisted upon wielding the moral force of the state to eliminate the very temptation to drink by outlawing the production and sale of alcohol.[8]

Why did prohibitionists break with Christian tradition by adopting such a radical approach of not only abstinence, but legal prohibition? The answer lies in part in the changes in religious sensibilities between the American Revolution and the Civil War. During that time, most Protestants in the United States increasingly based their faith on individualistic, republican, and common-sense readings of the Bible. This new consensus replaced more traditional Christian views (even among Protestants) that revered community authority, expert exegesis, and hierarchy. Mark Noll, Nathan O. Hatch, and others have observed that this alliance between representative government and Christianity was by no means obvious or natural but was remarkably innovative for a faith that had been defined through hierarchical relationships and community consensus. In short, most American Protestants had already broken dramatically with Christian tradition by aligning it to individualistic common sense, which made it more likely for American Christians to adopt innovations that were unconnected or even opposed to classical Christian teachings, including alcohol abstinence and prohibition.[9]

Various learned laymen across the nation took up the pen to expose prohibition as an innovation that had more to do with legalistic Islam than with classic Christianity. In 1867, John A. Andrew of Boston spoke out at a public forum against "those who would rest the hopes of humanity on the commandments of men" such as prohibition and pointed instead to "the promises of Gospel

Grace" as the effective means to live truly temperate lives. He also pointed to the positive reforms of England in that century, citing the people's "[r]eligious faith, Christian charity, philanthropic benevolence," and other virtues in all levels of society, which "now battle effectually against the vices of society, and the evil inclinations of human nature." "This progress," he claimed, "was not Jewish, nor Mohammedan, but it was Christian. It was not due to law, but to liberty." He believed the most effective way of combating vice among all classes was Christian faith and virtue stemming from liberty, not the legalism he saw in other religions.[10]

Some Christians in the South shared this perception. Alexander Watkins Terrell, a Texas state senator who later became a chief architect of the state's dry poll-tax law, also denounced prohibition in 1879. On the one hand, he claimed that centuries of Islamic prohibition on alcohol led to the gradual "physical and moral decay" of the Turks. On the other hand, he objected to banning wine, "which the Savior himself once made by his miraculous power, to cheer the heart of a bridegroom and his guests, and against the temperate use of which He never uttered a word during all his pilgrimage on earth." For Terrell and his constituents, temperate alcohol use was on the side of Jesus and freedom, while prohibitionists were on the side of Muhammad and regression.[11]

The Bible and Booze

As Terrell's reference to Jesus turning water into wine in John 2 indicated, wets could cite the Bible for their cause just as well as, if not better than, their dry opponents. This seems to challenge Mark Noll's observation that popular recourse to the Bible as authoritative for a major US political crisis occurred for the last time regarding slavery. The dominant approach in that theological and moral debate was a common-sense hermeneutic that valued individuals' interpretations of the Bible over church tradition and magisterial authority, which left only the violence of the Civil War as a viable option to overcome the impasse over slavery.[12] Following the conflict, ordinary people in the United States displaced debates over Bible passages from the public discourse because, without recourse to an outside authority like church tradition, it was open to conflicting interpretations and so failed to provide the means to resolve the issue of slavery apart from devastating Civil War.[13] When it came to prohibition, however, both drys and wets freely wielded the Bible for their cause, suggesting that the Bible still carried weight in the postbellum United States.

The American prohibition movement sprang not from literal interpretations of the Bible but from Americans' experience. Drinking became a serious problem for many churches around the nation after the Civil War, but most

Southern Baptists did not immediately call for prohibition, even if they did recommend abstinence from alcohol. The official newspaper of the Baptist General Association of Virginia recommended in October of 1865 that only teetotalism could prevent drunkenness, but five years later admitted that such behavior was not demanded by the Bible: "Total abstinence from intoxicating liquors, with certain limitations, is commended by expediency, the experience of multitudes, the opinion of many wise and good men, and by a fair application of certain scriptural principles." Still, they admitted "the Bible contains no prohibition of the use of wine and strong drink, and all attempts to draw such a prohibition from it is a perversion of Scripture, and injurious to the cause which it is intended to subserve."[14] In 1870, Southern Baptists had not yet claimed the Bible directly supported alcohol abstinence, much less prohibition.

Skepticism about the wisdom of using the Bible to insist on abstinence persisted among Southern Baptists until the 1880s. A few voices in major Baptist periodicals argued for moderate consumption of alcoholic beverages, including hard liquor, as late as 1884. After a consensus emerged that distilled liquors were unacceptable drinks for serious Christians, some Baptists continued to suggest that the best antidote for intemperance was moderate consumption of wine, beer, cider, and other malt drinks that occurred naturally and featured less alcoholic content. Even these modest allowances were frequently countered by observations that excessive drinking of any alcoholic beverage could easily lead to drunkenness.[15]

The hardest drink habit for Southern Baptists to kick was wine. Many southerners considered wine the most innocuous of alcoholic beverages. Farm columns in Baptist journals such as the Atlanta *Christian Index* included wine recipes and encouragement to produce diversified crops for the manufacture of wines from various fruits, including blackberries, strawberries, and scuppernongs.[16] Baptist writers also acknowledged that wine was encouraged in the Bible. St. Paul urged his protégé in 1 Timothy 5:23 to "take a little wine" for his health, and Jesus famously turned water into wine in a wedding in John 2. "We fully believe," wrote one contributor to the Richmond, Virginia, *Religious Herald* in 1879, "that the wine made by Christ at the marriage in Cana was intoxicating, if drunk to excess." Another stated, "That Christ drank wine during His stay on earth, no one can doubt."[17]

Nonetheless, many Southern Baptists insisted upon shunning wine despite the examples in the Bible because they interpreted their faith according to a common-sense understanding of their own times. Baptist icon John A. Broadus of Southern Baptist Theological Seminary granted that Jesus used wine in the first century but claimed that Christ only drank it because of cultural custom. Had Jesus lived in the present, Broadus insisted, he would have shunned wine and preferred more respectable drinks like tea or coffee. A Virginian editor in 1888 urged teetotalers: if they would focus on "present facts and present dangers" and "abandon all attempts to find an explicit Bible command, what a relief it would be to them and to the cause!"[18] By the 1890s, Southern Baptists had hardened their views against alcohol as the greatest vice, though this view sprang from experience rather than the Bible. The Florida Baptist Convention called alcohol the most "destructive curse of the 19th century, imperiling our homes, hostile to our churches, a constant menace to society, the prolific mother of vice and crime, the corrupter of politics, a breeder of anarchy in our government, and in all its dark record the offspring of the devil."[19] For Southern Baptist drys in the late nineteenth century, appeals to common sense and present realities trumped clear biblical examples condoning alcohol consumption.

Methodists banned alcohol consumption before Baptists, though experience and reason had more to do with the proscription than Scripture or tradition. John Wesley established the rule forbidding "Drunkenness, or drinking spirituous liquors unless in cases of necessity," for his followers in the eighteenth century. While British Methodists threatened to ban members for drinking liquor as early as 1795, American Methodists' book of discipline in use at that time did not mention drinking, though it did banish people who talked before church. By the 1870s, however, the white-led Southern Methodist and Northern Methodist denominations both included the rule against drunkenness and distilled drinks. Even then, "spiritous liquors" meant distilled beverages and excluded fermented drinks with lower alcoholic content such as beer and wine.[20]

In the nineteenth century, white and Black American Methodists began to embrace alcohol abstinence and then prohibition. The African Methodist Episcopal Church (AME), the first major Black denomination in the United States, had since the 1830s taught abstinence from all kinds of alcohol and since the 1850s backed prohibition laws to purify society at large.[21] By 1883, the main white Methodist group, the Methodist Episcopal Church, South (MECS), began treating not only drinking but also the production and sale of alcohol—and soon even renting property to those in the alcohol trade—as an evil worthy of church discipline.[22] These standards stemmed more from evolving understandings of the dangers of alcohol than the teachings of Scripture.

Dry organizations such as the Woman's Christian Temperance Union (WCTU) invoked the Bible freely to support their mission. A typical state-conference report of the Texas WCTU reveals the organization's heavy use of a common-sense evangelical approach to the Bible not only in rhetoric but in regular functions. The second page provides the "WCTU Benediction," an exact quote of the Aaronic Blessing from Number 6:24–26.[23] The use of these verses as the WCTU Benediction suggests their ritualistic function in concluding all manner of events by officially invoking God's presence and aid through the unambiguous use of the Bible as Scripture. The regular function of Scripture for the WCTU is made clear in the yearbook at the end of the report, which included a Bible reading for each week, with the verses taken from books throughout the Bible.[24] The fourth page of the report lists various "MEMORIAL DAYS," including "Flower Mission Day," quoting the uncited Bible verse Leviticus 23:4 as justification: "There are Feasts of the Lord, Even holy Convocations, Which ye shall proclaim in their season."[25] Like the use of the Aaronic Blessing in the benediction, this use of Leviticus lacks any cultural or historical context of the verses composed several millennia earlier yet demonstrates a common-sense evangelical hermeneutic. The women of the WCTU found a way to link their every deed to the Bible. This creative use of the Bible was not merely a pretext but inspiration: God was on their side, and their authority derived from the God of the Bible.

Some Christian drys believed that they had special access to God's will and ways. Frances E. Willard, who served as the WCTU president for nearly twenty years and grew it to be the largest woman's organization of the nineteenth century, was a devout evangelical Methodist. She attributed her support for "Home Protection," or women's suffrage, as a means to support prohibition, to a direct revelation from God: "Upon my knees there was borne in upon my mind from loftier regions, the declaration, you are to speak for the woman's ballot as a weapon of protection to her home."[26] For Willard and likeminded evangelical women, God granted them spiritual authority and wisdom to defend their God-given roles as women and mothers through political activism.[27]

The Texas WCTU's presidential address portrayed their fight as a simple matter of good against evil. The state president quoted in a single breath both the organization's aim "that each man's habits of life shall be an example safe and beneficial for every other man to follow," and the evangelistic text of John 3:16.[28] For many drys, that prohibition and the Gospel fit together was as self-evident and plain as the Bible itself. She continued with even more unambiguous language. The WCTU women relied "upon the promise of the One who is able to rescue us from the great curse of the liquor traffic," and waged even more "pitiless and relentless warfare" against saloons than Texas patriots had waged in the battles of the Alamo and San Jacinto. This great battle for prohibition pitted "righteousness against unrighteousness; the children of the living God against those who put material prosperity above the success and happiness of the sons and daughters of the land."[29] The WCTU slogan, "For God and Home and Native Land," though not itself a reference to Scripture, illuminates much about the WCTU's theology, which in turn influenced how it read the Bible.[30] For the WCTU and likeminded prohibitionists, the Bible, women's empowerment, and patriotism were forged together to battle the evil of alcohol.

Wets and drys both applied popular and scholarly analyses of Bible passages, particularly on the "two-wine thesis" that raged in the late 1880s. This thesis claimed that the Bible referred two kinds of wine: a nonalcoholic wine for all positive references, and an alcoholic wine for all negative references. Hundreds of educated American clergy around the nation objected to the two-wine thesis in 1888, including the Rev. Edward Hurtt Jewett. Using references to the original Hebrew and Greek texts of the Bible, Jewett argued that "the term *unfermented* wine, in Scripture phraseology, is a misnomer and self-contradictory," since wine was always presumed to have been fermented.[31]

Some years later, Edward R. Emerson, a winemaker, wrote *A Lay Thesis on Bible Wines* to echo and expand upon the arguments of Jewett and others. Emerson explained at length why the laws of fermentation, ancient authors, leading lexicons, and the best modern scholars give no support to the two-wine thesis, displaying considerable erudition and mastery of ancient texts, especially for a layperson. His first defense notes that "the Bible in unmistakable language commended wine," yet the innovation of anti-alcohol asceticism produced the two-wine argument.[32] Emerson claimed that, in making this distinction, "Reason, science, and the teachings of two thousand years were to fall apart as if cut with knives." In place of reason and tradition, "Linguistic legerdemain has been indulged in to such an extent that even many of the most watchful have failed to see the glaring absurdity and utter ridiculousness of the name they have chosen for their wine," namely "unfermented wine."[33] Drinking fermented wine, Emerson noted, was ubiquitous among the ancient Israelites and their neighboring nations.[34] He also noted that, throughout the Bible, the typical Hebrew and Greek words for wine (*yayin* and *oinos*) are always spoken of as "a blessing sent by God for the use of man" and "to be used in the service of God," such as in Isaiah 55:1–2, where the word functions "as a symbol of the highest spiritual blessing."[35] Other Hebrew and Greek words for wine, such as *'asis* (Isaiah 49:26), *tirosh* (Hosea 4:11), and *gleukos* (Acts 2:13), all imply intoxication, and no word for wine in the Bible ever refers to a nonalcoholic beverage.[36]

Emerson continued his reasoning with reference to many other Bible passages that referred to wine positively. The Bible "plainly said that Christ made wine" in John 2.[37] He refuted those who interpreted Jesus's parable of new wine into old bottles as a parable against fermented wine, pointing out that there is no basis in the text for such an interpretation, and the parable only makes sense if the wine in question is fermented.[38] Jesus himself was derided by his detractors as having come "drinking wine" in Luke 7:33–34, a fact to which Emerson attached great theological importance: "Jesus was no ascetic. He gave no countenance to asceticism. By drinking wine—freely using the blessings of God's providence—He testified against the error, afterward called Gnostic and Manichean, which would attach impurity to that which enters the mouth." Furthermore, Jesus thus "vindicated the liberty of His followers to use 'every creature of God' as good and fit for food, and to be received with thanksgiving by them as those who 'believe and know the truth,'" a direct reference to 1 Timothy 4:3–4.[39] Rather than merely arguing that the Bible allows and blesses alcoholic beverages, Emerson contended that prohibition went against the essence of Christian liberty as articulated in the Bible and Christian tradition. Emerson and likeminded wets avoided the extreme of prohibition not merely because they professed fidelity to the plain meaning of the text, but because they—unlike prohibitionists—refused to separate Bible interpretation from the church's tradition and ethics.

Among Southern Baptists, this two-wine argument raged especially between 1887 and 1890 and then abruptly ceased to attract significant debate. This debate on Bible wines either waned in 1890 because prohibitionists had won or, more likely, because Baptists agreed to disagree and focus on more important matters, since the debate over prohibition was not resolved in the SBC until 1896.[40] Wets like Jewett and Emerson interpreted the Bible through philology and history, yet they also argued from a plain reading of the Bible according to church tradition and common sense. Prohibitionists also appealed to philology and history to reinterpret the Bible, but the argument mattered only because many on both sides viewed the Bible as Scripture.

However, some nineteenth-century prohibitionists publicly rejected the Bible as Scripture, including Elizabeth Cady Stanton. An early advocate for prohibition, Stanton turned away from evangelical Christianity before reaching adulthood. By the 1890s, Stanton grew convinced that Christianity and the Bible were inimical to gender equality and had to be confronted. She initiated the *Woman's Bible,* a collaborative project in which she and other women offered commentary on Bible passages that dealt directly with women, especially those used by opponents of gender equality. Consequently, she and other religious radicals were marginalized from both the suffrage and temperance movements by the end of the nineteenth century. Nonetheless, the fact that heterodox women such as Stanton had played key roles in the earlier temperance movement suggested their continued presence in the movement in years to come.[41]

Prohibitionists who invoked the Bible differed on how literally to interpret it and on whether prohibition was primarily about saving individual souls or redeeming society. Temperance literature in the nineteenth century often contained variants of, "No drunkard . . . shall inherit the kingdom of God," from 1 Corinthians 6:10,[42] and a few leading drys repeated this claim in the twentieth century. Ferdinand Iglehart dedicated his celebration of prohibition, *King Alcohol Dethroned,* to the salvation of souls: "This book goes out with the hope that it may reclaim some drunkard . . . that some soul may be saved for time and eternity."[43] However, this fear of hell was not shared by progressive prohibitionists such as the modernist Presbyterian Charles Stelzle, who took a leading role in the Social Gospel movement to reform society according to Christian principles and modern scientific management. In his defense of dry laws, *Why Prohibition!,* Stelzle mocked the idea of people going to hell as something the fundamentalist revivalist "Billy Sunday says."[44] Thus, Christian prohibitionists were divided between fundamentalists like Sunday, whose concern to save souls through prohibition was rooted in a common-sense evangelical interpretation of the Bible, and modernists like Stelzle, who mocked their concern and shunned such a literal reading of Scripture.

The Bible could and did play on both sides of the prohibition divide, though some prohibitionists treated it as peripheral or nonessential to their cause while anti-prohibitionists at times invoked the Bible more effectively. Baptists sometimes admitted that one could not reasonably argue for prohibition from the Bible and that Jesus drank and made wine. Only by applying contemporary culture and experiences could Christians conclude that alcohol must be shunned. Christians on both sides often resorted to extra-biblical arguments rather than trusting Scripture alone to resolve the issue. Whether supported by the Bible or not, once prohibitionists viewed alcohol as evil, the struggle expanded beyond prohibition to the question of wine in communion.

Communion Wine

On Christmas Day 1838, in the Masonic Lodge of Matagorda, the first Episcopalian Eucharist in the Republic of Texas was celebrated. The priest, Fr. Caleb Smith Ives, in the prayer of oblation asked God "to bless and sanctify, with thy Word and Holy Spirit, these thy gifts and creatures of bread and wine." Then, after a hymn, the congregants knelt before the priest, who served them the bread and then the cup, saying, "The Blood of our Lord Jesus Christ, which was shed for thee, preserve thy body and soul unto everlasting life." Through participation in the Eucharist, also called the Lord's Supper or Communion, those Episcopalians received a sacrament—an outward and visible sign of an inward and spiritual grace—that assured them of fellowship with Christ and salvation.[45] Their use of sacramental wine was deeply rooted in ancient Christian tradition and the example of Jesus as recorded in the Gospel accounts of the Bible.[46]

Despite contemporary associations of evangelicals with grape juice in miniature plastic cups, it was not so in the beginning. The Christian tradition of wine in the Lord's Supper derived from the Jewish custom of Seder dinner, with its four cups of wine. Since at least the first century, ancient Christians began meeting together over bread and wine. The tradition gradually transitioned from a "love feast" meal to a highly structured ritual in which a priest distributed wafers and sips of wine. For most medieval peasants, communion wine remained in sight but out of reach, reserved for priests. Though greatly changed, two constants remained: bread and wine.

The Reformation democratized the Lord's Supper. The English *Book of Common Prayer* made worship more accessible in many ways: services were in the English vernacular, the altar became a table closer to the people, and everyone was encouraged to partake of both bread and wine weekly. Ironically, even as Protestant doctrine made the Eucharist more accessible, Protestant anxiety about taking the Eucharist improperly led to communion becoming less frequent and less important in Protestant worship just as the Council of Trent ordered every faithful Catholic to partake in communion at each mass.[47]

The centuries-old assumptions that communion should feature fermented wine came under attack in innovative America. In 1869, a British-born Wesleyan Methodist named Thomas Bramwell Welch invented a pasteurization method to prevent the fermentation of grape juice. Though other methods previously existed to create nonalcoholic grape juice, and Welch's own Wesleyan Methodist denomination had explicitly required nonalcoholic wine for communion since 1843, Welch's method could produce higher-quality juice in larger quantities than other techniques. Welch encouraged churches to use his "unfermented wine," and his sales increased commensurately with the growing popularity of prohibition.[48] As the nineteenth century closed, more American Christians came to believe that personal experience, common sense, and modern science were incompatible with the doctrine that alcoholic beverages should be used in the Lord's Supper. As Jennifer L. Woodruff Tait argues, the move to replace communion wine with grape juice among Methodists represented "the natural result of applying the common-sense worldview to the temperance problem."[49] Some churches forsook alcohol while others revered it. These divides over alcohol suggested that the historical peculiarities of denominations and theological traditions affected their approach to the issue of communion wine. Since Tait has provided an excellent description of these shifts in Methodist churches, much of the following analysis will focus on a few other Christian groups, starting with Baptists.

Some Baptists preferred to keep alcohol in their sacred wine. From 1886 to 1890, the main argument among Baptists had shifted from whether alcoholic beverages were generally permissible (they were not) to whether they should use wine or grape juice in communion. Though Baptists viewed communion as an ordinance, or command to be followed, rather than a sacrament, or a means of God's grace, they took ordinances seriously. The very name "Baptist" referred to their only other ordinance, baptism, on which they staked their denominational identity. Since Baptists insisted upon the biblical model of baptism—full immersion for believing adults only—how could they justify using anything other than wine for communion? "If we must have real water for baptism and not some substitute for it," a Baptist from Florida asked, "why not have real wine for the supper?"[50] Another insisted that replacing communion wine with grape juice was just as absurd as "substitut[ing] sprinkling for baptism"—a violation of *the* Baptist distinctive.[51]

Ironically, those who contended most firmly for baptism by immersion also tended to be those who insisted upon replacing wine with grape juice. To hold their view with any consistency, prohibitionists who claimed "literalist" views of the Bible fiercely advocated the two-wine thesis. This theory essentially argued that all the Bible's positive references to wine were to nonalcoholic juice while all the negative references were to alcoholic wine. Wets like Edward R. Emerson claimed that partaking of wine in communion was "the most sacred and solemn act that a human being can perform."[52]

Other Baptist drys, less willing to resort to exegetical gymnastics, took a more "liberal" view on Bible wines. This camp included John Broadus, who admitted that all wine in the Bible was alcoholic but used reason and experience to conclude that biblical authors and figures indulged only because doing so was necessary in their culture, but they would never have partaken in modern times, when such beverages were linked with vice. For this reason, and because communion was merely symbolic and using wine would cause total abstainers to stumble in their faith, grape juice could and should be substituted for wine in communion.[53]

After 1890, the argument over communion wine ceased to occupy much attention of most Southern Baptists, who largely agreed to disagree on the matter. A motion to insist on unfermented grape juice in communion at the 1891 convention of Tennessee Baptists was tabled. Various articles in Baptist journals in 1900 likewise failed to evoke responses or rejoinders. Baptists' congregational form of government allowed autonomy to local churches and prevented denominational leaders from dictating uniformity. Social sanctions and persuasion turned most Baptist ministers to grape juice in the Lord's Supper by the turn of the century, yet some celebrated their freedom by persisting with wine. Rather than consuming their energy on sacred wine, Baptist leaders instead focused their attention on acting against the liquor business generally.[54]

African American Baptists also divided on the issue of communion wine and embraced alcohol-free wine more slowly than their white co-religionists. Remarks in the minutes of the National Baptist Convention (NBC), the largest Black denomination (and for a time larger than the SBC), proved that many of its churches continued to use alcoholic wine in communion into the twentieth century. In their 1908 and 1909 reports, the NBC woman's auxiliary asked for the use of only unfermented wine in communion.[55] While most white Baptists had by this time either adopted grape juice in communion or made peace with those who persisted with wine, African American Baptists remained divided on communion wine into the twentieth century.

Some Catholics, on the other hand, insisted on Eucharistic wine to *enable* alcoholic abstinence. Official records of the Catholic Total Abstinence Union of America (CTAU), founded in 1872, called for abstinence from alcohol, but encouraged regular use of the sacraments—including the wine-bearing Eucharist. J. B. Purcell, the first US bishop personally committed to total alcohol abstinence, emphasized that one could remain abstinent only by "the frequent use of the Sacraments," and other priests with similar advice appeared frequently in CTAU records.[56] For Catholics, who believed in transubstantiation, Eucharistic wine was not wine in substance, but transformed into the blood of Christ. For such Catholics, doing away with wine in communion did not help but rather would hinder the cause of abstinence, because the Eucharistic wine was an essential part of their connection with God in Christ, and that connection was necessary for their sobriety.

Columbia University professor John Erskine expressed an objection to nonalcoholic communion wine typical of high-church traditions: if the Eucharist with bread and wine was a central Christian practice, then taking away wine diminished that practice. The essence of Christian faith for Erskine was expressed in the "beautiful metaphors" of Christ from the Gospel of John—"I am the Bread of Life" and "I am the true Vine"—and there was no better way to express that truth than in communion with bread and wine.[57] Erskine claimed that "prohibition by professed Christians would be impossible if their faith were still warm in the heart or clear in the head, and that it has come now only because that faith is dead."[58] Ministers, he continued, "still read out in the churches that Christ celebrated the Passover with His disciples, with the bread and wine of the ancient sacrifice," and he then quoted the related Bible passage.[59] By objecting "to the wine as improper, as a temptation and a snare," they are "giving up, logically if unconsciously, any further concern with the mythical or metaphysical aspects of His nature, or with that inner sustenance of which the bread and wine were to be outward or visible signs."[60] Such an approach simplifies Christian faith so that "perhaps nothing will remain of it but an ecclesiastical system or a body of ethical doctrine for such as still revere the life [of Jesus] spent in Galilee."[61] If the mystical and spiritual union of the believer with Christ in communion was the essence of the Christian faith, then prohibitionists were gutting the heart of Christianity.

For Erskine, as for Emerson, prohibitionists misinterpreted not only the Bible, but the tradition of the church. Since the catechisms for Episcopalians, Presbyterians, Lutherans, and Catholics alike explicitly mentioned wine as one of the elements to be received in communion, prohibitionists should insist upon reforming their catechisms before supporting prohibition.[62] Only by divorcing themselves from the traditional teachings of the church could Christians devote themselves so wholeheartedly to the innovation of prohibition. If Christians could select their communion elements at will, Erskine implied, then Christians denied that those elements had any meaning apart from what the church today felt like ascribing to them. Such a faith could pick and choose its practices and doctrines at will. By removing wine from the Eucharist, prohibition proved itself not to be a form of conservative Christianity, but a thoroughly modern innovation. In short, Erskine wondered "whether the Eighteenth Amendment [for federal prohibition] is an amendment to the Constitution or to the New Testament."[63]

Christian Liberty
On August 15, 1885, a fifty-six-year-old Episcopalian addressed a crowd of thousands in Waco, Texas, on the evils of political preaching. If pastors strayed from the Gospel into politics, "Flog them back!" he cried to cheers and loud applause. "Flog them back!" he repeated, to continued acclamation. The target of his ire was the campaign—led by prominent clergy—to dry the area in a

29

local option election, which he claimed would result in a union of church and state. The speaker, Richard Coke, had considerable clout: he was a current US senator, the governor who ended Reconstruction in Texas, and a Confederate veteran who had served on Jefferson Davis's staff. Coke attacked prohibition as a northeastern invention, such as churches' support for abolitionism, which he believed had caused the Civil War.[64] Richard Coke's denunciation of prohibition as dangerous to personal liberty and a precursor to overly invasive government was consistent with Jefferson Davis's open letter against statewide prohibition in 1887.[65] In the 1880s South, many southerners, including Democratic leadership, accused political preachers of trying to unite church and state.

Still, a significant and growing minority in Texas saw the issue differently. Waco First Baptist Church's pastor, Benajah Harvey Carroll, who led the drys, bristled at Coke's accusations. Carroll accurately countered that southern Democrats had written the local option in the Texas Constitution of 1876; there was nothing northern about it. He also argued that prohibition did not threaten a union of church and state but simply fought against a union of whiskey and state.[66] In the 1880s, however, Coke represented the white majority, and prohibition efforts floundered.

Of all the Christian ideas that mobilized opposition to prohibition, none enjoyed more invocation than liberty. Liberty became a rallying cry for anti-prohibitionist Christians in several ways. Anticlericism, or an insistence upon separation between church leaders and the state, predominated among Christians in the South. Also, many Christians had championed liberty as limited government, while drys sought to impose morality by a powerful activist government.

Several historians have traced the dominance of anticlerical views in the South through the nineteenth century. Joe Coker argues that the South initially resisted prohibition in the late nineteenth century because, among other reasons, most southern whites believed in the spirituality of the church. This doctrine insisted that churches should not address or advocate directly on political issues, including prohibition, but was overcome by dry evangelical activism from the 1880s to the 1910s, transforming the region from a wet bastion to a dry stronghold.[67] Joseph Locke further develops this idea, contending that activism on prohibition played a key role in reshaping the South from an anticlerical region suspicious of the union of church and state to one that revered political preaching on many issues. Notwithstanding southern white evangelical ministers' support for slavery, secession, the Confederacy, and the Lost Cause before prohibition, the latter issue was instrumental in creating a distinctive form of religious politics of the "Bible Belt," which did not exist until the early twentieth century.[68] Following Locke, Robert Wuthnow briefly contends that prohibition activism was a prominent element in empowering political preaching in the South in the late-nineteenth and early twentieth centuries.[69] Coker studied the eastern South (Georgia, Tennessee, and Alabama) while Locke and Wuthnow focused on Texas, altogether demonstrating how this religious and political transformation of the South into the Bible Belt occurred across the region around the issue of prohibition.

Episcopalians, the epitome of elite whites in both the South and the North, generally believed that preachers should stay away from politics. Richard Coke, a Texas governor, US senator, and strident wet who was raised Episcopalian, articulated the popular view that wets were for southern, Democratic, and Christian values against foreign innovation and tyranny, an echo of the Confederate argument for regional self-determination on slavery.[70] Other Episcopalians agreed. An Episcopal newspaper, Austin's *Texas Churchman,* declared itself "emphatically in favor of temperance" yet against legal prohibition. "Will prohibition meet the case and convert the people into a nation of teetotalers? Vain delusion!" True temperance, the paper declared, could only be achieved by the church, not the state. In any case, it was not the church's business to interfere in politics.[71]

Even as American Protestants increasingly pursued personal abstinence from alcohol in the late nineteenth century, many declined to endorse prohibition. For much of the nineteenth century, many Baptists around the nation, white and Black alike, shared the theological precepts of J. Newton Brown's 1853 Church Covenant. That covenant was officially endorsed by the Black-led National Baptist Convention (NBC) in 1900, suggesting strong grassroots support for it in the decades leading up to that endorsement. The covenant explicitly called for members "to abstain from the sale and use of intoxicating drinks as a beverage." However, it said nothing about prohibition laws. For many African American Baptists at the close of the nineteenth century, alcohol abstinence was a matter of personal piety and church practice, not public policy.[72]

While anticlerical views reflected Protestant fears of Catholic influence, many American Catholics embraced the separation of church and politics. As a minority in a democratic society dominated by Protestants, Catholics in the United States generally sought a less intrusive government so they could work out their own salvation. Because Catholic tradition held that alcohol was not inherently sinful, Catholic temperance advocates generally preferred voluntary abstinence out of extraordinary need or piety rather than legal prohibition. Such was the norm in the largest Catholic temperance group in the nation, the Catholic Total Abstinence Union of America (CTAU). Founded in 1872 by clergy from around the nation, the CTAU was both anti-alcohol and anti-prohibition. The opening convention of the CTAU in 1872 issued an "Address to the Catholics of America" insisting upon the motto of "Moral Suasion" while shunning "Prohibitory laws, restrictive license systems, and special legislation against drunkenness."[73] At that same convention, Rev. James McDevitt of the District of Columbia argued that Catholics must work for abstinence "on a strictly Catholic basis, discard all political considerations or means, and labor for the amelioration of the victims of intemperance through religious principles only."[74] Catholic religion, not political prohibition, guided Catholic temperance.

A peculiarly Catholic element in the CTAU's abstinence pledge—a requirement for all CTAU members—was the thirst of Christ on the Cross. The pledge began: "I promise, with the Divine assistance and in honor of the Sacred Thirst and Agony of Our Savior, to abstain from all intoxicating drinks."[75] The pledge implied that, by the agonies of abstaining from drink even in moments of weakness, pledge takers relied upon Christ's help as they identified with his sufferings on the cross.[76] By 1907, the CTAU had enlisted over a 100,000 Catholics with chapters in many southern states, including Louisiana and Alabama.[77] Even in the Deep South, some Catholics embraced alcohol abstinence—but through their church, not by legal prohibition through the state.

Evangelical Protestants' theological differences with Catholics and more liturgical Protestants influenced their views on prohibition. Evangelicals believed in a sudden conversion experience, immediate moral change, and the aspiration of ever-greater holiness for all believers. However, Catholics and more liturgical Protestants tended to view salvation as sacramental, to see holiness as the result of slow progress rather than a sudden event, and to tolerate vices such as heavier drinking habits. Attempting to impose rapid moral development on all people by strict religious laws fit better with the rapidly changing circumstances and evolving theology of American Protestants than with traditionally minded high-church Episcopalians, Lutherans, and Catholics.[78]

In addition to questioning the politicization of the church for prohibition, many Christian wets in the South believed that dry laws violated their liberty by abandoning the sacrosanct principle of limited government. White southerners throughout the nineteenth century typically held to the Jeffersonian view that divisive moral issues such as alcohol were best left to individuals, families, communities, and local government rather than the state or federal government. This localist critique had roots in the American Revolution and carried weight in the South, which had fought the Civil War to protect their regional practice of slavery and long after the war invoked the rights of each state and locale to settle contentious moral issues.

The notion of limited government also had roots in classical Christian theology, which taught that individuals built righteous character by overcoming temptation through self-control, Christian community, and divine assistance. This traditional Christian position opposed prohibition, which attempted to use the state to prevent sin by removing temptation. Rather than merely exhorting parishioners to overcome bondage to drunkenness by moderate drinking or voluntary abstention, dry ministers saw demon rum as inexorable, requiring not merely individual willpower or church support but state intervention. For prohibitionists, the locus of godly social reform thus shifted from the church to the state, with the church playing a secondary role as a pressure group to ensure the progressive advancement of human morality—not through the regeneration of souls by the power of the Holy Spirit but the coercion of bodies by the power of government. By replacing the roles of God and the church with the state, prohibition made government control all-important, turned the issue into a holy culture war that justified almost any means to achieve its end, and effectively secularized the church's function while attempting to sacralize the state.

Prohibition's rise prompted church leaders to clamp down on dissident voices and enforce ideological uniformity on a political issue. This happened not only among Methodists, who already had a top-down structure, but increasingly among liberty-loving Baptists, who celebrated congregational autonomy and soul liberty to follow one's individual conscience on secondary matters. Even Baptists, who in colonial Virginia had sometimes been imprisoned for defying the Anglican establishment, sought to impose their own moral vision on the South a century later as they gained cultural and political power.

By the 1870s, some Southern Baptists began advocating prohibition, yet they were out of step with most Baptists and Christian tradition. Baptists generally agreed that wine was permitted in the Bible and even consumed by Jesus, yet dry Baptists primarily relied on arguments from common-sense reasoning and contemporary experience. In 1875, the Baptist State Convention of Texas's Committee on Temperance cataloged the evils of the liquor traffic: it wasted $900 million and murdered more than sixty thousand people annually; it generated 75 percent of crime and most of the poverty and insanity; and was "corrupting the ballot box," "hastening monopoly," and even "planting the seeds of communism."[79] These concerns were all contemporary and contingent—particularly matters such as elections, monopolies, and communism—rather than being based on eternal values from Scripture or tradition. Still, many Southern Baptists then favored moderate drinking, believed only the Gospel could cure a drunkard, and shunned politically lobbying for prohibition. Southern Methodists in the mid-1870s likewise focused more on strict abstinence among their members than in passing prohibition laws.

White Baptist preachers defended prohibition advocacy as their Christian duty to resist evil. Responding directly to Senator Coke's call to put political preachers in their place, the "old time Baptist" preacher I. B. Kimbrough pronounced in 1887 at the Baptist State Convention that he would rather "live on corn cobs and stump water" than "allow any politician to put a padlock on my mouth."[80] The language inverted the wet rhetoric against political preachers as power-hungry and gave them the moral high ground as saints suffering for freedom of speech. While southern clergy asserted regional distinctiveness, their dry campaign also tied them into a national movement to advance Christian values.

The issue of prohibition also led Baptist churches to modify their traditional emphasis on congregational autonomy. Though state conventions of the Southern Baptist Convention (SBC) had never before exercised authority over local congregations, according to historian Rufus Spain, various state conventions in the 1870s began threatening to cut off churches who did not properly discipline their members to avoid involvement in the alcohol trade. While Baptist churches had long since punished saloon operators and drunkards, Baptist churches began using social sanctions against those involved in the alcohol industry more generally: brewers, distillers, liquor wholesalers, or even property owners who rented land to them. Florida passed such a resolution in 1872, followed by Georgia in 1873, Texas in 1876, and Mississippi in 1878. While churches or individuals could flout them, such resolutions had an overall chilling effect on those involved in the alcohol trade. Still, in the 1870s, these were just several states in the SBC, not the whole denomination.

The turning point for white Methodists and Baptists across the South on prohibition was 1886. That year, the Methodist General Conference (Southern Methodists) denounced the manufacture and sale of alcoholic drinks as sins. After that, the denomination plunged into prohibition advocacy even as they continued using moral suasion within their churches.[81]

While the Methodist hierarchy backed prohibition, some lay Methodists opposed it. Roger Quarles Mills, a Methodist from Corsicana, had been an ardent prohibitionist with his own dry monthly paper, *Prairie Blade*. One 1855 issue compared the argument that liquor is good because it brings in tax revenue to the argument that "a maiden should sell her virtue or a man his honesty for gold or silver."[82] Yet by 1887, Mills, a former US representative and future US senator, had joined the wet "True Blues," contending that legal prohibition undermined Jeffersonian democracy. Mills withdrew from the Southern Methodist denomination to protest constant "political preaching," and in a debate with B. H. Carroll retorted, "Hell is full of better preachers than that man, so full that their legs are hanging out at the windows."[83] While some Methodist laymen were convicted by their preachers to vote dry, others grew alienated and left because of the political preaching.

As with Methodists, the SBC's first temperance resolution in 1886 was a sea change. Support for local option laws slowly morphed into support for statewide and national prohibition by the 1890s. Nonetheless, Southern Baptists did not see temperance as all-important: most denounced the Prohibition Party for undermining white supremacy by threatening the Democratic Party's stranglehold on the region.[84]

The endorsement of legal prohibition among Baptists represented a decisive shift from church-led moral suasion to state-enforced laws. As the Texas Baptists' Temperance Report from 1886 stated, the phrase "'moral suasion' has been rung in our ears so long by those who never did anything *for* moral suasion" (emphasis original) that it "has ceased to be potent."[85] The report also noted that the government had never enforced local prohibition laws and saloon operators often flouted them—a curious argument to lobby for *more* laws. Baptists must "as citizens VOTE against this hydra-headed monster," since "it is our duty as Christians to vote for prohibition" and "for God, and home, and native land" (the motto of the WCTU). If dry activism should lead to a backlash, the committee urged, "let us force the boycott." The report then invoked Psalm 2 ("let the heathen rage") and the Declaration of Independence ("let us pledge our lives, our fortunes and our sacred honor") to inspire their comrades against "this greatest of all iniquities"—alcohol. Texas Baptists adopted the whole report, indicating that the time for old-fashioned moral suasion was over.[86] Their American experience and identity had redefined the very meaning of Christian liberty.

Then in 1896, the SBC itself issued a resolution that not only endorsed prohibition, but also promised action against any Baptist who did any business with the liquor traffic. The resolution read:

> We announce it as the sense of this body that no person should be retained
> in the fellowship of a Baptist church who engages in the manufacture or
> sale of alcoholic liquors, either at wholesale or retail, who invests his money
> in the manufacture or sale of alcoholic liquors, or who rents his property

to be used for distilleries, wholesale liquor houses or saloon. Nor do we believe that any church should retain in its fellowship any member who drinks intoxicating liquors as a beverage, or visits saloons or drinking places for the purpose of such indulgence.

Though the SBC had no mechanism to enforce compliance, the power of state conventions could bar individual churches from their fellowship. By 1900, every Southern Baptist state convention save North Carolina had passed similar resolutions, which pressured their churches to comply. With these declarations, prohibition advocacy became a defining issue of Southern Baptist identity. It seems fitting that the main nineteenth-century social issue on which Southern Baptists demanded new government regulations also led state conventions to exert more direct control over churches. Baptists' increasing advocacy for alcohol prohibition by law paralleled their diminishing tolerance of dissenting views on alcohol in church government.[87] Rather than pursuing anticlerical politics and limited government, white evangelicals in the South reinterpreted temperance to mean a total war against alcohol that demanded its unconditional surrender through state-mandated prohibition.

While more traditionalist Christians favored working out their salvation apart from state interference, prohibitionists insisted that an enlarged government played a necessary part in attaining salvation from demon rum. Scholars like Richard Hamm, Ann-Marie Szymanski, and Lisa McGirr have made clear how prohibitionists contributed to the development of a more powerful federal government.[88] Prohibition also profoundly changed the South's perception of progressive, interventionist government on the state level. Despite the South's reputation for Jeffersonian Democracy and local rule, various scholars have pointed out how prohibition in the South was profoundly linked to the progressive movement and trademark streamlining of government. As Szymanski observed, the South grew more progressive through embracing prohibition, but she rejects the claim that the South's turn to progressivism came from chiefly northern influence, as William A. Link, Paul L. Harvey, and others have contended. Instead, she argues persuasively that southern progressives' approach to prohibition by gradual measures and local option often were more effective than more sudden and statewide approaches popular in the North. As a result, prohibition laws lasted much longer in the South than the rest of the nation. Whether or not progressivism in the South was mostly indigenous or imported, it was profoundly linked to radical changes in how southerners looked to government, from child labor laws to taxation reform. Thomas R. Pegram sums up a consensus among prohibition scholars by putting the reform at the forefront of a dramatic change for the Jeffersonian South: "[P]rohibition was a doorway to a host of reforms that entailed expanded state regulation over personal liberty."[89]

Conclusion

Traditional Christian views on temperance, the Bible, communion wine, and liberty all resisted the American innovation of alcohol prohibition. Despite citing Scripture to suit their own purposes, drys broke with classical morality, the example of Jesus, Christian ceremonies, and American traditions to advance their novel Gospel of prohibition. The truly traditionalist Christians were not drys, but wets.

The communion wine question still divides Christians today. Millions every Sunday imbibe grape juice at communion without considering how truly modern that drink is. Given the fierce debates within Baptist and Methodist churches over the issue, it is remarkable that during national prohibition neither federal nor state governments sought to prevent the production or consumption of sacred wine. It remains an open question how much of their Christian past prohibitionists left behind when they chose the cup of Dr. Welch over the cup of their spiritual forebears.

Decades after the Civil War resolved the theological and political crisis of slavery, Christians who read the same Bible and prayed to the same God continued to deploy theology and Scripture on both sides of a culture war, this time over prohibition. White evangelical drys continued to approach the Bible the same way most US citizens did up to the Civil War: with an individualist, republican, common-sense hermeneutic. This hermeneutic democratized the interpretation of the Bible and gave readers a sense of the certainty of their readings directly with the text apart from the traditional teachings and practices of the church.[90] Many today still invoke Christian faith for contemporary politics, and then as now, they do so on both sides of the culture wars.

Having taken a stance against Christian tradition for prohibition, white evangelical drys throughout the South took the political offensive in the 1880s, testing their political strength for the first time through a series of statewide and local prohibition campaigns. These referenda challenged southern traditions in three other areas: race, gender, and party unity. While drys' early efforts to dry up the Bourbon South mostly failed, they began a movement that challenged the region's norms and would eventually transform it into the Bible Belt.

2
"Dark and Peculiar"

RACE, GENDER, AND PROHIBITION IN THE 1880S SOUTH

JOHN B. RAYNER'S LETTER of March 17, 1887, was political dynamite. He wrote to Dr. Benajah Harvey Carroll, a fellow Baptist minister and the white leader of the Texas drys, that to win the upcoming election on statewide prohibition he needed Black support. Rayner, a self-professed "Prohibitionist by deep religious principle" and fellow Baptist, warned Carroll that "the negro vote is quite an item and will play an important part in the coming election." Rayner, an African American himself, advised Carroll how best to win the Black vote: enlist as many African American ministers and newspapermen as possible.[1] Soon thereafter, prominent Black ministers, including African Methodist Episcopal (AME) Bishop Henry McNeal Turner of Georgia, were campaigning in the state for prohibition. Rayner himself campaigned heavily in Robertson and surrounding counties.[2] As in North Carolina, Georgia, and Tennessee, drys in Texas in the 1880s initially sought to achieve prohibition through a multiracial coalition of voters. Interracial cooperation seemed to be working until early June, when wets obtained Rayner's secret letter and published it. One wet editor accused, "That Rayner letter and the presence of Bishop Turner needs, nay, demands explanation," and concluded, "Politics which mix up religions [sic] like that are dark and peculiar, and Dr. Carroll ought not to be in the business."[3] As with other prominent prohibition votes that year around the South, the Texas vote led to loss for the drys and resulted in white backlash to multiracial politics.

Prohibitionists in the 1880s South fought an uphill battle not only against racial conventions but also against gender norms. While southern traditions in the postbellum period put white women on a pedestal yet denied them basic civil rights, drys drew much of their support from women, both white and Black, and many drys advocated for women's suffrage. Women used the temperance movement to denounce abuse in the home and justify public activism as a necessary extension of their domestic sphere. Black women also sought racial uplift, middle-class solidarity, and feminine respectability by making common cause with their white sisters for prohibition. The intertwined social constructions of race and gender in the conservative Bourbon South militated against prohibition, particularly when it aligned with political empowerment for women and African Americans. Prohibition was too radical and transgressive for the 1880s South. To understand why the interracial prohibition campaigns of the 1880s mostly failed, however, one must first consider an essential piece of context: the racial history of prohibition in the Old South.

Origins of Southern Prohibition

Prohibition's slow progress in the Bourbon South stemmed in part from its old association with controlling nonwhite bodies. Long before most white southerners seriously contemplated limiting the access of fellow whites to alcoholic beverages, colonial legislatures in the South passed laws prohibiting the sale of alcohol to African American slaves. In the wake of the Stono Rebellion the year before, South Carolina's Slave Code of 1740 included such a provision. Section XXII strictly forbade a retailer to "give, sell, utter or deliver to any slave, any beer, ale, cider, wine, rum, brandy, or other spirituous liquors, or strong liquor whatsoever, without the license or consent of the owner, or such other person who shall have the care or government of such slave." Punishment for violation included payment, increasing for repeated offenses, which could result in up to three months of jail time.[4] In this respect, the colonial South was not distinctive from the colonial North. Massachusetts also had a law against selling spirits to any "Negro, Indian or mulatto slave" in 1751.[5]

Aside from slaves, colonial prohibition laws also targeted Amerindians. Despite believing that moderate alcohol consumption was "wholesome and necessary" for whites, British colonists across North America sought "to reduce and finally prohibit the sale or gift of intoxicating liquors" to indigenous peoples. According to Anti-Saloon League statistician and historian Ernest H. Cherrington, alcohol wrought "havoc" among Amerindians, indicating "clearly and emphatically their possibilities for evil" and proving that "it was all but impossible for the Red Man to drink in what the white man considered moderation." Colonists cared about this issue regarding Amerindian alcohol abuse only because "serious trouble with the savages . . . menaced the safety of the whites." Besides indigenous peoples, servants (including slaves) were also targeted for alcohol bans, since their drunkenness stole the labor that "belong[ed] to others."[6] The only colony that banned ardent spirits (distilled beverages) outright was Georgia, but even that was linked to class: it began as a penal colony, and the restrictions on alcohol were lifted in the 1750s, when restrictions on slavery were also lifted.[7]

The Old South had a few temperance organizations, but they failed to achieve much success in laws restricting alcohol sales, except for slaves.[8] And, as Lee L. Willis put it, slaves across the region "already lived under prohibition" before emancipation.[9] Tennessee's 1838 "quart law," the first ban on selling small quantities of intoxicating beverages in the United States, had only a modest impact. The quart law allowed purchases of larger quantities, resulting in effective prohibition for the poor but not the rich. The state legislature repealed the quart law in 1846 and replaced it with the old licensing system, along with a requirement that liquor dealers had to swear to not sell to slaves, allow gambling, or sell drinks on Sundays. The quart law was briefly reinstated between 1856 and 1857 before finally being consigned to oblivion.[10] As with the quart law, Mississippi enacted in 1839 a "gallon law" to ban liquor sales of less than a gallon. The law's severe penalties—a $200 fine and at least a week in jail for a first offense, $500 and a least a month in jail for subsequent convictions—prompted an angry mob to burn the law's sponsor, Henry S. Foote, in effigy in Jackson. The gallon law was replaced in 1842 by a law allowing sales by a licensed liquor seller—who had to be "a free white person."[11] Texas acquired an early taste for dry laws as well. In 1843, the Republic of Texas passed the first local option law in North America, allowing cities and counties to vote to ban alcohol for themselves. An 1845 Texas law banned saloons, though it was never enforced and was repealed by 1856. Prohibition laws in the Antebellum South were limited in scope, faced tremendous backlash, and were invariably repealed.[12]

When racial chattel slavery was overthrown by the Thirteenth Amendment to the US Constitution, former Confederates sought to salvage white supremacy through Black Codes to control Black labor—and drinking habits. A Mississippi law from November 1865 stated that any person of color who was convicted of selling "spirituous or intoxicating liquors" would be fined between ten and one hundred dollars and could be imprisoned up to thirty days, while any white person convicted of providing a person of color with weapons or an intoxicating drink could be fined up to fifty dollars and faced imprisonment of up to thirty days. Likewise, a South Carolina law in December 1865 prohibited African Americans from owning even part of a business that distilled or sold spirituous liquors or being employed as a distiller or seller of those drinks. While that act punished a person of color who engaged in such business with beating or hard labor at the discretion of a district judge or magistrate, there was no punishment for a white distiller who employed that person of color. Slave codes sought to control slaves' drinking habits through coercing white collaborators while benignly neglecting free Blacks, yet the Black Codes directly targeted alcohol access for all people of color.[13]

Given the racial connotations of alcohol control in the South, it is unsurprising that the prohibition movement originated in the North and initially met resistance in Dixie. In the early nineteenth century, the temperance movement was one of many causes, including abolitionism, developed and advanced by the evangelical reform nexus in the North. The Union victory in the Civil War brought some of these northern reform-minded evangelicals South through organizations such as the American Tract Society, African Methodist Episcopal Church (AME), African Methodist Episcopal Zion Church (AMEZ), American Baptist Home Mission Society, the American Missionary Association, and the National Temperance Society. While most of these groups were organized by whites, the AME and AMEZ were Black-led denominations, and all of these groups sought to provide African Americans in the South with spiritual and practical assistance. Missionary schools, public schools, churches, and fraternal lodges all encouraged Black leaders to embrace the convictions of the northern evangelical reform nexus, including alcohol prohibition, thus linking racial uplift with interracial reform.[14]

While laws targeting Black drinking disappeared under Congressional Reconstruction in the late 1860s and early 1870s, dry groups formed around the South. In addition to many of the antebellum reformist organizations mentioned above, other groups also came South and had chapters throughout the region by 1870, including: United Friends of Temperance, International Order of Good Templars, Sons of Temperance, Band of Hope, and Temperance Council. Dry newspapers such as Houston's *Temperance Family Visitor* (around 1871) cropped up around the South, and other local press gained sympathy for the movement.[15] The prohibitionist impulse was not limited to African Americans and so-called carpetbaggers but began taking root among southern whites.

After Reconstruction, white-supremacist Democrats wrote new state constitutions, many of which introduced local option laws. These laws, promoted by Jeffersonian Democrats and prohibitionists, empowered cities, counties, and other locales to prohibit or allow alcohol within their borders, usually by plebiscite. This arrangement produced a patchwork quilt of fully wet, bone-dry, and mixed "moist" locales across southern states, with towns and counties sometimes flipping back and forth between banning and legalizing alcohol. Some states resisted local option, such as Tennessee, which did not include it in the 1870 constitution, and the state's governor in 1873 vetoed a local option law.[16] Yet other states embraced the Jeffersonian arrangement of local option votes. Alabama had twenty-two dry counties by 1874. The 1876 Texas Constitution permitted local option laws, finding first success when Jasper County voted to go dry in December of that year.

The local option laws in several southern states, though modest in practical scope, marked a turning point for prohibition's racial dimension in the region. For the first time in southern history, blanket prohibition laws were imposed with votes from all the people they affected, including people of color. African Americans in the South, who had for generations been told by white overlords what they could not drink, could now vote in elections determining not only their own right to drink, but the rights of their white neighbors as well. For Black voters, postbellum prohibition contests offered a heady cocktail of freedom and power.

Meanwhile, many southern white evangelicals also came to appreciate the empowering possibilities and moral necessity of prohibition reform by the 1880s. While the connection of prohibition with causes such as abolition impeded its progress among southern whites before the Civil War, the end of slavery and then the end of Reconstruction by 1877 encouraged white evangelicals to focus less on securing white dominance through Democratic rule (which had already been achieved) and more on expanding their moral authority. Despite persisting regional denominational divides among Methodists and Baptists, many white evangelical clergy and laity sought to cooperate with their northern co-religionists to institute a sort of moral reconstruction in the decades after 1877. By the 1890s, white southern evangelicals' priorities mirrored the evangelical reform nexus, with most southern federal legislators backing laws against gambling and polygamy and for closing the World's Fair on Sunday.[17]

This transformation among white evangelicals took time. Robert Wuthnow argues that Texas churches were for most of the nineteenth century too focused on bringing order to a wild frontier by building institutions and instilling moral character to invest much in direct political activism, but by the early twentieth century, the landscape had changed. Fostered especially by Baptists and Methodists, the notion of liberty of conscience became a major part of civil religion, and both wets and drys claimed to uphold individual rights. Wets argued that each person should have free reign over whether to drink, but the church had no place demanding laws to force compliance with religious teaching. Drys, however, defended individuals' right to live upright lives free from alcohol addiction and moral degradation. Prohibitionists also argued that saloons corrupted politics through their collusion with political machines, that brewers and distillers were dominated by "foreigners" who undermined American liberty, and that leading dry organizations were not churches but nonsectarian and nonpartisan. By framing themselves as warriors for heaven and the homeland above the everyday fray of politics, drys increased their political clout and cultural influence as they sought to reshape the South in their own image.[18]

Threats to Bourbon Rule: African Americans and Women

The interracial prohibition movement in the South occurred in the broader context of other political threats to conservative Democratic rule in the South. During Reconstruction, African Americans experienced a new birth of freedom through emancipation, citizenship rights, public education, modest economic opportunities, the franchise, and—for the select few—offices in local, state, and federal government. Though white supremacists denounced "black rule" during Reconstruction, African Americans very rarely made up more than a minority of state and local officers in any given state at any time. Nonetheless, the elevation of Black Americans from slaves to state officials in a few short years surprised everyone in the South. Coupled with support from white Republicans—both northern-born "carpetbaggers" and southern-born "scalawags"—African Americans held the balance of political power in every state that underwent Congressional Reconstruction.

Since Republican rule in the Reconstruction-era South depended upon interracial coalitions of whites and Blacks, white-supremacist Democrats employed terrorism, intimidation, trickery, and fraud to wrest control in state after state. By 1877, all the formerly Confederate states were under Democratic control and remained so until the mid-twentieth century, nearly a century later. While Republicans still held some seats in localities, state legislatures, and even Congress, their representation dwindled. Southern white Republicans debated whether to have an interracial "Black and tan" party or go "lily-white" to have a chance at power, and eventually the lily-whites won out. By the 1890s, interracial politics in the South appeared finished.

Before southern Republicans had completed their abandonment of African Americans, the most serious opposition to conservative Bourbon rule in the early post-Reconstruction South came from a movement outside of the Republican Party. Founded by the former Confederate general and railroad tycoon William Mahone, the Readjuster Party from 1879 to 1883 dominated Virginia state politics. When the Virginia Republican Party collapsed in the state after the election of 1877, the dominant Conservative Party (essentially Democrats), called "Funders" for their intent to pay the state's debt in full at a fixed interest rate, dominated the state legislature and angered poorer Democrats who sought to refinance the state's debt and so reduce the burden of repayment on taxpayers. Mahone saw an opportunity to win over disaffected Democrats and disorganized Republicans by forming a new party, named Readjusters because of their commitment to readjusting payment of the state's debt. In addition to controlling the state legislature, the Readjusters elected five men to the US House, two to the US Senate—Mahone in 1880 and Harrison Holt Riddleberger in 1882—and a governor, William Evelyn Cameron. While limited to Virginia, this new party posed the most serious challenge at that time to Bourbon rule anywhere in the South.[19]

The Readjusters not only challenged the economic order but also promoted interracial political cooperation. In addition to other issues, the Readjusters abolished public whippings and ended Virginia's poll tax, both of which disproportionately burdened African Americans. By 1881, one-third of delegates to the statewide Readjuster convention were African Americans, and the white delegates mingled with their Black compatriots on terms of casual equality. As Nicole Meyers Turner observes, Mahone courted support from Black churches, who in turn played a crucial role in providing margins of victory for the Readjusters in the 1881 governor's election. But no good thing lasts forever. The Readjusters lost heavily in the 1883 elections when Democrats rallied most of the state's whites around the banner of white supremacy, and Readjusters lost their political clout in subsequent votes. Mahone's 1885 bid for governor likewise resulted in defeat. Like the Populist-Republican Fusionists in North Carolina in the 1890s, Virginia's Readjusters were a potent interracial political threat to Bourbon Democratic rule, and white supremacists put down the threat ruthlessly.

A lesser but potential threat to white-only Democratic rule in the 1880s South was the nascent Prohibition Party. Founded in 1869 by members of the Independent Order of Good Templars, the National Prohibition Party originated in northern states and has fielded a presidential candidate ever since 1872, making it the oldest extant national third party in the United States. However, the Prohibition Party never gained much traction in the South because most southern white drys were Democrats. They saw other parties as a potential threat to white-only rule by splitting the vote and giving racial minorities the power to swing elections. B. H. Carroll, a faithful Democrat, represented this "non-political" strain of dry activism in the South, though he worked with Black allies such as Rayner to win African American votes in special prohibition elections. By contrast, Carroll's friend and fellow Southern Baptist minister, J. B. Cranfill, was a "political" prohibitionist because he backed the Prohibition Party. Though Carroll's stance, by far the more typical of white southern drys, sought to distance prohibition from partisan politics, Carroll's articles for Cranfill's newspaper in the 1880s helped wets paint all prohibitionists as anti-Democratic.[20] While the specter of the prohibition question splitting the white vote and giving a decisive role to Black voters frightened some white southerners, it roused African Americans who saw an opportunity to regain the political clout they enjoyed during Reconstruction.

Looking back from the perspective of 1920, the ASL's Ernest H. Cherrington concluded that the Prohibition Party could never have succeeded as a party but succeeded in its great cause. From his perspective, the Prohibition Party founders "were not politicians; they were crusaders." While "Partyism" depends upon "opportunism" to "attract the largest number of voters," the Prohibition Party faithful "never knew the meaning of policy, prudence, or diplomacy." He further reflected that party loyalty was too strong. "Christian voters who are favorable to prohibition refuse nevertheless to leave the political party with which they are affiliated and vote for a new party, although that party may advocate the thing in which they believe." Though the Prohibition Party failed, they laid the groundwork for others to finish the work through "a great non-partisan political movement" that allowed "men to remain in their own political parties and yet give political expression to their Prohibition sentiment."[21] Yet the Prohibition Party stood not only for bans on alcohol, but also on suffrage for the most reliably dry demographic: women.

Women's Christian Temperance

Women turned the nation's attention to temperance in the 1870s and 1880s. A dramatic combination of prayer and social action took place in the "woman's crusade," when Eliza Jane Thompson led dozens of women on a tour of Ohio towns in December 1873 and early 1874 to kneel, pray, and sing in front of saloons until they shut down. This "Whirlwind of the Lord," as Frances Willard later called it, led directly to the creation of the Woman's Christian Temperance Union (WCTU) in 1874. Originally led by Annie Turner Wittenmyer, the WCTU grew to over a thousand chapters around the nation in five years.

The WCTU had focused exclusively on anti-alcohol activism until 1879, when Frances Willard became president and broadened the organization's focus to include women's suffrage. Willard justified the controversial goal of votes for women as a necessary means of "Home Protection" from the abuse, neglect, and family decline wrought by drunken husbands and fathers. Frances Willard, a devout Methodist, believed the idea was God-given during a prayer. Under her leadership, hundreds of thousands of women across the nation, including many culturally conservative women, joined in an activist movement for the twin radical reforms of women's suffrage and alcohol prohibition. The activism of Christian women suggested a holy alliance between women's activism and the explicitly Christian purification of culture.[22] While the first wave of temperance activism had little impact on the South, this second wave begun by the WCTU finally began making serious inroads in the US South.

Many women, both Black and white, despite not having the right to vote, also campaigned for prohibition, though for different reasons. White women drys were divided between radicals like Willard and conservatives, who dominated the WCTU in the South. In 1881, Willard made a tour of the South, including North Carolina during a statewide prohibition election, mobilizing WCTU women to advance the twin goals of prohibition and women's suffrage. "Everywhere the Southern white people desired me to speak to the colored," Willard recalled, but her aims differed from her white Democratic hosts. Willard desired to "liberate the suppressed colored vote" and "divide the white vote on the issues" and make a partisan "realignment" uniting drys North and South.[23] In short, Willard advocated for a multiracial Prohibition Party to challenge Republicans and Democrats alike.

Willard's radical advocacy for the Prohibition Party led to the founding of a nonpartisan WCTU by Judith Ellen Foster. The first woman admitted to practice law in Iowa in 1872, Foster served as a delegate to the first WCTU convention in 1874 and rose to become a legal advisor to the organization by 1880. Though like Willard she was a Methodist and a proponent of women's suffrage, Foster objected to Willard aligning the WCTU with the Prohibition Party for a simple reason: she was a dedicated Republican. In protest of its support for the Prohibition Party, she resigned from the national WCTU in 1884 and soon became the president of the Iowa state chapter. In 1888, she founded the Woman's National Republican Association and served as its president until her death in 1910. Frustrated by the WCTU's continued support for the Prohibition Party, she led the Iowa state chapter to split from the national WCTU in 1889 and founded a Non-Partisan National WCTU in 1890. The latter group never posed a serious threat to the dominance of the main WCTU, and the two groups reconciled after Willard's death in 1898. Though temporary, the split revealed the difficulty of holding a third party together around prohibition when women could advance their interests within the two-party system.[24] While northern white women like Foster sought to link prohibition with the Republican Party, most southern white women sought to tie their cause to the Democratic Party, which stood for white-supremacist rule.

For their part, many Black women sought prohibition not only for "Home Protection" from alcoholic men but also for racial uplift. The WCTU offered a respectable forum for activism and represented middle-class womanhood. For women subject to both sexual and racial double standards, asserting their Victorian morality while organizing for social reform alongside prominent white allies (particularly northern radicals like Willard) could seem very attractive. One leading Black voice in the North Carolina WCTU was Sarah Dudly Pettey, who electrified mixed-gender crowds with her oratory. One Black man cited her as a fine example of "womanly womanhood" and "a brilliant Frances Willard." In short, African American women joined the WCTU primarily to assert their equality with middle-class Christian whites.[25] While they were not opposed in principle to interracial politics and women's enfranchisement, which the Prohibition Party supported, many Black women preferred to back the Republican Party, which offered more practical avenues for racial uplift.

More conservative southern white women, meanwhile, seemed more interested in preserving racial hierarchy through the Democratic Party even as they reached out across the color line for votes on prohibition. For example, the white women running a prohibition club meeting in a Methodist church in Concord, North Carolina, in June 1881 invited Black women—to segregated seating in the balcony.[26] The ordering spoke loud and clear: white women wanted support from Blacks, but only as inferiors. After the 1881 statewide vote, the WCTU in North Carolina organized white and Black chapters, resulting in a state structure in which chapters of both races interacted as equals. However, as Glenda Elizabeth Gilmore has observed, southern white women saw African American women as their inferiors. By 1883, when Willard returned to the state, she anointed white supremacy by how she reorganized the local chapters into a statewide structure. All Black chapters were shunted into a department called "Work amongst the Colored People," which was led by a white woman.[27] Formerly engaging as near-equals, Black women in the WCTU were now treated as objects of missionary work and racial uplift under white supervision: separate and clearly unequal.

An 1889 schism in North Carolina's WCTU illustrated the difficulties of interracial cooperation on prohibition. Since the "Work amongst the Colored

People" was founded in 1883, the department head, Rosa Steele, was a white New England–born Methodist. She moved south when her husband, Professor Wilbur Steele, took a position teaching at a Black school. He later took a leading role in the state's Prohibition Party, and the couple sometimes dined with Black friends, for which the white press attacked him as "Social Equality" Steele.[28] Despite these credentials for interracial work, Rosa Steele adopted a paternalistic approach, critiquing Black chapters that organized and operated without white oversight, though in many cases no white women would volunteer for those positions. In 1888, Steele invited Sarah Jane Woodson Early, the Black superintendent of the national WCTU's "Colored Work for the South," to North Carolina. After five weeks of Early's campaign (funded by Black women), fourteen Black WCTU chapters stood strong around the state. Encouraged by Early's example and wearied by years of second-class treatment, these chapters seceded from the white-controlled state WCTU in 1889 and formed "WCTU No. 2." They intentionally "avoided using the word colored" in their name because they "believe[d] all men [were] equal."[29] The No. 2 held their own statewide conventions and reported directly to the national WCTU as an equal of the white state group.[30] Racial uplift and equality, more than unity with whites on prohibition, guided Black women on prohibition in the 1880s South.

As with male drys in other southern states, most dry men in Tennessee affirmed patriarchal politics and distanced themselves from claims that they supported votes for women. Wet papers called the WCTU a "great moral fraud," claimed that its members were "coquetting with politicians," and warned that drys sought women's suffrage. One dry Tennessee newspaper responded that "the women of Tennessee have no desire whatever to vote, and female suffrage has no place in the wishes of the prohibitionist of Tennessee." Since prohibition was "purely and simply a fight of the home against the saloon," it was "perfectly natural that the sympathies of every good woman in Tennessee should be for prohibition, and that they should use their united influence for its success."[31] For white dry southern men in the 1880s, the association of prohibition with women's suffrage was a political embarrassment, and they sought to distance themselves from women's political empowerment.

Nonetheless, branches of the "radical" WCTU under Frances Willard spread throughout the region after her 1881 tour of the South. Local WCTU unions arose in every southern state by 1883, while state unions took shape in Tennessee in 1881; in Georgia, Mississippi, North Carolina, and Texas, 1883; and in Alabama by 1884. These organizations addressed issues from "temperance Bible reading" to work with the press and "work among the colored people."[32]

Even more than lobbying for prohibition, the WCTU enjoyed some of its greatest impact through the indoctrination of children in churches and schools. Temperance discourses in the nineteenth century had proclaimed that alcohol abstinence was needed "to save the youth of our land from falling into the cruel bondage of strong drink,"[33] and the temperance movement had advanced this kind of education through sermons, books, and lesson plans from the 1840s to the 1920s.[34] The WCTU not only produced a flood of their own instructional material from the 1870s on but also pressured groups such as the International Sunday School Committee (ISSC), which was initially indifferent to their cause in 1881, to adopt it by 1887.

The Alabama state WCTU demonstrated how southern women could influence male-led denominations to join their cause. In 1885, the Alabama Baptist State Convention, with its 8,927 students in 249 Sunday school classes, endorsed the WCTU's plan for quarterly temperance lessons. Two years later, WCTU lessons appeared regularly in Southern Baptist periodicals around the nation. While the northern-based Methodist Episcopal Church (MEC) had embraced temperance lessons in 1880, Southern Methodists (MECS) from the North Alabama Conference in 1885 warmly received the WCTU missives and pledged to "teach temperance from the pulpit, in the Sunday-school, and from house to house until public opinion is properly educated."[35] Building on such pressure from states across the South, the MECS as a whole took a similar tack in 1886, and quarterly publications of the MECS included those lessons by 1887.

Presbyterians in Alabama proved more difficult to persuade. They took no direct action in 1885 on the WCTU's pleas, and Presbyterian promises in 1886 to produce explicit temperance lessons in denominational publications did not materialize until 1893. This delay came in part because Presbyterians sought to distance themselves from Methodists and Baptists, who retained fewer connections to Christian tradition than the old-fashioned Reformed faith of Presbyterians. They did, however, follow the ISSC's materials for Sunday school, so they effectively deployed some temperance education starting in 1887. In addition, the state WCTU worked with groups such as the Loyal Temperance Legions, Bands of Hope, and Kindergarten Schools to reach children beyond the church walls.[36]

Perhaps the most important area of the WCTU's reach was educating children in public schools. Mary Hanchett Hunt, who headed the WCTU's Department of Scientific Instruction, led the national effort to indoctrinate children in public education against alcohol by lobbying state legislatures to require anti-alcohol instruction. Hunt's moral crusade reaped remarkable dividends. By the 1880s, most states in the nation had compulsory temperance education, and by 1901 every state had it three times a week, indoctrinating twenty-two million children. Yet this battle was fought and won state by state at different rates. The Alabama WCTU, for instance, petitioned the state legislature for seven years, from 1884 to 1891, before it relented and required "instruction on the evil effects of alcohol on the body and mind." By 1908, nearly 259,000 white children and more than 127,000 Black children were being taught the horrors of alcohol in state-run schools.[37]

Hunt's curricula for students included abundant anti-alcohol material, some of it factually inaccurate and calculated to terrify children. One children's song chanted, "Tremble, King Alcohol; we shall grow up!"[38] The (mis)information campaign proved effective: one dry book later declared, "Constitutional prohibition was the result of a long process of education," and the WCTU fought at the forefront of that movement.[39] Yet in the 1880s, women in the South still could not vote while major prohibition contests emerged in states across the South and introduced perhaps the only political issue more controversial than prohibition or women's suffrage: interracial politics.

Race and Prohibition Campaigns in the 1880s

The 1880s were busy years for statewide prohibition campaigns around the nation, including the South. That decade witnessed referenda on state constitutional amendments about prohibition in many states.[40] Only three of these were in the South, and two of them, Texas and Tennessee, occurred in 1887. Yet Atlanta went through a pair of referenda in 1885 and 1887 that turned the city dry for a spell and then returned it wet. The first major contest in the region, however, was an 1881 vote on statewide prohibition in North Carolina (see table 1).

NORTH CAROLINA, 1881

Efforts at statewide prohibition in the South started with a flop in North Carolina. In 1879, the Good Templars there moved the Southern Methodists to pass a resolution urging a state law banning liquor, and the state's Southern Baptists pushed for a similar measure the next year. Due to a recent tax cut for alcohol sellers, prohibition sentiment was on the upswing in the state. North Carolina's Democratic Party had enough drys in the state legislature in early 1881 to push for a statewide vote on banning alcohol by law. The vote took place on August 4, turning the summer into an all-out contest about booze.[41]

The question cut against the grain of party lines, and Democrats were the most divided. The state's Democratic governor, Thomas Jordan Jarvis, expressed support for prohibition while denouncing any effort to divide white

Table 1. Major Prohibition Events in the US South, 1880s

DATE	STATE	TYPE	VOTES FOR	VOTES AGAINST
1881 Aug. 4	NC	Voters rejected statewide prohibition	48,370	166,325 (77.5%)
1885 Nov. 25	GA	Voters backed prohibition in Atlanta	3,829 (51.5%)	3,600
1887 Aug. 4	TX	Voters rejected statewide prohibition	129,270	220,627 (63.1%)
1887 Oct. 13	TN	Voters rejected statewide prohibition	117,504	145,197 (55.3%)
1887 Nov. 26	GA	Voters repealed prohibition in Atlanta	5,183 (56%)	4,061

Sources: Connor, ed., *A Manual of North Carolina Issued by the North Carolina Historical Commission for the Use of Members of the General Assembly Session 1913*, 1019–20; Robert Plocheck, "Prohibition Elections in Texas"; Endersby, "Prohibition and Repeal," 506; "Prohibition Vote in Tennessee," *New York Times,* October 18, 1887, 9; Thompson, *"A Stirring and Most Significant Episode,"* 184–87, 233, 235.

Note: As with other tables, statistics on some Texas elections missing in Plocheck are provided by Endersby. When their numbers differ, as for 1887 and 1935, I defer to Plocheck, whose numbers are confirmed in *Legislative Reference Library of Texas,* "Constitutional amendment election dates." Differences between Plocheck and Endersby are small—a few hundred or at most a few thousand out of hundreds of thousands—and results are never affected.

Democratic rule. As a speaker at the North Carolina State Prohibition Convention in May 1881, he said, "If this movement means to organize a political party, I do not go with it, but if it means to do the good work of eradicating vice, I go with it heart and soul."[42] Soon after the election, a South Carolina newspaper claimed that "decent government" depended on "keeping the whites solidly united" for the Democrats, but prohibition divided whites and strengthened the position of Blacks, who would elect legislators bringing "shame and disgrace" to the region.[43] One paper noted in May that the impending vote in North Carolina was "tearing both political parties in twain."[44] The prohibition question threatened politics as usual in the South.

At first, it seemed that North Carolina's Black vote would rally around prohibition in 1881, but by the election they went overwhelmingly wet. On June 25, a local paper noted: "Every colored newspaper in North Carolina" save one "favors prohibition. Is not this significant?"[45] This perspective was echoed by historian Glenda Elizabeth Gilmore, who stated that the Black press gave "nearly unanimous endorsement of prohibition."[46] By July, however, after the State Republican Committee declared itself against prohibition, both Black and white rank and file fell in for party unity. John Campbell Dancy, a Black politician, newspaperman, and popular temperance advocate from Tarboro, North Carolina, refused to campaign for the prohibition bill because "a very large majority" of his fellow Republicans were wet, and "under no circumstances would he fight the authorities of his party."[47]

Mr. Israel Braddock Abbott, a newspaper editor in New Bern and a former member of the state house, echoed Dancy. "I am a prohibitionist . . . yet I am a Republican, and stand, first by my party, then secondly by prohibition." Since the State Republican Committee opposed the bill, Abbott committed to using "all my influence against the prohibition bill" and believed that he and every other "true Republican" would always stand by the party "under any and all circumstances." The same newspaper reporting their views observed that, just weeks earlier, placards advertising dry events "were out in full blast—but at this writing we cannot hear of a single Prohibition speaker save Rev. J. C. Price." While that was hyperbolic—the same page noted that Dr. William Wells Brown of Boston, "probably the ablest negro orator living in America," would stump for prohibition—it did capture real decline for drys. Given the about-face of Black voters on prohibition, the only notable partisan divide by the August election was between white Democrats.[48]

North Carolina's 1881 election produced a landslide for the wets. While initial reports varied on the margin of victory, the final total was 166,325 wet to 48,370 dry for a margin of 117,955 votes of nearly 215,000 cast, or more than three-to-one for the wets.[49] How did the votes break down by party and race? According to the 1880 census, North Carolina had 807,242 white and 581,277 "colored" residents. Despite the minority position of the Republican Party since Reconstruction's end, tens of thousands of Black citizens there could still cast ballots in 1881.[50] One white-run South Carolina paper reported that white voters were divided while "the negroes were solid against" prohibition. While the paper also promoted Democratic rule against the "radicalism" of racial equality, its reporting on the united Black vote matched other sources such as the *New York Times,* which reported that virtually all Republicans, regardless of race, voted wet.[51] As historian Daniel Jay Whitener put it in the 1940s, "The consensus of opinion was that the Negroes voted almost solidly against prohibition."[52]

Most white Democrats also apparently voted against the measure. While one newspaper's claim that more than two-thirds of Democrats voted wet seems exaggerated, white Democrats almost certainly made up the majority of votes cast, and the vote was more than 77 percent wet, meaning that a strong Democratic majority was nearly certain.[53] Even without help from solidly wet Republicans, wets would have easily carried the day with Democratic support alone. That fact did not prevent some in the white dry press from blaming their failure on Black voters.[54]

The 1881 vote showed how the South inverted the typical partisan divide on prohibition in the 1880s. Outside the South, Republicans—from leadership to the rank and file—championed prohibition, and the Prohibition Party was more likely to siphon votes from the GOP. After all, the infamous jibe that Democrats were the party of "Rum, Romanism, and Rebellion" came from a New York Republican in 1884. However, partisan loyalties on alcohol flipped in the South. In 1881 North Carolina, a Missouri paper noted that the "curious thing about this Southern prohibition" is that it appeared to be "altogether a Democratic idea." Democrats were divided on the issue while Republicans—"nearly all of them, white and black"—opposed it, and the Prohibition Party chiefly threatened Democrats rather than Republicans.[55] At least in 1881 in the South, rum and Republicanism were allies.

ATLANTA, 1885 AND 1887

Four years later in neighboring Georgia, however, a coalition cut across partisan and race lines to enact prohibition in Atlanta, one of the South's largest cities. On November 24, 1885, Henry McNeal Turner, the AME's most prominent bishop, addressed a crowd of more than five thousand prohibitionists. Most of them, like Turner, were African Americans preparing to vote the next day on banning saloons in the city. In that election, Turner proclaimed, Black Americans were "on trial before the country to see whether they will vote as honest, sober men or whether they can be purchased with money and mean liquor." Rather than submit to the chains of corruption by white saloon men, Turner urged them to vote dry so that "if Abraham Lincoln looked down from heaven[,] he would not be ashamed of the people whom he set free."[56] The crowd went wild. The next day, Turner's version of Lincoln would have been proud: the final vote gave drys a margin of victory of just 229 votes out of 7,429 cast.[57]

For the first time since the end of Reconstruction, freely cast Black votes in Atlanta determined the margin of victory for a major policy issue. That election was, to borrow the title of H. Paul Thompson's book, "a stirring and most significant episode" in race relations in the South. Unlike in North Carolina in 1881, white votes were evenly divided on the issue. Similar municipal prohibition votes, which divided white Democrats and allowed African Americans to cast decisive votes, appeared throughout the South in the 1880s, including in Greenville, South Carolina.[58]

After African Americans in neighboring North Carolina voted overwhelmingly wet in 1881, why did most Black voters in Atlanta four years later support prohibition? The simplest answer is that Black voters believed that voting dry would better benefit their race. Bishop Turner pointed out in his speech that a vote for prohibition was a vote for Black manhood, proving in the sight of God and man that African American voters were pure and upright, fully deserving human and civil rights alongside the "better sort" of whites.

After the vote, it took time for prohibition to take effect, and its results were disappointing for Black voters hoping for visible racial uplift. June 1, 1886, marked the official start of prohibition in Atlanta, though enforcement of the law proved more difficult than voting for it. Despite the promise of great change, prohibition resulted in remarkably little change to the status quo. While white drys valued Black votes, they were more intent on keeping whites in power than advancing prohibition. This sense of betrayal led many African Americans to take a disillusioned attitude toward prohibition's promises of interracial cooperation. By 1887, a campaign to repeal prohibition took place, and this time wets prevailed, 5,183 votes to 4,061 for the drys. The results of the 1887 vote revealed that Black voters once again decided the election, though this time they went wet.[59]

TEXAS, 1887

Fulton County's temporary dry victory by a multiracial coalition in November 1885 inspired similar campaigns for statewide prohibition from neighboring Tennessee to faraway Texas. Not content to stay in Atlanta, Turner also campaigned in Texas and Tennessee in 1887 to spread the dry gospel. Along with many other Black drys, Turner urged the "best people"—namely, those who embraced middle-class Victorian morality, including prohibition—to unite across the race line. Even without John Rayner's letter encouraging Carroll to invite Turner to Texas for the prohibition campaign, Bishop Turner likely would have come there anyway to support racial uplift by aligning Black citizenship rights with prominent white prohibitionists.

In Texas, Baptists played major roles for prohibition. Dry leaders in 1886 appointed white Baptist minister James Cranfill to their committee on Texas Baptists. Most importantly, the Baptist preacher and former Confederate soldier B. H. Carroll became head of the drys in 1887.[60] With Carroll's blessing, Rayner enlisted African American Baptists for the prohibition cause.[61]

Prominent African American pastors, including the national leader of the AME, Bishop Henry M. Turner of Georgia, campaigned in Texas as well. At the same time, Rayner had warned Carroll that many African American Baptist ministers and newspapermen would side with the brewers if not first secured by the drys.[62]

While some white drys embraced interracial politics, some preferred the politics of racial exclusion. Cranfill, a white Baptist and member of the Prohibition Party, sabotaged Carroll's inclusive approach with a racist editorial, "The Native White Man," in his newspaper. The editorial sought to rally "the native, white, Anglo-Saxon elements of the South" for prohibition against the "bo-dutch," "nigger," and "low-bred foreigners."[63] Even after an official apology by Carroll, Cranfill's rhetoric helped push every ethnic and racial minority into the wet camp.[64] Interracial bridges were easier to burn than to build.

Perhaps the weightiest voice against prohibition for white southerners was the high priest of the Lost Cause, Jefferson Davis. Texas's current US senator and former governor, Richard Coke, had served on Davis's staff during the war and coaxed him to offer his input on the prohibition question in Texas. Davis replied with an open letter. While he admitted that temperance was good and alcoholism a great evil, prohibition tended "to destroy individual liberty and moral responsibility" and would effectively "eradicate one evil by the substitution of another," which was even "more fatal" than the other.[65] In short, the cure of prohibition was worse than the disease of drunkenness. The letter dominated news around the state for several days, and all parties believed it played a major role in the amendment's defeat. A similar letter by Davis spelled the same fate for prohibition in Tennessee. The former president of the late Confederacy was not merely political, but almost a religious leader for many southerners who embraced Lost Cause ideology. For them, Davis was more authoritative on the question than any preacher or politician, no matter how venerable.[66]

Wets deftly appealed to the white majority. The wet state committee's statement of principles claimed that prohibition was "at war with the fundamental principles of Anglo-Saxon civilization." Wets believed that white male supremacy was threatened by prohibition, and they were not entirely wrong. Not only did some drys promote women's suffrage, but the Prohibition Party threatened white supremacy by dividing white votes and undermining one-party rule.[67] Wets also attacked drys' interracial collaboration. In early June, wets obtained and published Rayner's secret letter to Carroll, claiming that African Americans were the brains behind the drys. One wet editor demanded explanation for the Rayner letter and Bishop Turner's political activism and denounced Carroll for mixing religion and politics, particularly across the race line.[68] "The success of the [wet] cause has never been doubtful for one moment," the Waco *Daily Examiner* crowed, "since Parson Rayner came to Parson Carroll's help with advice as to how to run the campaign."[69] Since both Black and white clergy fueled the drys' grassroots movement, they were susceptible to accusations of uniting church and state as well as undermining white supremacy.[70]

At the same time, African American speakers effectively mobilized many Black voters for the wets. Black Republicans such as J. C. Akers of McKinney and Melvin Wade stumped East Texas, giving wet speeches and debating drys. A former slave, Wade became a prominent Dallas businessman and led several state Republican conventions. According to him, white drys wanted to "curtail your freedom," but Blacks voted wet out of their "passion for freedom." Akers and Wade's contention that prohibition would further limit their already compressed liberty resonated with African American Republicans who recalled their days in bondage, their losses since Reconstruction, and the importance of liberty in American Christianity.[71]

The connection of liquor with liberty in the 1880s took clearest expression in Robert Reed Church Sr., the South's first African American millionaire, who began his Memphis career as a saloon owner. Like Ida B. Wells, Church was born in Holly Spring, Mississippi, to a slave mother. Church, however, was raised by his white father, owner of a steamboat fleet on the Mississippi River, where he gained entrepreneurial experience. By 1865, he had settled in Memphis and acquired a saloon while his wife, Louisa Ayres Church, opened beauty parlors. A white mob shot Church and left him for dead during the 1866 Memphis riot, but he survived and was determined to remain. During the 1878 yellow fever epidemic, when so many fled Memphis that the city was demoted to a taxing district, he stayed and was the first person to buy a $1,000 bond to help restore the city's charter. By 1887, Church had established himself as a philanthropist of stature in the city, and by the end of the century, he owned numerous saloons. While Church made most of his fortune in banking and real estate, his continuing connections to saloons linked beer with Black entrepreneurship, resilience, and racial uplift and doubtless inspired many African Americans to vote wet in 1887.[72]

Black activists, both wet and dry, used prohibition referenda as opportunities to divide the white Democratic vote and give Black voters a meaningful role in major political campaigns, especially at the state level. Norris Wright Cuney, the African American leader of Texas Republicans from 1884 to 1896, was offered a seat on Texas's anti-prohibition executive committee in 1887, but he declined the honor to avoid pushing Democrats into the dry camp. As he put it, he sought to avoid "giving the anti-prohibition movement political recognition and sanction, which has been so far avoided on both sides." Yet his personal stance on alcohol was not ambiguous. He drank claret each night before sleeping, and the invitation to join the wets showed his equally unambiguous public stance. Ever the politician, Cuney was shrewd enough to realize that his presence on the wet executive committee would likely push more racist whites into the dry camp and so be counterproductive.[73]

Texas wets issued a twenty-six-page pamphlet that advanced two old Christian ideas: limited government and temperance as moderate use rather than outright prohibition. First, it extolled a license system at the local level as the most effective way to limit drunkenness, particularly by encouraging lighter drinks such as beer and light wine against distilled liquors. Second, it denounced prohibition as counterproductive because the impulse to drink was natural and healthy, and any attempt to ban such drinks would only encourage citizens to subvert the law and overdrink. The pamphlet also cited authorities from James Madison to Alexander Hamilton and linked prohibition to then-radical movements like free love and women's rights. Above all, it argued that prohibition was tyranny: it took away God-given liberties.[74] Ideals of local government and classical Christian beliefs in moderation over abstinence persisted with a critical mass of southern voters in the 1887 elections.

Wets' shrewd arguments resonated with most Texan voters. The election on August 4, 1887, delivered a predictable result: 220,627 wet votes to 129,270 dry. That was a margin of more than 90,000 wet votes, or more than 63 percent of the vote going wet, nearly two to one.[75] While their victory was not as dramatic as in North Carolina six years earlier, wets demonstrated that they could still dominate the vote in the South. Yet another statewide prohibition election in the South was just a few months away in Tennessee.

TENNESSEE, 1887

After their failure in Texas, southern drys in 1887 tried their luck once more in a push for statewide prohibition in Tennessee, which had been growing in dry strength for years. Though the governor vetoed an 1873 law to allow local option elections on prohibition, the Volunteer State a few years later gained the Four Mile Law, perhaps the most advanced temperance legislation in the South. Sewanee, the University of the South, secured in 1877 passage of the Four Mile Law, which banned liquor sales within four miles of a school in an incorporated town. Four years later, the state supreme court ruled that the Four Mile Law could only be enforced around incorporated schools, not in the free schools of some counties. The founding of a state WCTU in 1882 signaled the growth of the dry movement in the state. By 1885, the state WCTU and other drys lobbied the Tennessee legislature to pass a prohibition amendment to the state constitution. The text of the amendment read: "No person shall manufacture for sale or keep for sale as a beverage any intoxicating liquors whatever, including wine, ale, and beer. The General Assembly shall by law prescribe regulations for the enforcement of Prohibition herein contained, and shall thereby provide suitable penalties for the violation of the provision thereof."[76] While a majority of the legislature voted for the amendment, the needed two-thirds majority could not be attained in the senate, and as in North Carolina in 1881, both parties in Tennessee preferred a plebiscite to avoid open division in their ranks. So, on September 29, 1886, an overwhelming majority voted to submit the amendment to a popular vote, which was scheduled to take place exactly a year later, on September 29, 1887.[77]

As in Georgia and Texas, Tennessee drys also attempted to distance their movement from partisan politics. One paper stated in early September that the prohibition movement "is not political party measure, and has not connection with any political party," despite the attempts of wet papers such as *New Era* to brand it as such.[78] Later that month, the same paper claimed that prohibition sentiment rang throughout the state, endorsed by "Democrats and Republicans, black and white" alike.[79] Drys claimed then, as they had for years before and decades since, that prohibition would conserve public resources by reducing the crime caused by saloons, which cost taxpayers more through prisons than it gained by liquor licenses. In 1887, drys convinced four hundred convicts in Nashville to claim that three-quarters of the state's criminals were incarcerated due to alcohol. Newspapers such as the limited-time *Woman's Appeal* and the popular Nashville *Banner* supported the dry cause. The Jonesboro WCTU sought to woo voters through music, festive decorations, and "free lunches on election day"—a transparent, if effective, effort at low-key bribery in an age before the secret ballot.[80]

Leading up to the vote, tensions rose and occasionally flared into violence. After drys insulted Betsy Ward, a saloon owner who stood fast against a Woman's Crusade in Greeneville, Tennessee, in 1874, her eighteen-year-old son, William Ward, fought with them, resulting in his death. Despite the drys' claims that alcohol led to violence and crime, they themselves contributed to the same in the killing of a teenage boy. Wets, for their part, maintained that prohibition would generate more crime by creating an illicit alcohol traffic, harm the economy, reduce public revenue, and undermine the basic principles of democratic liberty.[81]

The vote was closer in Tennessee than in Texas, but it still resulted in defeat for the drys. The tally had 145,197 wet votes to 117,504 dry, or 55 percent wet. According to the *New York Times,* it was the largest turnout of any election in the state's history up to that point.[82] Despite losing the state, the drys carried several counties in East Tennessee, showing their strength in the Appalachian region. Some drys blamed political machines of both major parties, while the state WCTU chair, Silene Moore Holman, declared that drys would have easily won if women only had the right to vote.[83]

Tallying the Votes

One common but dubious charge in all of these 1880s prohibition referenda was that Black voters were to blame for the defeat of the drys in every case. This charge was the least credible in North Carolina, in which most African Americans followed Republican Party directives and voted wet. Yet even so, the final tally was 77.5 percent wet, so overwhelming that most white voters, Republican and Democratic alike, also likely rejected prohibition. Nevertheless, some white drys implausibly tried to blame African Americans for their loss.[84]

In Atlanta, on the other hand, it was certainly true that Black votes made up the margin of victory in both directions. As H. Paul Thompson has examined at length, African Americans cast deciding votes to turn the county dry in 1885 as well as to turn it wet in 1887. Black voters who supported prohibition in 1885 because of the opportunity for interracial political cooperation grew disillusioned by the broken promises of whites. At the same time, the white vote also went wet in 1887, meaning both racial groups were equally responsible for the result.[85]

More ambiguous are the cases of Texas, which voted 63 percent wet, and Tennessee, which went 55 percent wet. Blaming Blacks for their defeat in 1887 had become a popular myth among white drys by the 1900s, as a letter B. H. Carroll in 1909 attests.[86] Yet whites at the time also baselessly blamed African Americans for prohibition's failure in the 1880s South, as W. E. B. Du Bois pointed out.

Du Bois, the first African American to earn a PhD from Harvard University, and a self-proclaimed prohibitionist, attested that most white drys immediately scapegoated African Americans for their 1887 defeats. In a seven-page handwritten "Open letter to the Southern People" dated that year, he flipped white drys' anti-Black narrative and blamed the losses on white folly. He noted that white drys only courted Black voters, whom they ordinarily regarded as animals, because they "saw that without the Negro vote prohibition would fail."[87] So, even though the Black man was "generally recognized as a man" and "cordially" entreated by white drys during the campaign, the appeal was "wholly without effect." True, some joined the drys' ranks: "The large majority of intelligent Colored men, the students of Fisk, Atlanta, Clark, and other schools, responded to the call and worked mostly for the cause." Nevertheless, "the wet majority of the Negro race . . . are *not* intelligent" (emphasis original), and so vulnerable to manipulation by wet operatives due to white leaders' "short-sighted policy which refused us [African Americans] education and oppressed us with caste prejudice."[88] In Du Bois's estimation, the Talented Tenth worked with the "better" sort of white prohibitionists, while the uneducated masses were seduced by ignoble wet operatives. Thus, southern whites' racist policies "recoiled upon its strongest advocates." Du Bois took the opportunity to echo the Bible and compare Black voters to Jesus: "The stone which the builders rejected had of length become the head of the corner."[89]

Another reason for African American hesitation to vote dry, according to Du Bois, was the close association of white-supremacist Democrats with the dry cause. As he put it, Black voters "saw, as an old Negro said to me, 'A heap too many dimocrats in dis yere ding!'"[90] While a few elite African Americans coordinated their dry campaigning with B. H. Carroll, the white leader of Texas drys, most Black voters were likely concerned because Carroll was a white Democrat. White southern Democrats' policies had led most African Americans to surmise "that whatever is for the benefit of the white man is to his detriment."[91] While the prohibition vote did not fall neatly along party lines, aligning Black voters with white Democrats was a hard sell.

Though correctly pointing out why most Black voters in 1887 trended wet, Du Bois incorrectly claimed that the "majority of the Whites" voted for prohibition in those contests.[92] At least for Texas, there is clear evidence that whites and Blacks voted along similar lines, with both groups voting wet independently. While scholars agree that Texas's 1887 prohibition amendment was soundly defeated,[93] they take different positions on just how wet African Americans, native-born whites, and foreign-born whites voted, so Texas merits more analysis than the other cases.

Texan historian Gregg Cantrell argues that native-born white Democrats were nearly evenly split on the issue while Blacks and foreign-born voters decisively rejected prohibition, so 74 percent of African Americans voted wet.[94] Jared Paul Sutton concluded that "black Texans voted heavily against every prohibition election,"[95] yet his data do not definitively prove that Black voters in 1887 were any wetter than white voters. A careful analysis of his raw data and other census information (see table 2) suggests that Black voters in 1887

Table 2. Comparing 1887 Texas Vote to Black Population in Select Counties

COUNTY	BASTROP	HARRIS	HARRISON	HOUSTON	REFUGIO	SABINE
Black % of total population 1887	41.6%	22.7%	59.4%	33.7%	30.7%	24%
% of total population voting wet in 1887	76.2%	74.1%	76.6%	66.7%	91.1%	42.3%
Total population, 1887	19,966	38,344	26,922	20,255	1,245	4,525

Source: Sutton, "Ethnic Minorities," 35, 80, 82, 86.

did not behave significantly differently from other voters, since there was no consistent correlation between the Black percentage of a county's population and the percentage of wet voters in that county.[96]

James Ivy has made the most thorough attempt to provide specific numbers for racial and ethnic groups in the 1887 election, and his numbers on African American voters deserve the most scrutiny.[97] Ivy tallied the Black vote total at 71,338 while placing their opposition to prohibition at over 83 percent, an even higher rate than in Cantrell's model, which had 74 percent voting wet. Even so, Ivy has confessed that his model is imperfect. To his great credit, Ivy granted that his model initially inaccurately calculated the foreign-born vote and "yielded an impossible result" of 122.3 percent wet, which he adjusted accordingly (to 91.3 percent wet, close to Cantrell's projection of effectively 100 percent wet). In addition, Ivy's estimate of the Black vote is suspect because of a sizable computational error elsewhere. His vote total for drys in the 1911 statewide vote inverted two crucial numerals: the actual number was 231,096 for Prohibition, but Ivy inverted the 3 and 1 to make 213,096, a difference of 18,000 votes. While understandable, that computational error nearly quadrupled the margin of victory from the actual 1.3 percent of the total vote to "over five percent" in his reckoning.[98] Given the admitted flaws of Ivy's model regarding foreign-born voters and his erroneous reporting of the 1911 results, it seems possible that his African American vote projection might also need correction.

If Ivy's Black vote projection is adjusted to reflect a contemporary estimate of the Black vote, Black voters were *drier* than the population at large. By lowering Ivy's African American wet vote percentage downward by the same proportion as his adjustment for foreign-born whites (about one-quarter), results come to about 62 percent of African Americans voting wet. That number very nearly fits the 60 percent figure given by the *Star of Zion,* an African Methodist Episcopal Zion (AMEZ) newspaper edited by John C. Dancy, just a few weeks after the 1887 election. The AMEZ paper conceded that, out of approximately 80,000 African Americans casting ballots in Texas, 60 percent of them voted wet.[99] While the dry paper might have overestimated dry support, its contemporary reporting and its willingness to give the wets a clear majority of the Black vote support its veracity. Tweaking that 60 percent number upward to account for bias and too-neat rounding, one arrives at something close to the 62 percent made by adjusting Ivy's total downward. Given that tweaked percentage, African Americans in 1887 Texas voted comparably to white voters. Contrary to scholarly assumptions that Black voters were wetter than whites, they were, at least in Texas, as dry if not *drier* than whites.

However, even if Ivy's high-end estimate of Black voters as 83 percent wet (or Cantrell's estimate of 74 percent wet) is correct, native-born white voters would have defeated prohibition all by themselves without help from racial and ethnic minorities. Ivy argues that native-born whites voted 55 percent wet and provided nearly two-thirds of the overall wet vote, while African Americans provided scarcely a quarter of the wet vote. Ivy's analysis thus effectively refutes Gregg Cantrell's deductions that native-born whites were evenly split in 1887; Ivy's 55–45 is a far cry from Cantrell's 50–50. And if the adjusted projections of the Black vote as 62 percent wet are correct, then even more than 55 percent of native whites voted wet, making the nonwhite vote even less consequential in the wets' victory. Despite fears among some whites in both the dry and the wet camps that Black participation in the election might imperil white supremacy, African Americans did not cast decisive votes in Texas in 1887.[100]

Given this context, claims by Du Bois and others that Black voters tipped Tennessee wet later that year must be taken with a grain of salt. According to a Tennessee paper (citing a Republican paper elsewhere), more than two-thirds of whites voted dry while about 92 percent of black voters went wet, so that drys would have won by 40,000 votes were it not for Black voters. However, the paper defended the integrity of African Americans; they were not "corruptly influenced" but voted wet because "they are not far enough away from the period of slavery to willingly take any risks where a question of individual liberty is in the remotest degree involved." Indeed, black voters were even *more* wary than whites of any movement that might seem to be "abridging their rights," including prohibition. Black voters in Tennessee went wetter than whites, the paper claimed, because their love of liberty was greater.[101]

Despite its charitable interpretation of why most Black voters went wet, this paper's claim that 92 percent of them opposed prohibition seems a bit high, particularly given the much more mixed African American vote in Texas earlier that year (62 percent wet). While African Americans might have provided the margin of victory in Tennessee, this seems implausible. The failure of Tennessee to produce effective statewide prohibition for several more decades, years after most Black voters had been effectively disfranchised, suggests that most whites had opposed prohibition since the 1880s and continued to do so for decades. A simpler and more plausible explanation is that white and Black votes in Tennessee both voted equally wet, but white drys sought to blame their failure on their Black neighbors—and wet Republicans sought to credit Black voters for their defense of liberty.

Rather than being caused by Black voters, the defeat of southern drys in the 1880s statewide votes was mainly due to white evangelical ministers failing to convince their parishioners. Methodist and Baptist laity were ambivalent about political preaching; the flocks had flogged back their shepherds. This pew-pulpit divide was laid bare in the title of the 1887 Baptist General Convention of Texas (BGCT) temperance report: "Attitude which Baptists *should* Occupy toward the Liquor Traffic" (emphasis mine). That report claimed that Baptists ought to confront the liquor traffic with "Truceless, uncompromising, eternal war," but this was aspirational, not descriptive.[102] For years after 1887, the committee spilled more ink recording the powers and evils of the alcohol lobby than progress against it.[103] Perhaps the most devastating admission was in the 1894 report: "the attitude Baptists *should* occupy" did not match "the attitude Baptists *do* occupy on this important subject" (emphases original). They admitted with sorrow that "the attitude of Baptists toward the liquor traffic is one of general apathy." Still, the committee affirmed the right of Baptists to dissent: "It is not competent for this Convention to dictate to any Baptist the attitude he should occupy on any question of conscience, but your committee announces its own position." While allowing dissent, the closing prayer urged Baptists to be "loyal and brave and true," implying that wets were disloyal, cowardly, and false.[104]

Decades later, white drys looked back on the 1887 campaigns as a turning point. In 1923, J. M. Carroll recalled the 1887 fight as a military affair which "affected the life and Christian standing of every denomination, of every church, of every preacher and of every individual within the State of Texas." More than affecting all peoples in the state, the campaign proved "a mighty revealer of men and things," not only who were "the real men" and who the "imitating manikins," but also "it revealed Satan, the one supreme personality back of the whole nefarious business."[105] Baptist ministers told to stay out of the political issue of prohibition remained convinced that they were merely expressing their right and duty to speak out against evil, and would rather endure privation and slander as real men than fail to resist Satan. However, southern white evangelical churches had more than a few "imitating manikins" who felt free to vote wet in 1887.

The perceived satanic threat posed by demon rum remained in 1893, when the BGCT temperance report gave the grimmest picture yet of the power of the liquor traffic. "Never before in the history of America," they declared, "has there been greater aggression or more compact organization on the part of the liquor sellers than now." Particularly in Texas, the "secret organization among saloon keepers has been perfected and has permeated every nook and corner of our state." The evil network "is to our state what the mafia was to New Orleans and what the nihilists are to Russia"; its "emissaries of evil are always at work and exercise more power in the state . . . than all the preachers in Texas."[106] The next year the committee "doubted whether there is in all the world a greater impediment to the spread of the gospel of Jesus than the saloon."[107] To fail to stand against the traffic "is like asking our mothers and their little ones to march in to the valley of the shadow of death and to the gate of hell," and accordingly the committee recommended "intolerance toward dram-drinking in our members" and living out total abstinence as "a chief aim" to assert the church's moral influence.[108] This shift toward putting their own house in order continued over the next several years, strengthened prohibition sentiment among white Baptists and white Methodists, and laid the foundation of a new generation of prohibitionists who would challenge the alcohol industry more effectively.[109] Yet in the 1880s, the "demon" of anti-prohibition sat comfortably in their pews.

Conclusion

In the South, the close tie between feminism and prohibition initially hurt drys. Women helped stir up the first major surge of interest for prohibition in the 1880s, though most southern white men wanted to keep women out of politics just as much as they wanted to keep out prohibition. As James Ivy argues, the close association of prohibition with socially disruptive "long-haired men" and "short-haired women" contributed to the defeat of prohibition in Texas in 1887, and dry leaders thereafter marginalized the role of women in future prohibition campaigns. Similar results in North Carolina and Tennessee that decade reinforced similar ideas across the region. Joe Coker argues that prohibitionists across the South gained success only because they adapted to uphold traditional gender roles, keeping women on a pedestal but away from the ballot box.[110]

While the 1887 campaigns failed by wide margins, they mobilized the Black vote and demonstrated that African Americans were sought after as a swing vote in elections on alcohol. Unfortunately, many white drys perceived the Black vote as a stumbling block to be overcome and sought to strengthen their position by joining a growing movement to disfranchise nonwhites. The 1880s campaigns thus generated a backlash that would eventually link prohibition in the South inextricably with Jim Crow.

Figure 1. John Baptis Rayner, a minister, prominent African American Populist, and major campaigner on both sides of the prohibition issue from the 1880s (as a dry) to the 1910s (as a wet). Library of Congress Prints and Photographs Division.

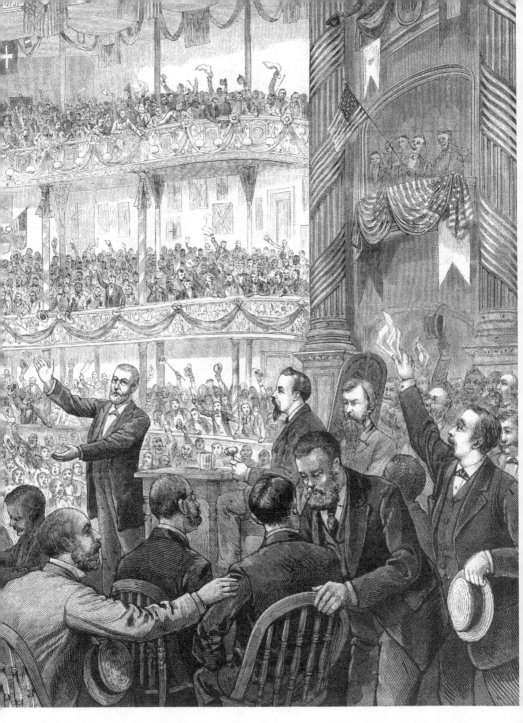

Figure 2. Readjusters in Virginia, who represented the most serious interracial threat to Democratic rule in the South between the end of Reconstruction and the Populist movement. Image from *Frank Leslie's Illustrated Newspaper* (June 25, 1881), courtesy of the Library of Virginia.

Figure 3. "Cotton Tom" Heflin, a US representative (1904–20) and US senator (1920–28) from Alabama, notorious white supremacist, and shooter of Mr. Lundy in 1908. Library of Congress Prints and Photographs Division.

Figure 4. Oscar Wilder Underwood, one of the most powerful opponents of national prohibition, women's suffrage, and the Klan in the South. He represented Alabama in the US House (1895–96, 1897–1915) and US Senate (1915–27). Library of Congress Prints and Photographs Division.

Figure 5. Cartoon from a dry newspaper after Texans voted down statewide prohibition in 1911. At left is "Justice" weighing votes on uneven scales tilting toward "Anti" (against prohibition). She peeks with her unblindfolded eye at a Black angel with "poll tax receipts" who hands her more votes, saying: "Here is some perfectly fresh ones mam." At top right is a "Portrait of a broad-minded (wet-foot Mexican) voter," showing a dark-skinned man in fancy clothes holding a poll tax receipt. These two images visually represent the common view among white drys that Black and Mexican votes fraudulently decided the referendum against prohibition. *Home and State*, Dallas, August 5, 1911. Courtesy of the Texas State Library and Archives.

SIDNEY J. CATTS
of DeFuniak Springs Florida

The People's Candidate for Governor of the State of Florida

Subject to the Democratic Primary 1916.

The Catt, The Catholics and Whiskey Men Are Fighting

Mr. Catts will speak at

Florida

To-Night at _____ o'clock on the issues here stated. Ladies, gentlemen and children are invited to be present. Especially the Democratic voters of the State are requested to hear him.

A native of Alabama, but he loves his adopted state—Florida, and will use his best endeavors for her betterment.

He is a Baptist preacher, a Woodman of the World, a Knight of Pythias and a Mason. He is also Chaplain of the First Florida Brigade of United Confederate Veterans, with the rank of Major. Mr. Catts is also State Manager of the Home's Friend, of Athens, Ga. He has been compared in his oratory to Wm. L. Yancey, who stirred the South to fury in 1858 to 1860; in his power to sway men by his eloquence, to Henry Ward Beecher at Plymouth, England, and in his power to charm by the beauty of his language, to the golden-tongued Frank F. Ellis, of Baltimore. Be sure you hear him speak during the campaign. Mr. Catts comes before the people of Florida on the following platform which he will present to the people of Florida alike, and live up to if elected:

1.—Economy in all parts of the State Government, so that the taxes of the people can be lowered constantly.

2.—Equalization of Taxation, so that the large corporations shall pay a juster proportion of taxation.

3.—To help the county, village and town schools in every way possible—by extending their terms, giving more money to them, giving better teachers and in every way possible supporting and strengthening them. Dry these schools up and you dry up the tides of the nation's power. Build them up and you build the nation up.

4.—Nothing in Florida above the Nation's flag. As Roman Catholicism puts her allegiance to the Pope above the flag, Mr. Catts stands against her invasion of the State of Florida in her politics. As Roman Catholicism opposes our public school system, Mr. Catts opposes Roman Catholicism in the State of Florida in the realm of education. As Roman Catholicism believes in the celibacy of the priesthood and the confessional, Mr. Catts stands squarely against them, and is ready to fight from the State of Florida this great menace to the peace of home, the maintenance of our public schools, and the enjoyment of quiet religion at all hazards.

5.—Be awake, vigilant and watchful in everything else that will make for Florida's good.

6.—Better Pensions for the Old Soldiers.

7.—Against the Gunboat over our Fishermen.

8.—In Favor of Prohibition.

Figure 6. A 1916 campaign flier promoting Sidney J. Catts for governor of Florida. Catts used virulent anti-Catholicism, populist rhetoric, and dry sentiment to become the only governor ever elected under the Prohibition Party banner. Though he was a Democrat, he embodied the budding links between anti-Catholicism and prohibition that bore their full fruit in the election of 1928 with the crushing defeat of Al Smith for president. Reproduced from *Florida Memory*, www.floridamemory.com/items/show/212322.

To the Friends and Supporters of CATTS

1. You want to be sure to pay all poll taxes and register so that you can vote for Catts in 1916.
2. You want to influence every voter in the State who loves his country and hates Catholic control of American politics, to vote for Catts.
3. The wives, mothers and sisters of the State who cannot vote, but whose influence is so great, want to get busy for Catts, for they are a great and silent power God bless our women and our homes. Sisters help Catts out in his heroic race.
4. The friends of Catts want to know that in four or more counties in the state there is danger of Catts being counted out at the poles. We must not allow a single vote CAST FOR HIM NOT TO BE COUNTED, or counted for some other candidate. The law allows three watchers at every voting precinct and the

CATTS MEN MUST HAVE ONE MAN

at every voting place in Florida, to see that Catts gets every vote cast for him.

THIS IS NECESSARY, DO IT SURE

What is this Cat Mewing for?

To be Governor of Florida.

Put him in Office, and Scratch for the

COMMON PEOPLE

If Texas had a Hogg for Governor why can't

Florida have a Catt for Governor?

Register Mr. Voter--Kill The Rats--

Pay Your Poll Tax and VOTE for CATTS.

Peninsular Printing Co.

Figure 7. Back of the 1916 campaign flier promoting Catts for governor.

Figure 8. Statue of Edward Ward Carmack in front of the Tennessee State Capitol, Nashville. The statue stood from 1925 until 2020, when it was toppled in a Black Lives Matter protest. Wikimedia Commons image.

Figure 9. Miriam Amanda Wallace "Ma" Ferguson, wife of impeached governor James Edward Ferguson and the first woman in the United States to be elected to a full term as governor (1925–27). Texans elected her again in 1933, and her second term overlapped with repeal at the federal and state level. She exemplified women's increasing ambivalence toward prohibition in the 1920s and 1930s. Library of Congress Prints and Photographs Division.

AND HE VOTED DRY!

Figure 10. "And He Voted Dry!" Women for repeal campaigned against the hypocrisy of holier-than-thou politicians who publicly voted for prohibition laws but personally drank alcohol. Image from Grace C. Root, *Women and Repeal: The Story of the Women's Organization for National Prohibition Reform* (New York: Harper and Brothers, 1934), frontispiece.

II
Gin Crow

PROHIBITION IN THE JIM CROW SOUTH

AS BOURBON RULE FELL in the early twentieth-century South, so did the old wet consensus to a new dry order that might justly be called "Gin Crow." Chronologically, statewide prohibition existed in the US South only during Jim Crow. More importantly, though, southern white drys endorsed Jim Crow laws in the 1890s in part because they believed it was the only reliable path to prohibition's success. The attempted interracial prohibition coalitions in the 1880s failed, leading white drys to blame Black voters for their failures. White drys increasingly sought to advance white supremacy through the punitive legal measures of Jim Crow, particularly voter suppression. Concern with suppressing Black votes permeated the publications of white drys. Many whites worried aloud that the prohibition issue could divide the white vote and so give a decisive role to African American voters in elections.

Because of the hardening of racial views among most white drys, African American participation in local and statewide prohibition elections during the early Jim Crow period was effectively a form of resistance to Jim Crow. White supremacists had effectively used Jim Crow laws to disfranchise the majority of African Americans by the first decade of the twentieth century, and white Democrats exercised a stranglehold on statewide offices and state legislatures throughout the region. Black men found in the wet movement at least one issue on which to ally with a powerful, white-dominated industry—brewers and distillers—to wield real political influence and protect Black suffrage. Even white supremacists in the wet coalition unwittingly helped to prop up interracial politics by protecting the alcohol lobby, which fought more to mobilize Black voters and to subvert Jim Crow poll taxes than any other white industry at the time. To oppose Gin Crow (southern prohibition) was to oppose Jim Crow, and that opposition was stronger and went longer than scholars have previously thought possible. Still, Black turnout eventually succumbed to voter-suppression tactics, dooming the region to Gin Crow.

Once statewide and national prohibition took effect, not only did law enforcement disproportionately target Black Americans for violations of dry laws, but white Protestant attacks against traditionally wet Catholics increased, particularly in the presidential election of 1928. The "Solid South" broke, with half of the formerly Confederate states joining with the GOP. The Democratic Party in the South had switched from "Rebels, Rum, and Romanism" to rebels against rum and Romanism.

While Black men lost suffrage, white women gained it. The Eighteenth and Nineteenth Amendments, for prohibition and women's suffrage, had gone hand in hand, and many dry men granted women the vote mostly because they hoped women would never permit alcohol's return by the ballot box. However, the failure of prohibition to bring a promised utopia, particularly during the Great Depression, prompted respectable women to organize against prohibition. From the first woman elected governor, Texan Miriam "Ma" Ferguson, to the Alabama organizer Pattie Ruffner Jacobs, southern women played leading roles in challenging assumptions that white women would always embrace prohibition.

Unlike the contests over prohibition's enactment, repeal in the South came with little discussion of race and virtually no major Black involvement. Even the Republican Party in the South, once a staunch defender of Black rights, had turned from a multiracial "black-and-tan" coalition to a lily-white institution. Gin Crow finally fell in part because it was no longer needed: Jim Crow laws had effectively disfranchised African Americans and imposed white supremacy. Before then, however, white drys had indelibly linked prohibition in the South with Jim Crow.

3
Gin Crow Begins

WHITE DRYS AND JIM CROW

ON MARCH 27, 1908, James Thomas "Cotton Tom" Heflin shot a Black man who had just drunk alcohol in front of a white woman. The day before, Heflin, who represented Alabama in the US House, had introduced a bill to extend Jim Crow segregation to the District of Columbia's streetcars. Just before the shooting, Heflin was on a streetcar in the nation's capital on his way to give a lecture at a Methodist church on "Temperance"—which in that context meant prohibition—when two Black men boarded the car. One of those men, Louis (or Lewis) Lundy, produced a flask, at which point Heflin berated him for drinking in front of a white lady. Lundy "replied that he'd take a drink if he felt like it." Everyone left the car at the next stop except Heflin, the unnamed white woman, Lundy, and an unnamed Black man. When Lundy rose to take a drink, Heflin engaged him, and Lundy grabbed him by the lapel. Heflin drew a pistol, hit Lundy on the head with the butt, shoved and kicked Lundy off the car, and fired two shots at him. One of the shots hit Lundy in the neck, and another ricocheted into a white bystander, Thomas McCreary.[1] While Heflin was briefly arrested, he was soon bailed out and charges against him were soon dropped.

In one sense, this behavior fit with Heflin's lifelong advocacy of white supremacism. As a delegate to the convention for the 1901 Alabama Constitution, Heflin successfully pushed for measures to disfranchise Black voters, stating:

"God Almighty intended the negro to be the servant of the white man."[2] While serving as secretary of state for Alabama in 1903, he publicly supported white men who had Black men fraudulently arrested and then forced them to perform slave labor through convict leasing, arguing that such efforts helped maintain white supremacy. As he represented his state in the US House from 1904 to 1920, he routinely spouted racist vitriol.[3]

More broadly, Heflin's vigilante action weaves together southern prohibition and Jim Crow in several ways. First, the incident highlights how prominent white southern drys used their power to promote white supremacism and Jim Crow laws, such as the streetcar law Heflin had introduced the day before the shooting. While Heflin, like many other "states' rights" southerners, later opposed *federal* prohibition, speaking on "Temperance" at a Methodist church implied his dry stance at the local and state levels. Other prominent white drys across the South likewise linked prohibition to white supremacism. Tennessee's prohibition "martyr" Edward Ward Carmack, Alabama's "Father of American Prohibition" Richmond Pearson Hobson, and Virginia's Southern Methodist Bishop James Cannon also numbered among white drys who advocated both prohibition and strict racial hierarchy.

Second, the shooting suggested how fears connecting racial disorder and gender, which inspired Jim Crow laws, also helped the cause of prohibition. Heflin attributed the incident to a Black man drinking alcohol in the same streetcar as a white woman, an allusion to fears of drunk Black men assaulting white women and to Black criminality generally. White drys had openly argued that legal segregation and banning alcohol would keep Black men docile and so protect the virtue of white women, thus preventing the need for lynchings. The notion of protecting white women's honor from inebriated Black men was a key component of prohibition advocacy in the South.

The shooting also reflected how white churches supported the values of Jim Crow and prohibition. While Heflin did not explicitly connect his white-supremacist violence to his faith, he was a white Christian on his way to a Methodist church to lecture on temperance when it happened. Instead of leading him to turn the other cheek or at least stay his hand, Heflin's convictions whipped him into a nearly lethal rage at the sight of a Black man who violated his racial, gender, and alcohol taboos. While it might be tempting for believers to claim Heflin's behavior was out of step with "true" Christian faith, religious and racial convictions are strands of a contingent and experiential fabric and are demonstrated by their fruits. Far more important than what Heflin himself did is how white Christians around the South responded. The lack of a serious rebuke from his peers indicated their tacit consent—if not nodding approval—for his near-murder of a Black man who had the temerity to sip alcohol in front of a white woman on a streetcar. White churches in the South and around the nation thus showed more support for a white champion of Jim Crow and prohibition than the Black man he nearly shot to death.

Support for Heflin was not limited to churches. Regardless of party or home region, Heflin's white colleagues in the US House heaped praise and sympathy on him. Southern white members excused his "impetuous temperament" and "his views on the race question." Within minutes of Heflin's arrest, offers to pay his $5,000 bond came from House members representing parts of Georgia, Louisiana, Mississippi, North and South Carolina, Tennessee, Texas, and most of the Alabama districts.[4] Other Democrats offering to pay Heflin's bail came from beyond the former Confederacy, including Charles Ferris Booher of Missouri and John Geiser McHenry of Pennsylvania. Sympathy for Heflin and regret for the incident came "from all quarters," including the Republican Speaker of the House, Joseph Gurney Cannon of Illinois.[5] Even the white man Heflin accidentally shot shared his white supremacism. When an ambulance took Lundy, the also-wounded McCreary ordered a separate carriage, since he refused to ride with a Black man to the hospital.[6] McCreary also dropped charges when Heflin offered to pay his hospital bills.[7] Whites regardless of party or region saw little need to punish Heflin for nearly killing a Black man who defied the racial order.

The ties between prohibition and Jim Crow were not limited to extraordinary incidents like this but extended to changing laws around the South. On New Year's Day, 1908, the first statewide prohibition law in the South went into effect. Georgia's state legislature voted overwhelmingly for the measure in July 1907. The Georgia House voted 139 to 39 in favor on July 30; then the Senate approved the amended bill 34 to 7, and the governor promptly signed it.[8] It seemed fitting that the state whose capital, Atlanta, was the first major city in the South to opt for prohibition in 1885 would also be the first southern state to go dry.

As far as Black voters were concerned, however, the 1885 and 1907 measures could not have been more different. While white drys and white wets competed for African American votes in the 1880s, Jim Crow laws in the 1890s and 1900s had marginalized Black voters in nearly all major political contests. Prohibitionist whites were particularly insistent on suppressing Black votes, which they blamed for their failures in decades past. As statewide prohibition laws spread throughout the South in the 1900s and 1910s, the dry movement became increasingly white and ever more entwined with Jim Crow. This sharp turn to Jim Crow—and prohibitionist "Gin Crow"—in the South can best be properly understood by way of a brief detour into the greatest interracial political movement across the region between the 1870s and the 1960s: populism. While not directly bearing on prohibition, populism reveals how interracial politics rose, nearly triumphed, and crashed dramatically, providing the immediate context for the white-supremacist alliance between drys and advocates of Jim Crow.

Political Prelude: Populists

After the failure of interracial cooperation in the prohibition contests of the 1880s, the next major effort at multiracial political coalitions in the South was the Populist Party or People's Party. According to Gerald H. Gaither, historians have generally fallen into three schools of thought on how Black men interacted with the populist movement. The progressive school of the 1920s and 1930s treated Black voters as tools of whites, more inclined to sell their votes than engage in the political process to achieve their own interests. The consensus school of the 1950s, however, emphasized the class solidarity of Black and white farmers and optimistically posited that interracial politics could have succeeded if events had only gone differently. A more pessimistic recent school since the 1990s has emphasized institutional racism over class and concluded that interracial politics between relatively marginalized Blacks and relatively more secure whites was doomed to failure. While surveying these three perspectives, Gaither argues that southern populism is "a many-faceted crystal that does not fit easily into any set historiographical formula."[9]

The Populist Party grew out of the Farmers' Alliance, a farmers' cooperative whose white leaders initially sought to win over Bourbon Democrats to support their cause. Founded in 1874 or 1875 in Lampasas County, Texas, the alliance sought to help small-time farmers through the hard times brought on by declining cotton prices. Charles William Macune grew the organization but sought to keep it "a strictly white man's nonpolitical secret business association."[10] Macune, a Democrat, denied Blacks membership in the Texas Alliance and sought to pressure Democratic politicians to advance farmers' interests, not turn it into a political party.

The alliance spread west, and by 1887 the Texas Alliance had fused with the Louisiana Farmers' Union, forging the National Farmers' Alliance and Co-operative Union of America, commonly called the Southern Alliance. By 1888, the enlarged Southern Alliance merged with another farmers' cooperative, the Agricultural Wheel. Two years earlier, in 1886, the Colored Farmers' Alliance (CFA) had been founded in Texas as a secret society working for the interests of Black farmers following the philosophy of self-help and racial uplift. By 1888, the white farmers of the Southern Alliance formally endorsed collaboration with the CFA, which aspired to represent the region's 4.5 million African American farmers. The CFA, for its part, depended on economic aid from whites to support most of its state exchanges to help farmers struggling with low crop prices. Even before the Populist Party was founded, there was limited interracial cooperation in the alliance organizations that preceded it.[11]

Despite the rhetoric of shared self-interest for Black and white farmers, however, most African Americans had difficulty making common cause with white farmers for racial and economic reasons. The racial order of the South prevented integration of the alliance organizations. Most southern white farmers refused to treat African Americans as their social equals, and most Black farmers preferred Black-only organizations to work for their common racial interest and to avoid sabotage by white interlopers. Despite the nonpartisan nature of the alliances, they did address lightning-rod political issues along racial lines. In 1890, white Southern Alliance members denounced a "Force Bill" that would have allowed federal supervision of southern elections, while the CFA endorsed it. While whites and Blacks both supported the Subtreasury Plan of federal aid to farmers with loans, crop storage, and price controls, the CFA also backed more radical measures such as a socialistic single tax to move land ownership to communal control, while the Southern Alliance preferred a more modest graduated income tax.

Economically, the vision of shared interests by all farmers in the South was little more than fanciful fiction. Many white farmers in the Southern Alliance were small landowners who were primarily interested in raising crop prices while most Black farmers were tenant farmers chiefly concerned about raising wages. By 1888, the Southern Alliance proposed to support the Colored Alliance to mobilize some while still upholding the doctrine of racial segregation. While several state branches of the CFA supported strikes by Black workers in 1891, the white Southern Alliances denounced the strikes. When push came to shove, differences of race and class divided southern farmers deeply.[12]

Nonetheless, the Populist Party, or People's Party, emerged from the alliance movement in the South due to Bourbon Democrats' refusal to implement alliance policies. Despite the efforts of Macune and others to keep the alliance nonpartisan, some supported a "People's ticket" that swept out Bourbon Democrats in Comanche County, Texas, in the summer of 1886. Local People's Party elections won in a few races until 1890, when several alliance organizations in the West and South endorsed the newly organized Populist Party. Texans such as James "Cyclone" Davis (white) and John Rayner (Black) eventually backed the new party as well. While Davis argued that the Populist Party platform came from the Democratic principles of Thomas Jefferson and Andrew Jackson, Rayner appealed to African Americans disillusioned with the Republican Party.[13]

Some African Americans in the South considered joining the Populist Party due to long-standing tensions with the Republican Party. While white Radical Republicans supported Black citizenship rights in the 1860s and 1870s, most white Republican elites soured on protecting African Americans. The Liberal Republican split-off in 1872 denounced federal interventions in the South that protected African American citizens from white terrorism, and the contested 1876 election resulted in a Republican president, Rutherford B. Hayes, who declined to send in federal troops when white supremacists violently seized power in Louisiana, Florida, and South Carolina. After white-supremacist Democrats took firm control of southern state governments in the late 1870s, some white Republicans reasoned that they needed to embrace white supremacy to have a chance at power in the region. These "lily-white" Republicans clashed with "Black and tan" Republicans, who embraced interracial politics. By the 1890s, most white Republicans, even in much of the South, had taken an ambivalent or hostile position toward Black political rights.[14]

For their part, some African Americans in the South had taken steps to distance themselves from the Republican Party in the 1880s. Robert Reed Church Sr., the South's first Black millionaire and a saloon owner, ran unsuccessfully for Memphis's Board of Public Works in 1882 on the People's Ticket and Independent Ticket—but not as a Republican.[15] John Rayner, a saloon operator and Republican politician in North Carolina in the 1860s and 1870s, dropped his GOP affiliation when he moved to Texas in the 1880s, preferring prohibition activism to partisan politics. Some African Americans even joined the Democratic Party. From 1878 to 1890, for example, twenty-one African Americans were elected as Democrats to the South Carolina House of Representatives. Nonetheless, most Black southerners still identified with the Republican Party in the 1890s.[16]

Despite its multiracial base, Populist leaders, both white and Black, insisted that they fought merely for political equality, not social equality. One white Populist in Alabama declared that the party was "further from . . . social equality, than any ballot box stuffer alive," and their opposition to racial mixing did "not relax at the going down of the sun." Rayner, the son of a white father and a Black mother, went so far as to deflect white southerners' fear of miscegenation onto the Democrats. He often opened his Populist stump speeches before white audiences by remarking on his light skin and declaring that "this is what he had received from the Democrats"—even though his father was a Whig, not a Democrat.[17] While the Populist Party welcomed white and Black votes, it also upheld racial segregation.

Rayner's support of the Populists embodied the hope of many Black southerners that it could be their best chance for political and economic progress in the South since Reconstruction. He seized the chance to become the greatest African American "orator, organizer, and political strategist" for the Populists from 1892 to 1898.[18] Rayner worked for negligible pay, planting African American Populist Party organizations and delivering powerful speeches for their cause throughout East Texas. As during the 1887 prohibition contest, he openly offered political advice to white comrades and attracted respect from white crowds. He also helped shift most African Americans' support from the Republicans to the Populists. Though just 20 percent of African Americans supported the Populists in 1892, 50 percent backed them four years later. For his efforts, Rayner was elected as the only African American delegate to the Texas Populists' state executive committee in 1896. As historian Charles Postel puts it, Rayner was "the most prominent" African American in the movement nationally.[19]

In the 1890s, Populists rose to prominence in state and federal elections throughout the South (see table 3). Georgian politician Tom Watson was elected to Congress in 1890 as an Alliance Democrat, loyal both to the party of white supremacy and to alliance issues, yet he faced furious opposition and defeat from Bourbon Democrats in 1892. In Texas, Populist gubernatorial candidate Thomas Nugent in 1894 received over 150,000 votes, or 36 percent of the total, displacing the Republicans as the most serious threat to Bourbon rule in the state. In 1894, Alabama Populists helped elect three men to the US House. Truman Heminway Aldrich, a Republican, ran for Congress with Populist backing against Democrat Oscar Underwood, while two outright Populists, Albert Taylor Goodwyn and Milford Wriarson Howard, also ran. Goodwyn and Aldrich lost due to fraud, though they both successfully challenged the results and took their seats for a few months from 1896 to March 1897. Howard, meanwhile, won clear majorities in 1894 and 1896, serving two terms.[20] Populists gained real political power throughout the South in the 1890s.

The Populists' greatest success in the South, however, was in North Carolina, but that story ended in tragedy for interracial politics. In 1894, Populists and Republicans combined forces to win most seats in both houses of the state legislature for a "Fusion" government. No fewer than six Populists were elected to Congress between 1894 and 1898, and Marion Butler, a powerful figure in the state and national populist movement, became the only member

Table 3. Populists in the South, 1890s

YEAR	REGION	POPULIST ACTIVITY
1874–75	TX	Farmers' Alliance founded as nonpartisan organization
1886	TX	Colored Farmers' Alliance (CFA) founded; some candidates beat Bourbon Democrats on "People's Ticket" in Comanche County
1887	TX, LA	Southern Alliance (SA) formed from Farmers' Alliance and Louisiana Farmers' Union
1888	South	Agricultural Wheel joined SA; cooperation between CFA and SA
1890	South	SA denounced "Force Bill" while CFA endorsed it; national Populist Party founded with SA and CFA support
1890	GA	Tom Watson elected to Congress as Populist and Democrat
1891	South	CFA branches endorsed Black workers' strikes while SA denounced them
1892	TX	John Rayner became most prominent Black Populist nationally
1892	GA	Tom Watson defeated for Congress by Democrat
1894	TX	Populist Thomas Nugent received 36% in governor's race
1894	NC	Populists and Republicans form "Fusion" ticket, control state legislature; Marion Butler elected to US Senate
1894	AL	Milford Wriarson Howard elected to US House
1895	AL	Truman Heminway Aldrich and Albert Taylor Goodwyn, who lost in 1894 due to fraud, took US House seats
1896	USA	Populists share presidential candidate with Democrats; defeat spells beginning of end for Populists nationally
1896	AL	Milford Wriarson Howard reelected to US House
1896	NC	Daniel Lindsay Russell (GOP-Populist) elected governor; George Henry White (GOP-Populist) only African American to Congress
1898	NC	Democrats took state legislature through terror and fraud; George Henry White reelected to Congress for last time; Wilmington Insurrection after GOP won city elections

of his party from the South elected to the US Senate, serving from 1895 to 1901. North Carolina Populists also helped deliver the governor's mansion to a Republican, Daniel Lindsay Russell, the only non-Democrat to serve as governor in that state between the 1870s and 1970s. African Americans took some seats in the upper and lower chambers of the state legislature, and George Henry White won a congressional seat in 1896 and 1898, becoming the only Black congressman at the time and the last African American in Congress from the South until the 1970s.[21]

Despite these initial successes, white supremacism overturned these gains by violence in 1898. Fomenting fears of "black rule" and race riots, Democratic leaders such as newspaperman Josephus Daniels and Furnifold McLendel Simmons helped organize Red Shirt clubs to achieve Democratic victory through intimidation, murder, and fraud, sweeping the 1898 state legislative elections. When Wilmington, North Carolina, the state's largest city with a Black majority, elected a Republican mayor and city council in 1898 despite the reign of terror, white supremacists took violent action. They burned down the city's Black-run newspaper, murdered at least a dozen people, forced the Republican officeholders to resign at gunpoint, and prompted thousands of African Americans to leave the city—enough to turn the city from majority-Black to majority-white, which it remains to the present day. As a reward for coordinating the white-supremacist coup, Simmons in 1901 took a seat in the US Senate, where he served for thirty years, and set up his powerful "Simmons machine" to reward his allies.[22] Despite this crushing defeat, North Carolina's Fusionists in the 1890s, like Virginia's Readjusters before them, had threatened conservative Democratic rule in the post-Reconstruction South in ways that the Republican Party alone could not.

Outside of North Carolina, 1896 brought doom for the multiracial Populist coalition as an effective opposition to the Democratic Party in the South. The national People's Party supported William Jennings Bryan, the same presidential candidate as the Democrats that Rayner and other Black voters so hated. Many white Populists placed white supremacy above their economic interests and voted Democratic, while African Americans split their vote between the Populists and the Republicans. That year also signaled the return of white supremacy in Rayner's Robertson County by fraud, intimidation, and violence. As in the 1894 Texas elections, white Democrats committed massive fraud, buying votes outright from Mexican Americans and deceiving illiterate African Americans to vote for the Democratic ticket. By 1898, the Populist Party in Texas was effectively dead, and with it the dream of a multiracial coalition overthrowing white-only rule. After one last brief flirtation in 1902 with a Populist campaign that never materialized, Rayner and most other African Americans were finished with Populist politics. Rayner and most other African Americans sought other avenues for advancement.[23]

The Populists' failure in the South owed much to white southerners' devotion to the Democratic Party and its policy of white supremacism. Tom Watson declared, "To be anything but a Democrat was in public opinion to be a traitor to the section and the white race." As the *Greensboro Daily Record* stated in 1892, the Democratic Party in the South was "a white man's party, organized to maintain white supremacy." As Rayner put it, "The faith the [white] South has in the Democratic Party is much stronger than the faith the South has in God."[24]

Southern white attitudes towards interracial politics soured with the rise and fall of the Populist Party in the 1890s. The Populists launched the first serious attempt at interracial politics in the South since Reconstruction in the late 1890s, but Democrats used fraud, intimidation, and violence to defeat it. As the twentieth century dawned, so did new restrictive voting measures to suppress turnout from the supposedly unworthy citizens—particularly (but not limited to) African Americans, who had provided essential support to the Populists. White Populists eventually rejoined the Democratic Party and infused it with a fiery commitment to exclude African Americans from politics entirely. As early as 1890, Edward R. Cocke, who led the Virginia Farmers' Alliance, petitioned to repeal the Fifteenth Amendment to stop Black voting. As Charles Postel put it, "The white Farmers' Alliance was a driving force behind the new Jim Crow segregation laws adopted across the South."[25] While initially seeking Black votes, most white Populists eventually joined with white Democrats to advance white supremacy by disfranchising and segregating from their Black former allies through a series of laws collectively called "Jim Crow."

Jim Crow

Repressive laws targeting African Americans in the former Confederacy began with the Black Codes. Pioneered by Mississippi's legislature in late 1865, in the aftermath of the Thirteenth Amendment's abolition of racial chattel slavery, Black Codes were adopted in southern states by former Confederates eager to salvage some form of legal white supremacism. The codes included vagrancy laws to force unemployed Black men into harsh labor, apprenticeship laws to force underage Black children into quasi-slavery, and other laws calculated to reduce Black freedoms. Though these laws were overturned by Congressional Reconstruction in 1867, white southern Democrats' ambition to treat Black Americans as second-class citizens by law emerged with a vengeance with Jim Crow.

Soon after the end of Reconstruction, white Democrats experimented with various disfranchisement measures to achieve white-only rule. Alabama adopted shifting residency requirements to ensure victory at the polls as early as 1875.[26] Virginia's 1884 Anderson-McCormick Elections Law, designed to prevent the Readjusters or Republicans from regaining control of the state legislature, handed control over local elections to appointed Democratic Party operatives. As the *Richmond Dispatch* noted, the bill was "in the interest of the white people of Virginia. . . . It is a white man's law . . . [that] operates to perpetuate the rule of the white man."[27] Given the stranglehold of the Democratic Party in that state, the law achieved its intended goal.

Another sneaky tactic was the Eight Box Law, which South Carolina adopted in 1882. A variety of literacy test, this law mandated eight distinct boxes for different offices in the election and required voters to put their ballots in the right box—on which instructions had to be read—or otherwise have their vote disqualified. While voting officials could aid voters with their choice, African American voters had little reason to trust white Democratic officers to direct them honestly. Even more nefarious was the law's lesser-known provision that all eligible voters had to *reregister* by June 1, 1882, or else be forever banned from voting. Given the broad powers of local officials in determining a voter's eligibility and an arduous appeals process, the disfranchisement aspect of the Eight Box Law was even more sinister than its eponym. Despite objections from Black legislators like state senator Thomas E. Miller of Beaufort and litigation by the US attorney for South Carolina, Samuel A. Melton, the state legislature followed Governor Hugh Thompson's advice to pay $10,000 to cover the legal fees of poll workers who were sued for abuse of Black voters' rights. Covered financially and politically by the white-supremacist state government, not a single poll manager was convicted for rights violations.[28]

Inspired by South Carolina's example, Florida followed with its own multibox law in 1889. This iteration not only created a separate box for each office and invalidated votes in the wrong box, but it only allowed voters only five minutes to choose the correct boxes. By 1895, when Florida composed a new constitution, the disfranchisement of Black voters had been so complete by existing measures that no new measures of voter suppression were introduced.[29] Fraud, intimidation, and trickery secured white-only Democratic rule to the southern states. However, many whites sought to reduce the corruption in elections while still minimizing the role of Black voters.

Jim Crow laws arose in formerly Confederate states in the 1890s to impose segregation and political suppression upon nonwhite people in a more systematic, more orderly, and less overtly corrupt fashion than previous methods.

These laws divided into two major categories: racial segregation and voter suppression. While racial social divisions had existed even during Congressional Reconstruction and considerable Black voter suppression had been achieved by fraud and terrorism since 1877, neither social division nor disfranchisement was systematically enshrined by legal code in the late 1880s. Jim Crow was, in short, an attempt to secure and advance white supremacism by law.[30]

Popular accounts of Jim Crow often focus on segregation in schools, bathrooms, drinking fountains, and other public accommodations, yet the Jim Crow statutes most relevant to prohibition concerned disfranchisement. Some of these laws—such as poll taxes, literacy tests, and grandfather clauses—were not explicitly racial, but their intent and application excluded African Americans from meaningful political participation.

The most widespread and obvious attempt at voter suppression was the poll tax (see table 4). Ostensibly levied to provide funds for education, taxes on all voting-age men had existed long before the Civil War, but they were often laxly enforced. Arkansas, for example, authorized a poll tax in its first state constitution in 1836 as well as its Confederate constitution in 1861. Reconstruction-era states reined in poll taxes. For example, Arkansas's 1868 Reconstruction constitution stated: "The levying of taxes by the poll is grievous and oppressive; therefore the general assembly shall never levy a poll tax excepting for school purposes."[31] Poll taxes were a flat fee and therefore regressive, disproportionately burdening the poor, particularly African Americans. As Reconstruction's interracial politics fell to white Democrats' campaigns of terror and fraud, new state constitutions opted to include poll taxes. Under this new order, poll taxes were more strictly enforced and receipts were required to vote.

The poll taxes in this era took two forms: opt-in and cumulative. Of the two, opt-in poll taxes allowed voting-age men to pay a flat rate to vote for the next year or six months, depending on the state. This option allowed voters to opt out of paying the poll tax for years—at the cost of not being able to vote—and then opt in for another voting period for a flat rate. Cumulative poll taxes, however, added up over time if left unpaid. Voters who skipped poll taxes for several years had to pay the cost of those years as well. In some states, the cost was capped at up to three years' worth of poll taxes, while others demanded payment for *every* year since a man turned twenty-one and thus became eligible to vote. Because cumulative taxes made a more onerous burden on the poor, both Black and white, they were more reliable at suppressing voter turnout than opt-in taxes.

Table 4. Select Voter Suppression Laws by Year and State, 1875–1902

YEAR	STATE	TYPE OF VOTING LAW
1875	AL	Changing residency requirements
1876	VA	Poll tax (repealed 1882 by Readjusters)
1877	GA	Cumulative poll tax, $1.50 per year
1882	SC	Eight Box Law: voters had to reregister, also form of literacy test—voters had to read instructions, cast vote in right box
1884	VA	Anderson-McCormick Elections Law: Democratic Party operatives oversaw local elections
1889	FL	Multi-box law: form of literacy test, voters had to read instructions, cast each office vote in right box under time limit
1889	FL	Opt-in poll tax, $2.00 per year
1889	TN	Opt-in poll tax
1890	MS	Opt-in poll tax, $2.00 per year
1892	AR	Opt-in poll tax, $1.00 per year
1900	NC	Poll tax, exempted all able to vote (or parents able to vote) before 1867 (year before African Americans could vote there)
1902	TX	Opt-in poll tax, $1.50 per year
1902	VA	Cumulative poll tax, $1.50 per year
1902	VA	"Understanding clause," type of literacy test

A pioneering state in poll taxes was Georgia, which adopted one as early as 1877. Georgia imposed a cumulative tax of $1.50 per person, requiring each person to pay a sum for every year since the law went into effect or since they turned twenty-one. Even earlier than Georgia was Virginia, which implemented its first round of poll taxes via constitutional amendment in 1876 at the behest of the Conservative Party (as Democrats were briefly called there), but a cross-racial coalition of Readjusters repealed the poll tax requirement in 1882.[32]

Populism's resurrection of interracial politics in the 1890s prompted white-supremacist Democrats across the South to take extreme measures, including poll taxes, to maintain their grip on power. Florida took the lead in 1889 with a $2.00 annual opt-in poll tax, followed later that year by Tennessee. While Tennessee's 1870 constitution permitted a poll tax, even the renowned white supremacist and former US president Andrew Johnson opposed it for its obvious potential to disfranchise poor whites, and a poll tax was not implemented by the state legislature until 1889. Still, Tennessee's poll tax was opt-in on an annual basis, lessening the potential to fully eliminate poor white voting. Mississippi followed suit with a $2.00 opt-in tax in its 1890 state constitution, while Arkansas adopted a $1.00 opt-in tax in 1892. While most Populists sought to repeal those poll taxes in the 1890s, the enforcement of them (along with blatant fraud) made it all but impossible for Populists to win major victories in those states.[33]

A few straggler states joined the poll tax movement around the turn of the century. In North Carolina, after the Red Shirts' takeover in 1898, systemic disfranchisement of Black voters was the next logical step. As Josephus Daniels, a proud supporter of the Red Shirts and purveyor of baseless racial fearmongering in 1898, claimed, "The greatest folly and crime in our national history was the establishment of negro suffrage immediately after the [Civil] War. Not a single good thing has come of it, but only evil."[34] Seeking to rectify that "evil," a 1900 vote approved a new poll tax law that explicitly excluded that tax for anyone who had, or whose parent had, been able to vote in 1867, the year before African Americans received the right there. Last of all came Texas and Virginia, where voters in 1902 approved poll taxes of $1.50. While Texas's poll taxes were opt-in by year, Virginia's were cumulative for up to three years.[35] By 1902, poll taxes were a weapon of choice for disfranchising Black voters.

Poll taxes were just one of many means to systematically suppress Black voters, however. Literacy tests provided an insidiously subjective quality to voter qualification. Article II of Virginia's 1902 Constitution included an "understanding clause," a provision limiting the vote to those who could read (or have read to them) and explain any section of the state constitution to the satisfaction of a local registrar. Of course, the satisfaction requirement provided ample latitude for discrimination. One delegate to Virginia's 1901–2 constitutional convention, Carter Glass, explained that the measures were designed to remove "four-fifths of the negro voters" from the electorate without "necessarily depriv[ing] a single white man of the ballot." He insisted that this would not be by fraud, but by "discrimination within the letter of the law, and not in violation of the law." Such discrimination, he stated, was "what the Convention was elected for—to discriminate to the very extremity" permitted under the US Constitution "with a view to elimination of every negro voter who can be gotten rid of, legally, without materially impairing the numerical strength of the white electorate." Another delegate, Alfred P. Thom, remarked explicitly: "I would not expect an impartial administration of the clause," but he expected a hard exam for Blacks and an easy one for whites to purge the voting rolls and create "an Anglo-Saxon electorate."[36]

They got their wish and then some. By 1904, due to the new voting measures, the white vote in Virginia (compared to four years earlier) had declined by about 50 percent, while the Black vote fell by about 90 percent. Because of its remarkably strict voting laws, Virginia began six decades of low voter turnout and rigidly conservative politics—even by southern standards—under the control of the Byrd Organization.[37]

While some challenged these repressive laws in courts, rulings generally favored Jim Crow laws. Two Mississippi-based cases involved African American men, John Henry Dixon and Henry Williams, who were convicted for murder by all-white juries, because the voter rolls had been purged of Black men by systemic disfranchisement. In *Dixon v. Mississippi* (1896) in the Mississippi Supreme Court, and *Williams v. Mississippi* (1898) in the US Supreme Court, the rulings upheld a cocktail of literacy tests, poll taxes, and other disfranchisement clauses on that grounds that they did not *on their face* discriminate on racial grounds. Even though the makers and enforcers of those laws openly expressed their intent to disfranchise Black voters, the courts held that there was no legal remedy for discriminator enforcement so long as the laws themselves were technically color-blind.[38]

Allen Caperton Braxton, who masterminded the disfranchisement mechanisms in the 1902 Virginia constitution, explained the virtue of color-blind laws as he echoed Populist (and fellow Virginian) Edward Cocke in denouncing the Fifteenth Amendment. In a speech delivered to the New York Southern Society in February 1903, Braxton called the Fifteenth Amendment just as "beyond right and reason" as slavery. He called the amendment "wrong in principle," impossible to enforce in areas with a majority of "the inferior race," "demoralizing to the negro," and "corrupting to the white man." Giving self-determination to African Americans would be "the greatest cruelty," while allowing them to rule over whites "would be a crime against nature and sin against God!" He called Black suffrage during Reconstruction "political bondage" of a "blind, unreasoning and thoughtless" mass, "like dumb, driven cattle," who threatened civilization—namely, white rule—itself. In this twisted perspective, African Americans' refusal to "*accept* political freedom forced the whites to *abandon* it" (emphases original) to blindly follow the white man's party regardless of its political stances. Whites then followed a "difficult, narrow but safe path" of Jim Crow laws to "achieve salvation and regain the Promised Land" of white supremacy. These restrictions were officially "irrespective of race or color" but "safely and perpetually shut out" the "vast sea of ignorant, venal, and vicious negroes." While he conceded that some African Americans could still vote, southern states had restricted "the negro's defects" so effectively that their vote had "been reduced far below the danger point" of deciding elections. He concluded that this brought greater goodwill between the races—or more accurately, suppressed Black dissent so effectively that whites ceased to hear of it.[39]

Southern white drys' support of this order came through unambiguously in a speech by a congressman from Mississippi, Eaton Jackson Bowers. On April 8, 1904, he delivered a notable speech on the US House floor praising Jim Crow laws for excluding African Americans from voting. He stated that several southern states' constitutions restricted the right to vote for Black citizens—including Alabama, Louisiana, South Carolina, North Carolina, Virginia, and Mississippi—because African Americans were not fitted for "equal social and political rights" with whites. Bowers claimed that Reconstruction's "decade of negro domination and misrule" furnished definitive proof that African Americans were "not fitted for governance" and should be "eliminated as a political factor." "I thank God," he said, that Mississippi had by its constitutional restrictions effectively "obstruct[ed] the exercise of the franchise by the negro race," which he called "the wisest statesmanship ever exhibited in that proud Commonwealth." Not only did he celebrate disfranchising "the ignorant and vicious black, but the ignorant and vicious white as well," so that only those "who are qualified by intelligence and character" to vote may do so."[40] Given such sentiments, it seems fitting that Bowers's grandson, Samuel H. Bowers Jr., who had idolized his grandfather, committed murder for white supremacy while serving as grand wizard of the Ku Klux Klan in the dying days of Jim Crow.[41]

The overall effect of these Jim Crow laws by the early 1900s devastated Black political participation across the South. Roughly three-quarters of South Carolina's African Americans were effectively disfranchised by the Eight Box Law and its aftermath. Of Alabama's 150,000 voting-age Black men, only 3,000 were registered to vote in 1900. In Louisiana, Black voter registration dropped from 130,000 in 1896 to just 1,342 by 1904.[42] While the populist movement brought out about 85 percent of the African American vote in Texas in 1896, the African American vote had plummeted to just 23 percent turnout in 1902, even before the poll tax was implemented.[43] Years before Georgia became the first dry state in the South in 1908, Black voters seemed to have lost their political voice in the region, due in no small part to white drys.

Gin Crow: White Prohibition in the South

As Jim Crow became the law of the land throughout the South, white drys increasingly backed voter suppression to realize their reform. Joe Coker argues that prohibition gained momentum throughout the South in part due to white drys' ability to harness white supremacy for their cause.[44] Although white drys in the 1880s eagerly sought Black votes to achieve prohibition, the failure of whites to win over most African Americans in any of those elections resulted in a white backlash against Black enfranchisement generally.

White Churches for Prohibition

While the ubiquity of Jim Crow laws distinguished the South from other regions in the United States, the South's turn to prohibition in many ways signaled its entrance into a national framework of moral reconstruction under white Protestant leadership.[45] The prohibition movement's turn to a broader theological spectrum by the early twentieth century is evident in the ecumenical tolerance of the national Anti-Saloon League (ASL), the most powerful dry political pressure group, founded in 1895. The ASL put its single issue above doctrinal purity and welcomed support from all, including Catholic drys such as Archbishop John Ireland.[46] Nonetheless, the ASL's ecumenism was limited at the popular level to mostly "Methodist, Baptist, Presbyterian, and Congregational churches."[47] The Federal Council of Christian Churches, which was founded in 1908 and included thirty Protestant denominations, consistently backed prohibition through the ASL until repeal in the 1930s, demonstrating widespread Protestant support for prohibition.[48] This growing ecumenism of the prohibition movement was mostly limited to white Protestants—excluding most Lutherans and Episcopalians.

As prohibition picked up momentum around the South, the situation grew better for political preachers of the white Protestant variety. In 1910, a leading southern dry, H. A. Ivy, laughed away the wet claim that prohibition would lead to "the union of Church and State." Ivy asked rhetorically whether Maine had a church-state union after fifty-eight years of state prohibition (the answer: no). The charge of church-state union that troubled preachers in the 1880s now amused Ivy so much that he wanted to tell wets, "these distinguished jokers, 'Quit yer kiddin'.'"[49] Baptists, who had long cherished the separation of church and state, ironically took a greater role than any other denomination in pushing for prohibition in the South.[50]

White evangelical preachers presided over an exploding population of white Baptists and Methodists, whom they gradually converted to the cause of prohibition by wedding it to righteous white rule.[51] An agent of the brewers confided to a Corpus Christi beer dealer in 1905, "We know the Methodist and [B]aptist members of your community are being very quietly worked by their preachers, local and foreign, to pay their poll taxes, as it is part of the prohibition propaganda."[52] After losing a "hopeless" September 1909 election in bone-dry Shelby County, the same agent sighed, "Darkest Russia is not any more under the domination of the Czar than is Shelby under the rule of the Baptist and Methodist Churches."[53] In 1911, even Alexander Terrell, who wrote Texas's 1902 poll tax laws while he was a wet, became a dry and denounced alcohol as a child-devouring demon.[54] Brewers knew it was only a matter of time before the double pressure of suppressing wet votes and converting the white vote would dry up the South.[55]

Taming the Devil: Race, Sex, Violence, and Class in Dry Rhetoric

To control Black bodies and suppress Black votes, white drys did not merely invoke the fear of the Lord but also fears of drunken Black men assaulting white women. As Joe Coker put it, "White hysteria about black brutes assaulting white women that swept the South in the early 1900s put the prohibition cause back in the public spotlight. Evangelical prohibitionists capitalized on this public concern over alcohol and successfully pushed prohibition as the solution to black savagery."[56] Michael Lewis sounded a similar note: "Drawing on the increasingly negative and animalistic portrayal of black men that accompanied the campaign for disfranchisement, anti-liquor campaigners wove tales of liquor-crazed black men ravaging and killing innocent white women."[57]

White evangelical drys sometimes countenanced lynchings as a proportionate if "unfortunate" response to Black men who violated racial taboos. References to lynching are sadly widespread in dry newspapers such as *Home and State,* the Texas ASL's official organ. As early as 1905, the paper's editor, G. C. Rankin, in his column "Progress of Reform" refused to condemn the lynching of a "negro brute" who allegedly "committed an outrage upon a white woman" and was convicted for rape yet granted a new trial "on a mere technicality." Rankin stated that the lynched man's guilt was "beyond doubt," but mob action was a "disgrace" for which he blamed the "careless" court for creating "the feeling of uncertainty produced by the granting of the new trial."[58]

White drys gave disproportionate attention to Black drinking, especially when connected to rape, murder, or both. A few sensational episodes reinforced the widespread idea among southern white Americans that alcohol turned otherwise docile Africans into rapacious, murderous monsters. "WHISKEY MAKES BLACK SLAYER THIRST FOR BLOOD" reads the headline concerning Clarence Cooley, who murdered Johannes Hansen and Louis

Teten after drinking two bottles of beer and a pint of whiskey. The article begins with a saloon that "soaked Clarence Cooley's black flesh with whiskey, fired his docile brain with the fumes of alcohol, and sent him forth to slay." The article ends with words of warning from Cooley: "Let booze alone. It made me kill."[59] The article at once removes Cooley's responsibility for his actions and prompts the reader to prevent such actions by removing the real killer: alcohol. The article makes this explicit when it states the price of Cooley's drink and adds: "That was the price of three human lives."[60] The story inspires the reader to take responsibility for the poor "negroes" who cannot help but kill once they have a few drinks. White drys did not see African Americans as three-dimensional people but as objects of scorn and pity to be protected from booze.

That story parallels an incident in Shreveport, Louisiana, where Charles Coleman, an African American man, was convicted and punctiliously hanged (legally) for raping and murdering a fourteen-year-old white girl, Margaret Lear. Coleman had been drunk. A reporter speculated (apparently without proof) that Coleman's drink had been "Black Cock Vigor Gin," an actual brand of cheap gin sold to African Americans that featured a scantily clad white woman.[61] According to a prohibitionist mindset, alcohol was to blame. By the same token, white drys argued that taking away alcohol would improve Black behavior and therefore reduce lynchings. In February 1928, *Home and State* printed a clipping stating that lynchings decreased due to prohibition, advancing the logic that proper legislation keeps alcohol out of the hands of Blacks and so keeps them docile.[62] For white drys, prohibition was yet another means to control the bodies of Black men.

While one may interpret white evangelicals' prohibition advocacy as trying to reduce racial violence, it may equally be viewed as another form of racial control. Joe Coker contends that white evangelicals in the South promoted prohibition as a "preemptive solution" to lynching which contributed to a "decline in racial rhetoric." Even so, he admits that white evangelicals were often "embracing and utilizing" the "prevailing racial attitudes of the region . . . for the advancement of prohibition."[63] In other words, even white drys' well-meaning efforts at avoiding unnecessary violence grew from an underlying commitment to white supremacism, and they deliberately used white-supremacist rhetoric to win over their white neighbors to prohibition.

White media justified not only lynchings but other forms of extralegal violence against Black men with alcohol by depicting them as deviants particularly prone to criminal behavior. Heflin's shooting of Lundy in 1908 was not technically an attempted lynching because it was not done by a group of three or more people,[64] but the incident illustrates this principle. As happened over a century later when unarmed Black men were shot by whites, some media outlets depicted the Black victim as a drug-tainted criminal and the white shooter as acting in self-defense. One *Washington Times* article, entitled "Wounded Negro Has Bad Record in Police Court," noted that Lundy "has been arrested time and again on charges of every character, and during the last few years much of his time has been spent in jail." Offenses included carrying concealed weapons, petty larceny, and various incidents of drunkenness, disorderly conduct, and "violating the police regulations." The newspaper called Lundy "surly," "a source of constant trouble to the police," and "one of the most persistent lawbreakers and one of the most desperate negroes with whom the police have ever come in contact."[65] The paper also reported that Lundy was drunk or high when he reached the hospital and that it required six men to subdue him with anesthetic—a clear parallel to latter-day warnings of drugs giving Black men unnatural strength. Heflin refused to speak to the press, but his authorized spokesman, fellow Alabama congressman Henry De Lamar Clayton Jr., claimed that Lundy was "under the influence of gin, cocaine, or some other drug."[66] Such reports described Lundy as both "uppity" and under the influence: a not-so-subtle warning that Black men with alcohol threatened law and order, a standard white argument for prohibition.

While major newspapers declined to interview the two Black men involved (or the white woman present) in Heflin's attempted homicide, close analysis of white accounts sufficiently undermines Heflin's self-defense claim. Clayton claimed that Heflin fought because the two Black men had planned to attack him. This theory made little sense, since the other Black man had earlier "attempted to take the flask away from" Lundy, showing that he was trying to defuse the situation by complying with Heflin's demand. While the *Times* stated that Heflin shoved and kicked Lundy off the car, South Carolina representative James Edwin Ellerbe claimed Heflin had scuffled with *both* men, who cursed Heflin "after reaching the ground," suggesting that Heflin had thrown them both off the car. Then Heflin fired while both men were on the ground—hardly a position requiring Heflin to shoot in self-defense.[67] To the media of that time, however, the violence deserved no closer scrutiny: the Black man on drugs inherently deserved excessive force from a white elected official. White drys promised greater white control of such Black men.

White drys sought to control not only Black men but also Black women who challenged the racial order. When Ida B. Wells denounced the lynchings of three African Americans in Memphis in 1892, Edward Ward Carmack, a prominent dry media personality, used his position as editor of the *Memphis*

Commercial newspaper to malign her as "the Black wench." In what might reasonably be described as incitement to riot, Carmack called for retaliation against Wells for daring to oppose the system of racial terror they represented. An angry white mob answered his call and destroyed the offices of her paper, the *Free Speech*. Fortunately, Wells was out of town at the time of the attack and so was unharmed, but the incident and subsequent death threats prompted her to live in exile in the North for thirty years. By inciting a mob against Wells, Carmack literally called for the destruction of *Free Speech* in the defense of white supremacism.[68]

Rather than hurting his reputation, the incident helped Carmack's political rise, and by 1908 he became the leader of the dry faction in the Democratic primary for Tennessee governor. He was only narrowly defeated by Malcolm R. Patterson, who led the state Democratic Party's wet faction. While Patterson easily won the general election, Carmack returned to working as a newspaper editor. In that role, Carmack launched several libelous attacks against a rival newspaperman, Duncan Brown Cooper. On November 9, 1908, when Cooper and his son encountered him on a Nashville street, Carmack opened fire. Carmack wounded Cooper's son, and Cooper shot Carmack dead. Carmack, who lived in vitriol and violence, became known as a "martyr" for the dry cause and earned a posthumous statue in front of the Tennessee statehouse from 1925 until its removal in 2020.[69] Violence on behalf of white supremacism and one's "honor" was a feature, not a bug, for southern white drys.

The "Father of American Prohibition," Alabama US representative Richmond Pearson Hobson, likewise linked prohibition to white-supremacist views in his most famous dry speeches to Congress. In his famous "The Great Destroyer" speech on the House floor in 1911, he spoke about "THE CURSE OF THE RED MAN AND BLACK MAN" and argued: "If a peaceable red man is subjected to the regular use of alcoholic beverage, he will speedily be put back to the plane of the savage." The answer for such problem was, in his Progressive mind, using government force to coerce right behavior: he remarked approvingly that "The Government long since recognized this and absolutely prohibits the introduction of alcoholic beverage into an Indian reservation." Hobson extended such thinking to African Americans as well: "If a negro takes up a regular use of alcohol beverage, in a short time he will degenerate to the level of a cannibal." Hobson conceded that liquor was not only a problem for racial minorities but also could affect "the noblest white men" regardless "how high the stage of evolution." Even this supposedly more-evolved white man with corresponding "great self-control," who is "considerate, tenderhearted, who would not willingly harm an insect," will be degenerated by regular use of alcoholic beverage to the point where he will strike with a dagger or fire a shot to kill with little or no provocation." The description of shooting to kill with little cause seemed an apt description of Heflin's attack on Lundy in 1908, a sober white man assaulting a Black man having alcohol. However, for white southern drys such as Hobson, alcohol was the prime culprit for such danger, and nonwhites were particularly "cursed" with the vulnerability to descend to "savagery" and lose their "self-control, self-respect, the sense of honor, [and] the moral sense."[70]

In a similar speech in 1914 entitled "The Truth about Alcohol," Hobson repeated and expanded on these white-supremacist themes. He claimed that alcohol has made "twice as many slaves, largely white men, today than there were black men slaves in America at any one time." In addition to minimizing the extreme terror and torture experienced by real slaves, he literally did not count the suffering of enslaved women and children in his "black men slaves" calculation.[71] He also bemoaned a "growing degenerate vote directly due to liquor" which menaced not only large cities but also the whole nation. Liquor "creates this degenerate vote" and purchases it, thereby "undermining the foundations of our [free] institutions."[72] While "degenerate" in this context likely included recent immigrant whites, he undoubtedly meant African Americans as well. He once again repeated the particular weaknesses of racial minorities to alcohol: it "degenerates the red man, throws him back into savagery," and "will promptly put a tribe on the war path," while it "will actually make a brute out of a negro, causing him to commit unnatural crimes," presumably including attacks on white women.[73]

Compared with his 1911 speech, this 1914 diatribe indicated a progression toward more violent descriptions of Amerindians ("the war path" has been added to mere "savagery") and insinuating drunk Black men would attack white women ("unnatural crimes" rather than "cannibalism"), in both cases suggesting violence directed at whites. His second speech, while also claiming that liquor could take the same effect on white men (though, "being further evolved it takes [a] longer time to reduce him to the same level"), now omits the old reference to drunken white men stabbing and shooting.[74] Hobson, prohibition's greatest promoter in the US House and an outspoken Progressive from the South, emphasized white suffering from alcohol, stirred fears of "degenerate" voters, increasingly stressed the threat of violence against whites from drunken African Americans and Amerindians, and muted his earlier concerns of violence committed by drunken whites. In short, the South's most prominent dry linked prohibition's success in the 1910s more and more to control of nonwhite bodies and votes.

Many drys, including Mexican Americans and Black Americans, linked prohibition to the rule of "better" social classes. The racial order articulated by Texan drys in *Home and State* assumed at least as much cultural and class superiority as racial superiority. Various articles in the paper argued against "the low negro and Mexican vote," the "Mexican and ignorant negro," and the like.[75] However, many drys distinguished between "low" and "better" minorities, especially regarding Mexicans and African Americans. A 1912 *Home and State* article entitled "Our Mexican 'Citizens'" focused on "the ignorant and unpatriotic Mexicans known as the 'Greaser Class.'" The author recognized that "among our Mexican citizenship there are many first-class men and women who are educated, intelligent, and loyal to our government and its situations," but in the rest of the article "no reference whatever is made to that [first] class."[76] In the context of a dry paper, such terms as "educated, intelligent, and loyal" were synonymous with prohibition while "ignorant and unpatriotic" signified opposing it. Mexican Americans may have been generally regarded with contempt by white Texans, but some dry whites saw middle-class dry Mexican Americans as respectable, in contrast with the wet majority.

Similarly, some African American clergy gained white favor by backing prohibition. Before white drys had opted for prohibition via Jim Crow, a good number of leading African Americans were dry. Rayner, Bishop Turner, and the Rev. J. W. Bailey were just a few of many Black ministers who sought to advance themselves and their race by working alongside the "best" whites. They followed in the tradition of Booker T. Washington, who tried to uplift his race by deferring to the southern racial order while seeking advancement through gradually expanding economic and practical educational opportunities. While some have criticized Washington for failing to speak out against injustices of his time, he was very influential and widely respected among both Blacks and whites.[77] White paternalists took up the "white man's burden" to civilize and Christianize their racial "inferiors" at home and abroad while African Americans sought to empower their race through economic progress, educational attainment, and increased respectability. "Racial uplift" could simultaneously serve the causes of white paternalism and Black advancement.[78]

In 1911, some Black clergy in Texas maintained that they had always been dry, in accordance with "the word of God and church laws against the use of liquor." In addition, they did "not want the public to wonder about our position," so they "most emphatically declare[d] that we favor prohibition."[79] There is no reason to doubt the veracity or sincerity of this declaration, since African American Baptists and Methodists shared many of the same beliefs and practices with their white co-religionists, and drunkenness was just as much a blight and burden on Black families as on white. Also, telling whites of their dry stance was a sure way for Black pastors to show common cause and seek alliances with wealthier and more powerful white neighbors.

Likewise, an editor of the *Home and State* in 1911 highlighted a letter by the Rev. J. W. Bailey, corresponding secretary of the Texas Negro Baptist Convention. The editor called Bailey "one of the strongest and best men of his race . . . a noble man . . . well informed, reliable, aggressive for the best things in Texas, and is always in harmony with the best people . . . against saloons, because they are against the best things in Texas."[80] While Bailey's stance endeared him to "the best people"—that is, white evangelical drys—Bailey's claim that the "negroes of Texas will be with you [drys] when the time comes" was at best wishful thinking and at worst disingenuous.[81] The typical complaints in *Home and State* against "the low negro" sprang in part from widespread dry white frustration that most Black Texans voted the "wrong" way on the issue. Even when embracing a select few Black Christians as allies for prohibition, the overall tenor of white dry sentiment in the South advocated marginalization and disfranchisement for their race as a whole.

White southern drys did not regard Black Christians, even those who backed prohibition, as their spiritual equals. Edwin DuBose Mouzon, a relatively progressive Southern Methodist bishop from Texas who promoted prohibition vigorously, confessed to his fellow bishop James Cannon Jr. in 1919 that "the negro is not in point of morals, or education, or religion, the equal of the white man, and to place him in the church on a position of equality would be a wrong to the negro and to the church." For his part, Cannon, who led the Virginia ASL to dry the state by 1916, expressed similar views. He described "the negroes as a people" as "a child race—immature, not fully developed" and justified extralegal action against "brute beasts . . . whose brutal assaults on white woman bring on rioting and bloodshed."[82] White evangelical drys may have occasionally welcomed Black support but believed whites should rule the church as well as the state.

Drying the Southland

Given the increasingly clear connection between white churches, white supremacy, and prohibition, most southern states turned dry within a few years, from 1908 to 1915. Georgia went dry on New Year's Day in 1908, and throughout that year several southern states opted to begin prohibition on January 1, 1909. After Birmingham's Jefferson County went dry by nearly eighteen hundred votes on Oct. 28, 1907, Alabama's legislature decided that the writing was on the wall and voted for statewide prohibition that November. Mississippi's legislature followed suit in February 1908.[88]

North Carolina distinguished itself by becoming the first southern state to opt for statewide prohibition by popular vote in 1908. The dry side brought together such unlikely allies as Governor Robert Broadnax Glenn and US Judge Jeter Connelly Pritchard, who had taken opposite sides on disputes about railroad monopolies. Nearly all of the state's Democratic congressmen also joined the drys. So, it was unsurprising that on Tuesday, May 26, 1908, North Carolinians voted for prohibition by a margin so large that newspapers predicted its victory before watching official results come in. With North Carolina's vote, half of the eight states in the nation that approved statewide prohibition were in the South—most if one includes the new state of Oklahoma.[84] While only three states nationwide (none of them southern) had statewide prohibition in effect at the start of 1907, within two years the South had leaped to the forefront of the movement.

The next several years demonstrated rapid progress for drys in the South. As with Mississippi and Alabama, North Carolina's dry law went into effect on January 1, 1909, and the year saw more successes for the drys across the South. On January 19, the Tennessee legislature overrode the governor's veto to ban alcohol within four miles of schools and ban alcohol production in state, which took effect the next year. In August 1909, a South Carolina election enacted partial statewide prohibition, allowing counties to opt out, and only six counties opted to stay wet with government-run alcohol dispensaries.[85] While a prohibition amendment to Alabama's constitution was defeated by the voters in November 1909, the state remained officially dry, even if dry laws were not consistently enforced.[86] Tables 5 and 6 give a fuller timeline for the success of prohibition in the region.

One constant throughout these campaigns for white drys was control of African Americans. As Lee L. Willis put it, "Restricting blacks' access to alcohol was a theme that ran through the temperance and prohibition campaigns in Florida."[87] Even in free-wheeling New Orleans, "the Gibralter [sic] of the liquor traffic in the South," where laws regulating saloons were "everywhere openly violated," prohibition laws reeked of Jim Crow's doctrine of racial separation.[88] Louisiana's Gay-Shattuck law, which regulated liquor licenses and ostensibly went into effect in January 1, 1909, prohibited the sale of alcoholic drinks to whites and Blacks within the same building. Though drys complained that the law was frequently ignored in New Orleans and other wet towns, the law on its face made plain that, as far as southern white drys were concerned, prohibition included racial separation.[89]

Table 5. Timeline for Statewide Prohibition across the US South, 1907–1920

YEAR	STATE	EVENT
1907	GA	July 31—legislature passed prohibition bill
1907	AL	November 22—legislature passed prohibition bill
1908	GA	January 1—statewide prohibition took effect
1908	MS	February 8—state legislature passed bill for statewide prohibition
1908	NC	May 26—voters approved statewide prohibition
1909	NC, MS, AL	January 1—statewide prohibition took effect
1909	TN	January 19—legislature overrode governor's veto to ban alcohol within four miles of schools ("Four Mile Law") and ban alcohol production in state; July 1—Four Mile Law took effect
1909	SC	August 17—voters approved letting counties opt out of statewide prohibition; six counties voted wet with county dispensaries
1909	AL	November 29—voters rejected statewide prohibition amendment
1910	TN	January 1—ban on alcohol production in effect
1913	AR	February 17—state legislature passed virtual statewide prohibition, blocked referendum to reverse it
1913	TN	October 17—state legislature passed prohibition enforcement laws
1914	AR	January 1—statewide prohibition took effect
1915	SC	September 14—voters approved statewide prohibition
1915	VA	September 22—voters approved statewide prohibition
1916	SC	January 1—statewide prohibition took effect
1916	VA	November 1—statewide prohibition took effect
1918	FL	November 5—voters approved statewide prohibition
1919	FL	January 1—statewide prohibition took effect
1919	TX	May 24—voters approved state constitutional prohibition
1920	LA	January 19—goes dry due to federal prohibition

Sources: Cherrington, ed., *Anti-Saloon League Year Book* (1908–19); "Dry," *Prescott,* AR, *Daily News,* July 31, 1907, 1; "Prohibition for Alabama Passes," *Prescott,* AR, *Daily News,* November 21, 1907, 1; "Alabama Prohibition," Newbery, SC, *Herald and News,* November 22, 1907, 3; "Prohibition in Mississippi," *Newport,* VA, *News,* February 8, 1908, 3; O'Daniel, *Crusaders, Gangsters, and Whiskey,* 17, 23; *Alabama Official and Statistical Register, 1911,* comp. Thomas M. Owen (Montgomery, AL: Brown Printing Co., 1912), 318–19; Cherrington, *History of the Anti-Saloon League,* 118, 134.

Table 6. Select Statewide Prohibition Referenda across the US South, 1908–1919

DATE	STATE	TYPE	VOTES FOR	VOTES AGAINST
May 26, 1908	NC	Statewide prohibition law (approved)	113,612 (62%)	69,416
July 25, 1908	TX	Submit proposal to state vote, Democratic primary (approved)	145,530 (50.7%)	141,441
Nov. 29, 1909	AL	Statewide prohibition amendment (rejected)	49,093	76,272 (60.8%)
July 23, 1910	TX	Submit proposal to state vote, Democratic primary (approved)	159,406 (54.8%)	131,324
Nov. 8, 1910	FL	Statewide prohibition (rejected)	24,506	29,271 (54.4%)
July 22, 1911	TX	Statewide prohibition amendment (rejected)	231,096	237,393 (50.7%)
Sept. 9, 1912	AR	Statewide prohibition law (rejected)	69,390	85,358
July 25, 1914	TX	Submit proposal to statewide vote, Democratic primary (rejected)	156,534	179,217 (53.4%)
Sept. 14, 1915	SC	Statewide prohibition law (approved)	41,735 (71.4%)	16,809
Sept. 22, 1915	VA	Statewide prohibition law (approved)	-90,183 (60%)	-59,818
July 22, 1916	TX	Submit proposal to state vote, Democratic primary (approved)	174,235 (50.3%)	172,222
Nov. 5, 1918	FL	Statewide prohibition amendment (approved)	21,851 (61.6%)	13,609
May 24, 1919	TX	Statewide prohibition amendment (approved)	159,723 (53.4%)	140,099

Sources: Connor, ed., *A Manual of North Carolina . . . 1913,* 1019–20; Robert Plocheck, "Prohibition Elections in Texas"; Endersby, "Prohibition and Repeal," 506; *Alabama Official and Statistical Register, 1911,* comp. Thomas M. Owen (Montgomery, AL: Brown Printing Co., 1912), 318–19; Cherrington, *History of the Anti-Saloon League,* 118, 134; *Report of the Secretary of State of the State of Florida,* ed. H. Clay Crawford (Tallahassee, FL: 1911), 16–22; *Report of the Secretary of State of the State of Florida* (Tallahassee, FL: T. J. Appleyard, 1919), n.p., edocs.dlis.state.fl.us/fldocs/dos/secretarystatereport/reportofsecr19171918flor.pdf; Cherrington, ed., *Anti-Saloon League Year Book* (1917), 221; Virginia 1915 estimates approximated from given margin of victory (30,365) and rough vote total (150,000) in Cherrington, ed., *Anti-Saloon League Year Book* (1915), 206–7.

Southern white drys had dramatically shifted their tactics on race from the 1880s to the 1900s. After the dramatic failure of attempts at interracial cooperation in the 1880s, white drys increasingly tended towards the exclusion of racial minorities from politics by intimidation and Jim Crow laws. Unabashed race-baiting grew increasingly effective in advancing prohibition in the South.

However, white drys encountered significant opposition in the 1900s and early 1910s. Christians of all races continued to resist Gin Crow's infringement of their God-given liberties. Black voters defied the Jim Crow laws that limited their voting rights and worked together with brewers to inflict stinging defeats on the drys. This multiracial and religiously infused wet coalition won a string of statewide votes that humiliated drys from one end of the South to the other during the early days of Jim Crow.

4
"Fidelity to That Liberty"
DEFEAT AND SUCCESS FOR GIN CROW

THOUGH "BAPTIST" HAD GROWN synonymous with prohibition by 1905, that year's Temperance Committee report of the National Baptist Convention (NBC) denounced prohibition. With over two million members in 1906, the NBC was then the largest Black-led denomination and the nation's largest Baptist denomination, with more members than the white-led Southern Baptist Convention.[1] Due to its demographic base before the Great Migration, most of the NBC's members resided in the South, including the author of the 1905 Temperance Committee report, Texan John Rayner. Though he had backed prohibition in Texas's 1887 referendum, Rayner reversed himself in 1905 and critiqued prohibition with arguments from Christian theology.

He declared in the report that any temperance "not from above" was "not Christian temperance," effectively insinuating that abstinence from alcohol came from changed hearts, not changed laws. Rayner further articulated ambivalence about prohibitory laws that made men "more anxious to procure strong drink" so that "they buy it in larger quantities." While implying that prohibitory laws were counterproductive, he advocated strongly for truly Christian temperance, which "can *only* be enforced by example, persuasion and dissuasion, expressed in personal Christian service" (emphasis mine).[2] Rayner thus affirmed the Baptist conviction that drinking was sinful while suggesting that Baptist churches had no need for state prohibitory laws if they would simply apply church discipline. Only upright Christian lives and education, not government power, he maintained, could make men sober. For Rayner, as for many traditionalist Christians before him, regulating such morality was the role of the church, not the state, and the church ought not try to use the government to remove a man's liberty to choose, even if he chose sin.

Rayner's 1905 report demonstrated that the same kinds of Christian arguments against prohibition in the nineteenth century continued to be reiterated in the early twentieth-century South. In that era, white and Black voters invoked old Christian traditions of true temperance, liberty, and the Bible to resist the spread of Gin Crow in countless local option and several key statewide elections. In Florida in 1910, Texas in 1911, and Arkansas in 1912, statewide prohibition was defeated by multiracial coalitions in which Black voters cast decisive votes. Dry whites' defeat in these races sparked a white backlash that suppressed minority votes, empowered white women to vote, and completed the South's conversion to a dry bastion. Nonetheless, the multiracial resistance to prohibition in the 1910s represented the last great show of Black electoral strength in the South against Jim Crow voting restrictions until the Voting Rights Act over half a century later. Before examining the contributions of African Americans to prohibition elections in the 1910s, however, we must revisit Christian resistance to prohibition across denominations and races.

Background: Christians Defying Gin Crow

While Jim Crow and the rise of prohibition advocacy had changed many aspects of southern culture, traditional wet arguments that carried so much weight in the nineteenth-century Bourbon South continued to matter in the early Jim Crow period of the 1900s and 1910s. As before, Christian wets invoked classical temperance, the Bible, and liberty to resist the imposition of statewide prohibition. Clergy as well as laity employed sophisticated and persuasive religious arguments. Some were Methodists defying the teaching of their denominational leaders while others were Episcopalians representing their denomination at the highest levels. Conservative Lutherans condemned prohibition as a modernist innovation while a Baptist seeking humanity's "transcendental perfection" argued that it would increase immorality. These Christian arguments formed a potent defense against prohibition and so kept alive the hopes of interracial politics in the South on that one issue for a few tumultuous years.

Despite drys' apparent monopoly on Christian virtue, many in the early twentieth-century South and around the nation invoked Christian liberty to denounce prohibition. These pious wets included prominent clergy, ranging from African American Baptist preachers to white Episcopalian bishops to Roman Catholic priests. Most of them, however, were laity, frequently politicians, who wielded Christian arguments against prohibition. Wets in the 1900s and 1910s recycled many of the same faith-based arguments from the 1880s, yet this time drys rather than wets had the religious momentum. From newspapers to stump speeches, anti-prohibition rhetoric sought to reclaim the banner of true Christian temperance from the drys.

METHODISTS

Perhaps the most prominent Methodist layman against prohibition in the 1910s South was Oscar Branch Colquitt, elected Texas governor in 1910. While most other Methodists championed legal bans on alcohol, Colquitt pledged in the opening speech of his 1910 campaign, even before he was first elected, to "do what was within my power, honorably," to prevent statewide prohibition.[3] Colquitt justified his opposition to prohibition by appealing to the Wesleyan Quadrilateral: reason, experience, tradition, and scripture. "Man is a free moral agent," he reasoned, "endowed by his Creator with a knowledge of good and evil, with power to choose between the two. No statute law can rise to a higher level than the rule prescribed by the Divine law." This very freedom to choose between right and wrong was the foundation of Christian liberty, while prohibitionists sought to limit that liberty. Since man is a free moral agent, "statutes can not cleanse his heart; this is the work of Christian grace." Indeed, a "doctrine of force," using the might of law to make men good, was "wrong in principle; it is intemperance; it is injustice," since "the application of political force tends to retard rather than to develop [the] growth" of "Christian grace." "We cannot make men good by law," he insisted. "It is only through education, [C]hristian and charitable influences and growth of intelligent consciousness and responsibility in the individual man himself that this can be done."[4] Colquitt argued that Christian doctrine opposed prohibition because it retarded one's spiritual development into a responsible Christian adult.

Colquitt's trump card, naturally, was Jesus. Quoting Matthew 15:11, Colquitt declared, "The Nazarine [Jesus] said 'not that which goeth into the mouth defileth a man; but that which cometh out of the mouth, this defileth a man.'" In Colquitt's interpretation, Jesus was opposed to prohibition because he saw evil as a condition of one's heart and words, not what one ate or drank. Prohibitionists, on the other hand, were like the Pharisees who rejected Jesus due to their focus on ceremonial righteousness. "Therefore," he deduced, "I am opposed to the application of force [prohibition] and believe that the correct doctrine is to preach temperance and to persuade men into the paths of soberness, honest and correct living."[5] Colquitt did not merely reach for a proof text but got to the heart of the matter: if Jesus said food and drink do not defile, why should the church insist upon the prohibition of alcohol?

Colquitt concluded his religious discourse with a reference to Jesus's best-known parable. "The best prohibition law the world has ever known," he said, "is the spirit of brotherly love and the best example of helping the fallen is the action of the Good Samaritan."[6] In that parable, which his audience would have known, the Samaritan found a man belonging to a hostile ethnic group who had been injured by thieves. Rather than judging or ignoring him, the Samaritan had compassion on him and paid out of his own pocket to provide the injured man medical care. Jesus concluded the story by calling on the audience to love their neighbors—including their enemies—as themselves. The implication was clear: alcoholics were more victims in need of help than enemies in need of punishment. Persuasion to right living by acts of love, not prohibition by force, was the path of Jesus. Wet Methodists could use Scripture just as well as, if not better than, drys.

Not all Methodists agreed. As Colquitt spoke against prohibition in the months leading up to the July 1911 statewide referendum, he aroused the ire of many, including a rising Southern Methodist pastor, Robert "Fighting Bob" Shuler. Having served as a minister in Virginia, Tennessee, and Texas, Shuler would eventually achieve national fame while pastoring Trinity Methodist Church in Los Angeles from 1920 to 1953. In 1911, however, Fighting Bob was in Temple, Texas, and he issued a sixty-page pamphlet, *The New Issue, or, Local Booze Government,* in which he lampooned the governor for his selective use of religion to support anti-prohibition. "Hon. O. B. Colquitt, the moist statesman," had "spasms like unto hydrophobia every time he thought about a preacher 'mixing in politics,'" yet "just hallelujahed" when Father Zell, a Catholic priest at Muenster, Texas, "made a political speech in the interest of Colquitt's candidacy" in 1910.[7] "In the estimation of the moist statesmen," Shuler continued, "it is terrible for preachers to 'meddle in politics' unless it is liquor politics, and then it is just heavenly."[8]

Shuler had a point: Colquitt did denounce preachers' involvement in politics—except when it benefited his campaign. On the eve of Texas's July 1911 statewide vote on prohibition, the governor gave a speech in which he denounced radical prohibitionists as "fanatics"; then he turned around and praised "the Bishops and clergy of the Episcopal and Catholic churches" in a list of anti-prohibition luminaries that included George Washington, Thomas Jefferson, and both of the state's US senators.[9] While Shuler rightly called out the governor's double standard, he also revealed an inconvenient truth: not all politically active clergy were drys. This conundrum led some dry ministers to pressure outliers like Colquitt to either conform or leave.

Even within officially dry Methodist churches, clergy differed a great deal on how much politics they put in their preaching. On one extreme was Bob Shuler. He issued pamphlets, gave stump speeches for prohibition, and involved himself in various local elections. His appointment to the pulpit of University Methodist Church in Austin drew a formal complaint from the church's board, which insisted their minister stick to the Gospel rather than indulge in politics. On another extreme was D. E. Hawk, Shuler's predecessor at University Methodist Church, who avoided politics and earned the quiet approval of the wet members of the church board.[10]

Somewhere in the middle and more representative of Southern Methodist clergy was Dr. W. D. Bradfield, pastor of First Methodist Church in Austin. Dr. Bradfield had prominent wets in the congregation, particularly Governor Colquitt, and largely shunned politics from the pulpit. Dr. Bradfield refrained from denouncing his most famous wet congregant even during the fierce 1911 statewide prohibition election, and a grateful Colquitt appointed him a trustee of the state's school for the blind. In 1912, Bradfield's bishop, Edwin DuBose Mouzon, called for an aggressive campaign for prohibition across Texas, partly encouraging a primary challenge to the sitting governor from a prominent dry, William Ramsey.[11]

Leading up to the 1912 election, likely under pressure from Bishop Mouzon, Dr. Bradfield finally spoke out against Governor Colquitt for his wet stance. When Colquitt won the race, he fired Dr. Bradfield from the school's board of trustees and formally left the congregation by requesting his membership letter be returned. However, he had difficulty finding a welcoming Methodist church, even though his political stance did not break any official Methodist discipline.[12] The episode demonstrated not only the divide between powerful anti-prohibition laity and dry clergy, but also the power of the Methodist hierarchy to convince apolitical clergy to speak out on a divisive issue even when they preferred silence.

Like Governor Colquitt in Texas, the Hon. Henry W. Long in Florida showed that lay white Methodists could deploy Scripture and tradition against prohibition. In September 1910, Long declared himself in favor of local option rather than statewide prohibition for several reasons. Most seriously, he claimed it defied the tradition of the Democratic Party, which "is not and never has been a prohibition party," but instead trusts people at the local level to determine whether they want alcohol. Indeed, the Florida Constitution provided that local option elections must be sixty days away from general elections to keep the issue nonpartisan. Implicit in his argument was the need to avoid divisions among white Democrats that would undermine white-only rule. Additionally, he argued that local option enjoyed great success due to the work of Democrats and temperance workers from organizations such as the WCTU, so statewide prohibition was unnecessary. He warned that prohibition laws "can not be enforced and maintained without a strong moral element behind it," which could only be given by the consent of "at least a majority of the citizens" in a locale. In all of these arguments, he pointed back to old-fashioned Jeffersonian Democratic ideals of local self-government. He capped his observations with an appeal to "broad-minded men" to consider his argument, as well as a crack against the "narrow-minded, egotistic crank" who was fixated on alcohol when there were more important issues at stake: expansionism, economic development, transportation revolutions, monopolies, and corruption, among others. He turned over those "cranks" to Jesus, who warned people not to give holy things to dogs or cast pearls before swine (a reference to Matthew 7:6).[18]

As with Colquitt, drys attacked the hypocrisy of Long. Some noted that Long had attended the Methodist State Conference the previous fall as a voting delegate, yet the resolution to back statewide prohibition had passed without a single no vote. Thus he either voted yes or was silent at the convention, yet now he took a prominent stance against it. The drys asked rhetorically: "is his present attitude consistent?" Much as Colquitt's pastor eventually denounced him for resisting statewide prohibition, so also the presiding elder (T. J. Nixon) and pastor (M. M. Lord) of Long's church (St. John's Ocala) called him out for a similar stance, this time with an open letter.

The letter began with respect for his long service to church and country but insisted that "the cause of truth and righteousness demand[ed]" a response, reminding him of the Southern Methodist (MECS) Florida conference's declared commitment to prohibition at all levels, including statewide prohibition. They, too, referenced Scripture, selectively quoting Habakkuk 2:15: "Woe unto him that giveth his neighbor drink, that puttest thy bottle unto him and makest him drunken also" (but omitted the context at the end of that verse: "that thou mayest look on their nakedness"). They admitted that they might not understand politics, but "we can understand a plain statement of the Bible, and a plain law of the church," and in the statewide prohibition vote "we are called on to vote" against liquor as "our Christian duty." More than that, it was "wrong for a church member to vote for liquor" under any circumstances. They continued: "No specious pleas for Jeffersonian democracy, local self-government, or broad-mindedness can justify a church member in violating the duties of his church and trampling under his feet the plain teaching of God's word." Long's opposition to state prohibition was "directly contrary to the principles of the Methodist church," yet his name was "published abroad as a leading Methodist," so he brought "reproach . . . upon [the church's] fair name," lending his influence to "perpetuate the infamous liquor traffic, the greatest enemy of the church." They appealed to him in the name of Sunday-school children, of the women of the state, and of God, to leave the ranks of "the enemies of temperance and prohibition" and join "those who live and labor for the salvation of men and for the glory of God." Their logic was clear: whoever was not with them was their enemy, on the side of the damned.[14]

The power of the Methodists' top-down church structure to quell dissent and demand political uniformity on prohibition held true for the northern-based and white-led Methodist Episcopal Church (MEC) as well as for Colquitt's white MECS. Because of its cultural alignment with the North and Republican politics, the MEC encompassed many African American congregations and ministers in the South, including (for a time) John Rayner. A Baptist minister for most of his adult life, Rayner joined the MEC from 1898 to at least 1903, yet he left the MEC and rejoined the more decentralized National Baptist Convention soon before he began openly questioning the wisdom of prohibition.[15]

While many African American Methodists in the South joined the MEC, many affiliated with Black-led Methodist groups. By 1916, while the MEC was the largest majority-Black Methodist denomination in five formerly Confederate states, the African Methodist Episcopal Church (AME) or breakaway rival group African Methodist Episcopal Zion Church (AMEZ) took the plurality in the other six states. Another substantial, Black-led group was the Colored Methodist Episcopal Church (later Christian Methodist Episcopal, always CME), which initially enjoyed considerable assistance from the white-led MECS. AME leaders had promoted prohibition at least since Bishop Henry M. Turner of Georgia stumped for prohibition in Atlanta, Tennessee, and Texas in the 1880s, and the denomination worked just as vigorously for prohibition as their white brethren in the Southern and Northern Methodist denominations. In North Carolina, where the AMEZ was the largest majority-Black Methodist church, ministers such as John C. Dancy and J. C. Price spoke out for prohibition in the 1880s as well. The CME joined its fellow Methodists in advocating for prohibition.[16]

By the 1910s, however, a few Black Methodist ministers worked against the new orthodoxy of prohibition. The Rev. Phillip C. Hunt, a prolific church planter and builder who was then pastor of St. Paul's AME Church in Beaumont, Texas, wrote to the brewers in 1910 to work with them to register voters.

His willingness to work with brewers may have hampered his ecclesial career, however; by 1916, Hunt had twice been nominated for the office of bishop of Texas, but he never attained the coveted position—perhaps the professional price he paid for transgressing the Methodist party line on prohibition. While most Black Methodist ministers bowed to the dry consensus, those like Hunt viewed political empowerment of the race as such a righteous cause that it merited working with brewers, if necessary, to achieve their political salvation.[17]

BAPTISTS

John Rayner's Christian opposition to prohibition was not limited to his 1905 Temperance Committee report at the National Baptist Convention, but took expression in his support for wet Methodist politician Oscar Colquitt. In a speech during Colquitt's 1910 run for governor, the African American Baptist minister John Rayner praised Colquitt for "guarding manhood's inalienable rights, and man's divine privileges," such as the liberty to imbibe alcohol, with "the faith and fortitude of a martyr."[18] While Rayner advocated for the restriction of distilled beverages, which he classed with "morphine, cocaine, bangue, and absinthe," he defended beer and wine as "very wholesome and refreshing" and denounced prohibitory laws against them as "immoral in principle, and unrighteous in legislation."[19] This claim signaled a significant shift from his 1905 NBC Temperance Committee report, in which he essentially agreed that drinking was sinful for Baptists who had taken the pledge; now he was affirming the essential goodness of fermented beverages while still denouncing distilled alcohol and other drugs.

Rather than bringing about a more just and Christian world, prohibition, Rayner argued, would ruin a thriving industry and increase immorality by encouraging casual drinkers to "make their own intoxicants, and a bacchanal revelry nightly will appear in too many homes."[20] While Rayner sympathized with many prohibitionists' desire to achieve "the final triumph of the Christian religion, and the transcendental perfection of humanity," he disagreed with legal measures to impose such a result: "God does not need the help of the ballot box in the furtherance and completion of his redemptive purposes."[21] While inconsistent with his former views that all drinking was wrong, he still insisted that only mild fermented beverages were acceptable alcoholic drinks and trusted in God to work salvation by means far greater than political activism.

His embrace of fermented drinks fit with many other Baptists, who continued to use wine in communion. Many churches in the NBC continued to use alcoholic communion wine, as indicated by indignant reports in 1908 and 1909 reports by the NBC women's auxiliary, which asked for the use of only unfermented wine in communion.[22] Their consternation indicated a push in the denomination towards grape juice in the Lord's Supper, but it also demonstrated the persistence of the millennia-long tradition of sacred wine. While white Baptists took the lead in the South for dry advocacy, African American Baptists displayed less ardor for total prohibition.

EPISCOPALIANS

Though traditionally skeptical towards prohibition, Episcopalians generally avoided the issue in their official church meetings. The journal for the 1910 annual convention for the Episcopal Diocese of West Texas did not reference any prohibition committee, nor did it once mention prohibition, temperance, or the coming statewide vote. Instead of prohibition, Bishop James Steptoe Johnston, a Confederate veteran, spoke of overcoming the divisions from the Civil War and focusing on uniting the churches of the nation.[23] The next year's conference in May, just three months before the monumental 1911 prohibition election, did not even mention church political and social activism, much less prohibition. Though stressing church unity, Episcopalians who avoided the prohibition issue seemed to revere the doctrine of the spirituality of the church more than practical collaboration with Methodists and Baptists on prohibition.[24]

Nonetheless, several other Episcopal bishops spoke out against prohibition leading up to Texas's 1911 statewide vote. The most prominent bishop in the state, George Herbert Kinsolving of the Diocese of Texas, announced his opposition to statewide prohibition in a nuanced articulation of his position in April 1911. While he supported high license fees for saloon operators, local option elections for some cities and counties, and strict enforcement of the law, he doubted the wisdom or expediency of statewide prohibition.[25] The bishop's statement drew the notice of Governor Colquitt. In a major speech just days before the statewide prohibition election, Colquitt mentioned Kinsolving by name as an example of the nobler kind of clergy who focused on holier matters than political bickering.[26] While Colquitt's statement was self-serving, the fact remained that a notable cleric had publicly rejected prohibition.

Not all the attention Kinsolving received was positive, however. In a remarkable episode of priestly insubordination, Episcopal minister J. T. Smith of Jacksonville, Texas, wrote an open letter in the *Dallas Morning News* in May chastising his bishop for defending the saloon, "the sum of all villainies," against the view of 99 percent of Protestant ministers in the state.[27] Since the only Episcopal congregation in Jacksonville was tiny, and Smith disappeared from church records, his bold clash with a popular bishop likely cost his career in the Episcopal Church.[28] Despite Smith's declamations, Bishop Kinsolving remained in his role until 1928, indicating that his stance did him no professional harm even years after prohibition had entered the US and Texas constitutions in 1919.

The head of the national Episcopal Church joined Kinsolving in speaking out against statewide prohibition. Bishop Daniel Tuttle, leader of the Episcopal Diocese of Missouri and presiding bishop of the Episcopal Church for twenty years (1903–23), denounced prohibition in 1911 as counterproductive, a statement that influenced voters in Texas that year, in Arkansas next year, and in contests throughout the nation. In response, the lightning-rod Methodist minister Bob Shuler castigated him. When a Christian minister refused to back prohibition, he inveighed, even non-Christian decent men would hold their noses and hide their faces at his approach.[29] Though Shuler's words had little influence on Tuttle's standing, the fact that the head bishop of the Episcopal Church would speak his mind on another state's prohibition statutes strongly suggests he spoke for his whole denomination.

Episcopal clergy who declined to express their view on the volatile political issue gave tacit approval to their presiding bishop and the bishop of Texas, and like Bishop Johnson of West Texas, they simply preferred to invest their words elsewhere. In the 1880s, Episcopal clergy stayed silent on prohibition while Episcopal laymen (including Jefferson Davis) played prominent roles in defeating statewide prohibition.[30] By 1911, however, several Episcopal bishops dared to speak out against prohibition, and virtually all Episcopal clergy declined to support it. While Methodist and Baptist ministers frequently denounced anti-prohibitionists as necessarily insane and immoral, Episcopalian bishops spoke in more measured terms, took moderated positions, and critiqued statewide prohibition as unnecessarily extreme.

CATHOLICS

As with Episcopalians, more traditionalist Roman Catholics rejected prohibition, yet they tended to do so quietly due to concerns of riling up anti-Catholic sentiment. In private, brewers sometimes consulted with Catholic priests, including an archbishop; the vast majority of Catholic clergy kept quiet on the issue.[31] Catholic priests generally avoided public engagement on divisive political issues such as prohibition, even if most of them shared sympathy with the brewers, to avoid infighting in a minority church or persecution from a hostile Protestant culture.

Father Zell, a Catholic priest in Muenster, Texas, illustrates the danger of Catholics speaking up against prohibition. He was repudiated by his own parish when he spoke up on prohibition in 1910—at least, according to a prohibitionist pamphlet by the Methodist minister Robert "Fighting Bob" Shuler.[32] Official Catholic records tell a different story: Father Zell served a church in Muenster, Texas, from 1904 to 1910 and resigned voluntarily out of exasperation at the division between the Knights of Columbus (KC) and the pro-German element, who feared the knights would "put an end to the 'Deutsche Muttersprache'" (German mother tongue).[33] The truth likely includes elements of both the official Catholic account and Shuler's dry propaganda.

The parish struggle between Father Zell and the local KC illustrated the broader struggle over how Catholics should engage prohibition, which was linked to whether Catholics should emphasize their new American identity or European traditions. Father Zell favored his European heritage. Born in Württemberg, Germany, he visited his birthplace in 1908 and doubtless sympathized with the pro-German group in Muenster against the Americanist KC. When he spoke out against prohibition—a cause much more popular in the US South than in Germany—he believed it would rally his divided parish together for a common cause. His plan backfired. As official Catholic records stated, Zell "tried his best to reconcile the opposing elements but not with much success."[34] Rather than winning over the KC, it alienated them because they either supported prohibition or feared that Catholic opposition to prohibition would arouse more anti-Catholicism from their dry Methodist and Baptist neighbors.

The KC sought to make Catholicism indelibly American and accepted by their Protestant neighbors. Michael J. McGivney and other second-generation Irish American Catholics, who faced bigotry due to their ethnic background and their faith, founded the KC as a secret society in the late nineteenth century. They named their fraternal order after Christopher Columbus as a sign of their dual American and Catholic identities. The organization was famous in its early days for combatting anti-Catholicism, especially as the anti-Catholic Ku Klux Klan's popularity and membership skyrocketed in the years following the release of the pro-Klan film *Birth of a Nation* in 1915.

The Knights of Columbus in the South were also known for adopting patriotic causes. In addition to the three original degrees of membership—unity, charity, and fraternity—the secret society in 1900 added the fourth and highest degree: patriotism. They held many flag-waving Columbus Day celebrations. They began a program to give away free supplies to US soldiers guarding the border with Mexico in 1916, and that program expanded into a national effort of the KC serving soldiers at home and abroad during World War I. When the war gave way to the Red Scare, the Knights around the nation were fiercely anti-Communist. In their zeal to combat prejudice against their beliefs, they at times enflamed prejudice against those with different beliefs. Above all, they put America first, not their European heritage.[35]

Some prominent Catholics urged assimilation into American culture by backing prohibition. Archbishop John Ireland, the most prominent Catholic dry of the age, believed that Catholics should gain respectability and influence in the United States by embracing "the sacred stigmata of patriotism."[36] US Catholics at the close of the nineteenth century were divided between traditional Ultramontanists, who viewed the Pope as an earthly authority above any state, and modern Americanists like Ireland who saw the US government as supreme in earthly matters. As Ireland put it, "Church and country work in altogether different spheres."[37] Ireland embraced America as "the providential nation" and applied to his favored nation (rather than God) the words of the old hymn: "America, how good, how great, thou art!"[38]

This Americanist brand of Catholic temperance at times echoed Protestant nativism against "hyphenated" Americans, as when Ireland labeled an "Irish-American, a German-American, or a French-American" as an "intolerable anomaly."[39] The archbishop further "frowned down" any efforts "to concentrate immigrants in social groups" and insisted upon Americanizing Catholic immigrants.[40] This claim to Americanization justified the dominance of Irish Catholics (like Ireland) in the American hierarchy over more recent immigrants. When Catholics in Europe expressed concern that Catholic immigrants in America were falling from the faith and urged the hierarchy to appoint more American bishops from diverse ethnic backgrounds, Americanist Catholics pounced at the "foreign" attempt to seize power. Among other distortions, one Ireland ally printed the headline "Foreign Countries Seeking to Rule the Church in America," and another ally in the US Senate denounced a German Catholic plot to "denationalize American institutions and plant as many nations as there are people of foreign tongues in our midst."[41] Archbishop Ireland even co-founded the powerful Anti-Saloon League (ASL), which exploited anti-German rhetoric during World War I to help advance national prohibition.[42]

The rise of prohibition in the 1910s throughout the South initially featured a few efforts for Protestant drys to align themselves publicly with Catholics to win over their votes. Drys invited a Catholic priest to speak to 1,500 prohibitionists at their statewide convention at Waco's Cotton Palace on April 21, 1911. The speaker, Fr. Patrick J. Murphy from Dalhart, Texas, expressed hope that his appearance at the event would inspire no less than 1,000 Catholics to switch to the "true side" of the prohibition question. The real issue was not "prohibition, regulation, or moderation," he argued, but "4,000 saloons against 650,000 homes." Father Murphy also addressed the 1913 national ASL convention on "Why Should We Do Away with the Saloon Business," and "copies of his speech were widely distributed," showing not only Murphy's personal commitment to prohibition, but also the desire of drys in the 1910s to publicize their Catholic support.[43] Once prohibition had been installed, however, dry invitations for Catholics across the South evaporated. The efforts of Catholic drys like Ireland and Murphy did not, however, fully dispel American Protestants' fear of Catholics, which only grew under prohibition's high-water mark of the 1920s.

Even some explicitly prohibitionist Catholics, however, took a more nuanced stance than most dry Protestants. In August 1912, Monsignor J. M. Lucey, a Confederate veteran, issued a sermon sympathetic to prohibition in the *Southern Guardian,* the official organ of the Catholic church in Arkansas. Lucey acknowledged that German Catholics—about half of the Catholic population in the state—would likely oppose prohibition, and he also noted that local priests should not "take a position on a public question" such as prohibition that would embarrass or disgrace their congregants "unless a principle was at stake," such as to "end the frightful evils which liquor has introduced." Even so, priests should speak "without dictating to the members of my congregation what they shall do." He also granted that there were "no doubt some good men among saloon keepers," though "good men in the saloon business are in the minority," and the industry supported many vices. Lucey also "conceded that a glass of beer or wine or even stronger drink is not sinful in itself, and becomes sinful only by abuse," though for the present time the traffic was so uncontrollable that "good citizens" should close it down until "the best people" could control it, so that a husband and wife could "enjoy a simple refreshment without loss of self-respect or public reputation," as was the case in Europe. Southern Catholics—both drys and wets alike—expressed the nuance of Christian tradition on alcohol in a way that most southern Protestant drys did not.[44]

LUTHERANS

As with Catholics, Lutherans' stance on prohibition also depended upon their ethnic and theological stances. German Lutherans—the overwhelming majority of Lutherans in Texas, for example—tended to hold to more traditional views and saw prohibition as "puritan legalism." On the other hand, Swedish Lutherans—who also had a significant presence in Texas—tended to support prohibition due to their pietism, which emphasized heart religion over tradition and so left them more open to innovations like prohibition. These cultural and theological fault lines prevented an attempted church union between the more conservative wet Missouri Synod (which, despite its geographically limited name, included churches in the South) and the more liberal Augustana Lutherans in the early twentieth century. The Augustana group was sympathetic to modernists, state-church unionists, secret societies, and prohibition—all of which the Missouri faction opposed.[45] For traditional Lutherans, prohibition was tainted with liberal theology and other dangerous ideas.

The most conservative Lutherans proclaimed prohibition antithetical to Christian liberty, with the Michigan Synod taking the lead.[46] The synod had in 1909 healed a brief but intense internal split, yet attacked prohibition directly at its annual conventions in 1911 and 1912, suggesting a wet stance united rather than divided at a sensitive time.[47] Under such circumstances, Director O. J. Hoenecke's report on prohibition in 1911, "Prohibition in the Light of Holy Scripture," indicated the widespread view of his denomination. "Correctly considered," he stated, "prohibition is basically nothing else but a renewed onslaught on the glorious liberty of the Christian, in that thereby the attempt is made to impose a yoke, similar to the old one from which he has been freed, once again on his neck and thereby put him in danger of losing entirely his freedom." Hoenecke took up all his allotted time at the conference speaking to this one point, and still had much to say about prohibition at the next annual convention. There, he argued that good Lutherans "dare not" allow "the precious blessing of Christian freedom be curtailed," and "therefore dare not and cannot make common cause with the advocates of prohibition, [but] must all the more oppose their dangerous error with the weapon of the Word in the areas assigned to us by God." While he denounced prohibition as a grave error, he also urged compliance with prohibition laws. When "prohibition agitation" pressures the state to make "laws forbidding the use, sale, etc., of potable spirits, then we for the sake of God [must] conduct ourselves as obedient Christians . . . in this matter" just as "in all things that do not conflict with God's Word." Obedience to the state did not preclude seeking to overturn bad laws, however. He still urged Christians to "continue our testimony against prohibition in so far as it presents itself as a moral demand."[48] Conservative Lutherans denounced prohibition as a form of legalism antithetical to Christian liberty.

The Michigan Synod's wet sentiment predominated in conservative Lutheran churches, including some the South, in the 1920s. In 1919, the Michigan Synod had joined several others to form the arch-conservative Wisconsin Evangelical Lutheran Synod (WELS), which also had churches in the South, and churches throughout this denomination denounced prohibition. By 1920, their hardline wet views represented "most of [WELS's] thinking and speaking and writing on the subject."[49] Like many Episcopalians and Catholics, most traditional Lutherans expressed their displeasure with prohibition by their silence on the issue, though a few prominent voices spoke up for traditionalists against prohibition, while a few embraced the modern innovation.

True Christian Temperance versus Islamic Prohibition

The traditionalist argument that prohibition undermined Christian liberty came not only from clergy, but also from secular newspapers in the South. A letter to the editor of the *Dallas Morning News* claimed in April 1911 that drys "say all the Church wants is legislation. . . . Well, that is the dangerous part of it to a man [who] wants his liberty or one who does not happen to belong to the Church that is in power." He further warned of "Church rule," where ministers "want to make it against the law to do anything the Church objects to." For many Texans, the greater fear was not the saloon, but the union of church and state. While Kansas had instituted prohibition years earlier, the writer stated, with not a little state pride, Texans cared more for religious liberty: "I hope to never see the day that Texas will be Kansasized."[50]

While some southerners worried that prohibition would make them like Kansas, others expressed the old concern that prohibition would replace Christian liberty with Islamic legalism. In 1907, an article in a Florida paper reported that centuries of prohibition made Muslims *less* able to resist intemperate alcohol use than Caucasians, whose centuries of experience with brewing gave them stronger willpower to consume alcohol temperately.[51] On the eve of a 1911 statewide vote on prohibition, Texas governor Oscar Colquitt gave a speech in which he denounced radical prohibitionists as "fanatics" and "Mohammedans," apparently because he thought they inappropriately mixed religion and politics.[52] Colquitt was not alone in his sentiments. By 1920, a newspaper in South Carolina reported that Mohammed "nearly spread prohibition over the world" by aggressively advancing the Muslim faith.[53] By the time prohibition took effect nationally in the 1920s, its connection with Islam seemed common knowledge.[54]

This view of prohibition being more Muslim than Christian was not limited to the South but spanned the country. An 1912 anti-prohibition ad in a West Virginia paper rejected the idea that, "when Mohammed denounced 'wine as the abomination of the works of Satin [*sic*],' he set a better example for mankind than Jesus Christ" and denied "that prohibition prohibits, except in Turkey."[55] In 1920, John Erskine, a professor at Columbia University, wrote in favor of "the Christian virtue of temperance," meaning moderate use, against "the Mohammedan discipline of prohibition," which unduly restricted individual freedom.[56] For Christians taking a more traditional perspective, prohibition came from legalism, not true Christianity, and the true cure for the moral decline from alcohol abuse was more liberty.

The prohibition-Islam connection was so pervasive that even the Anti-Saloon League's national newspaper mentioned it from time to time. In 1921, the *American Issue* reprinted a short article on how the world was looking to the United States to see if prohibition might succeed. However, the article claimed that American prohibition "accepts the famous judgment of Mohammed against strong drink and is curiously in line with the severe Puritanism attributed to authoritative Bolshevism in Russia." It is remarkable that the ASL felt comfortable reprinting an article that described prohibition as a mix between Islamic teaching, Puritanical severity, and communist authoritarianism. However, this indicated that ASL partisans were so excited to share an article about the spread of their dry Gospel that they either overlooked its religious and political critiques or did not care whether they were true.[57] Likewise, when William E. "Pussyfoot" Johnson (a prohibition enforcement officer known for sneaking up on bootleggers) visited Egypt in early 1927, he wrote to the ASL paper with glowing comments about his dry Muslim interlocutors and disparaging remarks about European "Christians" and Jews who sold alcohol in Egypt. When his Muslim friends there stated that "America, because of the Eighteenth Amendment, had become a Muslim country," these connections between prohibition and Islam amused rather than troubled him. When his guests insisted on taking a picture of him wearing "Moslem head gear," Johnson included the photo in the article and remarked: "Really it does not look so bad."[58] His overall assessment indicated that adherence to the dry Gospel was more important than Christian orthodoxy. Appearing—in convictions and apparel—like a Muslim was preferable to being a Christian who sold alcohol.

In addition to linking prohibition to Islam, wets also suggested that prohibition undermined Christian responsibility. Without a real choice between good and evil, Erskine reasoned, there was no virtue in an action at all, yet prohibitionists sought to make men good by removing temptation, and they claimed all who "would permit the opportunity to get drunk must be an advocate of drunkenness."[59] Yet Erskine contended that "drunkenness has never been more thoroughly condemned or more successfully combatted than when the ideal of freedom with self-control has been sincerely followed."[60] He located the "viciousness of prohibition" in its "resemblance to drunkenness, in that it also takes away the sovereignty of the mind and deprives character of moral responsibility," an affront to both Aristotelian Greeks and early Christians.[61] This virtue of temperance he derived not only from the church in general, but also from the Apostle Paul's teaching in Ephesians 5:18 to "Be not *drunk* with wine," rather than avoid drink entirely. He closed by citing Luke 7:33–34: "John the Baptist came neither eating bread nor drinking wine. . . . The Son of man is come eating and drinking."[62] Echoing ancient teachings and wet arguments from the 1880s, Erskine argued that prohibition undermined rather than advanced Christianity. Rather than fostering the temperance taught by Christ and the Apostle Paul in the Bible, prohibitionists were denying individuals their moral responsibility to choose between good and evil and thereby denying them the chance to make moral decisions at all.

Another advocate of Christian liberty against prohibition in the 1910s South was Alabama's Oscar Wilder Underwood, one of the region's most prominent politicians in the 1910s and 1920s. Underwood's political credentials were considerable. After launching a serious presidential bid in 1912 while serving as House majority leader, Underwood switched to the Senate in 1915 and by 1920 had become the leader of Democrats in the Senate, making him the only person to lead a party in both the House and the Senate. He was a renowned defender of states' rights against federal prohibition, which he denounced in 1914 as "an attempt to rob the states of their jurisdiction over police matters."[63]

Though Alabama first went nominally dry in 1909, Underwood repeatedly defeated dry opponents for the US Senate in several subsequent elections. The 1914 race for an open Senate seat pitted Underwood against prohibition's national champion in the US House: Richmond Pearson Hobson. Hobson had served along Underwood in the House for the previous seven years and advocated for many progressive reforms, including women's suffrage and direct presidential elections. Underwood claimed that the latter reform would diminish the electoral power of the South. Underwood easily prevailed in the Democratic primary with 89,470 votes to Hobson's 54,738. Underwood once again sailed to victory against another dry opponent, Lycurgus Breckinridge Musgrove, in the 1920 Democratic primary, even though prohibition had already become the law of the land nationally.[64] Underwood's persistent victories as an open wet in an officially dry state demonstrated that many white southerners could and did embrace wet politicians.

While personally a professed "Temperance" man, Underwood claimed that dry laws were ineffectual in advancing that cause. On the floor of Congress in 1914, he stated that great moral issues "have not been worked out at the point of the sword or with . . . governments," but rather come "from the heart, following the teachings of God, and not from the force of men."[65] Further, he contended, "Prohibition established by law does not produce Temperance," but "merely makes men outlaws instead of encouraging a respect for law and order."[66] A prohibition law lacking local support would simply be "a breeder of fraud and corruption and of contempt for constituted authority."[67] By his reasoning, the best way to generate real moral reform was through changing souls in church, while merely passing restrictive laws could generate more vice than virtue.

Even drys remarked that wets lay claim to the mantle of true temperance. They admitted that the wets' argument held a certain attraction *if* one could take their rhetoric seriously—but drys just laughed. "The cry of the liquor forces is now for temperance, temperance!" exclaimed the editor of the Texas Anti-Saloon League's newspaper. "Prohibition is held up as un-American, fanatical, unreasonable," while temperance, meaning moderate drinking, signified "the road to freedom, the ladder to achievement, the light of life, the measure of a man, the essence of charity, the soul of religion and the touchstone of true patriotism. This all sounds splendid, it's charming—it is almost SUBLIME."[68] Rather than engaging these claims, however, the *Home and State* dismissed them as so much smoke and mirrors, since only voting against the saloons could stop intemperance. The persistent lack of nuance is evident earlier on the same page: "The idea that a man can be a Christian and support a death trap of any kind in his community is monstrous."[69] While able to articulate wet arguments about liberty, drys preferred mocking them to seriously engaging them. After all, momentum was on their side. With Jim Crow reducing wets' voting power, what could stop prohibition across the South?

Protagonists against Prohibition: African Americans in Florida, Texas, and Arkansas

Just when it seemed that the rise of Jim Crow would have stifled the political activism of African Americans, they continued to cast decisive votes on statewide races from one end of the Deep South to the other into the 1910s. While they were barred from white-only primaries and outvoted in Democrat-dominated races for statewide office, there was one kind of election where they could still cast the winning votes: prohibition. In Florida in 1910, Texas in 1911, and Arkansas in 1912, African Americans tipped the scales in favor of wets in tight statewide referenda despite Jim Crow laws. Before covering these contests, however, it is crucial to understand why brewers and African Americans became strong political allies in the years leading up to these races.

African Americans apparently joined the wet coalition out of mixed motivations that changed over time. One motive was the stench of white supremacy in the dry camp, which grew so noxious that some Black ministers defected from drys to wets. Another reason was to protect individual liberty, including the right to drink, which became particularly pressing as African Americans watched their rights contract further. Joining the wet coalition also meant resurrecting the African American political activism rendered moribund by post-Reconstruction intimidation, fraud, and poll taxes. This miracle of reviving a meaningful voice in politics came with the enticing prospect of respect and material gain from powerful whites.

The potent combination of political clout and economic advancement, the double helix of racial uplift, took clearest expression among saloon operators. In the late nineteenth and early twentieth centuries, saloons built the foundations of political and financial empires. President John Fitzgerald Kennedy's grandfather, Patrick Joseph Kennedy, started his political career in Boston in the 1880s as the owner of three saloons. African Americans also found fame and riches through selling beer. The South's first Black millionaire, Robert Reed Church Sr., made most of his fortune in banking and real estate, but his first business was running a saloon in Memphis in the 1860s.[70] Particularly for ethnic and racial minorities, running a saloon meant not only profitable business but also the chance to wield influence among voting-age men.[71]

The shape of interracial politics looked different for each state. Some states, such as Virginia, North Carolina, and Alabama, had effectively eliminated the Black vote by strict Jim Crow laws, while other states had weaker practices in place than enabled more political participation. In Tennessee, poll taxes had effectively eliminated Black voting in rural areas, but it increased the clout of urban political machines that illegally provided poll tax receipts for poor African Americans and poor whites alike—in exchange for reliable election results. These corrupt political machines stymied reformers and led even ardent white supremacists to push for the repeal of poll taxes by the 1930s.[72]

After the opt-in poll tax arrived in Texas 1902, brewers there did more than any white-owned industry to oppose Jim Crow voting restrictions and mobilize Black voters.[73] Brewers formed the Texas Brewers Association (TBA) to secure their collective interests and from 1903 to 1911 hired a veteran of the Spanish-American War, Captain Ormund Paget, to manage campaigns and elections.[74] He opposed the constitutionality of the poll tax, oversaw the payment of poll taxes, disseminated literature, managed many operatives around the state, prevented or swayed elections, spread wet literature, influenced police officers, local officials, and Democratic conventions, and generally advanced the wet cause however possible.[75] Brewers did not oppose Jim Crow voting out of a sense of principle, but practicality. Nevertheless, through their dual opposition to Jim Crow voting restrictions and prohibition, brewers funded the resistance to Gin Crow.

Brewers received vital support from African American preachers. Brewers' correspondence reports that some of these preachers were not only personally wet but were paid by brewers to mobilize the African American vote, and they did their work well. One such preacher, D. R. Stokes, according to the brewers' correspondence, single-handedly saved at least two counties from going dry: Henderson County in 1908 and Leon County in 1909.[76] Captain Paget personally oversaw the latter contest, which he described as a "royal scrap" that wets had "very little hope of winning" but, despite being there himself, gave the glory to his African American comrade: "[T]he credit of the victory is largely due to D. R. Stokes, our colored preacher."[77] Stokes was one of four African American preachers employed by the brewers in 1910 to travel Texas full-time turning out the wet vote in crucial local elections, and he alone was entrusted to work all the territory west of Dallas. The brewers supplied their African American agents with poll tax cards, Lincoln posters, powers of attorney, African American voters' addresses, daily report sheets, envelopes, night telegraph, and sundry hand-outs. Paget praised these four African American preachers as "men" who "will, I believe, do the work and do it satisfactorily."[78] Brewers had worked for years with African Americans across the South in the 1900s, but that alliance would pay its richest dividends in a series of statewide elections in the South starting with Florida in 1910.

FLORIDA, 1910

The Sunshine State in 1910 was a sleepy backwater in the Deep South. The northern reaches of the state, particularly the Panhandle, mirrored the demographic of the Black Belt in neighboring Alabama. The previous November, Alabamans had voted overwhelmingly to reject statewide prohibition: 76,272 wet votes to 49,093 dry votes, or nearly 60 percent wet.[79] This overwhelming defeat of prohibition in a neighboring and demographically similar state boded ill for drys in Florida, yet they persisted with their plans to hold the vote a year later.

The local WCTU joined the Florida convention of Southern Methodists in endorsing statewide prohibition out of Christian duty—and implicitly, white supremacy. In early October, they urged citizens to register to vote and pay their poll tax by October 8, the last day to qualify to vote in the November election. They warned, "The liquor people have qualified every bum—white and black—that they can," and urged "every good citizen" to register and perform the "paramount duty" of voting for "yourself, your family, your state and your God." The assignment of lower classes of both races to the wets implied that drys were the "better sort," the "good citizens" who cared for God and family, while their opponents were not merely wrong, but dangerous sinners. Given the racial dynamics of the Jim Crow South, the threat of "equality" with such people carried sinister racial implications.[80]

On election day, the liquor traffic prevailed with help from Black voters. Floridians voting dry totaled 24,506 while 29,271 voted wet. Wet won by 4,775 votes or 8.9 percent of the total, meaning that only a few thousand African Americans could have swung the election.[81]

Unsurprisingly, the ASL blamed their loss in Florida on African Americans. The reasoning matched the data: the four counties with the most Black voters, which combined provided more than the margin of victory, voted overwhelmingly wet. As ASL national secretary Ernest Cherrington put it in 1914, prohibitionists were not overly worried about the result of the 1910 vote because they won the "majority of the white vote," and only "four counties containing the largest negro vote gave a majority of almost 5,000 against the amendment." Further, the language of being "not in any sense discouraged" by the result indicated that drys were only concerned about the white vote, since African Americans' votes could be easily suppressed by vigorous enforcement of Jim Crow laws. White drys in the 1910s—including northerners like Cherrington—also did not much care about persuading African Americans to embrace prohibition when the former could simply force it upon the latter.[82] The ideology of prohibition, based as it was on forcing others to be moral, took a particularly dark turn when applied against African Americans in the Jim Crow South. Such an attitude among white drys could not but encourage African Americans to seek political allies elsewhere.

TEXAS, 1911

The example of Florida was not encouraging for Texas drys, who had a difficult enough time just getting statewide prohibition on the ballot. After suffering a statewide rout in 1887, drys focused on local option elections until 1908, when they felt strong enough to lobby the state legislature to vote on a statewide vote. Since the Democrats controlled that state legislature and desired to prevent a party split on an issue, they resolved the issue by holding a statewide Democratic primary vote—keeping the issue in the hands of whites only. Despite the exclusion of African Americans (and Mexican Americans), the July 1908 primary narrowly defeated statewide submission, 145,530 against to 141,441 for. Two years later, drys won a more convincing victory for statewide submission, 159,406 for to 131,324 against, or nearly 55 percent for voting on prohibition. For the first time in Texas history, a solid majority of white Democrats supported prohibition.[83] However, the real test was the election a year away in July 1911, which would determine whether prohibition would enter the state constitution. In that election, however, African Americans could and would vote.

As with earlier local option votes, Texas brewers worked with Black Baptist ministers to get out the vote against prohibition. One particularly powerful preacher backed by the brewers was the independent Baptist Dr. John L. Griffin, one of Texas's best-known preachers as well as a gifted songwriter who often set his sermons to poetry and music.[84] Popularly called "Sin-killer" Griffin or simply "the evangelist," he was not without blemish: before 1910 he ingeniously founded the Rescue Association of the United States of America and Africa, an organization supposedly dedicated to "rescuing . . . fallen women" that in fact functioned as a front to "secure the payment of poll taxes by negroes" in order for them to vote in prohibition elections.[85] The organization was "endorsed by 125,000 members of Texas" and sometimes received aid from the brewers.[86] By November 1910, Griffin had led vigorous rallies in at least fifteen cities throughout the state, including four meetings in San Antonio, and often preached to crowds with African Americans and whites. He was so powerful in his speech that the national secretary of the brewers wrote, "we can't find a better man than Dr. Griffin to handle the people, both white and colored. 'Hear him.'"[87] African American preachers like Griffin who worked with brewers had various opportunities to speak to crowds of African Americans and whites alike, openly courting voters of every race.

Though the brewers left evidence of paying only a few preachers to spread the anti-prohibition gospel, just one dynamic African American apostle working for the brewers could quickly multiply allies in the African American churches across the state. Lectures by the Reverend Jim H. McKimil "urging the race to pay their poll tax" at St. Paul's African Methodist Episcopal Church in Beaumont, which had some four hundred "alive and energetic" members, prompted the church's prominent pastor Phillip C. Hunt to write a letter to the brewers who bankrolled McKimil. Hunt pledged the brewers in a December 1910 letter, "Now anything that I can do to aid the work" of registering African American voters "I will gladly do."[88] By all indications, his power to aid the brewers was considerable. Having earned his doctorate of divinity from Paul Quinn College in Waco—the hub of late-nineteenth-century prohibition sentiment in Texas—he had served as a licensed AME preacher in Texas since 1883 and personally brought in more than 1,500 members into the denomination, some 1,250 of whom he baptized. By 1916 Hunt had twice been a candidate for bishop, served over a dozen churches well by paying off their debt and organizing the construction of their church buildings, and was a politically engaged Republican. With an influential race man like Hunt offering his services to the brewers, many other pastors in the AME doubtless would follow his lead.[89]

Since McKimil spent several days lecturing and distributing literature at various African American churches in Beaumont, his assignment seems to have been to move from city to city, church to church, discreetly mobilizing parishioners to pay their poll taxes and vote against prohibition. According to Hunt, McKimil gave such "convincing" and "forcible" argument for paying the poll tax that "[n]o better man could have been found" for the job. Notwithstanding McKimil's ties to the brewers, Hunt directly "endorse[d] what [McKimil] said because he was right" and lauded him for doing "much good" in the city.[90] Support for the brewers' coalition among African American preachers—including Republicans like Hunt—spread well beyond those apostles the brewers sent forth to spread their gospel of liberty because many preachers saw African American political empowerment as a righteous cause, even if that meant allying themselves with a morally dubious industry. Such religion was neither merely otherworldly nor solely political but hopefully pragmatic, seeking the best for one's community in a world without ideal options.[91]

In addition to working with pastors, the brewers also allied with newspaper editors, teachers, and other African American leaders to advance their agenda.[92] Paget revealed in a January 1910 general report that the brewers' African American "friends" had infiltrated "every meeting of colored educational bodies" and "kept down with considerable trouble all resolutions opposed to your [the brewers'] interests."[93] Even given earnest cooperation from some quarters, many African Americans were apparently wary of cooperating with the brewers, but upon vigorous discussion they seemed to believe their interests and the brewers' were sufficiently compatible to do business with each other. Paget also declared in January 1910 that "meetings will be held in all communities where colored people are numerous, urging the payment of poll taxes."[94] Though pastors took the most prominent role in mobilizing the African American vote, leaders from every sector of the broadly evangelical African American community were involved in cooperating with the brewers to get out the African American vote.

In time, Texas brewers also won over two of the most influential African Americans in the state: E. L. Blackshear and John Rayner. Both men had supported prohibition in 1887, reversed themselves by the next major election in 1911, and were influenced by their ties to powerful whites. Blackshear was president of perhaps the most prominent Black college in the state, Prairie View Industrial College (now Prairie View A&M University). Blackshear claimed that he reversed himself on the issue due to "the frequent denunciation of negroes by Prohibition orators." In addition, pressure from the outspoken wet Oscar Colquitt, who as governor could have arranged for his dismissal from the presidency of a state-funded university, likely played a role in Black-shear's switch. A dry newspaper editor claimed Blackshear's defection to the wets "did more to mislead and confuse his race than any other one negro in Texas."[95] More than any—except perhaps John Rayner.

Rayner's story provides further insight into the shifting circumstances and pragmatic calculation that inspired various African Americans to join the wets. Before moving to Texas in 1880, Rayner was a liquor seller and Republican operative in North Carolina, where his white father had been a Whig congressman. Rayner counseled white Texan drys on how to gain the Black vote in 1887.[96] Rayner's reasons for this likely included his lifelong appetite for politics, ambition for personal prestige, and desire to keep the African American vote mobilized in the South after the rollback of Reconstruction.[97] When the third-party Populists offered the best chance for political and economic progress for African Americans since Reconstruction, Rayner became the leading Black operative for the movement. By 1902, Rayner began cultivating ties with paternalistic conservative whites, apparently reasoning that they were friendlier to African Americans than harshly racist white progressives, including former Populists.

Some of the paternalistic whites Rayner curried favor with were brewers. In 1904, Rayner became the financial agent of Conroe College, a Texan African American school modeled after Booker T. Washington's Tuskegee Institute, and collected money for the college by ingratiating himself with rich, powerful, conservative, and paternalistic whites, including prominent wets, the same kind of conservative "patricians" he had assailed as a Populist.[98] While Washington was a dry in Alabama, the equally pragmatic Rayner lived in the far wetter state of Texas. So, by 1905, Rayner had abandoned his previous dry stance and became a wet. The divergent stances of Rayner and Washington suggest that similarly pragmatic African Americans in the South behaved in radically different and even opposite ways depending upon their circumstances.[99]

Rayner's flexibility was reflected in his religious affiliation as well. Though baptized and raised an Episcopalian like his white father, Rayner was rebaptized and became a Baptist minister in 1880. While losing faith in the dying populist movement he helped lead, Rayner in 1898 joined the Methodist Episcopal Church (MEC), whose local newspaper praised him as "an able orator, a strong writer and a man of no mean ability" and invited him to write occasional articles.[100] By 1905 he had rejoined the Black-led National Baptist Convention (NBC), probably to avoid punishment from the Methodist hierarchy: decentralized Baptist church structure gave Rayner greater freedom to express himself on controversial issues such as prohibition.

In 1905, the same year Rayner issued his anti-prohibition Temperance Committee report for the NBC, he took up a busy schedule lobbying against prohibition throughout the Lone Star State. Though the Texas Brewers Association paid for his traveling expenses, Rayner insisted that he not receive a regular salary from the TBA, but rather whatever they thought him worth in a given situation, which gave him a reputation among the brewers as "patriotic" rather than a mere mercenary.[101] His alliance with the brewers promised Rayner opportunities for limited personal profit, vengeance against the white progressives who had betrayed populism to racist politics, and the mobilization of African Americans for political action. Perhaps the brewers' ethnic heritage gave Rayner a further reason to trust them: Adoue was a French immigrant and former resident of New Orleans, and Wahrmund was of German descent, highlighting the non-Anglo leadership of the brewers' coalition. While society still considered them white and him African American, the lighter-skinned Rayner had grown accustomed to navigating the manifold gradations of racial identity and might have seen these brewers as struggling, like him, to attain full acceptance as men and as American citizens.[102]

This interracial alliance paid rich dividends for the brewers in 1911. Of over 460,000 votes cast, 231,096 were dry and 237,393 were wet, providing a margin of victory of just over 6,000 votes or 1.4 percent of the total. Given Texas's relatively generous opt-in poll tax laws, lack of additional Jim Crow election laws beyond the poll tax, and strong connections between African Americans and brewers, the evidence is clear: African Americans determined the margin of victory.[103]

While some scholars have dismissed the significance of Black voters in the 1911 Texas election, a close analysis of the data shows that Black votes decided the referendum. Though Jared Paul Sutton argues that the poll tax neutralized the significance of Black votes in that contest, he also notes that brewers tried to pay the poll taxes of African and Mexican Americans while failing to analyze how much that work might have effectively countered the poll tax. He also does not attempt to give any statewide estimates of African or Mexican American vote totals, since his research focuses exclusively on a few counties.[104] Sutton's data are insufficient to verify his claim that Black votes did not decide the 1911 referendum.

Modest estimates of Black votes lead show that Black voters generated well above the margin of victory for wets in 1911. At the high-end estimate of Black turnout was Ernest Cherrington of the Anti-Saloon League, the most prolific number cruncher for prohibition, who noted that there were 126,000 eligible Black voters in Texas that year. He does not speculate on how many

Table 7. Black Votes in 1911 Texas Prohibition Election

MODEL	ELIGIBLE VOTERS	TURNOUT	VOTE OVERALL	OVERALL % OF VOTE WET	NET % OF VOTE WET	NET WET VOTE	% OF VOTE OVER MARGIN OF VICTORY
Rayner	126,000	-40%	50,000	80%	60%	30,000	476%
Payne	126,000	32%	40,000	80%	60%	24,000	381%
Barr	50,000	33.3%	16,667	80%	60%	10,000	159%

of those 126,000 voted, but his self-proclaimed "conservative" estimate had 80 percent of African Americans voters going wet (some contemporary papers put them at 85 percent wet), and he claims they decided the election. He also attributed the dry loss to the 7,000 Mexican voters who "were practically as a unit against the amendment," which likewise mirrored contemporary accounts in Texan newspapers.[105]

If there were 126,000 registered Black voters, how many showed up to vote? Sociologist Ann-Marie Szymanski calculated 48.9 percent overall turnout for the 1911 vote, and Black turnout was likely much lower. Three years earlier, John Rayner had promised to mobilize "at least 50,000 negroes in Texas to pay their poll tax in time" for the next statewide election, which amounted to about 40 percent turnout of the 126,000 number. The ever-practical brewers never doubted Rayner's figure in internal reports assessing his value, but instead stated, "we need him."[106] Texas historian Lewis L. Gould estimated 40,000 Black voters annually in the early poll tax period, or a turnout of roughly one-third of eligible voters, is the most likely number of African American voters in 1911. Granting this modest turnout and Cherrington's conservative estimate of a four-to-one wet-to-dry ratio, African Americans cast more than 24,000 net votes against prohibition, four times the deciding margin.

Even granting the most parsimonious estimate of Black turnout, Black votes still decided that election. Texas historian Alwyn Barr speculated that only 50,000 Black voters held poll tax receipts in 1911 (fewer than half of Cherrington's "conservative" number) and that only one-third of those likely voted that year. From these numbers, Barr suggests they did not affect the outcome. Yet even if fewer than 17,000 African Americans voted (as Barr supposes), and did so at an 80 percent wet rate, their votes would still have determined the outcome.[107] By all calculations, Black votes kept Texas wet in 1911 (see table 7).

ARKANSAS, 1912

In September 1912, the prohibition election in Arkansas provided the clearest case not only that African American votes decided statewide elections, but also that opposition to prohibition and to Jim Crow went hand in hand. The very same day that the prohibition vote was scheduled to take place, a grandfather clause was put on the ballot as well, which could have disqualified around three-quarters of the Black vote.[108]

Rather than seeking to win over the African American vote, the Arkansas ASL articulated an openly white-supremacist stance and explicitly sought to eliminate Black influence from politics. In May 1912, drys formed local ASL groups around the state, but explicitly limited their membership to "white persons." To make the point plainer, the superintendent of this organization, Mr. Barrett, clarified these leagues' purpose: "Agitation will be the order of the day from now on until the black is truly knocked out of Arkansas."[109] For leading white drys in Arkansas, their mission of eliminating saloons was intimately tied in with destroying the political power of African Americans.

Nonetheless, a few African Americans joined their white brothers in Christ for prohibition in Arkansas. Clergy in Garland County published a full-page ad in a local newspaper to advocate for state prohibition. Signatories included many white-led churches—mostly Baptist and Methodist, as well as Presbyterian, Salvation Army, and "Christian"—and a few Black church leaders, including two from Second Baptist churches (traditionally Black) and one from a CME church. The ad covered standard dry ground. It scoffed at the "personal liberty" objection to prohibition, declaring: "Personal liberty should end where it becomes a menace to the community." It also used the standard progressive argument that the alcohol lobby was a "gigantic trust" that must be subdued, and it mocked the claim that "prohibition does not prohibit." The ad also appealed to southern manhood: "when helpless woman and children suffer, it seems enough to stir men to go to the polls"; and: "Show your manhood and vote 'er right." Perhaps the most remarkable item in this ecumenical production was the lack of distinctively Christian or Bible-based arguments.[110]

The WCTU of Arkansas, meanwhile, trusted in white men to vote on behalf of white women. An article in an Arkansas paper in September 1912 by the state WCTU quoted a passage from Frances Willard, a proponent of women's suffrage, to plead with men to vote out the saloon on behalf of the "unrepresented class" of women. Such action is "manly," a "royal prerogative of citizenship," against "crime," and "sure to win . . . by your votes."[111] Nowhere in the article was advocacy for women's votes mentioned. While many women in the WCTU hoped to advance their enfranchisement through prohibition, they adapted their message in the South to encourage white men to fulfill their role of safeguarding white women's honor through opposing alcohol.

That September, however, the drys were disappointed: wets won a clear victory, with 85,358 wet votes to 69,390 dry votes, thanks to an alliance between brewers and Black voters.[112] The ASL admitted that it lost the Arkansas prohibition referendum because it coincided with a vote on a grandfather clause to disfranchise African Americans, and the liquor forces allied with Black voters to defeat both measures. As the ASL put it: "The negroes in Arkansas seldom vote, but this fall they swarmed to the ballot boxes in large numbers. A trade was made between the liquor forces and the colored voters by which the liquor men were to vote against disfranchisement and in return the negroes were to vote against prohibition."[113] The language of "swarmed" in reference to Black voters indicates the ASL's view that they were inferior to whites. However, there is no reason to doubt the factual accuracy of the claim of a deal between the alcohol traffic (as drys would say) and African Americans to preserve their rights. This fits with evidence from Texas and Florida of African Americans aligning with the alcohol lobby to advance their shared interests and makes more explicit than any previous election the connection between fighting prohibition and combating Jim Crow voting restrictions. In Arkansas in 1912, drys admitted that a multiracial coalition had once again defeated Gin Crow.

Tallying the Votes, Again

Taken together, the three statewide elections in Florida, Texas, and Arkansas demonstrated beyond a reasonable doubt the impact of African American voters on a level many scholars did not believe possible in the early Jim Crow period. Table 8 examines four statewide elections in the South between 1910 and 1912 where wets won, with particular attention to African American church-member populations in 1916, a few years after those votes took place. Given that Cherrington had estimated only 126,000 eligible Black voters in Texas's 1911 contest, and 1916 is several years after the contests, it seems reasonable that at least a quarter of the Black church membership in each state was registered to vote, and even modest turnout of that one-quarter meant thousands—or for Texas and Arkansas, tens of thousands—of voters, more than enough to tip each election. Since contemporary accounts clearly stated that Black voters carried the day in Florida, Texas, and Arkansas, it seems reasonable to conclude that they might have done so in other states as well.

Table 8. Southern Statewide Prohibition Referenda Won by Wets, 1910–1912

STATE	DATE	DRY VOTES	WET VOTES	MARGIN OF WET VICTORY (TOTAL %)	BLACK CHURCH MEMBERS, 1916
Florida	1910 Nov. 8	24,506	29,271	4,775 (8.9%)	138,055
Texas	1911 July 22	231,096	237,393	6,297 (1.3%)	396,157
Arkansas	1912 Sept. 9	69,390	85,358	15,968 (10.3%)	242,199

Sources: Alabama Official and Statistical Register, 1911, comp. Owen, 318–19; *Report of the Secretary of State of the State of Florida,* ed. H. Clay Crawford (Tallahassee: 1911), 16–22; Plocheck, "Prohibition Elections in Texas"; *Anti-Saloon League Year Book* (1913), 39; Cherrington, *History of the Anti-Saloon League,* 118, 134; Hunt and Bliss, eds., *Religious Bodies, 1916,* 139, table 52.

Aftermath: Gin Crow Triumphant

Despite the early strong resistance to drys' efforts, the potent multiracial wet alliance that forestalled statewide prohibition across the South in the early 1910s crumbled by the end of the decade, replaced by an order fulfilling Jim Crow's promised marginalization of Black voters and instilling legal alcohol bans on state and federal levels. Internal and external factors contributed to this decline. Internally, racial tensions roiled the wet coalition as brewers failed to treat their Black allies as equals and so generated resentment and disillusionment from a vital constituency. Externally, white drys cried out for more rigorous enforcement of Jim Crow election laws to neutralize the racial minority vote even further while calling for a political voice for white women to counteract "ignorant" wet voters.

Much of the failure of the wet coalition was the fault of the short-sighted alcohol lobby. Despite their shared success, ethnic white brewers could be just as condescending as white drys. Despite success in many local option elections and the 1911 statewide vote, fissures broke out between the brewers and Black activists who did not feel they were receiving appropriate respect for their work, and brewers paid the price. In Limestone County in August 1909, an unnamed operative of the brewers thought the county would stay wet in a local option election with 90 percent of the African American vote but regretted spending money to "play with the negro saloonkeeper."[114] By August 11, after the election, the operative had trouble explaining how the election that should have been won by two hundred was lost by ten. "The only way I can account for the result," he confessed, "is that the negroes took their money and retaliated by voting the pro ticket to even up for the treatment received by the negro Dave Johnson that [a brewer operative] put out of business after putting him in business."[115] The brewers learned the hard way that African American men could not be simply bought off; they wanted to be treated as men.

By the summer of 1912, even Rayner felt that he was being used. "You say 'you will have to excuse me [from giving more financial support],'" he wrote to the brewers that July, "but when you need a colored vote and call on me I shall need tell you to excuse me."[116] The brewers' bewildered response to his request for compensation demonstrates their incomprehension of the value of their African American allies, and the lack of additional correspondence from Rayner in the records indicates that he followed through on his threat.[117] Later that year, Rayner wrote an essay in a white newspaper in which he openly despaired, "Politics has nothing to offer the negro." Since some of their race aspired to become "protagonist[s] in politics," he bemoaned, African Americans generally were deceived by "utopian promises" and plunged into political activism, only to find their "political opportunities circumscribed" and "manhood proscribed." The word choice of "protagonist" fit his political record and echoed his irate letter to the brewers earlier that year, indicating that he saw himself as a naïf whose political activism against prohibition did not elevate his race, but rather degraded it further by provoking white backlash.[118]

Unable or unwilling to blame themselves for their defeats, white drys blamed African Americans for their political failures in the 1910s. Statements criticizing the "low negro and Mexican vote," the "Mexican and ignorant negro," and the like peppered the Texas ASL's newspaper, especially after the drys' loss in the 1911 vote. A cartoon from a dry newspaper after the 1911 election (reproduced in this volume) depicted Lady Justice peeking out of her blindfold, weighing votes on uneven scales tilting against prohibition, and receiving votes from a dark-skinned man who said, "Here is some perfectly fresh ones mam," while pocketing a pack of suspicious "poll tax receipts." In other words, the cartoon claimed that African American votes corrupted justice by tipping the elections, and someone else had paid their poll taxes.[119]

Instead of seriously courting Black votes, white drys doubled down on winning over whites while suppressing racial minority votes. White Baptist minister James B. Cranfill openly pined for "the kindly influence of the Christian slave-holder" upon a newly rebellious generation of African Americans so they might not vote wrongly. J. B. Gambrell, another white Baptist minister, argued that by voting wet "negroes degrade citizenship" and called upon whites to "look this matter straight in the face and meet it like the Anglo-Saxon race has met every great issue."[120] A letter to the editor of the *Home and State* by H. C. Park put the issue baldly regarding the 1912 US Senate race between a wet and a dry: the wet candidate "wanted the lower class of negroes and Mexicans to rule," but "the white Americans" would support his opponent, Morris Sheppard. Predictably, Sheppard won the race and soon became prohibition's champion in the US Senate.[121]

These white attacks on Blacks were not merely rhetorical but corresponded to increasing intimidation that reduced turnout. Whereas the populist movement brought out about 85 percent of the African American vote in Texas in 1896, the African American vote had plummeted to just 23 percent turnout in 1902, even before the poll tax was implemented. By the time voters approved statewide prohibition in 1919, their share was smaller still.[122] Voter suppression by white drys against minorities proved ruthlessly effective.

Public pressure to suppress African Americans' participation in politics contributed to the court case that doomed the wet coalition in Texas. A suit filed in January 1915 by the office of Texas attorney general B. F. Looney demanded the brewers pay over $21 million for violating the state constitution and various laws, both antitrust laws and laws limiting the use of corporate money to influence politics and elections. The *Abilene Daily Reporter* in 1915 highlighted the sensational claim that the brewers paid poll taxes for wet voters, "especially negroes."[123] In a January 1916 court settlement, the seven Texan brewers admitted to the charges, paid fines of about $290,000 (far less than the initially proposed sum), and forfeited their business charters for two years.[124] With that stroke, the wet coalition was all but finished in Texas.[125]

While Black votes shrank, prohibition swept the remaining dry southern states. In February 1913, the Arkansas legislature passed virtual statewide prohibition and blocked a referendum attempt to reverse it; prohibition took effect the next year. In October 1913, the Tennessee legislature passed laws to strictly enforce their Four Mile Law, which essentially enacted prohibition statewide. South Carolina had opted in 1907 for a dispensary system that limited alcohol distribution, brought in revenue to the government, and slowed dry sentiment in the state. Nevertheless, on September 14, 1915, over 70 percent of South Carolinians voters favored prohibition, and the law went into effect on New Year's Day 1916. While by 1912 the Virginia House voted overwhelmingly to submit an "enabling act" to allow a statewide vote on prohibition, the state senate beat the measure by 24 to 16. Finally, in 1914, a tie-breaking vote in the Virginia Senate approved the vote, which was held on September 22, 1915, and resulted in a majority of 30,365 for the drys. Prohibition took effect over a year later, on November 1, 1916.[126]

By 1918, Florida went dry by popular vote while Texas turned dry by a vote of the state legislature, and Texas voters added prohibition to the state constitution by referendum in 1919.[127] By 1918, every southern state except Louisiana had statewide prohibition. Without a powerful white interest group to protect them in the late 1910s, African Americans' influence on prohibition elections in the South shrank to near insignificance. Gin Crow—the rise of prohibition in the South at the expense of Black political engagement—had triumphed at last.

Conclusion

The racial dynamics of prohibition were complex and sometimes ironic. White prohibitionists increasingly sought to affirm a racial hierarchy, particularly keeping African Americans in their place. Meanwhile, embattled and desperate brewers, to save themselves, politically empowered those same minorities who were being oppressed. African Americans chose from a variety of responses to advance their individual and collective fortunes, switching from dry to wet according to the shifting circumstances, and significantly affected prohibition elections by their actions, especially from 1910 to 1912. These cases demonstrate the power of interracial wet coalitions in the early Jim Crow period across the South, from Deep South to the upper South and from the far western South to the far eastern South. Those cases also show that African Americans' votes against prohibition were integrally tied to their efforts to preserve their citizenship rights, particularly the right to vote.

The alcohol industry was a powerful ally of African American enfranchisement, but the alliance was self-interested for all parties and short-lived due to internal divisions and outside pressures. As Barry Hankins has aptly stated, "Culture wars create odd bedfellows and ever-shifting alliances," and preachers like Rayner lived out these shifting alliances.[128] African Americans forestalled statewide prohibition in several states for years.[129] The diverse coalition demonstrated the potential power of interracial politics in the South into the 1910s and briefly rekindled allegedly moribund African American political activism more than a decade into Jim Crow.

The losses of prohibition votes across the region by the late 1910s resulted in a powerful backlash that effectively silenced Black votes in statewide elections for decades. The decline in Black voting power for prohibition coincided with a rise in support for white women's suffrage in enough southern states—Texas, Arkansas, and Tennessee—to enshrine the Nineteenth Amendment in the US Constitution. By 1920, white women gained suffrage in the South while Black men lost it. Throughout the 1920s, the enforcement of prohibition laws in the South disproportionately targeted Black Americans, reflecting and reinforcing the prejudices of white drys. Law-and-order rhetoric flowed from the lips of lawless racial terrorists in the Ku Klux Klan and anti-Catholic firebrands like Governor Sidney Johnston Catts of Florida. Gin Crow not only worsened racial inequality through selective enforcement but also stirred up ugly religious prejudices as well, particularly against Catholic Americans. For the 1920s, the forces of racial and religious intolerance had the law firmly on their side.

5

Rebels against Rum and Romanism

YANKEE REPUBLICANS in the presidential election of 1884 infamously attacked Democrats as the party of "Rum, Romanism, and Rebellion" because of Democrats' support from the alcohol lobby, Roman Catholicism, and former Confederates.[1] Yet an increasing number of southern Democratic "rebels" turned against both alcohol and Catholicism from the late nineteenth to the early twentieth century. In 1894, Sidney Johnson Catts, a dry Southern Baptist minister in Alabama (and later governor of Florida), stated: "There is no question that rum and Romanism go together," and "the very stronghold of rum in this country is Romanism."[2] By 1926, J. Frank Norris, the pastor of First Baptist Church of Fort Worth, was denouncing the presumptive Democratic nominee for president in an article aptly titled "The Conspiracy of Rum and Romanism to Rule This Government."[3] Two years later, many southerners had not only banned rum long since and denounced Romanism in the present, but apparently repented of rebellion as well: Florida, North Carolina, and Virginia voted for a Republican president for the first time (and Tennessee the second time) since Reconstruction, while Norris's home state of Texas voted for a Republican president for the first time ever. What happened?

Southern Democrats were more tolerant of Roman Catholics before prohibition became law. Outside Louisiana, Democratic Protestants enjoyed overwhelming voting majorities throughout the South, so Catholics posed little electoral threat to their rule. Southerners in the late nineteenth and early twentieth centuries had more often accused prohibitionist Protestant clergy, not Roman Catholic politicians, of mixing church and state. Yet when prohibition took effect, Catholic wets found themselves on the wrong side of the law. Anti-Catholicism and prohibition dovetailed in the "law and order" rhetoric of politicians like Florida's firebrand governor, Sidney Johnson Catts. In addition to official censure, Southern Catholics—along with Jews, African Americans, and other minorities—faced persecution from a reborn Ku Klux Klan in the late 1910s and early 1920s. Finally, anti-Catholic rhetoric from drys reached a crescendo in 1928, when the Democratic presidential nominee was a wet, Catholic, Irish German New Yorker named Al Smith. For many Southern Democrats, Smith was too much to bear; they shattered the Solid South by voting for Republican Herbert Hoover, who was reliably dry and Protestant.

Anti-Catholicism and Prohibition

Scholars have debated how anti-Catholic the prohibition movement was. Most scholars have contended that prohibition generally set white Protestant drys against wet Catholics, Jews, African Americans, recent immigrants, and other racial and religious minorities. Jeanette Miller Schmidt went so far as to suggest that "the repeal of the Eighteenth Amendment in 1933 was symbolic of the end of rural Protestantism's dominance in the United States," while Mark A. Noll described prohibition as "the last gasp of Protestant hegemony" in the nation.[4] While Catholics tended to be wet, some Catholics embraced prohibition. Sometimes dry Protestants explicitly courted Catholic support, as when the dry leader in Texas's 1887 campaign, B. H. Carroll, shunned overt criticisms of any religious group, including Catholics, who formed about 18 percent of the state population.[5] While Carroll's attempts at garnering Catholic support were ineffective, at other times Catholics could and did support the dry cause.[6]

The Prohibition Party Governor: Sidney Johnston Catts

Prohibition activism and anti-Catholic prejudice together in the South took clear form in Sidney Johnston Catts, who was elected governor of Florida in 1916 as the Prohibition Party candidate, the only candidate of that party ever to win statewide office. Born into a prosperous Alabama family in 1863, he became a Baptist minister after a "born again" experience in 1886. Growing dissatisfied with parish life, Catts ran for Congress in a crowded 1904 special election, but he came in second to another demagogue, James Thomas "Cotton Tom" Heflin.[7] Sensing riper political opportunities in neighboring

Florida, Catts moved in 1911 to DeFuniak Springs, a city in the Panhandle with a similar racial composition and political orientation as the Alabama Black Belt where Catts grew up. He pastored the First Baptist Church until 1914, when he resigned due to a dispute with the congregation and became a traveling insurance salesman.[8] Like Alabama's Jim Folsom and Louisiana's Huey Long, Catts used his insurance job to prepare for political ascension. In October 1914, he announced the beginning of his campaign for governor of Florida—two years before the 1916 election. His campaign events resembled revival services—including a passing of the offering plate.[9] Catts combined an open appeal to the "cracker" vote with new technologies, roaming the countryside in a Model T equipped with a loudspeaker system to attract crowds of neglected voters. In the words of renowned southern historian Wayne Flynt, Catts "provided a voice for the inarticulate 'unwashed' against the carefully manicured and properly pedigreed."[10]

Catt's populistic style came out clearly on a campaign flier that combined anti-Catholicism, prohibition, and the Lost Cause. The flier, designed for distribution before all his campaign rallies during the Democratic primary, framed his campaign against rum and Romanism, prominently calling him "The Catt" whom "The Catholics and The Whiskey Men Are Fighting." His eight-point platform spent the most time on the point about opposing Roman Catholicism, the "great menace to the peace of home, the maintenance of our public schools, and the enjoyment of quiet religion." The flier appealed to every voter "who loves his country and hates Catholic control of American politics, to vote for Catts." The shortest point in the platform paired with the anti-Catholicism: "In Favor of Prohibition." In line with his dry stance, Catts proclaimed, "God bless our women and our homes" as he appealed to the "great and silent power" of "wives, mothers and sisters . . . who cannot vote" but still "help Catts out in his heroic race." He praised white women—but did not declare support for their suffrage. Catts also aligned himself with the Lost Cause. While he never fought in the war (he was born in 1863), he claimed the rank of major as chaplain for the First Florida Brigade of the United Confederate Veterans (UCV) and promised better pensions for veterans.[11]

Catts also used shameless gimmicks to appeal to the common man against the political establishment. Not shy about self-promotion, he compared his oratory with the "fury" of fire-eater William Lowndes Yancey and the "eloquence" of Henry Ward Beecher. Playing off his name, he produced one flier (reproduced in this volume) featuring a large picture of a hissing cat, a catchy jingle ("Kill the Rats—Pay Your Poll Tax and VOTE for CATTS"), and cheesy animal jokes ("If Texas had a Hogg for Governor why can't Florida have a Catt for Governor?"). The imagery of the tooth-and-claw-bearing cat and "Kill the Rats" line underscored his sense of embattlement, which was further emphasized in his overt mistrust of the political establishment. The flier stated that, in at least four counties, votes for him might not be counted "at the poles [*sic*]," and so demanded in giant, all-caps script, "CATTS MEN MUST HAVE ONE MAN" as a watcher at every polling station. To hammer home the point, the flier added: "THIS IS NECESSARY, DO IT SURE."[12] The flier celebrated in giant letters "COMMON PEOPLE" and repeatedly urged them to register and pay their poll tax, showing how Catts exploited neglected voters' mistrust of political elites.

The mistrust between Catts and the elites was mutual. The *Pensacola Journal* cautioned its readers in January 1916 that Catts was a "dangerous" man who espoused "revolutionary" and "anarchistic" ideas and would bring "calamity" to Florida. The article compared Catts unfavorably with South Carolina's erratic and particularly racist governor from 1911 to 1915, Cole Livingston Blease. While Blease merely disrupted the political peace, Catts threatened to disrupt the religious peace as well. His anti-Catholicism appealed to many of the state's forty thousand Baptists, whose hostility to Catholics (according to the paper) exceeded any other denomination. He also relied upon a growing anti-Catholic secret society whose numbers may have exceeded ten thousand. Worst of all, Catts was preparing "to make open war upon the Democratic Party and its candidates" who were "suspected of being under Catholic influence," which should alarm the "most patriotic thinkers." The paper also noted that Catts's main competition in the governor's race, state treasurer William Valentine Knott, was a devoted Baptist "of the highest character." Anticipating countercharges, the newspaper maintained that all the people working there were Protestants—never Catholic. Even while railing against Catts's anti-Catholic demagoguery, they admitted the power of that prejudice most eloquently by declaring their Protestant bona fides.[13]

Though he claimed back in 1914, "I am a Democrat always," Catts controversially lost the Democratic primary to Knott in 1916.[14] Catts led in the initial count, losing only after the Florida Supreme Court order a recount, which Knott narrowly won. Blaming (credibly) corrupt party elites for his loss, Catts campaigned as the true Democratic nominee, but also accepted the Prohibition Party nomination for the general election. His grassroots campaign explicitly courted the poor white rural "cracker" vote. As one of his slogans went, "The Florida crackers have only three friends: God Almighty, Sears Roebuck, and Sidney J. Catts!"[15] Southern historian Wayne Flint described the "almost psychotic anti-Catholicism" and expletive-laden rants in his campaign speeches, which alienated some audiences but stirred up support from the common people. On election day, Catts emerged with a strong plurality and nearly ten thousand votes more than Knott.

Catt's inauguration speech in 1917 affirmed the populist bent that would carry him through his four-year term. He invoked Scripture and epic history as he denounced opponents in politics and business, including the "press," "negro voters," courts, and "the Roman Catholic hierarchy." Catts framed his victory as a triumph for "the common people of Florida, the everyday masses of the cracker people."[16] While he claimed to fight corruption, he took care of his friends by firing enough old hands in the government to give jobs to his supporters. His use of the spoils system mirrored that of one of his favorite historical figures, Andrew Jackson. At the same time, Catts also promoted genuinely progressive reforms such as initiatives, referenda, recalls, regulation of big businesses, ending the notorious convict-lease system, and starting prison reform, and he was particularly effective in the last two efforts. Catts's politics embodied a quixotic mix of progress and regression.

Though he finished his political career in a failed run for US Senate in 1920 (losing the Democratic primary with less than 30 percent of the vote), Catts had demonstrated how a blatant appeal to religious, racial, and antiestablishment prejudice in the Gin Crow South could lead to electoral success. While Catts rose like a rocket and fizzled quickly, more stable politicians cleverly deployed the same sense of threat and appeal to deep emotions to promote strict prohibition enforcement as the path to peace through law and order.[17]

Law and Order against Racial and Religious Minorities

Even after prohibition was adopted into the constitutions of various states and the United States in 1919, it was still a major issue throughout the South. In the 1920 governor's race in Texas, for example, the Democratic primary pitted the progressive champion Pat Neff against Joseph Weldon Bailey. Bailey was anti-prohibition, anti–women's suffrage, anti-labor, anti–foreign entanglements, and generally an anti-progressive candidate representing the fiscally conservative and pro–states' rights Jeffersonian wing of the Democratic Party. The lesser candidates were two progressives, Robert Thomason and Benjamin F. Looney, the very state attorney general who had put Texan brewers out of business for two years with a devastating lawsuit filed in 1915. Bailey won the first-round primary, but Neff won enough votes to challenge him in a runoff, and the progressive backers of Looney and Thomason coalesced behind Neff, giving him victory by more than seventy thousand votes.[18] Bailey's remarkable performance despite his overt rejection of prohibition (then the law of the land) spoke volumes not only of his ability as a politician but also the persistent strength of anti-prohibition sentiment even as prohibition seemed inevitable.

Nonetheless, Pat Neff's success signaled how prohibition had conquered the southern political landscape. In the opening speech for his candidacy for governor, Neff declared that he would back "every measure that has for its purpose the enforcement of the prohibition amendment."[19] The measure enacted was the Dean Law, which took effect in October 1919. The law was stricter than the federal Volstead Act in some respects—criminalizing alcohol purchases in addition to alcohol production and sales—yet slightly more lenient in others—only banning drinks with more than 1.0 percent alcoholic content (Volstead banned anything with at least 0.5 percent alcohol).[20] On the whole, the Dean Law gave Texas some of the harshest prohibition penalties of any state, though the lack of clear procedures for apprehending and convicting violators made the law relatively ineffective.[21]

Neff's zeal for enforcing prohibition stemmed from his sense of responsibility to the Texas Constitution and his long experience denouncing alcohol. During his first run for governor, Neff expressed his dedication to the Texas Constitution's duties of governor, especially Article 4, Section 10: "He [sic] shall cause all of the laws to be faithfully executed."[22] In addition to executing the laws without partiality, he insisted upon respect for the law. "Whatever tends to weaken respect for the law," he stated, "imperils the nation." In the context of prohibition, he was critiquing hypocrisy from legislators who voted dry but personally drank.[23] Over a decade earlier, as chairman of the Prohibition Campaign Committee of McLennan County, he echoed typical hyperbolic rhetoric about the saloon. It was "the chronic criminal of the centuries" that had "turned more men into brutes, made more homes unhappy, bribed more courts, defied more laws, corrupted more ballots, caused more tears to fall and more blood to run than any other institution ever legalized by man."[24] As such, the issue of prohibition was simple: "saloons or no saloons."[25] Alcohol was poison, a pure evil, and "[n]o wrong should be legalized."[26] With this Manichean view on alcohol, Neff's push for prohibition included rigid enforcement, though he still believed in changing hearts and minds.

On the other end of the Democratic South, Governor Westmoreland Davis of Virginia shared Neff's concerns about overreliance on enforcement of prohibition laws. In 1922, Davis expressed frustration over confusion arising from concurrent enforcement of prohibition laws by the state and federal government. Davis in 1920 had reduced state funding for prohibition enforcement, since he believed the federal government would provide for it, but now he stated, "The Federal government so far has failed effectively to enforce prohibition." Davis then concluded that the states must take up the burden of enforcing the law, regardless of the cost, since failing to do so would amount to "a surrender of order to disorder" and chaos for law enforcement generally.[27] He approvingly cited a speaker for the National Law Enforcement Convention who called for governments to "drastically punish" offenders of prohibition laws, even as he agreed that "principally we must educate, and practice what we preach." Rather than blaming the poor and uneducated for violations, Davis claimed that "low brows" only provided liquor because of demand from "high brows" who bought it. The people, especially impressionable youth, followed "example rather than . . . precept," and Davis suggested that legislators and police themselves led others astray by their illegal drinking: "*Those who openly and habitually violate the law should not be chosen as law makers or law enforcement officers*" (emphasis original). Without addressing this "degeneracy caused by hypocrisy," he feared "the very foundation of our civilization [would] be shaken by an accepted disregard of law."[28] Neff had a copy of Davis's speech in his library, and they likely agreed that prohibition sorely needed strict enforcement but equally needed good examples from police and lawmakers.

Racial Law and Order

White drys' law-and-order rhetoric was not limited to enforcing prohibition but at root targeted threats to white supremacy. Enforcement of prohibition laws in the South disproportionately targeted African Americans. Historian Lisa McGirr described prohibition as an "unprecedented campaign of selective enforcement" in which the poor, immigrants, and African Americans "experienced the full brunt" of the law.[29]

In Virginia, the long-term jail population doubled from 1923 to 1931 due to prohibition convictions. Overcrowded prisons prompted the state to force convicts to serve on chain gangs building roads, and state regulations decreed that violators of dry laws could be sent to work on those chain gangs, particularly if they could not pay their hefty court fines. Instead of focusing on big-time dealers, law enforcement agents spent most of their time arresting poorer small-time offenders, particularly African Americans. One prohibition agent in Norfolk County, Virginia, arrested primarily African Americans in over a hundred raids in 1924. Even though white and Black workers shared risks together in the bootlegging underworld, African Americans were most often caught and charged with crimes. As one Black newspaper noted, "It is a certainty that a large percentage of the crimes with which the colored race is charged have to do with bootlegging for white men."[30]

148

Raids tended to target poor and Black populations, often raiding homes, while police received handsome rewards for more liquor-related arrests. The results were predictable. Police ranks swelled in cities like Richmond, doubling from 1914 to 1929. Officers issued warrants on flimsy grounds such as "information and belief," while many arrested for "possession and storage" of a few quarts of whiskey for personal consumption could be sentenced like distillers and bootleggers. Domestic workers and elevator operators seeking to earn a few dollars a day could receive fines of scores or even over a hundred dollars and weeks or months in jail. While the southern white middle class could purchase and consume these goods in relative safety, poor whites and African Americans could be targeted as dangerous drug dealers even when they, too, were just supplementing their income or keeping some alcohol for personal use.[31]

Despite the horrors of hypocritical and racist law enforcement, some African Americans braved the risks for the relative rewards. Flaunting prohibition laws not only earned money but embodied Black resistance to the unjust justice system of Gin Crow. Fannie Lou Hamer's father, for example, was both a Baptist minister and a bootlegger, teaching his daughter by example to pray, sing, and resist the white power structure. In the Gin Crow South, crime could pay better than playing by the rules, particularly for African Americans whose very skin put them on the wrong side of the law. As the Black newspaper *Pittsburgh Courier* stated in 1930, "For several years colored citizens here have suffered indignities from policemen and prohibition agents who crash into their homes unlawfully and make liquor searches and arrests in violation of the search and seizure provisions of the law on the pretext of quelling disorder."[32] If people of color complained about being targeted by police for prohibition violations in the North, how much was there to complain about in the Jim Crow South?[33]

White law enforcement in the South had little trouble shooting violators in the back, particularly African Americans. When John Normeley, a Black bootlegger operating near Richmond, fought with agents and then ran away, agents fired several shots into his back, killing him. The agents also murdered Normeley's unarmed wife by shooting her in the head. A late 1922 raid led by the same agent responsible for the Normeley killings reported shooting twice at a Black bootlegger running away; no attempt was made to excuse the shootings as defensive in any way. While performing their duty in the name of law and order, white agents showed no compunction when offered legal excuses to murder Black men and women who defied prohibition. As African American Edward B. Rembert wrote to President Herbert Hoover, it was hypocritical to insist on enforcement of prohibition laws while Black Americans were being lynched with impunity.[34]

Heavy enforcement of prohibition against Black Americans did not correspond to higher rates of drinking or drunkenness but rather reflected racists attitudes of law enforcement. Statistics from 1880s Tennessee and Georgia demonstrated that, though most Black men drank moderately, they were far less likely than white men to get arrested for being drunk.[35] This likely reflected the simple fact that whites drank more, often because they could more easily afford it.

While African Americans suffered from harsh prohibition enforcement, white southern drys celebrated the "noble experiment" by erecting a statue of the notorious white-supremacist Edward Ward Carmack, the Nashville newspaperman who had called Ida B. Wells "the Black wench" and urged violence against her when she spoke out against lynchings. Carmack was also a failed politician who unsuccessfully ran for governor in the Democratic primary as the dry candidate in 1908. When he was gunned down by a wet rival in a shootout (in which he shot first), and the wet governor pardoned his killer, drys transmogrified the trigger-happy white supremacist into an icon.

By 1925, while statewide and national prohibition were in effect, Carmack's admirers in the Anti-Saloon League and Woman's Christian Temperance Union backed a larger-than-life statue of him on the grounds of the Tennessee state capitol. As historian Patrick O'Daniel wryly observes, the statue's location is ironic: it resided right next to the Motlow Tunnel, which was funded by money from the estate of Jack Daniel, a famous whiskey distiller whose brand still bears his name.[36] The statue remained there for nearly a century until May 30, 2020, when protesters toppled it as a symbol of white supremacism. From the 1920s to 2020, however, the figure who united the values of racial hierarchy and prohibition watched over Nashville from the seat of state power.[37]

Other prohibitionists focused on compliance through law enforcement leagues, which were particularly active in 1921. Atticus Webb, head of the Texas Anti-Saloon League (TASL), promoted such leagues in February 1921 as both a carrot and a stick for police. On the one hand, they aimed to "rally the mass of the people to strong moral support of the efforts at law enforcement." On the other hand, they would "prod up any officials that are negligent of their duty." One such "law and order" meeting in Dallas solicited a telegram from Neff, which the crowd of hundreds received with "deafening" applause.[38]

"Law and order" in the South implied not only white supremacy, but also Anglo supremacy against recent immigrants. A November 1915 article on a wet parade in Chicago that month called the participants, among other things, "a crowd of undesirable hyphenated Americans, whose hyphen is bigger than their Americanism," who "have no respect for the law that requires their conformity to American customs and . . . American ideas." In sum, "Such people are in no sense Americans," since they are "nearly all of foreign birth, speaking a language that few Americans can understand."[39] For TASL leaders, to be truly American was to be an English-speaking Anglo. Such concern for "law and order" and "real Americans" echoed the concerns of a violent vigilante organization: the Klan.

Vigilante Drys: The Second Ku Klux Klan

According to Lisa McGirr, prohibition "enabled the Klan's rise to power."[40] While the Klan was originally founded in 1865 to oppose Black rights and Reconstruction generally, it faded away by the 1870s. A second Ku Klux Klan (KKK) was founded by William Joseph Simmons in Atlanta in 1915 months after the blockbuster film *The Birth of a Nation* praised the first Klan. The Klan rose to national political prominence by the early 1920s under the leadership of a southerner, Hiram Wesley Evans, who tightly associated the Klan not only with opposition to Black rights, but with white "native" Americanism, anti-Semitism, anti-Catholicism, and support for prohibition. Its support of prohibition helped justify racist and xenophobic vigilantism in the name of "law and order."[41]

While the second KKK grew around the nation, its cause was linked with southern white identity. The KKK made its first major public appearance in Texas in Houston in October 1920 at a parade celebrating the United Confederate Veterans. By 1922 Klan membership rose to some 150,000 in Texas alone and over a million throughout the nation. The Texas Klan, however, was not as virulently anti-Jewish or anti-Catholic as some of its counterparts further North: it did not burn crosses against Catholics or Jews as much as some Klans in the North did. Instead, the Texas Klan, as with chapters throughout the South, focused primarily on keeping Blacks "in their place" and promoting reforms such as prohibition. Nonetheless, in the Second Klan, anti-Catholicism and anti-Semitism was a matter of degree, not kind.

The swift ascension of a Dallas dentist, Hiram Wesley Evans, through the organization's hierarchy embodied the meteoric rise of the Klan in American life. He joined the Klan in 1920 and by 1922 had risen to state leader ("great titan"), national secretary ("imperial kligrapp"), and finally national director ("imperial wizard"), a role in which he continued until 1939. The year Evans became imperial wizard, 1922, he launched a program to elect Klansmen to offices across the South and across the nation. That year, the Klan dominated the city governments of Dallas, Fort Worth, and Wichita Falls, and likely controlled the majority in the Texas House of Representatives. Most brazenly, the Klan openly lobbied in the Democratic primary and general election for a fellow Klansman and staunch dry, Earle Bradford Mayfield, who won an election to the US Senate with the reluctant backing of the ASL. Even Texas governor Pat Neff, while generically denouncing extralegal violence and denying personal involvement with the Klan, refused to denounce the organization by name. The Klan seemed unstoppable.[42]

In its heyday, the Klan received positive attention from many Protestants, even pastors, though not all. Methodist clergy such as J. T. Renfro of Dallas and Alonzo Monk of Arlington abandoned their pulpits to lecture for the Klan, and with some regularity Klansmen in full regalia interrupted funerals and church services, sometimes giving pastors small amounts of money to express their piety. While most Protestant clergy said little against the Klan, some ministers were less than enthusiastic about the Invisible Empire. The Klan's excesses outraged even J. B. Cranfill, the aging militant dry famous for his racist comments in 1887. In April 1922, Cranfill wrote to a friend, "Never, until the advent of the Ku Klux Klan, did the Baptists persecute anybody"; but now, under Klan pressure, many Baptists "are joining in the persecution of the negroes, the Jews, the Catholics and the foreigners." While his blanket denial of Baptists persecuting anybody before the Klan is dubious, especially given his virulent diatribes against Blacks and Catholics, Cranfill's rejection of Klan violence as undermining Baptist principles is remarkable and unequivocal. When "any Baptist anywhere joins hands with any movement and sows the seeds of race prejudice and intolerance," he wrote, "then uses subterranean methods of procedure, by that much he loses his grip on the age-long principles of the Baptist people." The Klan's invective was so great that even bigots like Cranfill blanched. While many Methodists and Baptists joined or supported the Klan, at least a few ministers saw the clandestine organization as betraying the principles of their faith.[43]

One violent incident captures the multivalent bigotry of the Klan in Texas. In 1921, Hiram Evans and several other Klansmen dragged an African American bellhop, Alex Johnson, out of the Adolphus Hotel in Dallas and burned "K.K.K." into his forehead with acid. The atrocity (ignored by law enforcement) was an explicit attack on an innocent African American but was also an implicit attack on the German American beer baron Adolphus Busch, who built the European-style luxury hotel in 1912 at the behest of city founders. The titles of several works by then–imperial wizard Evans—*The Menace of Modern Immigration* (1923) and *Alienism in the Democracy* (1927)—indicate the

Klan's hatred of non-Anglo immigrants, including Texas's sizable German population.[44]

The Klan shared a complicated relationship with the broader dry movement. An excellent example of collusion between the Klan and the ASL was support for Earle Bradford Mayfield for US Senate from Texas in 1922.[45] The *New York Times* thought an alliance between the ASL and KKK for Mayfield in the Democratic primary was news enough to place the headline "'DRYS' AND KU KLUX COMBINE IN TEXAS" on the top of page 6. In the article, the editor absolved drys from the sins of the hoods: "[I]t is not their fault that the klan backs Mayfield and the klan has nothing whatever to do with their advocacy of him." However, since Mayfield was dry and his opponent, Jim Ferguson, was a corrupt wet, "there is no alternative for [the drys] except to back Mayfield." Even the ASL's general counsel, Wayne B. Wheeler, claimed not to know whether Mayfield was a Klansman and admitted, "Yes, it is peculiar that in this campaign we happen to be linked with the klan behind Mayfield, but this is a circumstance over which we have no control." Wheeler, ever the pragmatist, shrugged, "There are only two men in the field, and one or the other has got to be voted for," and Mayfield was "a high-grade man" supported by "all the decent forces in the State"—namely, drys.[46] For the national ASL, the Klan's intolerance was not an asset, but dryness trumped tolerance; even a Klansman was "a high-grade man" if he was the only viable dry candidate left.

Some leading southern drys were neutral on the Klan but backed Mayfield. The *Home and State* acknowledged in its columns that many "conscientiously . . . fear that the Ku Klux organization would prove a menace to our government" and that "there are many Prohibitionists who are deeply concerned over this issue, an issue concerning which the Home and State is absolutely neutral." Texas Senator John Morris Sheppard, the Senate's leading voice for prohibition since 1913 and an outspoken opponent of the Klan, demurred that "the alignment of the league about the klan was an oddity" but "came about merely because Mayfield was regarded as the best candidate."[47] As with many voters who expressed concern over Donald Trump's comments on race and women but voted for him in 2016 and 2020 over shared stances on culture war issues such as abortion, so drys in the 1920s were willing to support Klansmen for public office if they agreed on the issues.

It even seemed a few Klansmen worked in the upper ranks of the Texas ASL. According to *Home and State,* the Klan was not merely a phenomenon among Democrats, but Republicans had proportionately as many Klansmen as the Democrats. Texas Republicans had split into white-supremacist "lily-whites" and racially inclusive "Black and tan" factions before 1922, but the split itself does not show how much of the GOP was KKK. The *Home and State* article does not explain how the editor knew how many Democrats and Republicans were Klansmen, but it seems only a member of the secret society could make the claim with authority.[48] Despite the ambivalent official position of the Texas ASL, it seems at least some KKK members held leadership. Like Texas's two US senators after the 1922 election, there were two leading voices among Texas drys: the radically nativist types like the Klansman Mayfield, and the equally dry but anti-Klan Morris Sheppard.

As with Texas, Alabama's two US senators took opposite positions on the Klan. Oscar Underwood, Alabama's senior senator, claimed in 1924 that the Klan was "a national menace" that cannot coexist with the nation: "It is either the Ku Klux Klan or the United States of America. Both cannot survive. Between the two, I choose my country."[49] (Underwood's anti-Klan stance earned him the first episode of a 1964 television show, *Profiles in Courage*.)[50] Alabama's junior senator, James "Cotton Tom" Heflin, boldly endorsed the Klan. In 1926, he led a coalition that combined KKK and ASL supporters to sweep many of the Democratic primaries in Alabama.[51]

With a few exceptions, the Klan's influence in most of the South began to decline after 1923, and the next year its gubernatorial candidates in Texas faced defeat at the hands of Miriam A. "Ma" Ferguson. Ma was an unassuming woman whose iconic picture with an old-fashioned gray sunbonnet inspired her campaign song, "Put on Your Old Gray Bonnet," and her slogan, "a bonnet or a hood." After besting Felix D. Robertson of the Dallas Klan in the Democratic primary in July, she used her power as Democratic nominee to remove known Klan backers from positions of power in the state party. The Klan then backed GOP nominee George C. Butte, whom Ma defeated in the general election by eighteen points. Still, Ferguson's margin of victory was the narrowest a Democratic gubernatorial candidate in Texas had received against a Republican since the end of Reconstruction. The Klan was still a force to be reckoned with, and she moved swiftly to crush it.[52]

Unlike Pat Neff, Ma Ferguson took on the Texas Klan directly. She promised a draconian anti-mask law that proposed the death penalty for assault when wearing a hood, open publication of the organization's membership, and loss of tax-exempt status for any church that hosted the Klan. None of those ideas passed except the anti-mask law, a symbolic victory that signaled the end of the Klan's power in Texas politics. The state attorney general, Dan Moody, completed the anti-Klan purge by cleansing his office of its influence and appointing an anti-Klan head for the Texas Rangers.[53] A woman in a bonnet had emasculated the hoods.

By 1928, the Texas Klan had dwindled to twenty-five hundred members. Prominent citizens shunned association with it, and Klan membership had become a political liability, even in the Deep South. The Klan's decline helped associate prohibition with particularly unpleasant characters. As one historian put it, "The Klan's excesses in the mid-1920s turned public opinion against them as well as Prohibition."[54] Perhaps the Klan's last-ditch effort at relevance was taking aim at a Catholic candidate for president in 1928.

Drys against Al Smith: Anti-Catholicism in the 1928 Election

Anti-Catholic attacks by prohibitionists throughout the South became more overt with the presidential candidacy of Al Smith in 1924 and 1928. Al Smith, an openly wet Catholic from drenching-wet New York City and a grandchild of Irish and German immigrants, had been elected four times as governor of New York between 1918 and 1926. When he first ran for the Democratic nomination for president in 1924, Smith loudly denounced the violently anti-Catholic Ku Klux Klan. Meanwhile, southern delegates and the Klan itself backed William Gibbs McAdoo, the dry candidate (and Woodrow Wilson's son-in-law), who refused to renounce either the Klan's endorsement or the Klan itself. While the bitter divide between Smith and McAdoo led the convention to settle on a compromise candidate after a ten-day deadlock, Smith contented himself to serving four more years as New York's governor and gearing up for the Democratic nomination in 1928, where he was the overwhelming favorite. Despite being nominated for president in Houston, Texas, on the first ballot of the 1928 Democratic Convention, Smith won little favor among southern Democrats.[55]

The nomination of Al Smith in 1928 proved the focal point of accusations that Catholics would unite their church with the American state. Despite their differences, dry Protestant ministers across the spectrum defended political preaching in 1928 and denounced their critics as hypocrites. Despite claims that his opposition to the Catholic candidate was driven by concerns about the separation of church and state, Norris not only justified his political activism as a preacher but insisted upon the need for more "political preachers."[56] When the *Ohio State Journal* declared, "Christ's religion and practical politics don't mix," the Texas ASL's official newspaper, the *Home and State,* responded, "SURE THEY DON'T—THEY CLASH"—if by "practical politics" they meant opposing prohibition.[57] Even for ministers viewing their task as narrowly delivering souls from Hell, many saw political support for prohibition as a necessary extension of that mission and a heroic act of martyrdom. An October 1928 article in the *Home and State,* "Insulting the Ministers," claimed that hundreds of Protestant ministers in Texas had joined the campaign against Smith and called them "heroes of righteousness" who had "laid all upon the altar" to combat the evil of legal liquor that had, among other evils, "blocked the evangelization of countless millions" and "peopled Hell with lost souls."[58] The very last *Home and State* article on the preelection issue was "'Preachers in Politics,'" a story about how a pro-Smith politician left his church because the pastor preached prohibition, but that shows the man's hypocrisy: if the minister had preached in Smith's favor, the politician would "doubtless" have been "delighted" with the message.[59] Protestant ministers throughout the South in 1928 claimed that their faith compelled them to take a stand in politics and openly criticized those who opposed mixing preaching and politics. By 1928, it was Catholics, not prohibitionist Protestants, who needed to combat charges of uniting church and state.

The first signs of trouble came from the lack of southern support for Smith's nomination in Houston. Delegations from Virginia, North and South Carolina, Georgia, Florida, Alabama, Missouri, and Texas had all refused to endorse Smith, while Mississippi, Oklahoma, and Kansas split their support. Of all the southern states, only a few delegations from the upper and border South—Tennessee, Arkansas, and Maryland—had given unequivocal support to Al Smith, even though Smith surpassed the two-thirds threshold for nomination on the first ballot. Some of this lack of support is explained in a remark by Cone Johnson, one dry Texas delegate to the convention: "I sat by the central aisle while the parade passed following Smith's nomination and the faces I saw in that mile-long procession were not American faces. I wondered where were the Americans."[60] For nativist southern drys, anti-Catholicism fit naturally with their "100-percent" Americanism and anti-immigrant sentiment.

Despite the chorus of many southerners against Smith, Alabama's former US senator Oscar Underwood—a proud wet—backed Smith as early as 1927. In December 1927, Underwood believed Smith was "best qualified to fill the office" and would easily win both the party's nomination and the presidency. However, Underwood was by far the exception in the South. His opposition to the Klan in 1924 alienated many southern white voters, and he declined to run for reelection in 1926 rather than face almost certain defeat. A sign of the times was Underwood's successor, Hugo Black, who had been a member of the KKK from September 1923 to July 1925, when he resigned to run for the US Senate. Despite their different views on the Klan, Black shared one similarity with Underwood: both backed Al Smith for president.[61]

Anti-Catholic southerners continued to denounce Al Smith, and none more loudly than Fort Worth First Baptist Church's pastor, J. Frank Norris. He was a die-hard fundamentalist pastor with a booming congregation of five thousand and a penchant for attacking anyone more theologically liberal than he was (which was nearly everyone). His assaults against more moderate Southern Baptists led to Norris's expulsion from the Texas Baptist General Convention and alienation from the Southern Baptist Convention.

Yet Norris saved his worst vitriol for Catholics. As far back as 1922, in a sermon he detailed a slaughter of Huguenot Protestants by Catholics in the French Wars of Religion three and a half centuries earlier, then declared, "This same bloody beast now undertakes to control the politics of this country."[62] Then when Fort Worth tried to buy property from the Catholic Church in July 1926, Norris claimed that the city's mayor, H. C. Meacham, and city manager, H. B. Carr, were involved in a pro-Catholic conspiracy. His fight against Catholicism turned lethal that month when in his office he shot dead an unarmed D. E. Chipps, a Catholic and prominent businessman. Incredibly, Norris was acquitted by a jury that apparently bought his story: Norris fired in self-defense, since Chipps was part of a Catholic conspiracy to kill Norris for speaking out against them.[63]

By 1924 Norris had denounced Catholicism as "anti-American and unconstitutional" and declared that no Catholic could honestly take the oath of office to become president because Catholics obeyed the Pope above any terrestrial authority, including the United States.[64] Norris reiterated this claim in 1927: "No true consistent Roman Catholic, my friends, who actually believes in the doctrine of papal infallibility, can be true to any other government in the world."[65] While many respectable Protestants agreed with Norris on that point, he mingled rejection of Catholic theology with denigration of Catholic immigrants, whom he referred to as "low-browed foreigners." He also connected biblical Christian (Protestant) faith with true American patriotism: "As far as we are concerned," he bellowed, "we stand for 100 percent Americanism; for the Bible; for the home, and against every evil and against every foreign influence that seeks to corrupt and undermine our cherished and Christian institutions."[66] For a white dry Southern Baptist like Norris, for whom prohibition embodied "our cherished and Christian institutions," a German Irish Catholic wet Yankee like Al Smith running for president of the United States was anathema to everything southern whites held dear.

Norris trained his sights directly on Smith as early as 1926, when Smith was the presumed but not yet official nominee of the Democratic Party for president. In an article titled "The Conspiracy of Rum and Romanism to Rule This Government," Norris argued that Catholics believed their church was supreme in all things, infallible, and unalterable, then pointedly asked, "Are we ready to permit a man to occupy the highest office, the chief magistracy over this Government, who owes his first allegiance to a foreign power which claims these three things?"[67]

Norris was not alone in fearing that a Catholic president could not separate his earthly politics from his spiritual allegiance to a foreign Pope. In 1927, jurist Charles C. Marshall of New York wrote "An Open Letter to the Honorable Alfred E. Smith" in the *Atlantic Monthly* which essentially asked the same question Norris was asking (if in a different spirit): how could a Catholic who maintains the supremacy of the Catholic magisterium—particularly, the Pope—in earthly matters be a fully loyal US citizen, much less president? The open letter prompted Al Smith himself to issue a reply that was in turn published in major newspapers around the country. Norris reprinted Marshall's article—without Smith's reply.[68] Protestant concerns about a Catholic politician's ability to separate his duties to church and state had forced Al Smith, rather than Protestant "political preachers" like Norris, on the defensive.

Even before Al Smith became an issue, Norris's inflexible principles had led him to buck the Democratic Party, a nearly unforgiveable sin in the Solid South. The son of an alcoholic, Norris gained a fresh passion for prohibition politics when he met Morris Sheppard in 1919. Afterward, Norris was so touched by meeting prohibition's champion in the US Senate that he gave Sheppard a silver set boasting that his church had "the largest Sunday School in America"—and more importantly, Norris dove into prohibition politics. Norris clashed with a federal judge who supposedly sentenced bootleggers too leniently and backed Klan members like Mayfield for Senate in 1922 and Robertson against Ma Ferguson for governor in 1924. In the latter contest, he wrote articles with sensational titles like, "Is Liquor Coming Back?" and "Can You Vote with the Bootlegger?" Though Norris promised to respect the result of the Democratic primary after Ma Ferguson won, ads for her Republican challenger appeared in his paper.[69] It is unsurprising, then, that as early as the spring of 1927, Norris had coordinated with R. B. Creager, a member of the Republican National Committee, on how to defeat Al Smith at the polls, and in 1928 embarked on a regional tour to ensure the wet Catholic's defeat.[70]

Norris's most notorious and perhaps most revealing rant against Catholics in his campaigning for the GOP candidate, Herbert Hoover, occurred in August 1928 before a crowd of six thousand in Dallas. After a woman interrupted his speech with swearing and was removed, Norris roared:

> Now, we are prepared to have order here tonight. We are not surprised at the lowdown whiskey-soaked imps of Hell. The toe-kissing Tammanyites

are here for the purpose of creating a disturbance, and I will serve notice
on you now that this is Texas and not Mexico. Now, you who are here to disturb this meeting, get up on your hind feet and stand where we can see you.
. . . Now, we will proceed and I call upon all red-blooded white folks here
tonight, who love God, who love the flag, and who love order, to exercise
your rights as American citizens and see to it that none of this ring-kissing
Tammany Hall gang cause any more interference or disturbance.[71]

For Norris and his six thousand listeners, God was on the side of America, the "order" of prohibition laws, and Protestant "red-blooded white folks"
against Mexico, "whiskey-soaked imps of Hell," and the "ring-kissing Tammany
Hall gang" of recent Catholic immigrants. The campaign for Hoover was for
many southern Protestants a campaign against demonic, semi-animal, nonwhite, corrupt, and Catholic foreigners.

Norris was just one of thousands of Protestant pastors across the South
who opposed Al Smith in 1928 while claiming that Catholics, not themselves,
posed the real threat to the separation of church and state. Even Norris's erstwhile enemies in the Southern Baptist Convention did likewise. The president
of Southwestern Baptist Theological Seminary, L. R. Scarborough, wrote an
article in which he began with a careful evaluation of the state-church issues
and descended into claims of Smith's alcoholism before announcing his support for a more "Christian" (that is, Protestant) candidate, Hoover.[72] Baptists
were joined by clergy in the Methodist Episcopal Church, South (MECS), who
opposed Smith as a bloc. One survey of eighty-five hundred ministers of the
MECS throughout the South found only four who openly supported Al Smith
for president.[73] Church conferences across the South lined up against Smith.[74]
Even Protestant ministers who at other times squabbled with each other
formed a united front against the perceived menace of a Catholic takeover of
the US government. This army of white southern Democrats for Hoover took
on a new name: Hoovercrats.

One of the most prominent Hoovercrats in the South was a Southern Methodist bishop, James Cannon Jr. He had served as leader of the Virginia ASL,
helped turn that state dry by 1916, and was rewarded with the rank of bishop
in 1918. After the death of Wayne B. Wheeler in September 1927, Cannon became the most visible national leader in the ASL, and he regarded it as his
duty to stop Smith—whom he said would be a "Cocktail President"—at all
costs.[75] As early as November 1927, Cannon urged his fellow Virginia Methodists to buck the Democratic Party if necessary to preserve prohibition. After
Smith accepted the Democratic nomination and expressed his intention to

modify prohibition laws, Cannon joined with a Southern Baptist colleague, Arthur Barton, to denounce Smith and organize likeminded southern Democrats. He collaborated with C. Bascom Slemp, a Republican congressman from Virginia, to rally the anti-Smith forces. He also brushed off criticisms from southern traditionalist bishops such as Atlanta's Warren Candler and Richmond's Collins Denny that he should "Preach Christ and him crucified" instead of politics. In response, Cannon joined with other progressive bishops such as the Texan Edwin D. Mouzon to affirm their political preaching: "The moral forces of the country will not be driven from the field by the cry that they are 'brining the Church into politics.'" Cannon declared defiantly, "I absolutely decline to be muzzled." Cannon clashed with Virginia's powerful Byrd Machine, which remained faithful to Smith, particularly the lay Methodist politician and US Senator Carter Glass. And, aside from a few weeks' rest for his health, he campaigned hard not only in his home state of Virginia but across the South: Texas, Arkansas, Tennessee, Alabama, Mississippi, Georgia, and even Oklahoma.[76]

Cannon also joined in the chorus of anti-Catholic rhetoric. Smith provoked reaction by appointing John J. Raskob, a wealthy Republican, militant wet, and Roman Catholic, as chair of the Democratic National Committee and then giving a speech on September 20, 1928, in which he denounced the Klan and other detractors as anti-Catholic. Cannon and other anti-Smith Democrats bristled at the accusation that they were intolerant, then proceeded to attack Smith's faith. Cannon claimed that "Wet, Roman Catholic" bosses of northern cities—like the notoriously corrupt Tammany Hall—were taking over their Democratic Party. While many northerners joined in the anti-Catholic crusade, including Methodist minister Deets Picket, US prohibition enforcement generalissimo Mabel Walker Willebrandt and fundamentalist Baptist pastor John Roach Stratton, Cannon took on a prominent role in the South. Three weeks before the election, Cannon issued a circular rhetorically entitled *Is Southern Protestantism More Intolerant Than Romanism?* (Answer: no.) The circular was deliberately polemic, or as he put it: "I made it just as hot as I could." He charged Smith and Raskob were peddling "deliberate and malicious political falsehoods." After repeatedly denying he was bigoted, he claimed the Catholic Church was against American tolerance and democratic values, including "freedom of action, freedom of speech, freedom of the press, freedom of conscience, freedom of education, free Democratic Government as we have it, free church in a free state, and the salvation of any outside the Roman Church." While he was not the most virulently anti-Catholic voice against Smith, he certainly fought back fiercely when he felt he needed to defend his honor.[77]

An even more vituperative Hoovercrat than Cannon was "Cotton Tom" Heflin, whose white supremacism (including his attempted murder of a Black man in 1908) was matched only by his anti-Catholicism. In January 1928 on the floor of the US Senate, Heflin described attempts to denounce the Klan at the Democratic Convention in 1924 as dividing the party and "put[ting] Roman Catholic government above everything, above the Democratic Party, and above their country." Since by that time Al Smith was the favored nominee of the party, Heflin repeatedly called upon the American people to wake up and ready themselves for battle against Smith, who would help the Pope "control this country," "make America Catholic," and "lay the heavy hand of a Catholic state upon you and crush the life out of Protestantism in America." Heflin did not limit his attacks to the floor of Congress, but spoke to large crowds in Birmingham, Montgomery, and elsewhere to attack Smith, African Americans, and attempts to repeal the Eighteenth Amendment.[78]

Even before Heflin joined the Hoovercrats, another US senator from the South took a bold anti-Smith stance: Furnifold McLendel Simmons of North Carolina. As chairman of the Democratic state committee, Simmons had helped lead the white-supremacist campaign that led to the Wilmington Massacre of 1898 and disfranchised African Americans in the state for half a century. After taking a seat in the Senate in 1901, Simmons served there for thirty years, during which time he set up a powerful political machine. Upset by Smith's wet stance, connections with Tammany Hall, immigrant background, and cooperation with African Americans while governor of New York, Simmons refused to endorse Smith.[79]

Despite their strong Democratic leanings in the South, the ASL branches followed Bishop Cannon to vigorously oppose Smith. The *Home and State* printed articles by Methodist Church leaders as early as 1927, calling on Democrats not to vote for Smith the next year should he be the nominee. By September 1928, nearly the entire issue of *Home and State* was filled with anti–Al Smith rhetoric, including a report that the Texas ASL had formed a "Non-Partisan Hoover League of Texas" to oppose the Democratic nominee.[80]

Unlike Norris, however, the Texas ASL went out of its way to avoid explicitly criticizing Catholics as such but were openly paranoid about Smith's interracial record. While drys such as the fundamentalist lightning rod J. Frank Norris fiercely attacked the Democratic presidential candidate for his immigrant Catholic family, the *Home and State* scarcely mentioned Al Smith's religion or immigrant background.[81] After months of denouncing Smith as a wet, only one article in July 1928 obliquely objected to Smith's candidacy on the grounds of Catholicism, citing "the liquor and religious [that is, Catholic] issues."[82] Shortly after the election, the *Home and State* ran an article titled "Anti-Saloon League Not Opposed to Smith Because of His Religion," which speaks for itself. Another article on that same page, "WHO ARE THE TOLERANT?" argued that Texan drys love a number of Catholics—especially those who didn't support Al Smith—and above all the "people of Texas are tired of being called 'intolerant' because they are dry."[83] The ASL bristled at accusations of anti-Catholicism after the election and did not join in anti-Catholic rhetoric to the same degree as firebrands like Norris, yet by failing to denounce virulent anti-Catholicism before the election, ASL showed it placed greater value in electoral victory and washing its hands of blame than in treating Catholics fairly.

Race in the 1928 Election

In addition to anti-Catholic bias, race-baiting played a large role in white southern opposition to Smith. The *Home and State*, for example, hammered Smith especially for working in government with African Americans.[84] They reported in July that "Many Negroes [were] Supporting Al Smith" because he would push for "negro equality."[85] Then in September, the front page of the paper was full of articles expressing alarm at "negro" support for the wet Catholic: "TEXAS NEGROES TRY TO FORCE THEMSELVES INTO DEMOCRATIC PRIMARY"; "Negroes to Vote for Al Smith"; "TAMMANY HALL, NEW YORK, LARGELY COMPOSED OF NEGROES"; "Negro Organizations in the West Wire Pledge of Support to Al Smith"; "COLORADO NEGRO VOTERS' ADVISORY ASSOCIATION, DENVER."[86] On page 5 of that issue, Thomas B. Love—then Democratic nominee for lieutenant governor of Texas—expressed disgust that Al Smith's New York welcomed racially integrated schools, integrated dance halls, integrated marriages, "negro" teachers over "white" students, many "negro" voters, "negro" police, a "negro" civil service commissioner, "negro" elected representatives, and "great negro Democratic meetings." Love vowed no fewer than six times, "Tammany must pay the price of its negro help."[87] In the October edition just before the election, the *Home and State* put in another article on "Smith and the Negro" calling him "the best friend the negro has" (not a compliment) and once again recalled the state of race relations in New York, where, among other things, "blacks marry whites, mostly of alien orogin [sic]."[88] Perhaps dry whites' greatest issue with Smith, more than being wet, Catholic, urbanite, northern, or a child of immigrants, was his support from and for Black Americans.

Bishop Cannon and other Hoovercrats likewise attacked Smith for supporting racial mixing and immigrants. He claimed that, in New York, "white women in a dance hall were in the arms of negro men," and Black teachers taught Black and white children in the same classroom. Such examples clearly insinuated that Smith's presidency might undermine Jim Crow segregation in the South. When Virginia Democrats claimed that Hoover did not share their white-supremacist views, Cannon claimed that Hoover segregated workers by race while at Smith's Tammany Hall, white women worked as secretaries for Black men, a clear violation of gendered and racial taboos. Cannon also lumped Smith with recent immigrant groups. He told a Maryland crowd that old-stock immigrants were "people like yourselves—English, Scotch, Dutch and German—... honorable" people "who make good citizens," but that Smith wanted "the Italians, the Sicilians, the Poles and the Russian Jew," the kind that "has given us a stomach-ache." Because the latter are "unable to assimi-late ... we shut the door to them," but "Smith says, 'give me that kind of peo-ple.' He wants the kind of people that you find today on the sidewalks of New York." For leading southern drys like Cannon, upholding Jim Crow, keeping out recent immigrants, and promoting white evangelical Americanism were threads of the same fabric.[89] Hoovercrats such as US Senators Heflin of Ala-bama and Simmons of North Carolina joined Cannon in deploying anti-Black and anti-immigrant rhetoric against Smith.[90]

For their part, some Black leaders in the North supported the dry Repub-lican candidate in 1928. That September, Kelly Miller, a sociology professor at Howard University, wrote in September of 1928: "The Negro is the chief victim of the liquor demon," and the "Eighteenth Amendment ... has been a godsend to his race." Miller framed his argument in terms of Christian morality. The best argument for prohibition "for thoughtful Christian people" was "based on our responsibility for those who are not strong enough to resist temptation." For Miller, Christians could come to no other position than prohibition: "There is no escape for a Christian from the bedrock proposition that 'we who are strong ought to bear the infirmities of the weak and not to please ourselves,'" and as such, "The state should of right remove temptation from those who have not the inhibition to withstand temptation." Miller expressed the belief of some Black leaders as late as 1928 that prohibition, and therefore voting for the dry candidate Hoover, remained a Christian imperative.[91]

Looking back in 1935, however, Miller remarked that unequal policing pol-icies had a negative effect on Black communities. "Too often the policeman's club is the only instrument of the law with which the Negro comes into con-tact. This engenders in him a distrust and resentful attitude toward all pub-lic authorities and law officers."[92] Given the disproportionate enforcement of prohibition laws against poor and Black citizens in the South, Miller's remarks seemed to fit a critique of prohibition. Back in 1928, however, Miller's dry stance underlined many Black elites' lingering support for the Republican Party just a few years before the New Deal arrived and eventually shifted most Black support to the Democrats. With a critical mass of northern whites and Blacks and southern whites supporting Hoover, Smith's defeat seemed sure.

In the South, however, Black voters were so few that their votes apparently made little difference in the outcome. The disfranchisement wrought a decade earlier by prohibition and the end of their alliance with the brewers rendered most unable to pay poll taxes, much less pass other restrictive voting requirements. While white women had gained the right to vote (provided they, too, paid a poll tax), Black women were doubly disadvantaged, denied suffrage while their white sisters enjoyed it. In this prohibition-focused election, Black southerners were on the sidelines.

Election Aftermath

On election day, Al Smith was crushed by Republican Herbert Hoover, who took nearly half of the formerly Confederate states, including Florida, North Carolina, Tennessee, Texas, and Virginia. Old-stock white Protestants around the country opposed Smith for many reasons—he was a Catholic, wet, urbanite, and child of immigrants with a grating accent of New York's Fourth Ward. In their crusade against rum and Romanism, southern drys had finally turned against the Democratic Party itself. Yet the drys' victory came at a high cost. The contest's bitter rhetoric divided the South's overwhelmingly white voters and countless Southern Baptist and Methodist congregations down the middle. Some devoted Methodist laymen such as Morris Sheppard, champion of the Eighteenth Amendment in the US Senate, had supported Al Smith out of loyalty to the Democratic Party while figures like Norris remained Republican activists even after the election.[93] Though several southern states had broken their tradition of siding with the Democratic presidential candidate, the GOP win in 1928 did not fundamentally change the Democratic stranglehold on the region. Even while losing several states, Smith still carried the core of the South: Alabama, Arkansas, Georgia, Louisiana, Mississippi, and South Carolina.[94]

Some Hoovercrats suffered electorally for bucking the Democratic Party establishment, and they either exited politics or returned to the fold. In 1928, the once-promising US senator (and Klan member) Mayfield lost his primary election to Tom Connally. When Mayfield ran for governor in 1930, he placed seventh in a crowded field, and his political career was finished. North Carolina's senator Simmons helped tip his state vote for Hoover in 1928, but two years later he lost his Senate primary to a party loyalist, Josiah Bailey.[95] Alabama senator "Cotton Tom" Heflin suffered a similar fate in 1930. Heflin's predecessor in the US Senate was the late John Bankhead, and in 1930 he lost a primary against John Bankhead II, the former senator's son, by fifty thousand votes. Though Heflin claimed fraud and formally protested for years, his protest was dismissed. Heflin eventually reconciled with party elites, serving in various federal appointments in the 1930s and early 1940s. By 1948, near the end of his life, he reversed his antiestablishment stance of two decades earlier and supported the Democratic nominee, Harry Truman, against the insurgent Dixiecrats.[96] The absence of a Catholic on the ticket made it easier for erstwhile Hoovercrats to return to the party faithful in the 1930s and 1940s.

Drys took Hoover's victory as a national referendum on prohibition that settled the question, so most dry pastors withdrew from partisan politics thereafter. As Jeanne Bozzell McCarty has demonstrated in her study of Protestants and prohibition in Texas from 1919 to 1935, most drys, content that prohibition had been saved in 1928, still supported enforcement but in their everyday work tended more to the Gospel message. The editor of the *Baptist Standard* pleaded two weeks after the 1928 election for preachers to avoid the "conscientious compulsion" to perpetually engage divisive political issues and focus more on "Christ and Him Crucified."[97] The editor of another paper, the *Christian Courier,* which had openly supported Hoover in the campaign, echoed this theme, pleading: "let the servants of God turn with new energy to the every-day task of the church—the preaching of the gospel of Christ, the seeking of the lost, the edifying of saints. . . . Not Hoover, but Christ is the Savior."[98] Another issue of the *Courier* stated baldly, "Adios, Politics!" and restated the paper's commitment to focus on matters of salvation.[99] While support for prohibition did not waver among most Protestant clergy after the election, the emphasis of many shifted more towards soul-saving work and away from politics.

Conclusion

In the South, opposition to Catholics played an increasing role in prohibitionists' rhetoric, and suspicion of a union of church and state shifted from Protestant "political preachers" to Catholic politicians. Anti-Catholicism was incidental before prohibition became law, expressed mostly indirectly at "foreign" ethnic groups such as Germans and Mexicans, and prohibitionists openly courted Catholics, some of whom drys celebrated when they came out in favor of prohibition. Only in 1928 did Protestants in the South seriously link Catholic religion with anti-prohibition and unleash a full barrage of rhetoric questioning the loyalty and American credentials of all Catholics. A similar story held for shifting accusations of who was mixing church and state. Initially, dry Protestants were defending themselves against charges of wrongly mixing church and state, but by 1928 prohibition was the law of the land, and anti-prohibition Catholics were responding to that charge.

Rather than featuring coalitions along more or less static religious and cultural lines, polarizing political moral issues like prohibition can produce evolving cultural and religious alliances that alternately woo and demonize certain constituencies. Even accusations of uniting church and state can rebound from advocates of a moral reform to its detractors, particularly when the reform has changed from fringe view to established law. Southern Democrats once accused of supporting "Rum, Romanism, and Rebellion" just a few decades later denounced alcohol, maligned Catholics, and voted Republican.

Drys' triumph in 1928, however, proved a pyrrhic victory. Public opinion gradually shifted against prohibition as it failed to live up to its promises of a better world and grew increasingly associated with its most extreme and vitriolic champions. While prohibition initially reduced drinking in the early 1920s, many came to believe that prohibition had betrayed its millennial hope for social improvement and instead only made society worse by insistence upon draconian laws. A growing emphasis on strict enforcement of the law marginalized efforts to change hearts and minds. The Ku Klux Klan in Texas in the early 1920s tainted prohibition with its strange mix of law-and-order rhetoric with extralegal violence. Aggressively dry pastors like J. Frank Norris, who pushed for prohibition at all costs in the 1928 election, created a backlash against prohibition. As his biographer described it, Norris by 1929 had shown "an almost pathological anger in the face of continued attacks on prohibition."[100] The pugnacious style of drys like him drove many moderates to shy away from prohibition by the end of the decade. Increasing skepticism towards prohibition's ever more pugilistic champions dovetailed with growing affection for repeal. When prohibition repeal came South in the 1930s, some of its champions came from a demographic once thought to be the cornerstone of a permanent dry majority: white women.

6
Lily-White Repeal

WHITE WOMEN AND THE DECLINE OF GIN CROW

IN THE 1932 TEXAS GUBERNATORIAL RACE, a sitting governor lost the Democratic primary to a woman. The incumbent, Ross S. Sterling, was temperamental and unpopular, and his opponent—Miriam Amanda Wallace "Ma" Ferguson, wife of former governor James Ferguson—was herself a former governor. Ma Ferguson had become the first elected female elected to a full term as governor in the United States in 1924 and returned in 1932 to do what women were expected to do: clean up politics. True, her husband had been impeached for corruption, and she had campaigned in 1924 on the platform of putting him back in the seat of power. Still, Ma Ferguson campaigned as a respectable white woman who ran not for personal glory but to defend the reputation of her wronged husband, and so commanded the respect due to her sex, which then was praised for a higher moral sense than men.

Ma Ferguson did not, however, follow the conventional wisdom that every respectable woman would support prohibition. It was no coincidence that the Nineteenth Amendment for women's suffrage was ratified in 1920, just a year after the ratification of the Eighteenth Amendment for national prohibition. Many assumed that women's enfranchisement ensured prohibition's perma-nence, and dry groups such as the ASL had lobbied hard for women's right to vote. Yet Ma Ferguson drew critique as early as 1924 for not openly backing prohibition. As governor, she did not seek to repeal statewide prohibition or to gut state laws for strict prohibition enforcement, but during both of her terms as governor she prolifically pardoned all kinds of crimes, especially transgressions of alcohol bans. By the time she took the governor's seat again in 1933, the South was turning against prohibition. Ma Ferguson's governorship illustrated how women, who had been perceived as a firewall of support for prohibition, became a divided constituency on the issue by the 1930s and contributed across the South to the fall of federal and statewide prohibition. Just as the Democratic Solid South shattered in the 1928 presidential election, so the once-solid voting bloc of women for prohibition began to crack after that vote. Once the dry wall of women's opinion on the issue split, wet sentiment trickled into and soon flooded the South.

While issues of race and ethnicity carried great weight in issues of prohibition from the 1880s to the 1920s, one remarkable aspect of the repeal debates of the 1930s is their relative absence of discussions of race. The effects of Jim Crow, the loss of political support of brewers, and years of disproportionate enforcement of drug laws had demoralized African Americans and rendered their voting totals negligible in the debates over prohibition's overturn. Instead, white women gained a new voice as the new swing vote in the region. Their rise had come somewhat at the expense of Black men, as the rhetoric of white supremacy played no small role in their political empowerment. Still, southern white drys had remained divided on the radical reform of women's suffrage even in 1920. The argument that women were needed to keep prohibition in place played a decisive role in their initial empowerment—even though they, rather than African Americans, eventually tipped the scales to end Gin Crow in the South.

Political preaching also suffered a decline in the 1930s. While drys continued to claim God on their side, wets tended more toward secular language of motherhood and pragmatism. Wets occasionally garnished their claims with Christian language and lampooned the false piety of drys, but they mostly abstained from citing the Bible as an authority or otherwise engaging in substantive appeals to Christian tradition. References to the Lost Cause and the moral authority of their feminine status easily outnumbered Bible verses. This ecumenical approach allowed Catholic wets, who were not welcomed into the Protestant-run Woman's Christian Temperance Union (WCTU), to take prominent roles in repeal organizations. Religious drys appeared as old-fashioned, and political preaching took a back seat to economic concerns about the Great Depression. The women's suffrage movement in the 1910s South demonstrates connections between race, religion, and gender during the gradual replacement of African American men with white women as deciding forces in the prohibition contests between the 1910s and the 1930s.

Votes for (White) Women

Some white drys responded to their narrow statewide losses of 1909 to 1912 by increasingly supporting the political rise of white women, in the name of all good and holy. Even undecided women began embracing the cause of women's suffrage as a Christian necessity. Mrs. S. J. Sweeny of Waco, a seventy-three-year-old woman who had "never advocated woman's suffrage," wrote to Texas ASL's newspaper on September 13, 1911, that she was driven to support women's suffrage due to the narrow defeat of statewide prohibition. Despite her age, she vowed to become a militant "W.C.T.U. evangelist." She justified her position by invoking Scripture and the need of women to arise when men neglected their duty to win the battle for righteousness: "Is there no David to meet this Goliath? No Elijah to call down fire from heaven?" Since the men had failed to halt the liquor traffic, she called for women to complete God's work. "When men's hearts failed" in the Old Testament book of Judges, chapters 4 and 5, "there arose a 'Deborah who judged Israel for forty years,' and the land had peace." Sweeny then paraphrased Jeremiah 6:14 against the wets, who "cry peace, but there can be no peace under the saloon reign"—a reference to God's judgment when Israel's leaders failed to follow God. Sweeny finished with a voluble plea for women's suffrage gained by "Christian courage . . . being careful never to bring reproach upon the Church we love or the Christ we serve," doing it all "for God and home and native land."[1] For pious Christian drys like Sweeney, the failure of men to vote for statewide prohibition necessitated giving white women the vote to purify the ballot.

A year later, Sinclair Moreland of Austin wrote an article in that paper that took up almost the entire front page, titled, "Woman Suffrage." The opening paragraph proclaimed: "The fetters and shackles of the enslaved are being loosed. The emancipation proclamation is being written. The dogmatist and reactionary are in retreat. The hosts of Deborah are marching on."[2] Rather than reaffirming traditional gender roles, Moreland declared that God made man and woman equal in the Garden of Eden. Moreland then anticipated dry criticisms of suffrage: "We hear it said that women's sphere is the home." But Moreland argued that woman's success in the limited sphere of the home justified expanding her sphere to suffrage: "The unsolved moral, social and political problems will find their solution in the suffrage of the American woman." He set the situation for suffrage in the direst terms: non-suffrage is slavery and suffrage is liberation; men have failed to reform the nation, so women must rise to slay the serpent of public vices whose "coils are tightening around the vitals of the Nation." Moreland concluded with a cry: "Awake! Woman, awake! Awake from your lethargic sleep—the dawn of your morning has come."[3] The desperate failures of drys in several southern states to win through male votes alone stirred them up to embrace women's suffrage as a spiritual and moral imperative.

As in Texas, the drys' loss of a statewide prohibition vote in Alabama in 1909 inspired prominent white women to advocate for their suffrage. Disappointed by that defeat, Mary Partridge of Selma founded the first chapter of the National American Woman Suffrage Association (NAWSA) in the state later that year. In response, Dr. Anna Howard Shaw, NAWSA's president, wrote to her expressing her gladness as well as recognizing the difficulty of such work. She confessed that "very little has been done for suffrage because of the great conservatism among the women of the South," despite their "absolutely helpless and unprotected position," but was glad for "the temperance agitation" for "arousing a great many women over all the country."[4] Afterward, Ms. Partridge sent out a call for more Alabaman women to join the movement, and by October 22, 1911, Birmingham women had responded by forming the Birmingham Equal Suffrage Association, with Pattie Ruffner Jacobs as its president. The Selma and Birmingham associations in turn formed the nucleus of the Alabama Equal Suffrage Association (AESA), founded October 9, 1912, again with Jacobs as president and Partridge as first vice president and state organizer. At just over thirty-seven years old, Jacobs was the youngest woman at that time to preside over any statewide women's suffrage organization.[5] Spurred on by the defeat of statewide prohibition, elite women like Jacobs turned their socialite prowess to achieving home protection—and white women's empowerment—via women's suffrage.

Jacobs continued to climb from statewide prominence to a national platform as she fought for women's suffrage. Despite attempting to retire from the AESA in 1914, she was reelected to the presidency, an indication of how popular and indispensable she had become. In 1915, the AESA relentlessly lobbied state lawmakers to submit an election on a state constitutional amendment for women's suffrage, gathering more than ten thousand signatures for the effort. With support from Ms. Chappel Cory, the president of the United Daughters of the Confederacy, the AESA also invoked Lost Cause religion to gain white women the vote. Despite winning a majority of fifty-two to forty-three votes in the state house, the women fell short of the three-fifths majority needed to submit the amendment for a vote. Since the Alabama legislature met only every several years to consider such matters, Jacobs and other women now set their sights on national women's suffrage.

In 1916, Jacobs had stepped down from her leadership of AESA to join the NAWSA board as second auditor, a role through which she extended her work across the region and the nation. That year, she helped organize NAWSA branches in West Virginia, North Carolina, and Mississippi. Over the next two years she worked on NAWSA's congressional committee to lobby legislators for a constitutional amendment giving women the right to vote, which was eventually realized in 1920 as the Nineteenth Amendment. After the United States entered World War I in April 1917, Jacobs was appointed by Treasury Secretary William Gibbs McAdoo to chair Alabama's Woman's Liberty Loan Committee, taking the same strategic path of others women's suffrage advocates around the nation of supporting the war effort in exchange for support for their cause.[6]

This pragmatic bargain paid dividends for woman's suffragists after the war. Jacobs resumed her leadership of AESA from 1918 to 1920, at the critical juncture when states could ratify the Nineteenth Amendment. After passing through Congress on June 4, 1919, Alabama's legislature considered the measure in July. Many prominent Democrats supported the measure, including southern-born President Woodrow Wilson, who had pledged support for women's suffrage before being narrowly reelected in 1916.

More Lost Cause support for women's empowerment came from Navy secretary Josephus Daniels, a notorious white supremacist from North Carolina, who urged Alabamans to join with other southern states, particularly Texas and Missouri, rather than risk "a loss to southern chivalry and southern prestige" by failing to advance the reform.[7] Nonetheless, the measure was easily defeated in the state legislature. Disapproval of women's suffrage was even stronger among the state's congressional delegation. After the departure of Richmond Pearson Hobson from the US House in 1915, only one Alabaman congressman, William B. Oliver of Tuscaloosa, dared to support the Nineteenth Amendment in 1919. The rest of Alabama's congressmen followed Oscar Underwood, the outspoken opponent of national prohibition and of women's right to vote.[8]

Notwithstanding Underwood's strain of southern conservatism, the concomitant rise of women's suffrage and prohibition in the 1910s South was dramatized by two nationally recognized champions of prohibition: Alabama's Hobson and Texas's Morris Sheppard. Hobson was prohibition's early champion in the US House of Representatives and was the most nationally renowned progressive from the state. He represented Alabama's Sixth

Congressional District from 1907 to 1915, advocating progressive causes such as graduated income tax, the direct election of US senators, regulating big businesses, and women's suffrage. He believed, as many progressives did, that such reforms would contribute to human evolution and make a more enlightened society. Yet Hobson's greatest passion was the prohibition of alcohol. Though he left the House before national prohibition was realized, he continued to campaign for it for decades. He authored a book on the subject, *Alcohol and the Human Race,* wherein he argued that alcohol stunted human development and resulted in a degenerate society. After the Eighteenth Amendment settled the issue to his satisfaction in the United States, he focused on spreading the anti-liquor crusade throughout the world and banning other drugs, such as heroin and opium.[9]

While Hobson advanced national prohibition in the US House, Sheppard advanced it in the Senate. A thoroughgoing progressive who proudly supported women's suffrage, he was first elected to the Senate in 1912 and served there for several decades. He wrote or helped write various national prohibition bills, including the Webb-Kenyon Act (1913) against interstate shipping of alcohol into dry states, the Sheppard Bone-Dry Act (1916) banning alcohol in the District of Columbia, and the Eighteenth Amendment, which he successfully introduced in the Senate. Sheppard's advocacy earned him the title "the father of national prohibition."[10]

The gap between support for prohibition and women's suffrage in the South appears most clearly in a comparison of states' ratification for the Eighteenth and Nineteenth amendments. On the Eighteenth Amendment, which established federal prohibition, southern states took the lead. Mississippi and Virginia were the first two states to ratify it, in January 1918. Among formerly Confederate states, seven lay among the first fifteen states to ratify it, and every single one had ratified it by January 16, 1919, when the needed three-quarters of the states ratified. Southern support for the Nineteenth Amendment, which granted women's suffrage, was far more subdued. While Texas and Arkansas were the ninth and twelfth states, respectively, to adopt the Nineteenth Amendment, the rest of the South was anti-suffrage territory. Georgia, Alabama, South Carolina, Virginia, Mississippi, and Louisiana (along with Maryland) all rejected it, and Florida and North Carolina did not even bother to vote on it. Despite this resistance, the amendment was ratified by thirty-five of the necessary thirty-six states by March 1920 and needed only one more state's approval. Months later, in August 1920, lobbyists for both sides descended upon Tennessee, which by a narrow vote became the only formerly Confederate state east of the Mississippi River to ratify the amendment.

No more southern states did so until the 1950s, and Mississippi resisted ratifi-cation until 1984.[11] While most of the South held out against women's suffrage, three of its states provided the tipping point for its ultimate success.

Even in Texas, the first southern state where the legislature affirmed wom-en's suffrage, most voters did not. Texan women could vote in the Democratic primary (but not general elections) starting March 1918. Then, on May 24, 1919, voters split their decision on two related measures. Out of roughly 300,000 votes cast, a state constitutional amendment for prohibition won by 20,000 votes, but the state amendment for women's suffrage lost by 25,000 votes. Where the popular vote failed to enfranchise women, the state legislature intervened, ratifying the Nineteenth Amendment in June 1919.[12] While prohi-bition and Jim Crow laws helped make white women's political empowerment palatable enough for several southern states to embrace it, a profoundly pa-triarchal system persisted in the South.

From WCTU to WONPR: White Women Flip on Prohibition

In 1920, few people had reason to believe that women would ever vote against prohibition. First Wave feminists from Susan B. Anthony and Elizabeth Cady Stanton to Frances Willard had connected women's suffrage and pro-hibition for nearly a century. As the nation's most prominent organization of Christian women, the WCTU provided moral clout for prohibition, which gained momentum around the nation by the turn of the century and helped dry up states in every region of the country by the 1910s. The yellow-and-black-ribboned advocates of women's suffrage joined in jubilation with their white-ribboned prohibitionist sisters in the twin political advances for women in 1920. The Eighteenth Amendment took effect in January 1920, and by Au-gust the Nineteenth Amendment to the US Constitution granted women suffrage in every state in the Union.[13] With women's suffrage established, WCTU leaders believed white women voters would never permit prohibition to be overturned.

Morris Sheppard, the "father of national prohibition" in the US Senate, was also a champion of women's rights before, during, and after the 1920s. He not only supported the Nineteenth Amendment but also the Maternity and Infancy Act of 1921, which was originally sponsored in 1918 by Jeanette Rankin, the first woman to serve in Congress and a Montana Republican. After Rankin left Congress, Sheppard continued her cause by sponsoring the bill, which provided money to hospitals to care for birthing women and newborns, both of whom suffered high mortality rates. By 1929, Sheppard had become the Democratic Whip in the Senate, one of the four most influential men in the chamber.[14] With Sheppard in the Senate, like Hobson in the House before him, the South had a powerful political advocate for prohibition and woman's political empowerment.

While southern politicians helped link women's empowerment with prohibition, one of the most politically empowered women in the South used her clout to overturn prohibition. Born Pattie Ruffner in 1875, she was by 1898 already drawing attention in local papers as Mrs. Solon Harold Jacobs and renowned for her beauty, clever outfits, participation in local women's clubs, and hosting of high-society events such as card parties and Japanese tea ceremonies. Though her initial relative fame did not suggest a political turn, by 1910 Jacobs joined thousands of white southern women who leveraged their good press and good looks for greater causes such as women's suffrage.[15]

Once women's suffrage was about to be realized nationally, Jacobs led the change to transform NAWSA and AESA into the League of Women Voters (LWV) and pursued other political reforms at a national level. In 1920 alone, she traveled well beyond the South to locales such as Omaha, Nebraska, to organize women voters.[16] Despite Alabama's resistance to giving women the vote, party leaders there appointed her as the first woman to represent their state at the Democratic National Committee. At the same time, she served on the national board of the LWV as secretary. A thoroughgoing progressive, Jacobs used her platform to protect other vulnerable members of society by advocating the end of the convict-lease system and child labor. She also served with reformist groups such as the Southern Council and Woman's National Trade Union League.[17] Not content to gain women the vote, she intended to wield those votes to expand women's influence in politics. At that time, however, respectable white women were expected to support prohibition.

In the early 1920s, progressive politicians like Texas governor Pat Neff illustrated the intimate connection between women's suffrage and prohibition. When he first announced his candidacy for governor, Neff declared in the same breath that he had supported both prohibition and women's suffrage. Since women's suffrage was still controversial in the South, however, Neff promised to safeguard it by supporting "every bill that seeks to put an unpolluted and unintimidated ballot into the hands of our women."[18] The "our women" doubtless referred to white women, not women of color. He reiterated his commitment to "pure and unhampered" elections with women's suffrage, which he believed would lead to "many laws both to purify and to dignify the ballot box."[19] His terminology implies concern that his anti–women's suffrage and anti-prohibition opponent, Joe Bailey, would intimidate white women voters and continue saloons' and brewers' corrupt brand of politics. After all, the most notable women in the federal government in the 1920s was Mabel Walker Willebrandt, the assistant attorney general of the United States and the most public face of prohibition enforcement in the nation. With white women fully enfranchised, most progressives believed, alcohol-tainted politics would finally face a reckoning.

Women's suffrage empowered not only dry, progressive women, but women across the political spectrum. The first elected female governor, Ma Ferguson, attracted support from wets and dismay from progressive drys when she won the Texas governor's race in 1924, challenging views that women, particularly southern women, would blindly support prohibition. Because her husband was an outspoken wet, many believed that she would not enforce the state's prohibition laws. While she did not gut Texas's strict Dean Law enforcing prohibition, Ma Ferguson continued her husband's tradition of giving pardons at an unparalleled rate, particularly for prohibition violators. One somewhat hagiographic history of Ferguson recounts how Neff's strict enforcement of prohibition and other laws filled the jails with petty offenders and did not let off offenders for good behavior, but Ferguson sought to correct the system and was "besieged" by petitions for clemency.[20] Others observed that her average of one hundred pardons per month, like her state highway contracts, were highly irregular, and some accused her of accepting bribes and kickbacks to award them. This was too much for the public, who voted in Dan Moody as governor in 1926 on a platform of cleaning up politics. Most women voters supported Moody more than Ma Ferguson, in part because he promised to enforce prohibition laws strictly and not hand out so many pardons. In the mid-1920s, most southern women sided with law-and-order rhetoric and strict prohibition enforcement over solidarity with a fellow woman such as Ma Ferguson.[21]

Repeal Goes South

Though the early 1920s maintained a comfortable link between prohibition and women's suffrage, 1929 provides a turning point after which white southern women turned from a dry bloc to split on the issue. After Al Smith's candidacy brought the prohibition question back into the public sphere the year before, a movement led by elite women began to deploy conservatively gendered language against prohibition. The main figure who sparked this shift was Pauline Morton Sabin, a New York Republican who in 1929 founded the Women's Organization for National Prohibition Reform (WONPR). The WONPR shattered the glass wall of women's unity on the issue and seized the moral high ground for repeal.

Sabin, a wealthy heiress, had fundraised for Republican presidents from Harding to Hoover, had taken a high position in Hoover's reelection campaign, and was the first woman ever elected to the Republican National Committee. As director of the Women's Republican Campaign in the East, Sabin had worked hard for Herbert Hoover's election over Al Smith in 1928 with the understanding that Hoover would investigate the effects of prohibition on the justice system and modify dry laws. Her insistence on prohibition reform shows that some women voters, even some Hoover voters, were not necessarily keen on strictly enforcing the Eighteenth Amendment. After Hoover won in 1928, he broke his promise to revisit prohibition enforcement, insisting that the current law needed no major reform. "I made up my mind I was fooled," Sabin said, and resigned her position in party leadership at once. The next day headlines around the country read, "Mrs. Sabin out to battle Drys!"[22] In a world that had associated women's suffrage with prohibition under the WCTU's slogan of "Home Protection," no powerful woman was expected to oppose prohibition publicly.

Undeterred, Sabin founded the WONPR in May 1929 with the implicit idea that temperance (meaning moderate drinking or abstinence) was a good ideal but legal prohibition was counterproductive for achieving it. The WONPR's first working name, the Women's League for True Temperance, implied that the means of prohibition would never achieve the ends of temperance. As the first prominent woman to come out against prohibition publicly, Sabin soon discovered she had spoken for "thousands of other women . . . ready to be organized, wanting to be organized," she said. "And the road before me was so plainly indicated I could not turn back from it."[23] Like other women contemporaries, she successfully framed her activism not as a selfish endeavor for personal power or fame, but as a selfless act of service, like a mother caring for her children.

That same year, a breach of racial etiquette involving women irrevocably turned southern Democrats, particularly women, against Hoover. The same day Hoover was elected president, another Republican, Oscar Stanton De Priest, became the first African American in the twentieth century elected to Congress, representing the Illinois First District. Since the First Lady had traditionally entertained congressmen's wives and daughters of the Congressional Woman's Club (CWC) for a tea party at the White House, First Lady Lou Henry Hoover invited De Priest's wife, Jesse L. De Priest, to join as an equal with the white women present on June 14, 1929. The event was the first time since President Roosevelt's invitation of Booker T. Washington to dinner in 1901 that an African American dined as a guest at the White House, and the result was equally scandalous for southern whites, particularly women.

This incident virtually guaranteed that most southern whites would vote for nearly any Democrat against Hoover in 1932, even a wet.

Democratic "Hoovercrats" who had backed the Republican presidential candidate in 1928 over prohibition and other issues were dismayed. Their ranks included Southern Methodist bishop James Cannon Jr., North Carolina's senator Furnifold M. Simmons, and Alabama's senator "Cotton Tom" Heflin. Simmons called the inclusion of Mrs. De Priest "exceedingly unfortunate and much to be regretted," while Senator Heflin said, "I deplore it very much; it was a mistake."[24] A 1929 convention of one thousand Hoovercrats in Virginia just days after the White House event called for strict enforcement of prohibition and adopted an indirect reference to "racial integrity and condemning social contact between whites and Negroes," but stopped short of a direct denunciation of Mrs. Hoover for inviting Mrs. De Priest to a tea party. I. C. Trotman, who claimed the De Priest incident had cost the Republican Party twenty-five thousand votes in the state, resigned from the organizing committee when the convention failed to condemn the First Lady more directly.[25] For many Hoovercrats, white supremacy trumped prohibition, and Hoover's embrace of social equality for Blacks, even at a tea party for congressmen's wives, was an unforgiveable sin.

Southern Democrats who had remained loyal to Smith in 1928 also denounced the equal treatment of a Black woman among white women. Texas Senator Morris Sheppard declared, "I regret the incident beyond measure. It is recognition of social equality between the white and black races and is fraught with infinite danger to our white civilization." North Carolina Senator Lee Slater Overman, who led the infamous Overman Committee during the Red Scare and successfully filibustered the Dyer Anti-Lynching Bill in 1922, called the incident "a great blow to the social stability of the South."[26] Texas governor Dan Moody likewise mocked the idea, advanced by Texas Republican R. B. Creager, that Mrs. Hoover should be excused because she was only following precedent by inviting Mrs. De Priest. "If the custom had been broken and the people of the Illinois district took offense," he huffed, "they should have been told to elect a white man to Congress."[27]

Perhaps the most vulgar response came from a South Carolina US senator, Coleman Blease. A protégé of "Pitchfork" Benjamin Tillman, Blease read aloud a resolution on the Senate floor that included parts of the poem, "Niggers in the White House." When Senator Hiram Bingham III of Connecticut denounced Blease's speech as "indecent, obscene doggerel" and successfully demanded it be stricken from the record, Blease withdrew the resolution, but claimed it was only because of the offense taken by Senator Bingham, not because of offense taken by African Americans.[28] This was in keeping with other statements by Blease, such as his 1930 rejection of constitutional rights that undermined white supremacism: "Whenever the Constitution comes between me and the virtue of the white women of the South, I say to hell with the Constitution."[29] (Blease also laid the groundwork for Section 1325, the piece of federal law that turned unauthorized border crossings into crimes, thus creating the category of "illegal immigrant.")[30] In his view, human and Constitutional rights came second to preserving a social order with native-born whites on top.

White women took prominent roles in denouncing the race mixing at the White House. On June 15, Senator Margie K. Neal, a Texas Democrat and the only woman in the Texas Senate, introduced the first of many state resolutions across the South against De Priest's welcome to the White House. The resolution bemoaned that "social recognition of a member of the Negro race accorded by women whose official and social positions are unsurpassed [that is, First Ladies] is fraught with the greatest consequences conceivable to amicable relations of the two races." The action seemed "calculated to greatly disturb [race] relations, widen the breach between Negroes and the white race and cause untold bloodshed"—mostly likely meaning, whites lynching Blacks. Her resolution concluded with "shame and regret" to "express in the strongest and most emphatic terms at our command, condemnation and regret at the conduct of the White House mistress and her associates." In addition, Senator Neal's resolution indirectly scolded Hoovercrats, who had been "warned of the danger of racial equality recognition at the National Capital through the election of the Republican candidate." The implication was clear: Republicans' support of racial equality undermined white supremacy, so white voters who broke with the Democrats to send the Hoovers to the White House were partly responsible for the race-mixing event. Senator Neal's resolution was adopted with just two dissenting votes, linking white women's empowerment in the South to white supremacism.[31] Other state legislatures in the South took a similar tune.[32]

Some lily-white Republicans, including some northern women, shared the white-supremacist rhetoric. When the wife of Albert H. Vestal, Republican congressman of Indiana, heard that Mrs. De Priest would be invited to the event, she introduced a resolution to alter the CWC's constitution to ban "undesirable persons"—namely, Mrs. De Priest. Not to be outdone, George M. Prichard of North Carolina, another GOP member of Congress, refused a room in the House office building adjacent to Representative De Priest. Unsurprisingly, De Priest nixed both Prichard and Vestal from the invitation list to his speech that year for the NAACP, though all other GOP Congressmen were invited. White southern Democrats were united against racial equality, and lily-white Republicans joined them.[33]

The De Priest incident accomplished two feats. First, it brought many Hoovercrats across the South back under the Democratic banner of white supremacy. Provided that the Democrats nominated someone other than Smith, the Solid South was likely to vote for a Democrat in 1932. Second, it demonstrated that white women's political empowerment, particularly though not only in the South, came at the explicit expense of Blacks. Given the lingering legacy of Jim Crow laws in the 1930s, women's suffrage in the South meant *white* women's suffrage.

Women Gone Wet

Even with southern whites' increasing opposition to Hoover, it was still embarrassing for women in 1929, South or North, to be seen opposing prohibition. Sabin recounted later that many women of Maryland whom she asked to join the WONPR in 1929 had said, "We are heart and soul with you, but don't put our names down!"[34] Even the WONPR official history claimed that in 1930 "there were few optimists in the country (aside from the so-called fanatics in the Association Against the Prohibition Amendment and WONPR) who thought the Eighteenth Amendment could be changed within ten years." In September 1930, the dry senator Morris Sheppard famously quipped: "There is as much chance of repealing the Eighteenth Amendment as there is for a hummingbird to fly to the planet Mars with the Washington Monument tied to its tail!"[35] The quote demonstrated the absolute commitment to prohibition from Sheppard, then the Senate minority whip and one of the most powerful figures in the Democratic Party.

The "hummingbird" quote also revealed the attitude of most people at that time: it would seemingly take a miracle to repeal the Eighteenth Amendment. Even the anti-prohibition American Federation of Labor, for example, aimed for the more realistic goal of modifying existing laws rather than repeal, which they deemed an "impossible goal" until 1932.[36] After prohibition had been so quickly defeated, the WONPR's official history remarked, "It is hard to believe that but three years ago such a crusade was necessary among the women of America," yet recalled "the uncertainty and timidity which existed about Repeal so short a time ago."[37] Public perception of anti-prohibition women shifted dramatically in just a few years from disreputable drunkards to defenders of the home, and the WONPR played no small part in that shift.

Women for prohibition's repeal struggled against negative stereotypes due to shifting gender norms in the Roaring Twenties that linked alcohol use and libertine lifestyles. Journalist Frederick Lewis Allen reported in 1931 that more women were smoking, drinking, kissing many men casually, petting, taking rides in the newly released closed car with young men late at night, and that a "bumper crop of sex magazines, confession magazines, and lurid motion pictures" added fuel to the fire of teenage and young-twenties' rebellion against their ancestor's mores.[38] As Paula Fass and Beth Bailey have noted, contemporaries other than Allen also looked with dread at the changing sexual, drinking, and other habits of increasingly liberated young women. Whereas the typical saloon before prohibition had served exclusively male customers, the elicit nature of the speakeasies of the Jazz Age broke down gender barriers. If the rise of the automobile enabled greater sexual independence, prohibition had ironically facilitated the new phenomenon of women drinking beside men. Prohibition, therefore, accidentally helped spur a revolution in drinking equality for men and women.[39]

In this context, it is little surprise that drys attacked the women of WONPR as libertines representing the very worst of their nation. Dr. Mary Armor, dubbed "the Georgia Cyclone," served as the WCTU president in her state and assailed "Mrs. Sabin and her cocktail-drinking women." Dr. Armor boasted, "we will out-live them, out-fight them, out-love them, out-talk them, out-pray them and out-vote them."[40] Clergy also assailed the character of women wets. The secretary of the Methodist Board of Temperance, Dr. Clarence True Wilson, was described as believing that "the great home-loving, church-going Americanized body of women would stand by Prohibition through thick and thin." He stated, "The little group of wine-drinking society women who are uncomfortable under Prohibition, will have as much influence in assaulting the Constitution of their country as they would have blowing soap bubbles at Gibraltar."[41] Other than their love for drinking, these voices suggested, why else would women want to repeal prohibition?

Repealist women in the WONPR, however, seized the moral high ground for the wets. In contrast to earlier repeal groups, the WONPR was the first well-organized group led exclusively by respectable women, and it posed the first credible organized threat to the WCTU claim to speak for all upstanding women in the nation. Despite accusations by the WCTU to the contrary, WONPR women generally had no material interest in the alcohol lobby, and even drys called their leaders "personally above reproach."[42] Unlike libertine women such as the Molly Pitcher Club, who defended alcohol on the grounds of individual freedom, the women of the WONPR co-opted the WCTU's conservative rhetoric of home protection and true temperance.

The WONPR's Declaration of Principles committed to objectives eerily like the ASL but even broader in scope. While the ASL sought to destroy the saloon and its attendant vices, the WONPR explicitly sought to prevent the return of the pre-prohibition saloons as well as to wipe out the speakeasies that prohibition produced. In addition, the WONPR denounced prohibition for being wrong in principle and "disastrous" in its consequences. First, prohibition violated Jeffersonian localism—a key conviction of southern whites— by arrogating too much power to the federal government and imposing law without support from the "moral sense and the common conscience of the communities affected by it." Second, prohibition did not work in practice. It led to more hypocrisy, corruption, death, and crime; stunted the steady growth in temperance before prohibition; had a "shocking effect" upon youth; impaired individual rights; and weakened "the sense of solidarity between the citizen and the government which is the only sure basis of a country's strength."[43] The WONPR thus turned the tables on the drys by arguing that prohibition, the supposed cure for societal decline, had made matters worse. WONPR did not seek to undermine the WCTU's Victorian model of womanhood in which women were the moral guardians of society, but rather expropriated it for a radically new political goal for women at a time when the concept of womanhood was shifting in other respects.

Like drys in the 1910s, the WONPR was also relentless in its advocacy. One speaker at the 1932 WONPR convention proposed to "take a leaf from the book of the Anti-Saloon League [ASL]. . . . Work for any candidate of any party who promises to vote for Repeal. Vote against any candidate who refuses to promise."[44] The WONPR emulated the calculating tactics and single moral purpose of the ASL while fighting against it. By combining the ASL's political shrewdness with the WCTU's moral authority, the WONPR thus appropriated the strongest traits of the two leading dry groups to effectively fight for prohibition's repeal.

By copying the tactics and rhetoric of drys, WONPR women were able to convert dry women to their cause. WONPR women set up booths at state and country fairs, often placing their booths fittingly "opposite those of the WCTU, which had long ago discovered this method of advertising." According to official WONPR report, at one such county fair in New York State, a prohibitionist woman "loudly called out that [a WONPR worker] must be a childless woman if she wished to get liquor back." When she woman "replied that she was working against Prohibition because she had four children, and asked the dry worker how many children she had," the latter hung her head, confessed she had none, and walked off. She later returned to apologize and sign the WONPR member pledge.[45] While the story may be apocryphal, it accurately reflects how women for repeal had to contend with charges that they were deviants—and how the WONPR turned this narrative on its head. By showing themselves to be "truer" women and mothers than many in the WCTU, the WONPR won them over. Once "the home had been both purified and equalized" by prohibition and suffrage, women used their newfound political power to decide for themselves the best way to cleanse their homes.[46] The WONPR thus framed its politically radical goal of turning women against prohibition within the conservative language of safeguarding motherhood.

One issue that animated Sabin and her followers was the hypocrisy of prohibition. Sabin allegedly founded WONPR because her disgust with broken promises among dry leadership compelled her to push for repeal. "I had started out believing in the Eighteenth Amendment," she said, but when she saw politicians "who would vote for prohibition and stricter enforcement and then half an hour later would be seen taking a cocktail," she "just couldn't stand anything so doubled-faced."[47] Prohibitionists like Wayne B. Wheeler and his ASL had long tolerated hypocrisy among "wet-dry" politicians who personally drank but voted dry, and WONPR women decried prohibition as a prodigious producer of hypocrisy. While dry newspapers like the Boston *Christian Leader* criticized H. L. Mencken's suggestion "that prohibition will not last long if we can have an exposure of all the hypocrites who are supporting it," the paper confessed: "undoubtedly, there is some truth in the remark," not least because many pastors preached with the assumption that some of their parishioners were also patrons of bootleggers.[48] Hypocrisy and lax enforcement not only bred disillusionment for prohibition, the WONPR claimed, but undermined the very spirit of the law. Women with WONPR followed their matronly duty to stand for purity against double standards.

Such sentiment against the hypocrisy of prohibition was common among the WONPR literature. It was most humorously featured in the cartoon opposite the title page in their official history (see figure 10). In that picture, dated 1930, a huge male figure has his hands clasped in prayer, a fake halo shining above his cowboy hat, and the word "LEGISLATOR" written on the belly of his fine suit shirt. A fashionably yet modestly dressed woman with a modern hat uses one hand to hold a sign emblazoned "WOMEN'S ORGANIZATION FOR PROHIBITION REFORM" while her other hand lifts the legislator's suit tails to reveal a bottle of whiskey in his pocket. The cartoon is simply titled: "AND HE VOTED DRY!" The message is simple: intended to reverse the moral decline brought on by alcohol abuse, prohibition had attended the rise of a slew of other vices, especially political hypocrisy.[49]

Armed with such rhetoric, the ranks of the WONPR rapidly swelled to 100,000 by April 23, 1930, then tripled to 300,000 a year thereafter, then doubled to over 620,000 by April 12, 1932, and finally doubled again to 1,326,000 by April 5, 1933—at that time the largest women's activist group in American history. Even the WCTU at its height in 1927 had reached a dues-paying membership of only about 766,000.[50] By enlisting more women than the WCTU ever had while WCTU membership slipped, the WONPR demonstrated that publicly supporting prohibition repeal, which had been embarrassing for respectable women in 1929, had within a few years become not only possible but increasingly fashionable.

While claiming old-fashioned values, the WONPR was also media savvy. The WONPR shamelessly juxtaposed its attractive women with their frumpier counterparts in the WCTU. Many praised Sabin's beauty in contrast to the unattractiveness of the head of the WCTU at the time, Ella Boole. One unnamed senator had welcomed Sabin's anti-prohibition activism with the remark, "Thank God, a pretty woman in politics at last."[51] This sentiment is reflected in a pair of pictures in the official history of the WONPR that contrasts a stunning portrait of "Mrs. Charles H. Sabin" with an unflattering figure of the WCTU president, "Mrs. Ella Boole." Sabin appears like a movie star with elegantly placed fingers, a refined pearl necklace, a white gown, part of her collarbone showing, an intent stare, and a dreamy haze that gives the impression she is wearing a halo. Boole, by contrast, has hands fumbling over books, a simple necklace buried in a dark drab coat, a double chin, a toothy smile, and spectacles that all convey the impression of an elderly, tottering, and old-fashioned woman.[52] Other prominent WONPR women, like Jacobs in Alabama, were also renowned for their beauty—an indispensable political asset in the age of movie stars. Women for repeal also employed "radio, moving pictures, special feature articles and daily press releases" as well as newsletters to members "from coast to coast and from Canada to Mexico" through their National Publicity Department.[53] While the WONPR with one arm clung to the rhetoric and some of the tactics of the WCTU, with the other it embraced modern media.

In 1929, repeal was a hard sell in the South, particularly in Morris Sheppard's home state of Texas. The WONPR had women working in bone-dry Texas as early as May 1929, led by Helen Edmunds Moore, a Catholic woman whose influence in Texas politics mirrored that of Sabin nationally. Though Moore was born in Wisconsin in 1881, she was a faithful Democrat who integrated well into the one-party system of the South after moving to Texas with her husband in 1905. A remarkable parallel to Jacobs in Alabama, Moore entered politics as she fought for women's suffrage through the Texas Equal Suffrage Association; then she became president of the League of Women

Voters of Texas in 1923 and served as a delegate to the Democratic National Convention in 1924 and 1928. The later convention is particularly noteworthy, as the Democratic nominee for president that year was, like Moore, both a wet and a Catholic. Not until Sabin founded the WONPR in 1929, however, could Moore join a well-organized, bipartisan, national organization against prohibition led by women. Despite Moore's stature in women's organizations in Texas, both her Catholicism and her wet stance made her an outlier. Nevertheless, she managed to win election to the state House in 1928 and 1930, when Sabin had named Texas a "hopelessly dry" state. While Moore lost her reelection bid in 1932 due to her wet stance, she was known as an unusually dispassionate politician, neither making emotional speeches (as did state representative Sarah Tilghman Hughes of Dallas) nor crying when she lost her seat (as did Senator Neal of the anti–De Priest resolution).[54] Undaunted by temporary setbacks, Moore and others in the WONPR pressed on with forming organizations and gaining members there and in every southern state.

Repeal gained real ground in the South when southern belles who had worked with the WCTU joined the WONPR. Her strong progressive credentials would have led one to expect Jacobs to be a proponent of prohibition. Indeed, in 1920, to celebrate the Nineteenth Amendment's ratification, Jacobs's LWV joined with the WCTU in a massive victory-day parade, apparently cementing the alliance between prohibition and women's suffrage.[55] Yet by 1933, Jacobs led the repeal forces in Alabama as the state chair of the WONPR. Joining her in the Alabama WONPR was Mrs. W. L. Muroch of Birmingham, a fellow progressive who had been a member of the WCTU. People like Jacobs and Muroch were part of a chorus of women across the South who broke fellowship with prohibitionists by the 1930s.

In March 1933, Mrs. Lillian V. D. Moore, chair of the national information service for the WONPR, boasted that no state—except perhaps Kansas— would be ignored by the repeal movement. Moore specifically mentioned the WONPR's growth in southern states: North Carolina, South Carolina, Georgia, Virginia, Tennessee, Texas, Mississippi, and Alabama. By April, Jacobs took a key role among nearly a thousand prominent women from across the nation who gathered in Washington, DC, for the WONPR national banquet. She joined southern luminaries such as Mrs. D. H. Foresman, former head of the Mississippi Federation of Women's Clubs, and Mrs. Ada Moore Healy of Atlanta among a handful of attendees featured from across the nation.[56] Southern women literally took center stage in the fight for repeal.

Jacobs and her comrades were not the first women in the South to take a notable stance against prohibition. In 1907, some women in Alabama had attracted press coverage for opposing alcohol bans in the name of the Lost Cause and children's education. After the Alabama House voted overwhelmingly for statewide prohibition on November 18, 1907, women officers of Mobile schools lobbied the state senate to reject the bill because their schools would close without state revenue from liquor licenses. Among those women were Miss A. Kirkland and Mrs. E. Semmes Colston, daughter of famed Confederate admiral Raphael Semmes, who as captain of the commerce raider CSS *Alabama* captured a record sixty-five prize ships during the war. Their advocacy reflected two positions that girded anti-prohibitionist arguments in the South. First, they contended that prohibition, rather than helping women protect children and families, would harm them—in this case, by cutting off the necessary revenue to educate them. This argument became far more persuasive once the Great Depression had begun in 1929, since wets promised that legalizing alcohol sales would provide needed jobs and tax revenue for recovery. Second, the women implicitly argued that anti-prohibitionists were the true inheritors of the Confederate legacy. While this second point was not particularly gendered and in this case was only implicit by virtue of Colston's parentage, women's unique role in advancing the Lost Cause narrative since the 1890s, particularly through the United Daughters of the Confederacy, has been well established by historians.[57]

These dual arguments—protecting women and Lost Cause religion—became potent arguments for breaking down the "wall of prejudice in the South" for prohibition. In 1931, a WONPR member in Kentucky happened upon an old clipping of Jefferson Davis's public letter against prohibition from the 1887 Texas campaign. Davis's message, with its emphasis on personal liberty and moral responsibility, was widely circulated and resonated with whites throughout the South.[58] With leadership by dynamic women like Jacobs and arguments tailored to southern white women, the South went from a stronghold of drys to a contested region for prohibition repeal.

A common WONPR argument that particularly resonated with the South was local self-rule. A major reason southern states supported repeal of federal prohibition—even while some of them opted for statewide prohibition for several more years—was aversion to federal intervention. Southern whites had claimed for decades that "states' rights" (rather than slavery) was the main reasons the Confederacy resisted the Union in the Civil War, and the trope took on mystic proportions in the South by the early twentieth century. Playing on that chord, the WONPR contended that national prohibition impinged upon "local home rule" by banning alcohol across the nation rather than letting states and locales decide for themselves how best to deal with

185

alcohol. The language of "home rule" echoed the conservative WCTU slogan of "Home Protection" and reflected the WONPR's desire for the death of saloons and speakeasies that prospered during prohibition.[59] Like other repeal groups advocating the "restoration of temperance," the WONPR described the repeal of prohibition as the only way to achieve "true temperance," by which they meant moderate alcohol use closely regulated by the government.[60]

In contrast to dry organizations like the WCTU and ASL that trumpeted their Christian identity, the WONPR embraced secular rhetoric. This secular language mirrored the broader cultural disillusionment with the millennial hopes of prohibition. Most US citizens were still Protestant at that time, and many of those rethinking their dry stance were liberal Protestants who grew increasingly alienated from prohibition by the vitriolic harangues of dry evangelicals throughout the 1920s. A typical liberal Protestant remarked at a 1928 prohibition convention that he was leaving because Congregationalists and most other denominations were "merely scenery at this convention; it is altogether a Methodist and Baptist movement."[61] Secular language for the WONPR was not merely a neutral stance on religion, but a rejection of the sectarian language of the most virulent drys that alienated other religious groups. This shift toward a more religiously inclusive politics signaled the rise of the New Deal coalition, which included the endorsement of the Democratic candidate for president in 1932 by the WONPR.

This more inclusive, less sectarian language opened the WONPR coalition to more religious groups than the exclusively Protestant WCTU. Roman Catholics, Jews, and Episcopalians, among other religious groups, had deeply rooted beliefs valuing alcohol and (legally) maintained the use of sacramental wine throughout prohibition. Jews and Christians alike noted the absurdity of prohibiting a drink that traditional teachings, the Bible, and even Jesus approved.[62] Catholics had been particularly embittered by the ugly presidential election of 1928 that pitted Protestants for Herbert Hoover against the Catholic Al Smith, and they welcomed a discussion of prohibition that took anti-Catholicism out of the equation.[63] Catholics also valued the family and community over the individual as the cornerstone of democracy, yet largely opposed prohibition, and so could naturally agree with the ostensibly secular rhetoric of the WONPR that prohibition was bad for the family.[64] It was no coincidence that Helen Moore, WONPR president for Texas, was a Catholic in a state that had narrowly voted against a Catholic for president in 1928. The WONPR was part and parcel of a seismic shift in the cultural acceptability of non-Protestants in politics, even in the South.

While one scholar has asserted that "the morality of the WCTU was deeply religious, whereas the moral system of the WONPR was strictly secular," the WONPR could indulge in religious rhetoric from time to time.[65] The first page of the WONPR's authorized account declared that, by 1927, many people had realized that "prohibition had, after all, not brought the millennium," a direct critique of the religious optimism that equated the Kingdom of God with prohibition.[66] That account later recalled how letters written back to sincere but misunderstanding critics of the WONPR resulted in "many 'conversions' or near-conversions," demonstrating the continued use of religious language by a "secular" movement.[67] Sabin herself used religious language for the WONPR, at times calling upon the "crusading spirit of every member" or saying "I prophesy" to describe her predictions for women's political empowerment.[68] On occasion, the women of the WONPR compared their cause to a fight between God and Satan. While encouraging women to resist the ASL and WCTU with their own tactics, WONPR leaders cried, "Fight the Devil with his own weapons."[69] Despite using more secular rhetoric than the WCTU, WONPR leaders did not hesitate to employ decidedly Christian language to recast their struggle as one of good against evil, language that resonated in the 1930s South. As in the 1880s and 1910s, religion continued to play on both sides of the culture war in the 1930s South—with women finally starring on both sides as well.

The greatest opportunity for repeal opened during the presidential campaign of 1932. The Democrats nominated Franklin Delano Roosevelt (FDR), a Protestant patrician who benefited from the urban inroads of the Smith campaign four years earlier while avoiding the anti-Catholic prejudices that doomed Smith's candidacy. Capitalizing on the crisis of the Great Depression, FDR advocated the repeal of national prohibition to create more licit jobs and government tax revenue from alcohol sales to fuel recovery programs. The GOP renominated Hoover, who took a more ambiguous stance on prohibition, trying to split the difference between wets and drys with a "moist" platform that promised some loosening of prohibition enforcement. Given a desirable change in prohibition with either candidate, male-led wet organizations refused to endorse a presidential candidate. The WONPR, however, decided to endorse FDR to hasten the total repeal of prohibition. Though risky, the decision bore immediate fruit: soon after declaring its support for FDR, the WONPR received 150 resignations but gained 137,000 new members. More importantly, the WONPR helped unite wet women voters around FDR, who promised outright repeal, rather than split their vote with Hoover, who tinkered with it. When FDR and other wets swept into power that November, the momentum had shifted decisively for repeal, vindicating the bolder stance of the WONPR over their timorous male allies.[70]

When WONPR reached its membership high-water mark in 1933, Congress had already passed a repeal resolution. Through a series of direct statewide elections, three-quarters of the states voted to repeal the Eighteenth Amendment by means of the Twenty-First Amendment by December 1933.[71] The battle to ratify the repeal amendment, however, seemed to be a hard sell in many states, particularly in the South.

While the WONPR welcomed racial and ethnic minorities in the North, the organization in the South was lily-white. Black Protestants found welcome in northern WONPR chapters and joined in considerable numbers. The Michigan branch included "Greeks, Russians, Roumanians, Ukranians, Poles and Negroes."[72] By harnessing the power of minority communities that had been demonized by drys in the past, the WONPR built a winning national coalition that mirrored the early New Deal coalition: diverse elsewhere, white in the South.[73]

As FDR and his wet coalition began dismantling prohibition in 1933, the governor's mansion in Texas welcomed back a white woman: Ma Ferguson. Though a teetotaler personally, she continued her practice from her first term of generously pardoning violators of prohibition laws. "Pardon seekers filled the waiting room" outside her office, and sacks of gifts arrived from those seeking pardons for their loved ones behind bars. One sob story she received was from a mother of five who had been abandoned by her husband and made a living selling home brew but was wrongly caught by a deputy when another man left his whiskey stash at her place. On one occasion, when criticized for pardoning twenty people in one day, she responded by pardoning forty the next day.[74] The "feminine" virtue of compassion—perhaps, her detractors suggested, as a cover for selling pardons to the highest bidder—was on full display in Ma Ferguson's second term. At the same time, the WONPR in Texas and throughout the South worked closely with other wet organizations and made use of the newest technologies, such as radio, to relay their message.[75]

Prohibition's zealous evangelical defenders, however, continued scorched-earth arguments against alcohol to a people already burnt out by them. Since Methodists had made the earliest pushes for prohibition, it was not surprising that they were particularly tenacious in opposing repeal. The North Texas Annual Conference of the MECS seconded uncompromising comments by Bishop James Cannon Jr. and the MECS national convention earlier in 1932. "Methodism has ever been in the forefront of every battle" for prohibition over the past century, they declared. Every level of the church from the pulpit to general conference has "recorded relentless opposition to the traffic and invincible determination to outlaw it as the common enemy of the [human] race." Whatever other groups might do, they declared, "Methodism will not lower her standards or agree to give a legal status to the traffic anywhere under the flag."[76] Nationalist sentiment and religious loyalty meshed for Methodists who would rather go down in a blaze of glory for prohibition than surrender to the pressures of popular opinion.

Gin Crow Ends

Go down they did, even across the South. Prohibition was overturned in three phases. The first step was modifying prohibition to allow low-alcohol fermented beverages, such as beer and wine. While the Volstead Act interpreted the Eighteenth Amendment's forbidden "intoxicating beverages" as anything with up to 0.5 percent alcohol, the Cullen-Harrison Act, signed March 22, 1933, and effective April 7, allowed beer of up to 3.2 percent alcohol by weight (4.0 percent by volume). Also, most state prohibition laws mirrored the Volstead Act, requiring legislative action to change them. Second, states ratified a constitutional amendment to repeal federal prohibition. After wets swept the 1932 elections, Congress on February 20, 1933, proposed what became the Twenty-First Amendment, which three-fourths of the states (thirty-six of forty-eight) had to ratify, a process that virtually necessitated cooperation from some formerly Confederate states. To circumvent the stranglehold of dry lobbyists like the ASL on state legislators, the Twenty-First Amendment was the first amendment to be ratified by convention, meaning that the people of each state would vote for delegates, who in turn would follow the voters' will to reject or ratify the amendment. Third, statewide prohibition laws were overturned, allowing the sale of distilled liquors with higher alcoholic content. While legalizing light beer and wine and repealing of federal prohibition were achieved across most of the South in 1933, repeal of state prohibition took years longer.

The first phase, legalizing light beer, was an easy sell, even in many southern states. Initially, some states' rights southerners balked at allowing beer just because Congress did so. A week after the Cullen-Harrison Act was signed, Arkansas attorney general Hal L. Norwood flatly rejected beer shipments into the state and promised that to keep Arkansas "as dry as a camel's tonsils" until the state laws were changed.[77] By 12:01 a.m. on April 7, nineteen states and the District of Columbia legalized the sale of beer, but no formerly Confederate states did so. Louisiana became the first such state to legalize beer on April 13, while North Carolina turned on its taps on May 1.[78] By April 1933, the Tennessee legislature passed a bill to legalize beer and wine with up to 3.2 percent alcohol, and the law went in effect on June 1. After a July special session of Alabama's legislature failed to approve beer, the leader of the Association Against Repeal, Dr. L. E. Barton, spoke of the contest in martial terms: "We ask no quarter and will give none."[79] Still, wet forces continued to gain ground. On August 24, the Arkansas legislature voted to legalize beer and light wines, and two days later Texans voted to approve the same. By September, most southern states, including Florida, South Carolina, and Virginia, enjoyed legal light beer. Only four states in the nation, including Alabama, Georgia, and Mississippi, still banned beer by the end of 1934.[80] A narrow majority of Georgians voted to allow beer in May 1935.[81]

The next step, ratifying the Twenty-First Amendment, also met with rapid success across most of the South, though the process was slower than in the rest of the nation. Whereas seven formerly Confederate states were among the first fifteen to ratify the Eighteenth Amendment, none were among the first fifteen for repeal. On July 18, Alabama and Arkansas—though still banning beer in their states—were the first in the South to reject federal prohibition (see table 9). Two days later, on July 20, Tennesseans narrowly voted to ratify, with wet turnout from Memphis and Nashville offsetting the dry bastion of East Tennessee. Texas voters decided in two simultaneous August elections to approve both the Twenty-First Amendment and the sale of beer. In October, Virginia offered a convincing two-to-one vote for repeal, while Florida provided the most convincing vote for repeal yet, with nearly 80 percent support.

The South, which had led the nation in its early support for the Eighteenth Amendment, lagged far behind the rest of the nation in its repeal. The only states in the nation whose voters rejected the amendment were North and South Carolina, while Georgia, Louisiana, and Mississippi never voted on the amendment. By December 5, however, the required thirty-six states had ratified the Twenty-First Amendment, including most in the South.[82]

While the battle for light drinks and national repeal had been won through most of the South by the end of 1933, the battle for repealing statewide prohibition took years longer. A few southern states got an early start on repealing their state prohibition laws. Virginia repealed state prohibition in October 1933, at the same time that it ratified the Twenty-First Amendment.[83] Louisiana—like many other states in the North and West—never enacted a state prohibition law; it was left up to local option, and wet locales such as the Big Easy allowed all kinds of alcoholic beverages as soon as the Twenty-First Amendment was ratified. In 1934, voters overturned state prohibition in South Carolina in August and in Florida by November. The next February, Arkansas narrowly joined the wet column through a legislative session marred by

Table 9. Timeline for Southern States Ratifying the Twenty-First Amendment (Federal Prohibition Repeal)

STATE	MONTH IN WHICH VOTERS REJECT FEDERAL PROHIBITION
AL, AR, TN	July 1933
TX	August 1933
VA, FL	October 1933

shouting matches and near-brawls.[84] When Texans finally repealed statewide prohibition in 1935, the margin of victory was 297,597 for repeal to 250,946 against—even narrower than the vote to repeal national prohibition two years earlier. Still, the tide had turned against prohibition (see table 10).[85]

Yet it was not all success for wets in the South. Several states initially rejected attempts to overturn statewide prohibition. By December 1935, only eight states in the nation were somewhat dry (excluding beer and light wines), most of them in the South—Alabama, Georgia, Mississippi, North Carolina, and Tennessee—and voters in six of those eight rejected attempts that year to turn their states wet. Georgia narrowly rejected repeal again in June 1937, thanks to rural voters.[86]

To hold back the growing wet tide, drys used plausible economic arguments. Despite promises to the contrary, the Great Depression had not been dramatically improved by the legalization of beer in 1933. Legalizing more heavily alcoholic drinks than beer seemed unlikely to make a major economic impact. The leading Southern Methodist paper for Texas in February 1935 cited the failure of alcohol legalization to assuage the Depression as well as reduced milk sales since 1933 as economic reasons to oppose repeal in Texas. For stalwart drys, however, the issue was a simple choice between order and chaos, between law and lawlessness.[87]

Most voters in southern repeal elections may have been more concerned about the economy than morality. James Endersby has demonstrated that voters' ideological values in prohibition elections were more important in 1919, when prohibition won the popular vote in Texas, than in the 1930s, when these factors were overwhelmed by the economic concerns of the Depression. While Endersby interpreted prohibition sentiment in general as more closely related to economic status than to religious affiliation, his analysis included only one religious variable—Catholic percentage of the population—so further research on other factors is needed, particularly the percentage of Baptists

Table 10. Select Statewide Repeal Referenda across the US South, 1932–1937

DATE	STATE	TYPE	VOTES FOR	VOTES AGAINST
July 23, 1932	TX	Submit proposed repeal to state vote, Democratic primary (approved)	405,198 (69.5%)	177,618
July 18, 1933	AR	Repeal federal prohibition (ratify 21st Amendment)	57,835	36,913
July 18, 1933	AR	Repeal federal prohibition (ratify 21st Amendment)	100,269 (58.7%)	70,631
August 26, 1933	TX	Permit sale of beer under prohibition (approved)	316,340 (62.9%)	186,315
August 26, 1933	TX	Repeal federal prohibition (ratify 21st Amendment)	304,696 (61.3%)	191,966
November 7, 1933	NC	Repeal federal prohibition ratify 21st Amendment (rejected)	115,482	300,054 (72.2%)
July 21, 1933	TN	Repeal state prohibition (approved)	123,516 (52%)	113,817
February 26, 1935	AL	Repeal state prohibition (rejected)	93,985	102,151 (52.1%)
August 24, 1935	TX	Repeal state prohibition (approved)	297,597 (54.3%)	250,946
August 24, 1935	TX	Establish state liquor dispensary system (rejected)	247,198	373,919 (60.2%)
September 23, 1937	TN	Repeal state prohibition (rejected)	35,250	91,872 (72.3%)

Sources: Plocheck, "Prohibition Elections in Texas"; Endersby, "Prohibition and Repeal," 506; initial, incomplete Arkansas results from "ARKANSAS AND ALABAMA JOIN MARCH FOR REPEAL," *Indianapolis Times,* July 19, 1933, 1; *Alabama Official and Statistical Register, 1935,* comp. Owen, 764–65; London, comp. and ed., *North Carolina Manual, 1935,* 113; "TENNESSEE IN 'WET' COLUMN BY SLIM VOTE," *Hendersonville, NC, Times-News,* July 21, 1993, 1; using incomplete early results from 1,602 of 2,280 precincts for 1937 Tennessee vote, "TENNESSEE VOTES 4 TO 1 TO KEEP BANS ON WHISKEY SALES," *Hendersonville, NC, Times-News,* September 24, 1937, 1.

Table 11. Timeline for Statewide Repeal across the US South, 1933–1966

YEAR	STATE	EVENT
1933	TN	April 6–12—Legislature legalizes beer and light wines
1933	LA	April 13—Legislature legalizes beer
1933	NC	May 1—Legislature legalizes beer
1933	TN	June 1—Law legalizing beer and wines goes into effect
1933	AR, TX	August—States legalize beer
1933	FL, SC, VA	September—States legalize beer
1934	MS	Voters reject repeal of state prohibition
1935	GA	Voters reject repeal of state prohibition
1936	Birmingham, AL	November—City refuses to enforce state prohibition law
1937	NC	February—Legislature scraps state prohibition law
1937	AL	March—Voters approve repeal of state prohibition
1937	TN	September 23—Voters reject repeal of state prohibition
1937	GA	Voters reject repeal of state prohibition
1938	GA	February—Legislature repeals state prohibition
1939	TN	March 2—Legislature overrides governor's veto to allow wet counties to sell distilled drinks
1952	MS	Voters reject repeal of state prohibition
1966	MS	Legislature allows local option exceptions to statewide prohibition

and Methodists, before a determinative judgment can be reached on the subject.[88] Still, his main argument holds: for many southern whites in the 1930s, money trumped morality.

Within a few years, however, even the bone-dry states grew moist, mostly because of action by state legislatures (see table 11). Birmingham, Alabama, overturned its dry laws in November 1936, ending local police enforcement of state prohibition for the city and turning the city wet in all but name. Caught in the untenable position of having its largest city openly defy its prohibition laws, Alabamans voted out prohibition by a modest margin the next March, making it the last state in the South to repeal by popular vote. Given North Carolina voters' overwhelming rejection of the federal repeal in late 1933, wets looked to the legislature for relief from prohibition. Legislators finally took the bold step to scrap the state's bone-dry law in February 1937, and county-operated stores opened in wet counties by April. Repeal in Georgia was stymied by two referenda in 1935 and 1937 that upheld state dry laws. Wets finally triumphed in February 1938, when a law was signed allowing the manufacture and sale of liquor in wet counties.[89]

Tennessee took even longer to overturn statewide prohibition. In April 1935, the legislature only reluctantly raised the allowed alcoholic content for local beers from 3.2 percent to 5 percent when told that the state was losing money to out-of-state brewers. However, the arrival of beer and the end of federal prohibition that December did not mean that most Tennesseans wanted the return of more potent distilled liquors. In September 1937, after months of delay by dry forces, a referendum resulted in more than 70 percent of voters rejecting a repeal of state prohibition for distilled beverages. Not until March 2, 1939, did state legislators finally overcome a governor's veto and effectively replace state prohibition with local option.[90] In most cases, the driest spots of the South let go of state prohibition only via their legislatures, not by popular referenda.

The final dry holdout was Mississippi. Voters rejected prohibition in referenda in 1934 and 1952, even though the state had taxed alcoholic drinks since 1944. Its legislature seriously debated repeal several times, in 1960 and 1964, but did not permit localities to take exception to statewide prohibition until 1966.[91] However, this was the exception that proved the rule. By the end of the 1930s, prohibition was all but finished in the South. Even Frank Norris admitted in 1935 that prohibition would prevail not in this lifetime, but only when Christ returned to usher in his millennial reign.[92] Heaven on earth would have to wait, thanks to white women going wet.

White women served as bellwethers and trailblazers for the shift of popular opinion on prohibition in the South. Under Ma Ferguson's last term as governor, Texas repented of federal prohibition, with the state's WONPR being "responsible in large measure" for pushing through the Hughes-Moffitt bill that submitted the amendment to the Texas citizens for a vote.[93] And while Texas state representative Helen Moore had lost her seat in 1932 due to her wet stance, she won it back in 1934 on a platform of overturning state prohibition, which she helped achieve a year later.[94]

The Vanishing Race Card

As white women took prominent roles in repeal, African Americans were conspicuous by their absence. One account of repeal in Alabama in 1937 noted, "Apparently the race question did not figure in the election" because "some of the counties having large Negro population voted for repeal."[95] The author's assumption seems to be white voters in majority-Black counties might be expected to vote dry as a means of racial control, since African Americans were expected to vote wet. Of course, in Alabama in 1937, virtually no African Americans could vote in those counties. But the fact that whites in notoriously repressive places like "bloody" Lowndes County supported repeal provides strong evidence that Gin Crow was no longer needed to exercise effective control of Black bodies. For most whites, wet and dry, race had moved from a major issue in the 1910s prohibition votes to a nonissue in repeal debates of the 1930s because nonwhites had been effectively eliminated from politics.

In Texas, rhetoric of some white drys in the 1930s showed the continued longevity of race baiting. The Southern Methodist flagship newspaper in the South, the Dallas *Southwestern Advocate,* prophesied that the end of prohibition would herald the return of the dubious tactics of the brewers before prohibition. The article cited letters between brewers and African Americans in the 1900s and 1910s, revealing the (then) scandalous work of Black ministers to mobilize the African American vote.[96] The implication was clear: good white citizens should vote down prohibition's repeal to keep whites in power and nonwhites out. The paper further accused liquor forces of organizing fraudulent payment of poll taxes and urged "every good citizen" to register to vote and keep liquor illegal.[97] The threat of interracial politics was more potent in Texas, where most African Americans could vote simply by paying an opt-in poll tax, than in other southern states like Alabama, which had more rigorous voting-restriction laws.

However, these race-baiting tactics by desperate drys proved ineffective in preventing repeal in Texas, which won by a comfortable margin in 1935. Race-baiting failed in the 1930s not because white supremacism had become outdated but because it had been so firmly established. Years of rigorous enforcement of Jim Crow laws and the end of the coalition between Blacks and brewers had neutralized interracial voting in the South. Once brewers and distillers came back to legitimate power nationwide in 1933, they no longer needed Black votes for their survival and did not seek them out. While white drys needed Jim Crow to create Gin Crow, southerners no longer needed Gin Crow to supplement Jim Crow.

Sharp declines in voter turnout strongly suggest that African American voters played virtually no role in the prohibition elections of the 1930s. Table 12 shows the depression in voting turnout from the 1880s to 1930s in prohibition elections in just one state, Texas. Its poll taxes hit hardest for poorer voters, particularly African Americans. While no exact numbers are available

195

Table 12. Turnout in Texas Statewide Prohibition Referenda

DATE	VOTES CAST	REGISTERED VOTERS	% REGISTERED VOTERS	TOTAL OF VOTING AGE	% OF-AGE WHO VOTED
1887 August 4	349,897	n/a	n/a	508,277	68.8
1908 July 25	286,271	646,113	44.4	950,245	30.2
1911 July 22	468,489	630,926	74.3	1,031,451	45.4
1919 May 24	297,889	703,576	42.3	1,256,203	23.7
1933 August 26	496,662	775,236	64.1	3,413,169	14.6
1935 August 24	548,543	872,500	62.9	3,541,535	15.5

Source: Plocheck, "Prohibition Elections in Texas."

Note: Ann-Marie E. Szymanski has alternate numbers for turnout: 77.7 percent in 1887, 48.9 percent in 1911, and 26.5 percent in 1919 (*Pathways to Prohibition,* 15). The lack of a clear number of registered voters available in 1887 helps account for the large discrepancy for that year, and for 1911 and 1919 the numbers are comparable. Both accounts show the same overall pattern of declining turnout, which was more dramatic in Texas than any other state in Szymanski's table 1 except for North Carolina—another formerly Confederate state. Even using Plocheck's figures, which are more conservative in terms of decline from the high of 1887, the drop in voter participation is dramatic.

along racial lines, the sharp decline in voting participation between 1911 and 1919—whether measured by total votes, percentage of registered voters, or percentage of voting-age eligible people—indicated the sharp exclusion of African Americans and poorer whites from the 1911 vote, which narrowly rejected state prohibition, and the 1919 vote, which established state constitutional prohibition. By 1933, despite the dramatic increase in voting-age population due to natural growth, immigration, and the newfound ability of white women to vote, the registered voter totals increased only modestly, and the percentage of voting-age people who voted sank to the mid-teens. If even Texas, with its relatively generous opt-in poll tax laws and lack of literacy tests or grandfather clauses, had voter participation sinking to dangerously low levels for everyone in the 1930s, including whites, African American voters must have been virtually nonexistent. If Texas's relatively weak Jim Crow prompted feeble attempts by drys to bring up race as an issue in the 1930s, states with more ruthless disfranchisement laws scarcely discussed race because the issue had been settled.

Conclusion

Prohibition, which had begun with such utopian promise, fizzled by the 1930s as white women, once believed its most loyal constituency, divided on the issue. As white women across the South gained the vote and political prominence, some questioned whether they needed the prohibition movement that helped gain them suffrage. Ma Ferguson, a Texas Democrat, wielded her husband's unique brand of popularity to take the governor's seat twice during prohibition's reign and weaken enforcement of prohibition by generously pardoning offenders. On the national stage, Pauline Sabin suavely channeled her resentment at broken promises to reform prohibition into a national antiprohibition movement that made it respectable for women to openly reject prohibition. And in the eastern South, women like Pattie Ruffner Jacobs led statewide efforts to overturn prohibition. Such women affirmed the rhetoric that women were the moral guardian of the home even as they opposed prohibition, which had been proposed as a safeguard for the home. By wielding the rhetoric and tactics of dry groups against prohibition, female wets were able to win over voters even in the region that remained prohibition's final holdout: the South.

In addition to changes in women's righteous rhetoric, the economic pressures of the Great Depression and the evident failures of prohibition pushed more southerners out of support for prohibition. The desperate need for legitimate work and tax revenues to fund relief programs in the nation's poorest region nudged millions of white southerners to put aside their former preference for prohibition and consider legalizing the notorious alcohol industry once again. Though the Solid South had split its presidential votes in 1928 due to the Democrats nominating a wet New Yorker, it united four years later to vote for another wet New Yorker—albeit a Protestant, not a Catholic. Four years of Depression and social change had radically altered the political appetites of southern whites. Within another seven years, only one southern state remained dry in law, if not in fact. A few counties and towns have remained dry to the present, but prohibitionists have fought a rear-guard action of gradual retreat over the decades. While prohibition's repeal seemed impossible in 1930, like "a hummingbird to fly to the planet Mars with the Washington Monument tied to its tail," in the words of Morris Sheppard, it soon became taken for granted. Seeming certainties of politics, even entrenched positions of a culture war, in a few short years faded and were forgotten like flowers of the grass.

Despite the changes in prohibition laws and white women's empowerment, however, the racial picture of the South remained much the same. While the

197

New Deal coalition gave them more clout in the Democratic Party in the North, African Americans would have to wait decades longer for their votes to make a powerful impact across the South again. The delay of southern prohibition in the 1910s owed much to African American votes, but prohibition's repeal in the South, like both Republican and Democratic parties there in the 1930s, was lily-white.

Epilogue

PROHIBITION IN THE SOUTH had come full circle in many ways from 1885 to 1939. The tenacity of conservative Protestants for prohibition and teetotaling has contributed to the popular misconception that prohibition was reactionary. Yet prohibition started as an innovation in theology and politics, challenging millennia of Christian tradition and decades of Jeffersonian democracy. As such, prohibition took root in the South more slowly than in the rest of the nation. Drys sought solutions for real social ills through an activist state that regulated personal consumptive habits and intervened in the economy so far as to ban a major US industry. The drys' two greatest organizations were the Women's Christian Temperance Union (WCTU), which championed the progressive reform of women's suffrage, and the Anti-Saloon League, which reinvented political lobbying. But by the mid-1930s, prohibition had become an old-fashioned relic associated with conservative Southern Baptists and the Roaring Twenties, a noble but misguided experiment ill-fitted to the ecumenical priorities of the Great Depression and the New Deal. Prohibition began as thoroughly progressive and modern but ended as reactionary.

Prohibition also incited prejudice against Catholic Americans, whose traditional religion and cultural mores led most of them to embrace alcohol. The Solid South split in 1928 when many formerly Confederate states voted for the dry Protestant Republican presidential candidate against the wet Catholic Democrat. The flood of support for the Democrats' wet candidate in 1932 reunified the South politically and quieted the fierce anti-Catholicism that prohibition incited four years earlier. If prohibition's imposition symbolized Protestant hegemony, its repeal marked the entrance of Catholics into the cultural mainstream, even to some extent in the South.

In addition to signaling changes in religion and politics in America, prohibition also marked the evolution of racial politics in the South. Black and white drys in the 1880s worked together to push for—and in Atlanta, briefly establish—prohibition in the South. Like the Readjusters and Populists, prohibitionists threatened white-supremacist Democratic rule in the South by dividing the white vote and allowing African American voters to decide elections. White drys increasingly blamed Black enfranchisement as an obstacle to prohibition and so transformed their crusade from multiracial Christian reform to white-supremacist Gin Crow. In response to this shift, African Americans increasingly joined with traditionalist white Christians and self-interested brewers in opposing dry laws, effectively forestalling Gin Crow's rise in three statewide votes in the 1910s and in countless local option elections throughout the South. Despite their best efforts at defying Gin Crow, however, voter suppression of racial minorities and conversion of white Christians to the dry gospel combined to impose prohibition in the South, effectively ending the last effective political resistance to Jim Crow for decades.

Gin Crow's enforcement and repeal marked equally significant milestones for racial politics in the South. Enforcement of dry laws—as with other laws—disproportionately targeted African Americans, foreshadowing the mass incarceration of latter-day Jim Crow during the War on Drugs. When repeal came in the 1930s, African Americans were conspicuously absent from most political rhetoric and from the polls. White southerners repealed Gin Crow in part because Jim Crow was secure without it.

Race cannot be fully understood without reference to gender, and prohibition in the South simultaneously contributed to the decline of Black men's political rights and the empowerment of white women. The WCTU linked the dry cause to women's suffrage, yet its segregated organization in the South and racist comments by its white leaders made it clear that the women voting would be white. Dry white rhetoric linked alcohol with Black rapists attacking white women and so helped justify lynchings, Jim Crow, and dry laws. Prohibition's rise powered the political enfranchisement of women in 1920, and everyone expected women to vote dry as a bloc. While the South resisted women's suffrage more than any other section, a few southern states tipped the balance to ratify the Nineteenth Amendment in 1920, thanks to the WCTU's linking of women's votes with prohibition. Yet women's loyalties shifted over time, and women provided crucial votes for repeal. The turn of millions of women against prohibition demonstrated that the votes of women, like any other demographic, could never be taken for granted, but changed over time according to their own priorities and needs. With white women able to vote for themselves, and with Jim Crow laws effectively enforcing the racial hierarchy, most white voters felt that legal alcohol no longer posed a substantial threat to the now-secure white-supremacist order.

Dry Another Day

Despite Gin Crow's demise at the state level in the 1930s, the South did not turn from completely dry to entirely wet in the 1930s. Much of the South remained officially dry due to local option laws, and skirmishes on that level continued into the early twenty-first century, though they mostly led to triumphs for wets.[1] Repeal did not overturn many local and state alcohol regulations, which remained in effect, while new laws arose to regulate when, which, and where alcoholic beverages could be purchased and consumed. As of 2021, hard-liquor stores in Texas still cannot open on Sundays until noon, encouraging those whose flesh is weak to stop by church before drinking off the rest of the weekend.

Even as prohibition laws were repealed, recalcitrant drys sang the praises of bygone comrades. Josephus Daniels, the famed newspaperman who incited the Wilmington Massacre in 1898, wrote in 1943 the dedication for an academic book on prohibition in North Carolina. He praised Robert Heriot Clarkson, who was the state's leading dry figure for the ASL since 1904, the unofficial leader of the successful 1908 campaign for statewide prohibition, and eventually a judge on the state Supreme Court from 1924 until his death in 1942.[2] Even years after prohibition had been defeated in the South, drys were still helping shape the narrative of prohibition in the region.

Southern drys did not die out; they evolved. Texas's prohibitionists reorganized as the United Texas Drys (UTD), which produced literature to combat demon rum, such as a curiously titled 1938 book, *Drinking and Its Moral Lessons,* which admitted drys' relative impotence on the issue: "[S]ince repeal they [the brewers] have been ignoring us and trying to create the impression in the minds of the people that prohibition is a closed issue."[3] Despite this fact, the UTD remained convinced that prohibition had failed only because it focused too much on enforcement and not enough on education. "If we supply [temperance education]," they wrote, "other phases of our program will take care of themselves."[4] Unable to lobby as the ASL had, Texan drys comforted themselves by thinking that information alone would lead to prohibition. In some ways, this strategy bore impressive fruits: as late as 1953, 142 of Texas's counties were dry while 82 were partly dry and just 30 entirely wet. Yet in the long run, the optimism of drys proved unfounded. The UTD's efforts were merely a defensive holding action. The UTDs had by the 1970s changed their name to Drug Prevention Resources, Inc., and shifted their primary focus from alcohol to other drugs. The number of dry counties in Texas continued to shrink, falling from 128 in 1970 to just 35 in 2008. Still, a few states, such as Arkansas and Kansas, have seen a significant increase in dry counties over the same period, showing that prohibition's demise has been neither universal nor inevitable.[5]

In the 1980s, a movement convinced states around the nation to raise the legal drinking age from eighteen to twenty-one when the US Congress in 1984 tied the higher age limit to highway funding. Subsequent laws have required labels on alcohol bottles warning potential buyers of the dangers of drink.[6] As Lisa McGirr has noted in *The War on Alcohol,* the War on Drugs owed much to prohibition. So long as government seeks to criminalize and sharply regulate widely consumed drugs, prohibition will never truly end.

Racial Reorder

The shift of several former Confederate states into the Republican column in 1928, though sparked by political battles over prohibition and religion, fore-shadowed a political realignment of the region from reliably Democratic to a hotly contested battleground to finally a Republican stronghold, a realignment based largely upon race. While prohibition's repeal did not immediately empower racial minorities—brewers became re-legalized without help from minority voters and saw no reason to support their suffrage a second time—the same New Deal that rolled back prohibition also persuaded most African American voters to switch their allegiance from the Republican to the Democratic Party permanently. In 1934, the only Black congressman, the Republican Oscar De Priest, was defeated in the general election by a Black Democrat, Arthur Mitchell. Since then, the vast majority of African Americans elected to public office have been Democrats. Ten year later, the Supreme Court ruled eight to one in *Smith v. Allwright* to end the white-only Democratic primaries across the South. Black voting registration began climbing slowly in most southern states. In 1948 and 1960, white Dixiecrats dissatisfied with the civil rights advocacy of the national party carried a few Deep South states, while GOP presidential candidates poached several southern states in 1952, 1956, and 1960. Then the modern civil rights movement—particularly the Civil Rights Act of 1964, the Voting Rights Act of 1965, and decisions by liberal federal courts in 1966—overturned Jim Crow laws such as poll taxes, removing the last legal barriers to Mexican Americans and African Americans registering to vote across the South. By 1968, the National Democratic Convention recognized only racially integrated state parties, and the battle for the political soul of the South began in earnest. For the first time since the anti-prohibition coalition half a century earlier, racial minority voters played key roles in tightly contested elections throughout the South.

As African Americans gained political clout in the South by the 1970s, so too did Latino Americans. Beginning in the 1920s, the activism of the Primer Congreso Mexicano helped inspire Tejano (Mexican Americans from Texas) independence from political bosses and greater Tejano interdependence through mutual aid societies. Groups like the Order of the Sons of America (OSA) and the League of United Latin American Citizens (LULAC) cultivated US citizenship for Tejanos in a white-dominated society, and especially LULAC (which Canales helped found) gave Tejanos mechanisms for political activism. Cesar Chavez and Dolores Huerta founded the Latino-led United Farm Workers union in the 1960s, demonstrating the economic and political muscle of Latino Americans in the US Southwest beyond Texas. By the late twentieth century, Tejanos and other Latino Americans throughout the nation had gained considerable social, economic, and political influence.

Signs of the growing importance of racial minority voters and candidates in the Deep South became apparent in the early twenty-first century. When Barack Obama was elected the first African American president of the United States in 2008, he carried three formerly Confederate states—Virginia, Florida, and North Carolina—and comfortably carried the former two again in 2012. The next year, Republican Tim Scott became the first Black US Senator to represent South Carolina or any southern state since Reconstruction in the 1870s. After narrowly winning a 2017 Alabama special election (by fewer than 22,000 votes out of over 1.3 million cast), Doug Jones became the first Democrat to be elected in the deeply Republican state to the US Senate since 1992. Jones, who is white, had made a name for himself prosecuting former Klan members, and his election was made possible by African Americans, who made up 29 percent of the overall votes and 96 percent of whom (including 98 percent of Black women) voted for him.[7] Then in 2018, Congressman Beto O'Rourke nearly unseated Ted Cruz from his Senate seat (losing by less than 3 percent out of 8.3 million cast) thanks to unprecedented turnout, particularly from young and racial minority voters: 65 percent of women under forty-five years old, 69 percent of Latino voters, and 90 percent of Black voters backed O'Rourke.[8] As it was with the wet coalition a century earlier and the civil rights movement a half-century ago, it seems that even the most solidly Republican parts of the South are once again becoming political battlegrounds, thanks to racial minority voters.

By 2020, racial minorities enjoyed more opportunities for political advancement in both the Republican and the Democratic parties. That year, fully one sixth of Texas's US Representatives were African Americans, and every other formerly Confederate state except Tennessee and Arkansas had at least one representative in the Congressional Black Caucus. In that same 116th Congress, thirteen Latinos and Latinas from both parties represented Florida and Texas, including US Senators Ted Cruz and Marco Rubio, both Republicans of Cuban descent. Then in January 2021, two US Senate runoffs in Georgia resulted in narrow victories for both Democratic candidates, including Rafael Warnock, the first African American Democrat to represent a southern state in the US Senate. If voting turnout for racial minorities around the South continues to increase, the region might not remain dominated by a single party, and racial minorities may continue to play decisive roles in statewide elections.

Another transformative moment in race relations in the South came from reactions to acts of violence against racial minorities. The Black Lives Matter movement (BLM), which arose in 2014 in the wake of police killings of unarmed Black men and women, launched protests across the nation for systemic change of the criminal justice system. The aftermath of the Emanuel AME Church shooting in 2015, in which nine Black parishioners were murdered by a white supremacist, resulted in a backlash against Confederate symbolism. Even conservative Republican politicians such as South Carolina's senior US senator Lindsey Graham and Governor Nikki Haley eventually supported removing the Confederate battle flag from the state house that year. Another sea change occurred in May 2020. Significant media coverage of the police killing of George Floyd sparked one of the largest protest movements in US history.

In addition to calling for an end to police brutality and killings of Black Americans, the protests also resulted in the removal of more statues of Confederate and other white-supremacist symbols that year. Protesters toppled many monuments, including Nashville's statue of the dry "martyr" and white-supremacist Edward Ward Carmack, which fell on May 30, 2020, almost a century after its erection.[9] On June 10, NASCAR, a refuge of the "politically incorrect," banned the use of the Confederate battle flag at its rallies.[10] While President Trump reiterated his support for Confederate symbols and monuments in a June 20 rally in Tulsa,[11] a popular tide was turning against them.

On June 19, the National Collegiate Athletic Association (NCAA) instituted a rule against postseason college games in Mississippi unless it removed the Confederate flag from its state flag. On June 23, the Mississippi Baptist Convention—which represents twenty-one hundred churches with more than half a million members—agreed, arguing that changing the state flag was "not merely a political issue," but was necessary a matter of "biblical morality."[12] Under intense pressure from these and other groups, the Mississippi legislature voted that year to remove Confederate imagery from the state flag, one of the last formerly Confederate states to do so. While the Lost Cause still carried weight among many white southerners, its luster had dulled considerably.

The Bible Belt(s)

While prohibition faded after the 1930s, the political engagement of churches (across the political spectrum) did not. The kind and degree of political preaching differed by denomination. Southern and Northern Methodists eventually joined in 1939, then formed the United Methodist Church after another merger in 1968. Their united denomination advocated for many social reforms throughout the twentieth century as the largest member of the progressive National Council of Churches (NCC). By 1972, Methodists maintained a commitment to many reforms, but prohibition was not among them: while previous editions of the Methodist Book of Discipline mentioned the sin of drinking, that year the mention of it abruptly vanished. While Methodists' relative influence in the South declined during and after the Great Depression, Southern Baptists' more independent and flexible church leadership helped the SBC gain undisputed numerical and cultural dominance in most of the South by the 1950s and spread throughout the nation. As prohibition faded and Methodists became increasingly mainline, their political influence declined. The only exception to this trend of shrinking political capital was perhaps the most famous Texan Methodist of the early twenty-first century, President George W. Bush, the candidate "you'd want to have a beer with" but personally was a teetotaler.[13]

Southern Baptists were less inclined than Methodists to adopt a wide range of reforms, and increasingly became champions of social, theological, and political conservatism. Unlike Southern Methodists, Southern Baptists never reunified with Northern Baptists (now ABCUSA), and the SBC's Foreign Mission Board kept its distance from the NCC in 1950. The SBC was easily the nation's largest Protestant denomination by 1979, when its bottom-up governance enabled grassroots conservatives to begin seizing power from moderate denominational leaders, which they did after a decade of struggle.

However, the overwhelmingly white SBC, which was founded to support slavery, famously apologized for its stance in 2000 and elected its first Black president, Fred Luter, in 2012. Still, the conservative style of political preaching by Southern Baptists is a venerable tradition with national influence, from J. Frank Norris, the pastor of First Baptist Church of Fort Worth who boldly backed the GOP in 1928, to Robert Jeffress, the Trump-praising pastor of First Baptist Church of Dallas in 2016. Conservative Baptists have influenced the modern Christian Right from the 1920s to the present, and prohibition activism established the norm for political preaching in the Bible Belt.

After prohibition's demise, Catholics enjoyed more widespread acceptance in the South. The Catholic hierarchy maintained its relative aloofness on most political issues, yet a few partisans showed willingness to work alongside similarly aligned Protestants. Even Frank Norris, who in 1928 crusaded against Al Smith, in 1945 embraced the Catholic Church as an ally against communism (the greater threat) and even enjoyed a brief audience with Pope Pius XII in 1947.[14]

The election of John Fitzgerald Kennedy in 1960 ended the taboo of Catholics in the White House. Even Texans repented of their anti-Catholic presidential streak; this time, they voted for the Catholic Democrat (then with a Texan running mate) against the reliably Protestant Republican.[15] By the late 1970s, evangelical Protestants joined conservative Catholics against abortion, gay rights, and evolving moral norms. Liberal Protestants, meanwhile, rallied with liberal Catholics to seek social justice for the poor and exploited at home and abroad. Few noticed in 2010 that the Supreme Court had six Catholics but no Protestants, and fewer noticed in 2012 when both Republicans and Democrats chose Catholics for their vice-presidential nominees. When Joe Biden became the second Catholic president after JFK, his Catholic faith attracted scant media attention.[16] Catholics in politics have become a commonplace.

Episcopalians, once the guardians of traditional Protestantism and outspoken opponents of prohibition, had by the 1970s become famous for progressive theology in everything from gender equality to gay rights. In 2003, the Episcopal Church consecrated Gene Robinson, their first bishop openly in a same-sex relationship, and thereafter touted itself as the vanguard of progressive inclusivity in American religion. Like the United Methodist Church and other mainline denominations, the Episcopal Church has declined in numbers and influence since the 1960s, but what the denomination lacked in numbers it has always made up for in dynamic cultural and political figures in the South: in the 1880s, it had Jefferson Davis; in the 1980s, it had the elder George H. W. Bush. Perhaps Episcopalians' greatest constant is their continued fondness for wine both in and beyond the Eucharist.

Religious arguments over prohibition also exposed the divide between pulpit and pew that merits further attention from historians, especially on culture-war issues. Church history that focuses on sermons, denominational minutes, and other official sources captures a few voices, yet leaves out lay figures who wielded theological arguments and Bible verses with equal if not greater alacrity and influence. The wet rhetoric of lay white Methodists like Texas governor Oscar Branch Colquitt and Florida judge Henry Long carried at least as much weight among laypeople as did the pronouncements of Methodist bishops, who were probably less recognizable than the governor, even among Methodists. Other extra-denominational sources such as secular newspapers with religious arguments, pamphlets like Bob Shuler's 1911 diatribe against *Local Booze Government,* and popular books are not only fair game for historians examining religion and culture, but essential sources for uncovering the views of everyday people who may have been regular church attendees but also dissented from their church's official teachings. The divide between most clergy and most lay voters on the prohibition issue was evident in Black and white churches alike. Sources that have been underutilized in traditional church history deserve further scrutiny, particularly where denominational unanimity has been assumed.

The tendency of evangelicals to oppose vehemently a practice that the Bible did not explicitly condemn—such as drinking alcohol—continued into the twenty-first century. While alcohol became increasingly accepted (except in communion), other taboos arose, from the use of other drugs to abortion—which concerned most evangelicals only since the late 1970s. On culture-war issues like sexuality, as with prohibition before, Christians of every persuasion have used historical and biblical arguments to invoke God on their side.[17] Religion now as then plays on both sides of the culture wars.

Takeaways

Religiously inflected culture wars can dramatically affect and be affected by issues such as race and gender. Women provided the moral core of the dry movement yet also tipped the nation's moral balance against prohibition. Black voters tried to serve their race by making their votes indispensable to white allies but divided their support between wets and drys. Brewers' myopic self-interest led them to defy white-supremacist norms and work with thousands of Black voters to decide statewide prohibition elections. The most decisive impacts by thousands of Black voters on statewide prohibition elections in the South came years into Jim Crow's enactment, yet the very fact of their newfound significance contributed to a backlash that removed what few voting rights most of them still had.

The relationship between religion and politics in the South is ever-shifting, and how one frames the starting and ending point of a study there greatly shapes one's conclusions. Starting consideration of prohibition in the South before the 1880s reveals that anti-alcohol views broke profoundly with Christian tradition, and even Baptists used to have a remarkable range of views on communion wine. Comparing prohibition in the 1880s with the 1910s reveals how white drys eagerly sought Black votes before trying to purge them with Jim Crow laws. This shift in white attitudes explains why John Rayner, an African American pastor who masterminded the get-out-the-vote effort for Black voters across Texas for drys in 1887, reversed course two decades later. By 1912, he claimed that he and thousands of other Black voters saved the state from prohibitionists. Also, ending a study of religion and prohibition in the 1930s rather than 1920 reveals that the power of political preaching in the region has not enjoyed a constant upward trajectory since prohibition, but ebbs and flows according to circumstances.

Religion, race, and politics in the South was then, as now, full of apparent contradictions. While white evangelicals normalized political preaching, so too did their wet opponents, be they Black Baptists, Episcopal bishops, or Catholic laymen. Even within white evangelical churches, lay people could use the Bible just as ably—if not more so—against prohibition as for it, and unanimity could never be taken for granted. Religious dry organizations such as the WCTU and ASL have given the impression that the church served on only one side of the prohibition battle; a closer examination of the evidence reveals that religious ideas, leaders, and practices served on both sides. And the same arguments about liberty that animated wets in the 1880s, including Jefferson Davis, resurrected in the 1930s. When examining apparently simplistic issues, such as the relationship between Christianity and prohibition in the South, looking for complexity and diversity of views can yield a fruitful harvest.

Also, culture-war issues like prohibition have repercussions on issues as diverse as race, politics, gender, and religion well after the original debates have faded into obscurity. Even for supposedly long-dead dinosaurs like prohibition and Jim Crow, the story is never over. A seemingly victorious or vanquished movement can always evolve, make new allies or enemies, adapt to changing circumstances, and come back with a bang or fade out with a whimper.

Further, the roles of racial minorities in subfields of history must be reexamined. When I began this study, I believed—as most scholars did—that African Americans played no major part in prohibition contests. As I investigated, however, the sources showed that Black voters played crucial roles in forestalling statewide prohibition throughout the South much later than scholars had believed, even during Jim Crow. Furthermore, sources attesting to the significance of African Americans were not buried in inaccessible archives; much of the evidence rested in freely available and text-searchable documents on the Internet. The only thing most of these discoveries required was a different lens through which to look for sources and interpret them.

Even on the specific confluence of race, religion, and prohibition in the South from 1885 to 1935, this book is a beginning rather than an end to the story. Religion in the past as well as the present can always play on both sides of culture wars, and careful readings may detect significant religious threads in a side or debate previously seen as primarily secular. More attention to relatively quietist Christian groups such as Catholics, Episcopalians, and Lutherans may reveal profound impacts on American politics that have been understudied because the links between faith and policy have been muted or subtle. Careful attention to surprising exceptions may change views on larger trends, such as exactly when and why African Americans ceased large-scale voting in the Jim Crow South. The true depths of southern prohibition's connections to Jim Crow merit far more exploration—and challenge—by other historians. More Black Americans in the thick of prohibition contests deserve further examination, particularly in the Arkansas contest of 1912. The links between the decline of Black voting and the rise of white women's voting in the South merit far more study, as does the common cause between women and racial minorities to overturn poll taxes later in the twentieth century. While it is now a truism that Black Lives Matter, more African Americans' past contributions await (re)discovery by historians. On this and other related matters, many revelations remain hiding in plain sight until we have the eyes of faith to see them.

Notes

Preface

1. Just to name a few: James H. Timberlake, *Prohibition and the Progressive Movement, 1900–1920* (Cambridge, MA: Harvard University Press, 1963); Norman H. Clark, *Deliver Us from Evil: An Interpretation of American Prohibition* (New York: W. W. Norton and Co., 1976); Gaines M. Foster, *Moral Reconstruction: Christian Lobbyists and the Federal Legislation of Morality, 1865–1920* (Chapel Hill: University of North Carolina Press, 2002); and H. Paul Thompson Jr., *"A Most Stirring and Significant Episode": Religion and the Rise and Fall of Prohibition in Black Atlanta, 1865–1887* (DeKalb: Northern Illinois University Press, 2013).

2. One fruitful approach to non-Christian wet religion is Marni Davis, *Jews and Booze: Becoming American in the Age of Prohibition* (New York: New York University Press, 2012).

Introduction

1. John Rayner to Otto Wahrmund, July 9, 1912, in B. F. Looney, ed., *The Brewers and Texas Politics* (San Antonio, TX: Passing Show Printing Co., 1916), vol. 1: 68–69. Rayner's full name given by Gregg Cantrell, *Kenneth and John B. Rayner and the Limits of Southern Dissent* (Urbana: University of Illinois Press, 1993), 178; see also Jack Abramowitz, "John B. Rayner—A Grass-Roots Leader," *Journal of Negro History* 36, no. 2 (April 1951): 160–93; Gregg Cantrell, "RAYNER, JOHN BAPTIS," *Handbook of Texas Online* (Texas State Historical Association), tshaonline.org/handbook/online/articles/fra52 (accessed June 15, 2010). Rayner was "the most prominent" African American Populist according to Charles Postel, *The Populist Vision* (New York: Oxford University Press, 2007), 189. Rayner started working for the brewers in 1905, according to

Gregg Cantrell, *Feeding the Wolf: John B. Rayner and the Politics of Race, 1850–1918* (Wheeling, IL: Harlan Davidson, 2001), 104; Looney described Rayner as "a negro preacher" who had "been in the employment of the breweries for many years," *Brewers and Texas Politics* 2: 602. The "earlier letter" is from 1908, wherein Rayner had promised to mobilize "at least 50,000 negroes in Texas to pay their poll tax in time" for an upcoming prohibition election; Rayner to Zane Cetti, November 14, 1908, in Looney, ed., *Brewers and Texas Politics* 1: 263; two weeks later an internal brewers' report admitted, "we need him in three counties holding elections this next year" (Looney, ed., *Brewers and Texas Politics* 1: 264).

    2. Looney, ed., *Brewers and Texas Politics* 1: 69.

    3. Kristin Kobes Du Mez, *Jesus and John Wayne: How White Evangelicals Corrupted a Faith and Fractured a Nation* (New York: Liveright, 2020), 10.

    4. Robert A. Orsi, *The Madonna of 115th Street: Faith and Community in Italian Harlem* (New Haven, CT: Yale University Press, 1988); David D. Hall, *Worlds of Wonder, Days of Judgment: Popular Religious Belief in Early New England* (New York: Knopf, 1989); Leigh Eric Schmidt, *Consumer Rites: The Buying & Selling of American Holidays* (Princeton, NJ: Princeton University Press, 1995); R. Marie Griffith, *God's Daughters: Evangelical Women and the Power of Submission* (Berkeley: University of California Press, 1997); David D. Hall, ed., *Lived Religion in America: Toward a History of Practice* (Princeton, NJ: Princeton University Press, 1997). Even Pope Emeritus Benedict XVI (when he was merely Joseph Ratzinger) sounded a somewhat similar note in 2004, observing that the Christian faith cannot be expressed outside of a cultural context. Joseph Ratzinger, *Truth and Tolerance: Christian Belief and World Religions* (San Francisco: Saint Ignatius Press, 2004), 85–105.

    5. This mirrors Aaron Griffith's comment about "the political import of evangelical soul saving, often overlooked by scholars who characterize the movement's conversionism as neglectful of issues and social change" but which "influenced their politics of crime and punishment." *God's Law and Order: The Politics of Punishment in Evangelical America* (Cambridge, MA: Harvard University Press, 2020), 5.

    6. Ann-Marie E. Szymanski, *Pathways to Prohibition: Radicals, Moderates, and Social Movement Outcomes* (Durham, NC: Duke University Press, 2003), 16.

    7. Howard Rabinowitz, *Race Relations in the Urban South, 1865–1890* (New York: Oxford University Press, 1978), 314–18; Richard F. Hamm, *Murder, Honor, and Law: Four Virginia Homicides from Reconstruction to the Great Depression* (Charlottesville: University of Virginia Press, 1995), 58–96.

    8. Joe L. Coker, *Liquor in the Land of the Lost Cause: Southern White Evangelicals and the Prohibition Movement* (Lexington: University of Kentucky Press, 2007), 123–230.

    9. Lisa McGirr, *The War on Alcohol: Prohibition and the Rise of the American State* (New York: Norton, 2015). Howard Rabinowitz and Richard Hamm contend that African Americans' tendency to vote against prohibition, especially in close elections, was a major argument for their disfranchisement, which in turn helped prohibition succeed in the South. Rabinowitz, *Race Relations in the Urban South*, 314–18; Hamm, *Murder, Honor, and Law*, 58–96. Ann-Marie Szymanski sums up the scholarly consensus: "disfranchisement of blacks principally enhanced the opportunities for dry success by eliminating one of the leading rationales for Democratic unity in the South." Szymanski also claims that African Americans' impact on prohibition elections in the South is difficult to verify since drys lost statewide referenda in Alabama (1909), Florida (1910), Texas (1911), and Arkansas (1912) "despite the diminished voting power of southern blacks"

(*Pathways to Prohibition,* 16; the four referenda mentioned by Szymanski are listed on p. 225n73). However, that same evidence could also suggest that wets won in those states precisely because African Americans continued to vote despite restrictive voting laws. Even H. Paul Thompson in *"A Most Stirring and Significant Episode,"* the most extensive treatment of Black voters' impact on prohibition elections, stops his narrative in the 1880s and misses early Jim Crow.

10. Szymanski, *Pathways to Prohibition,* 16.

11. Griffith, *God's Law and Order,* 4.

12. Michelle Alexander, *The New Jim Crow: Mass Incarceration in the Age of Colorblindness* (rev. ed., New York: New Press, 2012); McGirr, *War on Alcohol,* 71, 73–74, 80–89, 97–100; Patrick O'Daniel, *Crusaders, Gangsters, and Whiskey: Prohibition in Memphis* (Jackson: University Press of Mississippi, 2018), 6, 13–16, 34, 38–41, 45, 47, 86, 140, 171, 218, 241–42, esp. 93–95.

13. Barry Hankins, *Jesus and Gin: Evangelicalism, the Roaring Twenties, and Today's Culture Wars* (New York: Palgrave Macmillan, 2010), 170; see also 21–40.

14. Those noting prohibition's progressivism include Timberlake, *Prohibition and the Progressive Movement;* Clark, *Deliver Us from Evil;* McGirr, *War on Alcohol;* Lewis L. Gould, *Progressives and Prohibitionists: Texas Democrats in the Wilson Era* (Austin: University of Texas Press, 1973). One source covering the theological development of drys is Thompson, *"A Most Stirring and Significant Episode";* however, Thompson focuses on the growth of prohibitionism through the evangelical reform nexus.

15. Coker, *Liquor in the Land of the Lost Cause,* 37–122; Joseph Locke, *Making the Bible Belt: Texas Prohibitionists and the Politicization of Southern Religion* (New York: Oxford University Press, 2017); Robert Wuthnow, *Rough Country: How Texas Became America's Most Powerful Bible-Belt State* (Princeton, NJ: Princeton University Press, 2014).

16. Robert P. Shuler, *The New Issue, Or, Local Booze Government: Being a Collection of Articles on "Prohibition"* (Temple, TX: Temple Printing and Office Appliance Co., 1911), "The Antis and the Preachers" section.

17. McGirr, *War on Alcohol,* xx.

18. Peter H. Odegard, *Pressure Politics: The Story of the Anti-Saloon League* (New York: Octagon Books, 1966), 18; Mark A. Noll, *A History of Christianity in the United States and Canada* (Grand Rapids, MI: William B. Eerdmans, 1992), 135; Jeanette Miller Schmidt, *Souls or the Social Order: The Two-Party System in American Protestantism* (Brooklyn, NY: Carlson Pub., 1991), 199.

19. Darren Dochuk, *Bible Belt to Sunbelt: Plain-Folk Religion, Grassroots Politics, and the Rise of Evangelical Conservatism* (New York: Norton, 2010); Kevin M. Kruse, *One Nation Under God: How Corporate America Invented Christian America* (New York: Basic, 2015); David L. Chappell, *A Stone of Hope: Prophetic Religion and the Death of Jim Crow* (Chapel Hill: University of North Carolina Press, 2004); Charles Marsh, *God's Long Summer: Stories of Faith and Civil Rights* (Princeton, NJ: Princeton University Press, 1997).

20. Originally, "the South" meant any of the states south of the Mason-Dixon line that separated Pennsylvania and Maryland, which by the 1820s was also a euphemism for states with racial chattel slavery. Then, during the Civil War, it particularly referred to the eleven Confederate states, even though five southern slave states—Missouri, Kentucky, West Virginia, Maryland, and Delaware—fought for the Union. After the abolition of racial chattel slavery and the end of Reconstruction, the emergence of an overwhelmingly Democratic (and therefore white-supremacist) "Solid South" resuscitated a broader definition of the South. Some

definitions expanded the region to include Oklahoma due to its geographical and cultural similarities with neighboring Texas and Arkansas. Indeed, the 2010 US Census definition of the South included Oklahoma, West Virginia, Maryland, Delaware, and all former states in the broader "South" except for Missouri. US Census Bureau, "2010 Census Regions and Divisions of the United States," revised August 20, 2018.

21. The Eighteenth Amendment was ratified by the thirty-sixth state (then three-quarters of the forty-eight states) on January 16, 1919, but Texas did not vote for prohibition in their state constitution until May 1919. Robert Plocheck, "Prohibition Elections in Texas," *Texas Almanac,* Texas State Historical Association; K. Austin Kerr, "ANTI-SALOON LEAGUE OF TEXAS," *Handbook of Texas Online,* www.tshaonline.org/handbook/online/articles/vaa02 (accessed November 28, 2012); Ernest H. Cherrington, ed., *Anti-Saloon League Year Book: An Encyclopedia of Facts and Figures Dealing with the Liquor Traffic and the Temperance Reform* (Westerville, OH: American Issue Press, 1918), 207.

22. Robert A. Slayton, *Empire Statesman: The Rise and Redemption of Al Smith* (New York: Free Press, 2001), 237–328; Christopher M. Finan, *Alfred E. Smith: The Happy Warrior* (New York: Hill and Wang, 2002), 189–230; Kerr, "ANTI-SALOON LEAGUE OF TEXAS"; Cherrington, ed., *Anti-Saloon League Year Book* (1918), 207.

Part I. Bourbon Rule: The South before Prohibition

1. While this book usually employs a limited definition of "South" as formerly Confederate states, Kentucky certainly counted as southern during the antebellum period, as it had been a slave state. In any case, the land was technically part of Virginia when bourbon was first brewed there in the 1780s, as Kentucky did not become a state until 1792.

2. Quote from Sara Havens, "Best Driving Vacations: Kentucky Bourbon Trail," *Columbus Monthly* (March 19, 2019). Flaget M. Nally, "Bourbon," in *The Kentucky Encyclopedia,* ed. John E. Kleber (Lexington: University Press of Kentucky, 1992), 103–4; "Bourbon Whiskey," *The New Encyclopedia of Southern Culture,* vol. 7: *Foodways,* ed. John T. Edge (Chapel Hill: University of North Carolina Press, 2007), 128; Henry G. Crowgey, *Kentucky Bourbon: The Early Years of Whiskey-Making* (Lexington: University of Kentucky Press, 1971), chap. 7. Michael R. Veach claims the "bourbon" name emerged from Bourbon Street in New Orleans, where much of the product was shipped and sold, though this is speculative. Most historians prefer the simplest explanation: bourbon was named after where it was produced. Veach, *Kentucky Bourbon Whiskey: An American Heritage* (Lexington: University of Kentucky Press, 2013), chap. 2; Laura Kiniry, "Where Bourbon Really Got Its Name and More Tips on America's Native Spirit," *Smithsonian Magazine* (June 13, 2013), www.smithsonianmag.com/arts-culture /where-bourbon-really-got-its-name-and-more-tips-on-americas-native-spirit-145879/?no-ist.

1. Old-Time Religion: Christian Tradition against Prohibition

1. Nally, "Bourbon," in *Kentucky Encyclopedia,* ed. Kleber, 103–4; "Bourbon Whiskey," *New Encyclopedia of Southern Culture,* vol. 7: *Foodways,* ed. Edge, 128; Crowgey, *Kentucky Bourbon,* chap. 7.

2. Ira "Jack" Birdwhistell, "Elijah Craig," in *Kentucky Encyclopedia,* ed. Kleber, 238–39; John Taylor, *Baptists on the American Frontier: A History of Ten Baptist Churches,* ed. Chester Raymond Young (3rd ed., Macon, GA: Mercer University Press, 1995), 90.

3. John Erskine, *Prohibition and Christianity: And Other Paradoxes of the American Spirit* (Indianapolis: Bobbs-Merrill Co., 1927), 16–19; Aristotle, *Nicomachean Ethics* 2.7–8, trans. W. D. Ross (Oxford, UK: Clarendon Press, 1925), Internet Classics Archive, *classics.mit.edu/Aristotle /nicomachaen.2.ii.html*; Aquinas, *Summa Theologica* 2.142.1.

4. Clark, *Deliver Us from Evil,* 9. Mark Noll, *One Nation Under God? Christian Faith and Political Action in America* (San Francisco: Harper and Row, 1988), 129.

5. Ernest H. Cherrington, *The Evolution of Prohibition in the United States of America: A Chronological History of the Liquor Problem and the Temperance Reform in the United States* (Westerville, OH: American Issue Press, 1920), 10.

6. Cherrington, *Evolution of Prohibition in the United States,* 11.

7. Cherrington, *Evolution of Prohibition in the United States,* 98.

8. W. J. Rorabaugh, *The Alcohol Republic: An American Tradition* (New York: Oxford University Press, 1979); Noll, *One Nation Under God?* 130–33.

9. Mark A. Noll, *America's God: From Jonathan Edwards to Abraham Lincoln* (New York: Oxford University Press, 2002); Nathan O. Hatch, *The Democratization of American Christianity* (New Haven, CT: Yale University Press, 1989).

10. John A. Andrew, *The Errors of Prohibition: An Argument Delivered in the Representatives' Hall, Boston, April 3, 1867* (Boston: Ticknor and Fields, 1867), 48, 65–66; Erskine, *Prohibition and Christianity,* 32.

11. Terrell's comments were from a speech on a floor of the Texas State Senate in 1879 but republished in *Galveston Daily News,* September 10, 1885; see also *Austin Statesman,* September 22, 1886, and Lewis L. Gould, *Alexander Watkins Terrell: Civil War Soldier, Texas Lawmaker, American Diplomat* (Austin: University of Texas Press, 2004), 75–76, 78, 112. Incredibly, given his comments about the degradation of the Turks, Terrell later became the US ambassador to the Ottoman Empire from 1893 to 1897.

12. This hermeneutic is explained by Mark Noll, *The Civil War as a Theological Crisis* (Chapel Hill: University of North Carolina Press, 2006), esp. 40–50, 157–62. Noll explains an essentially identical approach under a different name, the "Reformed, literal hermeneutic," in his earlier work *America's God,* 367–85.

13. Noll, *Civil War as a Theological Crisis,* 161–62.

14. Quote from Richmond *Religious Herald,* August 18, 1870, 2; see also October 19, 1865. See also Rufus B. Spain, *At Ease in Zion: Social History of Southern Baptists* (1967; rpt. Tuscaloosa: University of Alabama Press: 2003), 177–78.

15. Richmond *Religious Herald,* November 21, 1872, 1; October 27, 1881; November and December 1882; March 18, 1886, 2; April 19, 1888, 1. Raleigh, NC, *Biblical Recorder,* September 13, 1876, 2. Louisville *Western Recorder,* February 14, 1884, 3. Meridian, MS, *Baptist Record,* April 29, 1886, 6. See also Spain, *At Ease in Zion,* 178–79.

16. A scuppernong is a kind of grape. Atlanta *Christian Index,* May 24, 1866, 88; December 6, 1883, 14. See also Spain, *At Ease in Zion,* 179–80.

17. First quote, Richmond *Religious Herald,* July 3, 1879, 2; second quote, November 21, 1872, 1. See also Spain, *At Ease in Zion,* 180–81.

18. Quotes from Richmond *Religious Herald,* April 26, 1888, 1; Broadus in April 8, 1875, 1.

19. Florida Baptist Convention, *Minutes, 1895,* 69. See also Spain, *At Ease in Zion,* 178.

20. British 1795 position in Wesleyan Methodist Association, *The Constitution of Wesleyan Methodism as settled in 1795 and 1797* (London: Egerton Smith and Co., 1835), 10. Eighteenth-century American position in *A Reprint of the Discipline of the Methodist Episcopal Church for 1787* (Cleveland: W. A. Ingham, 1900), 40. Southern Methodist position in *The Doctrines and Disciplines of the Methodist Episcopal Church, South* (Nashville: Southern Methodist Publishing House, 1878), quote 29; details of Wesley's involvement, 28. Northern Methodist position in *Doctrines and Disciplines of the Methodist Episcopal Church* (New York: Carlton & Porter, 1864), 30.

21. Thompson, *"A Most Stirring and Significant Episode,"* 35.

22. The 1886 version of the MECS *Doctrines and Disciplines* added a new chapter addressing "the extirpation of the great evil of intemperance," which called on all members to "abstain from the manufacture or sale of intoxicating liquors to be used as a beverage" and threatened discipline against offenders "as in cases of immorality." *The Doctrines and Disciplines of the Methodist Episcopal Church, South* (Nashville: Southern Methodist Publishing House, 1886), 123–24. Compare with *Doctrines and Disciplines of the Methodist Episcopal Church, South* (1878), 28–39.

23. Woman's Christian Temperance Union of Texas, *Twenty-Seventh Annual Report* (Marlin, TX: n.p., 1909), 2.

24. WCTU of Texas, *Twenty-Seventh Annual Report,* 80–94.

25. "Flower Mission Day" commemorated the "birthday of Jennie Cassiday, National Superintendent of Flower Mission work," by "taking flowers, with text cards, to prisons, jails, almshouses and to the poor and sick everywhere," certainly noble work. WCTU of Texas, *Twenty-Seventh Annual Report,* 4.

26. Jean H. Baker, *Sisters: The Lives of America's Suffragists* (New York: Hill and Wang, 2005), 164. For the heterodoxy of Stanton and Anthony, see Kathi Kern, *Mrs. Stanton's Bible* (Ithaca, NY: Cornell University Press, 2001).

27. Daniel Okrent, *Last Call: The Rise and Fall of Prohibition* (New York: Scribner, 2010), 37.

28. WCTU of Texas, *Twenty-Seventh Annual Report,* 32.

29. WCTU of Texas, *Twenty-Seventh Annual Report,* 34–35.

30. WCTU of Texas, *Twenty-Seventh Annual Report,* 3.

31. Edward H. Jewett, *The Two-Wine Theory Discussed by Two Hundred and Eighty-Six Clergymen on the Basis of "Communion Wine"* (New York: E. Steiger & Co., 1888), 126–27, *"unfermented"* emphasis his.

32. Emerson, *A Lay Thesis,* 5–6.

33. Emerson, *A Lay Thesis,* 7.

34. Emerson, *A Lay Thesis,* 52.

35. Emerson, *A Lay Thesis,* 52.

36. Emerson, *A Lay Thesis,* 54.

37. Emerson, *A Lay Thesis,* 7. He states it was in "St. John xi. 9," but the correct reference is to John 2:9, in which Christ turns water into wine at a wedding in Cana; the reference to 11:9 was undoubtedly a typo, especially since he later references Christ turning water to wine in "John ii," on page 52.

38. Emerson, *A Lay Thesis,* 22–26. The passages in question are Matthew 9:14–17, Mark 2:21–22, and Luke 5:33–39. While most translations now have "wineskins," "bottles" is used in the KJV, the most popular version of the Bible in the early twentieth century.

39. Emerson, *A Lay Thesis,* 52.

40. Spain, *At Ease in Zion,* 177–82.

41. Kern, *Mrs. Stanton's Bible.*

42. See Amos D. McCoy, "The Effects of Intemperance on Woman," *A Series of Temperance Sermons, Delivered in the City Hall, Lowell, by the Several Clergymen of the City* (Lowell, MA: Leonard Huntress, E. A. Rice & Co., 1841), 214, and Rev. James B. Dunn, ed., *Moody's Talks on Temperance with Anecdotes and Incidents in Connection with the Tabernacle Temperance Work in Boston* (New York: National Temperance Society and Publication House, 1877), 122.

43. Ferdinand Cowle Iglehart, *King Alcohol Dethroned* (Westerville, OH: American Issue Publishing Co., 1919), vii–viii.

44. Charles Stelzle, *Why Prohibition!* (New York: George H. Doran Co., 1918), 85.

45. Quote from the standard order of worship in that church for most of the nineteenth century: Episcopal Church, *Book of Common Prayer* (New York: Isaiah Thomas and E. T. Andrews, 1789), 58–61. Lawrence L. Brown, "Protestant Episcopal Church," June 15, 2010, tshaonline.org /handbook/online/articles/iep01.

46. Matthew 26:20–30; Mark 14:12–26; Luke 22:7–22.

47. The Council of Trent, Sess. XXII, chap. vi. The Catechism from the Council of Trent, pt. II, c. iv, n. 58. See also Thomas Scannell, "Frequent Communion," *Catholic Encyclopedia,* vol. 6 (New York: Robert Appleton Co., 1909); and Kevin Knight, *New Advent,* "Frequent Communion."

48. Karen B. Westerfield Tucker, *American Methodist Worship* (New York: Oxford University Press, 2001), 151.

49. Jennifer Lynn Woodruff Tait, *The Poisoned Chalice: Eucharistic Grape Juice and Common-Sense Realism in Victorian Methodism* (Tuscaloosa: University of Alabama Press, 2011), 3.

50. Florida Baptist Convention, *Minutes, 1895,* 69. See also Spain, *At Ease in Zion,* 178.

51. First quote, Atlanta *Christian Index,* October 13, 1887, 1; second quote, Selma *Alabama Baptist,* April 2, 1885, 1. See also Spain, *At Ease in Zion,* 181.

52. Emerson, *A Lay Thesis,* 5–6.

53. For examples of the "two-wine" thesis, see the Columbia, SC, *Working Christian,* April 12, 1877, 3; Meridian, MS, *Baptist Record,* September 18, 1884, 1; Selma *Alabama Baptist,* February 19, 1885, 1. For more on the "liberal" position, see Richmond *Religious Herald,* April 8, 1875, 1; *Alabama Baptist,* April 2, 1885, 1; *Baptist Record,* July 9, 1885; and Memphis *Baptist,* May 19, 1888, 8. See also Spain, *At Ease in Zion,* 181.

54. Spain, *At Ease in Zion,* 181–82.

55. *Twenty-Eighth Annual Session of the National Baptist Convention, Eighth Annual Assembly of the Woman's Convention, Auxiliary to the National Baptist Convention, September 16–21, 1908,* 308. *Twenty-Ninth Annual Session of the National Baptist Convention,* 317.

56. Joseph C. Gibbs, *History of the Catholic Total Abstinence Union of America* (Philadelphia: Penn Printing House, 1907), 28, 19.

57. Erskine, *Prohibition and Christianity,* 27; cf. 24–27.

58. Erskine, *Prohibition and Christianity,* 15.

59. Erskine, *Prohibition and Christianity,* 15. Cf. Matthew 26:26, Mark 14:22, and Luke 24:30.

60. Erskine, *Prohibition and Christianity,* 15.

61. Erskine, *Prohibition and Christianity,* 15. For Erskine, "faith in Christ, the vital use of the sacrament, must have been abandoned before prohibition could be supported" (*Prohibition and Christianity,* 16).

62. Erskine, *Prohibition and Christianity,* 22–24.

63. Erskine, *Prohibition and Christianity,* 12.

64. Editorial, *Austin Daily Statesman,* August 16, 1885, cited in H. William Schneider, "Dr. James B. Cranfill's Prohibition Activities, 1882–1887," MA thesis, Baylor University, 1971, 40–41. See also Locke, *Making the Bible Belt,* 1.

65. Editorial, *Austin Daily Statesman,* August 16, 1885; James D. Ivy, *No Saloon in the Valley: The Southern Strategy of Texas Prohibitionists in the 1880s,* Waco, TX: Baylor University Press, 2003), 98–99.

66. B. H. Carroll, *Prohibition: Dr. B. H. Carroll's Reply to Senator Coke* (Austin, TX: J. B. Link, 1885), 2–16, in Schneider, "Dr. James B. Cranfill's Prohibition Activities," 41–42. See also Thomas J. Brian, "The 1887 Prohibition Crusade in Texas," MA thesis, Baylor University, 1972, 18.

67. Coker, *Liquor in the Land of the Lost Cause.*

68. Locke, *Making the Bible Belt.*

69. Wuthnow, *Rough Country,* 77, 103–10.

70. The paper regards him as an Episcopalian because he was likely raised as one, though later in life he attended Baptist churches. John W. Payne Jr., "COKE, RICHARD," *Handbook of Texas Online,* www.tshaonline.org/handbook/online/articles/fc015 (accessed December 13, 2013).

71. *Dallas Morning News,* May 8, 1887, 6, in Brian, "1887 Prohibition Crusade in Texas," 25.

72. Charles W. Deweese, *Baptist Church Covenants* (Nashville: Broadman Press, 1990), 71. That covenant, a modification of the 1833 New Hampshire Covenant, was still very popular with Baptist churches as of the 1990s, though some have excised the phrase about abstaining from alcoholic beverages (65–76). Proving beyond a doubt that this is the covenant to which Rayner refers, the 1909 Temperance Committee report quotes a "covenant" with the exact same wording, though the order is slightly changed by swapping the words "use" and "sale." *Twenty-Ninth Annual Session of the National Baptist Convention,* 192. Thanks to Bill Summers and Taffey Hall at the Southern Baptist Historical Library and Archives for bringing my attention to their resources on church covenants.

73. Gibbs, *History of the Catholic Total Abstinence Union,* 20. Cf. Sister Joan Bland, *Hibernian Crusade: The Story of the Catholic Total Abstinence Union of America* (Washington, DC: Catholic University of America Press, 1951), 8.

74. Gibbs, *History of the Catholic Total Abstinence Union,* 16.

75. *History of the Catholic Total Abstinence Union,* 25, cf. 27.

76. Bland, *Hibernian Crusade,* 8.

77. Gibbs, *History of the Catholic Total Abstinence Union,* 20. See also Bland, *Hibernian Crusade,* 4, 8, 238; E. Dana Durand, ed., *Religious Bodies, 1906: Part 1—Summary and General Tables* (Washington, DC: US Bureau of the Census, 1910), 272.

78. Larry Jerome Watson, "Evangelical Protestants and the Prohibition Movement in Texas, 1887–1919," PhD diss., Texas A&M University, 1993, 145–46. Locke, *Making the Bible Belt.*

79. Baptist State Convention of Texas, *Minutes of the Thirty-eighth Annual Session* (Dallas, 1875), 32, in Brian, "1887 Prohibition Crusade in Texas," 47.

80. Both quotes in J. M. Carroll, *A History of Texas Baptists, Comprising a Detailed Account of their Activities, Their Progress and their Achievements* (Dallas: Baptist Standard Book Pub. Co., 1923), 663n1.

81. Hunter Dickinson Farish, *The Circuit Rider Dismounts: A Social History of Southern Methodism 1865–1900* (Richmond, VA: Dietz Press, 1938), 317–24; see also 5, 98, 367, and 398.

82. *Prairie Blade* quote from *Baptist Standard* (Austin, TX), June 2, 1887, 1. See also Brian, "1887 Prohibition Crusade in Texas," 38.

83. Ray Jefferson, *B. H. Carroll* (Nashville: Sunday School Board Press, 1927), 122; while a hagiographic work, it seems faithful in most details and was written by a man who knew Carroll well and likely heard a report of the event from Carroll himself. See also Brian, "1887 Prohibition Crusade in Texas," 38–40, 45; and Schneider, "Dr. James B. Cranfill's Prohibition Activities," 89–90. For more on Mills, see Alwyn Barr, "MILLS, ROGER QUARLES," *Handbook of Texas Online*, www.tshaonline.org/handbook/online/articles/fmi40 (accessed December 14, 2013).

84. Spain, *At Ease in Zion,* 174–97.

85. Texas Baptist Publishing House, *Proceedings of the First Annual Session of the Baptist General Convention of Texas* (Dallas: Texas Baptist Publishing House, 1886), 9. Thanks to the staff at the Texas Collection Library of Baylor University for providing this and related sources on Baptists in Texas.

86. *Proceedings of the First Annual Session of the Baptist General Convention of Texas,* 10.

87. Quote from Southern Baptist Convention, *Proceedings,* 1896, 45. Spain, *At Ease in Zion,* 184–85. See also Florida Baptist Convention, *Minutes,* 1872, 16; Georgia Baptist Convention, *Minutes,* 1873, 22.

88. Richard F. Hamm, *Shaping the Eighteenth Amendment: Temperance Reform, Legal Culture, and the Polity, 1880–1920* (Chapel Hill: University of North Carolina Press, 1995); Szymanski, *Pathways to Prohibition;* McGirr, *War on Alcohol.*

89. Quote from Thomas R. Pegram, "Temperance Politics and Regional Political Culture: The Anti-Saloon League in Maryland and the South, 1907–1915," *Journal of Southern History* 63 (February 1997): 64. Ann-Marie Szymanski, "Beyond Parochialism: Southern Progressivism, Prohibition, and State-Building," *Journal of Southern History* 69, no. 1 (February 2003): 107–36; see also William A. Link, *The Paradox of Southern Progressivism, 1880–1930* (Chapel Hill: University of North Carolina Press, 1992); George Harrison Gilliam, "Making Virginia Progressive: Courts and Parties, Railroads and Regulators, 1890–1910," *Virginia Magazine of History and Biography* 107 (Spring 1999): 189–222; Paul L. Harvey, "Southern Baptists and the Social Gospel: White Religious Progressivism in the South, 1900–1925," *Fides et Historia* 27 (Summer–Fall 1995), 59–77.

90. Noll, *Civil War as a Theological Crisis,* esp. 40–50, 157–62; and *America's God,* 367–85.

2. "Dark and Peculiar": Race, Gender, and Prohibition in the 1880s South

1. J.B.R. to B. H. Carroll, San Antonio *Daily Express,* July 27, 1887; Cantrell, *Kenneth and John B. Rayner,* 193.

2. For more on Turner, see Paul Harvey, *Through the Storm, through the Night: A History of African American Christianity* (Lanham, MD: Rowman & Littlefield, 2011), 78–83.

3. San Antonio *Daily Express,* July 7, 1887; Cantrell, *Kenneth and John B. Rayner,* 196; 193–98; Cantrell, *Feeding the Wolf,* 27–28.

4. *1740 South Carolina Slave Code, Acts of the South Carolina General Assembly, 1740 #670,* South Carolina Dept. of Archives and History, Columbia, digital.scetv.org/teachingAmerhistory /tTrove/1740slavecode.htm.

5. Cherrington, *Evolution of Prohibition in the United States,* 35.

6. Cherrington, *Evolution of Prohibition in the United States,* 11; cf. 12–15, 20–21, 23–35, 37.

7. Cherrington, *Evolution of Prohibition in the United States,* 35, 37.

8. The American Temperance Society (ATS), founded in New England in 1826, within a year had auxiliaries in Virginia, North Carolina, and various states in the border South, and by 1831, only five states in the Union did not have ATS chapters. Various fraternal orders for temperance sprang up around the nation in the 1840s and 1850s, most notably the Sons of Temperance and the Independent Order of Good Templars. Cherrington, *Evolution of Prohibition in the United States,* quote 98; 93–100.

9. Lee L. Willis, *Southern Prohibition: Race, Reform, and Public Life in Middle Florida, 1821–1920* (Athens: University of Georgia Press, 2011), 3.

10. Eric Russell Lacy, "Tennessee Teetotalism: Social Forces and the Politics or Progressivism," *Tennessee Historical Quarterly* 24 (Fall 1965): 219–20; Grace Leab, "Tennessee Temperance Activities, 1870–1899," *East Tennessee Historical Society's Publications* 21 (1949): 52. ASL historian Cherrington claims Tennessee passed an 1837 law making the sale of liquor a "misdemeanor" (*Evolution of Prohibition in the United States,* 120).

11. Thomas Jefferson Bailey, *Prohibition in Mississippi: or Anti-Liquor Legislation from Territorial Days, with Its Results in the Counties* (Jackson, MS: Hederman Bros., 1917), 21–23; Cherrington, *Evolution of Prohibition in the United States,* 121.

12. Wuthnow, *Rough Country,* 59.

13. Edward McPherson, ed., *The Political History of the United States of America, During the Period of Reconstruction* (Washington, DC: Philp and Solomons, 1871), 32, 35.

14. Thompson, *"A Most Stirring and Significant Episode,"* 1–153.

15. Leab, "Tennessee Temperance Activities," 52–56; Wuthnow, *Rough Country,* 59; Thompson, *"A Most Stirring and Significant Episode,"* 88–90.

16. Leab, "Tennessee Temperance Activities," 53–54; W. Calvin Dickinson, "Temperance," *Tennessee Encyclopedia,* tennesseeencyclopedia.net/entries/temperance/ (updated March 1, 2018); Matthew Downs, "Prohibition in Alabama," *Encyclopedia of Alabama,* www.encyclopedia ofalabama.org/article/h-4126 (September 6, 2019); Wuthnow, *Rough Country,* 59.

17. Foster, *Moral Reconstruction,* 113–30.

18. Wuthnow, *Rough Country,* 88–90, 103–10.

19. The five Congressmen were John Paul, Robert Murphy Mayo, Benjamin Stephen Hooper, Harrison "Harry" Libbey, and Henry Bowen. Nicole Meyers Turner, *Soul Liberty: The Evolution of Black Religious Politics in Postemancipation Virginia* (Chapel Hill: University of North Carolina Press, 2020), 106–43.

20. Alan J. Lefever, *Fighting the Good Fight: The Life and Work of Benajah Harvey Carroll* (Austin, TX: Eakin Press, 1994); Schneider, "Dr. James B. Cranfill's Prohibition Activities," 87–89.

21. Cherrington, *Evolution of Prohibition in the United States,* 168–69.

22. Quote from Baker, *Sisters,* 164. For women in the 1840s, see Philip Neely, "Idella Pemberton, or the Prayer of Faith," in *Series of Temperance Sermons, Delivered in the City Hall, Lowell,* 291–98. For all else, see "A Nation of Drunkards," *Prohibition,* produced by Ken Burns and Lynn Novick, PBS Video.

23. Frances Willard, *Glimpses of Fifty Years: The Autobiography of an American Woman* (Toronto: Rose Publishing Co., 1889), 373–74; see also 378.

24. "Quay for Chairman: Meeting of the Republican National Committee," *Waterbury* CT *Evening Democrat,* July 12, 1888, 1; "THE NON-PARTISAN W.C.T.U.," *Evening Star,* Washington, DC, March 24, 1890, 8; "MRS. J. E. FOSTER DEAD," Edgerton *Wisconsin Tobacco Reporter,* August 19, 1910, 8; "Foster, J. Ellen (1840–1910)," Encyclopedia.com, CENGAGE, www.encyclopedia.com /women/dictionaries-thesauruses-pictures-and-press-releases/foster-j-ellen-1840-1910 (updated August 23, 2020).

25. Salisbury, NC, *Star of Zion,* July 23, 1896, in Glenda Elizabeth Gilmore, *Gender and Jim Crow: Women and the Politics of White Supremacy in North Carolina, 1896–1920* (Chapel Hill: University of North Carolina Press, 1996), 48.

26. Concord, NC, *Temperance Herald,* June 16, 1881, in Gilmore, *Gender and Jim Crow,* 46.

27. Gilmore, *Gender and Jim Crow,* 46–50.

28. Daniel Jay Whitener, *Prohibition in North Carolina, 1715–1945* (Chapel Hill: University of North Carolina Press, 1945), 85; Gilmore, *Gender and Jim Crow,* 50.

29. Gilmore, *Gender and Jim Crow,* 52.

30. Gilmore, *Gender and Jim Crow,* 51–53.

31. McMinnville, TN, *Southern Standard,* September 3, 1887, 4.

32. James Benson Sellers, *The Prohibition Movement in Alabama, 1702 to 1943* (Chapel Hill: University of North Carolina Press, 1943), 53–54. Sellers also claimed that the WCTU had by 1883 "organized unions in every state except North Carolina and Mississippi" (53), yet proof of state WCTUs in North Carolina and Mississippi are given in Gilmore, *Gender and Jim Crow,* 48–50, and Bailey, *Prohibition in Mississippi,* 59–60. Several of the other states are confirmed to have state WCTUs in Lacy, "Tennessee Teetotalism," 220; Wuthnow, *Rough Country,* 59; Lula Barnes Ansley, *History of the Georgia Woman's Christian Temperance Union from Its Organization, 1883–1907* (Columbus, OH: Gilbert Printing Co., 1914), 56. Given these sources, it seems safe to say that every state in the South had at least local WCTUs by 1883.

33. Louis Albert Banks, *Seven Times Around Jericho: A Series of Temperance Revival Discourses* (New York: Funk & Wagnalls Co., 1896), 12.

34. "I use the word *education* in the broadest sense, and mean by it every thing which teaches a man to understand his nature, which developes [*sic*] his tastes, brings into play the moral powers, makes him see the dominion which his reason and conscience are to have over his passions and propensities, which trains in habits of self-control, gives him resources of thought, sentiment and happiness in himself, and unfolds to him the infinite number of subjects of curious inquiry and wonderful interest which are to be found in all parts of God's works." Henry A. Miles, "Causes of Intemperance" in *Series of Temperance Sermons,* 117. Educational books include Benjamin W. Richardson, *The Temperance Lesson Book, a Series of Short Lessons on Alcohol and Its Action on the Body, Designed for Reading in Schools and Families* (New York: National Temperance Society and Publication House, 1880), and Deets Pickett, *Alcohol and the New Age: An Elective Course for Young People* (New York: Methodist Book Concern, 1926).

35. *Minutes of the North Alabama Conference of the Methodist Episcopal Church, South* (1885), 23, cited in Sellers, *The Prohibition Movement in Alabama,* 55

36. Sellers, *The Prohibition Movement in Alabama,* 54–56. Most southern Presbyterians descended from the "Old School" side of a denominational split in the 1840s, and their faith was more old-fashioned even than most of their northern "New School" co-religionists.

37. Sellers, *The Prohibition Movement in Alabama,* 57.

38. "A Nation of Drunkards," *Prohibition*, produced by Burns and Novick.

39. Pickett, *Alcohol and the New Age*, 5.

40. These states were Connecticut, Iowa, Kansas, Maine, Massachusetts, Michigan, Nebraska, New Hampshire, North Carolina, North Dakota, Ohio, Oregon, Pennsylvania, Rhode Island, South Dakota, Tennessee, Texas, Washington, and West Virginia. Thompson, *"A Most Stirring and Significant Episode,"* 283n3.

41. Whitener, *Prohibition in North Carolina*, 73; *Salt Lake Herald*, August 7, 1881), 7; Hillsborough, NC, *County Observer*, May 14, 1881, 2. Cf. Lee Allan Craig, *Josephus Daniels: His Life and Times* (Chapel Hill: University of North Carolina Press, 2013), 56.

42. *Fair Play*, Ste. Genevieve, MO, July 16, 1881, 2.

43. *The Newberry*, SC, *Herald*, August 24, 1881, 2.

44. *Orange County Observer*, Hillsborough, NC, May 14, 1881, 2.

45. *Goldsboro*, NC, *Star*, June 25, 1881, 3.

46. Gilmore, *Gender and Jim Crow*, 46.

47. *Goldsboro*, NC, *Star*, July 9, 1881, 3.

48. *Goldsboro*, NC, *Star*, July 9, 1881, 3. Abbott served in the state house from 1872 to 1874 according to J. D. Lewis, "North Carolina State House of Representatives, 1872-1874," *Carolina*, www.carolana.com/NC/1800s/nc_1800s_house_1872-1874.html (accessed July 24, 2020*).* Abbott's full name from Catherine W. Bishir, "Abbott, Israel Braddock (1843–1887)," *North Carolina Architects and Builders: A Biographical Dictionary* (2009), *ncarchitects.lib.ncsu.edu/people/P000443* (accessed August 29, 2020).

49. Robert Digges Wimberly Connor, ed., *A Manual of North Carolina Issued by the North Carolina Historical Commission for the Use of Members of the General Assembly Session 1913* (Raleigh: E. M. Uzzell and Co., 1913), 1019–20. Incomplete tallies of votes in the *Newberry*, SC, *Herald*, September 7, 1881, 2; *Knoxville*, TN, *Daily Chronicle*, August 21, 1881, 1; "NORTH CAROLINA'S ELECTION," *New York Times*, August 11, 1881, 1.

50. Francis A. Walker and Chas. W. Seaton, *1880 Census: Volume 1, Statistics of the Population of the United States* (Washington, DC: US Dept. of the Interior, Census Office, 1883), 405.

51. *County Paper*, Oregon, MO, August 26, 1881, 4; "THE NORTH CAROLINA ELECTION," *New York Times*, August 5, 1881, 1.

52. Whitener, *Prohibition in North Carolina*, 50.

53. As reported in "NEWS ITEMS," Sumter, SC, *Watchman and Southron*, August 16, 1881, 1.

54. Gilmore, *Gender and Jim Crow*, 46; Whitener, *Prohibition in North Carolina*, 61–80.

55. *Orangeburg*, SC, *Times*, August 11, 1881, 2.

56. Thompson, *"A Most Stirring and Significant Episode,"* 183.

57. Thompson, *"A Most Stirring and Significant Episode,"* 187.

58. Stephen A. West, "'A Hot Municipal Contest': Prohibition and Black Politics in Greenville, South Carolina, after Reconstruction," *Journal of the Gilded Age and Progressive Era* 11 (October 2012): 519–51.

59. Thompson, *"A Most Stirring and Significant Episode,"* 188–240.

60. Carroll, *History of Texas*, 663n1. The note concludes with "-EDITOR," which refers to J. B. Cranfill. J. A. Reynolds, "CARROLL, BENAJAH HARVEY," *Handbook of Texas Online*, www.tshaonline.org/handbook/online/articles/fca63 (accessed December 13, 2013).

61. J.B.R. to B. H. Carroll, San Antonio *Express,* July 27, 1887; Cantrell, *Kenneth and John B. Rayner,* 193.

62. For more on Turner, see Stephen Ward Angell, *Bishop Henry McNeal Turner and African American Religion in the South* (Knoxville: University of Tennessee Press, 1992); and Andre E. Johnson, *The Forgotten Prophet: Bishop Henry McNeal Turner and the African American Prophetic Tradition* (Lanham, MD: Lexington Books, 2012).

63. Editorial, Waco *Daily Examiner,* May 27, 1887.

64. Ivy, *No Saloon in the Valley,* 89–101.

65. *Dallas Morning News,* July 27, 1887, 1. See also Brian, "1887 Prohibition Crusade in Texas," 62.

66. Ivy, *No Saloon in the Valley,* 98–99; Brian, "1887 Prohibition Crusade in Texas," 62–63. For more on Lost Cause religion, see Charles Reagan Wilson, *Baptized in Blood: The Religion of the Lost Cause, 1865–1920* (1980; Athens: University of Georgia Press, 2009), and Gaines M. Foster, *Ghosts of the Confederacy: Defeat, the Lost Cause, and the Emergence of the New South, 1865 to 1913* (New York: Oxford University Press, 1987).

67. Ivy, *No Saloon in the Valley,* 98–99.

68. San Antonio *Daily Express,* July 7, 1887; see also Waco *True Blue,* July 1, 1887; Waco *Daily Examiner,* June 18, 1887; Cantrell, *Kenneth and John B. Rayner,* 195.

69. Waco *Daily Examiner,* July 2, 1887; see also Cantrell, *Kenneth and John B. Rayner,* 195.

70. Cantrell, *Kenneth and John B. Rayner,* 193–98; Cantrell, *Feeding the Wolf,* 27–28; Waco *Daily Examiner,* June 18 and July 2, 1887; Ivy, *No Saloon in the Valley,* 45–51.

71. Quotes respectively from Waco *Daily Examiner,* May 31, 1887, August 4, 1887; and Victoria *Advocate,* July 9, 1887; all in Gregg Cantrell, "'Dark Tactics': Black Politics in the 1887 Texas Prohibition Campaign," *Journal of American Studies* 25 (April 1991): 89.

72. Ronald A. Walter, "Robert R. Church Sr.," *Tennessee Encyclopedia,* tennesseeencyclopedia.net/entries/robert-r-church-sr/ (updated March 1, 2018); Elwood Watson, "Robert Reed Church, Sr. (1839–1912)," *Black Past,* November 19, 2007, www.blackpast.org/african-american-history/robert-reed-church-sr-1839-1912/ (accessed May 7, 2020); O'Daniel, *Crusaders, Gangsters, and Whiskey,* 13; Darius J. Young, *Robert R. Church Jr. and the African American Political Struggle* (Gainesville: University of Florida Press, 2019), 9; see also Preston Lauterback, *Beale Street Dynasty: Sex, Song, and the Struggle for the Soul of Memphis* (New York: Norton, 2015).

73. Quote in Denison, TX, *Sunday Gazetteer,* May 15, 1887, 1. Cuney's concerns about party division in Cantrell, "Dark Tactics," 86. Cuney's wine habit in Maud Cuney-Hare, *Norris Wright Cuney: A Tribune of the Black People* (New York: n.p., 1913), 84.

74. *Drink and the Drink Question: A Discriminating License the True Policy; Prohibition a Fraud and Failure* (Dallas: [Texas] Anti-Prohibition State Convention, 1887).

75. Plocheck, "Prohibition Elections in Texas"; *Legislative Reference Library of Texas,* "Constitutional amendment election dates." Cf. James W. Endersby, "Prohibition and Repeal: Voting on Statewide Liquor Referenda in Texas," *Social Science Journal* 49 (December 2012): 506.

76. Leab, "Tennessee Temperance Activities," 62.

77. Lacy, "Tennessee Teetotalism," 220–21; Leab, "Tennessee Temperance Activities," 58–64. While Lacy (220) claims the state WCTU was founded in 1881, Leab (60) appears more plausible because she provides more specific information, including the date of its founding: October 22, 1882.

78. *Southern Standard,* McMinnville, TN, September 3, 1887, 4.

79. *Southern Standard,* McMinnville, TN, September 24, 1887, 5.

80. Leab, "Tennessee Temperance Activities," 63.

81. Leab, "Tennessee Temperance Activities," 56, 63.

82. "Prohibition Vote in Tennessee," *New York Times,* October 18, 1887, 9. Leab, "Tennessee Temperance Activities," 63–64, tallied 135,197 wet votes. The *Times's* number is used here.

83. Leab, "Tennessee Temperance Activities," 63–64.

84. Gilmore, *Gender and Jim Crow,* 54, 250n75.

85. Thompson, *"A Most Stirring and Significant Episode,"* 184–87, 233, 235, 238–40.

86. Benajah Harvey Carroll to Benjamin Franklin Riley, May 3, 1909, cited by Locke, *Making the Bible Belt,* 137, 239n61.

87. William Edward Burghardt Du Bois, "An Open Letter to the Southern People," 1887, W. E. B. Du Bois Papers, ser. 3: Articles, University of Massachusetts, Amherst, 2. See also Thompson, *"A Most Stirring and Significant Episode,"* 245.

88. Du Bois, "Open Letter to the Southern People," 3.

89. Du Bois, "Open Letter to the Southern People," 4.

90. Du Bois, "Open Letter to the Southern People," 4.

91. Du Bois, "Open Letter to the Southern People," 1.

92. Du Bois, "Open Letter to the Southern People," 1.

93. The most widely accepted vote total is 129,270 for to 220,627 against: Cantrell, "Dark Tactics," 91; Jared Paul Sutton, "Ethnic Minorities and Prohibition in Texas, 1887–1919," MA thesis, University of North Texas, 2006, 42; and Plocheck, "Prohibition Elections in Texas." There are two slight variants of totals: first, 128,342 for to 221,488 against in Endersby, "Prohibition and Repeal," 506; second, 128,835 for and 219,961 against in Ivy, *No Saloon in the Valley,* 93. Wuthnow, *Rough Country,* 61, merely notes that the measure failed by more than 90,000 votes, on which all accounts agree.

94. Cantrell estimates that native-born whites voted 33 percent for and 33 percent against prohibition while 34 percent abstained (a 50–50 vote split for native whites), but 64 percent of foreign-born voters voted no while the rest abstained (100 percent wet vote for foreign-born whites). Endersby incorrectly claims: "Cantrell . . . estimates that white voters were divided equally on the issue," but Cantrell actually states: "*Native* whites were divided evenly" (emphasis mine). Cantrell's makes the issue even clearer, distinguishing between "native-born whites," who voted about evenly wet and dry, and "foreign-born voters," who voted almost entirely wet. Endersby, "Prohibition and Repeal," 505; Cantrell, "Dark Tactics," 91, esp. note 23.

95. Sutton, "Ethnic Minorities," 38. Sutton's five counties for analyzing the African American vote are all in table 2, except Sabine County; I included his information from Sabine County as a counterpoint.

96. For example, Harrison, Bastrop, and Harris counties all voted roughly 75 percent wet, but the Black population varied between about 60 percent, 42 percent, and 23 percent. If the African American vote was consistently higher than the white population, one would expect significant variations in the vote for higher numbers of African Americans. Refugio voted 91 percent wet while Houston went only 67 percent wet, despite both being about 30 percent Black. Likewise, Sabine and Harris counties were both about 23 percent Black, yet Sabine was safely dry while Harris was solidly wet. The common denominator in the 1887 county

results was not so much Black population as urbanization: the four most populous counties voted between 66 percent and 76 percent wet, a bit more—but not shockingly more—than the statewide average of 63 percent wet, while mid-sized Sabine County went dry, and tiny Refugio went wettest of all. Of those four more populous counties, the proportions of African Americans varied widely (Harrison 60 percent, Bastrop 42 percent, Houston 34 percent, Harris 23 percent), yet their totals were within about 10 points of each other. In short, while Sutton's evidence strongly suggests that most Black voters consistently opposed prohibition, he has not demonstrated what percentage did so in any given election. Most significantly, his data cannot tell us definitively whether African Americans voted more wet than white voters in 1887 ("Ethnic Minorities," 35, 80).

97. Ivy, *No Saloon in the Valley,* 92–98, 140n10–144n19.

98. Ivy, *No Saloon in the Valley,* 142n13 (quotation); estimated vote totals, 93; comparison with white vote, 92–96; incorrect 1911 vote total, 117; explanation of the weaknesses of his model, 142–43n13. Correct numbers for 1911 vote in Plocheck, "Prohibition Elections in Texas."

99. *Star of Zion,* Salisbury, NC, August 25, 1887, 2.

100. Ivy, *No Saloon in the Valley,* 92–96.

101. *Bolivar,* TN, *Bulletin,* October 14, 1887, 2.

102. Texas Baptist Publishing House, *Proceedings of the Second Annual Session of the Baptist General Convention of Texas* (Dallas: Texas Baptist Publishing House, 1887), 43.

103. *Second Annual Session of the Baptist General Convention of Texas,* 5. A year later the BGCT committee abbreviated its title to "The Attitude of Baptists toward the Liquor Traffic," but its reports for years after remained terse and mentioned no progress against that traffic. Texas Baptist Publishing House, *Proceedings of the Third Annual Session of the Baptist General Convention of Texas* (Waco, TX: Baylor University Printing Co., 1888), 5, 26; Texas Baptist Publishing House, *Proceedings of the Fourth Annual Session of the Baptist General Convention of Texas* (Dallas: Texas Baptist Publishing House, 1889), 47; Texas Baptist Publishing House, *Proceedings of the Fifth Annual Session of the Baptist General Convention of Texas* (Fort Worth: Mail Publishing Co., 1890), 75; Texas Baptist Publishing House, *Proceedings of the Sixth Annual Session of the Baptist General Convention of Texas* (Dallas: Jas. A. Dorsey & Co., 1891), 51–52.

104. Texas Baptist Publishing House, *Proceedings of the Ninth Annual Session of the Baptist General Convention of Texas* (Waco, TX: Baptist Standard Printing House, 1894), 52.

105. Carroll, *History of Texas Baptists,* 663.

106. Texas Baptist Publishing House, *Proceedings of the Eighth Annual Session of the Baptist General Convention of Texas* (Waco, TX: Baptist Standard Book Pub. Co., 1893), 63.

107. Texas Baptist Publishing House, *Proceedings of the Tenth Annual Session of the Baptist General Convention of Texas* (Waco, TX: Baptist Standard Print, 1895), 47.

108. Texas Baptist Publishing House, *Proceedings of the Tenth Annual Session of the Baptist General Convention of Texas,* 48.

109. Texas Baptist Publishing House, *Proceedings of the Eleventh Annual Session of the Baptist General Convention of Texas* (Houston: Dispatch Printing House, 1896), 65–67.

110. Ivy, *No Saloon in the Valley,* 1, 7–23, 28, 31, 47–52, 56–64, 68, 89–90, 100–101, and esp. 118: "By 1911 [prohibitionists] could reject the assistance of women because they were confident that they could accomplish their goal without them"; Coker, *Liquor in the Land of the Lost Cause,* 1–3, gender and women 199–229; Wuthnow, *Rough Country,* 171. See also James D. Ivy, "'The Lone

Star State Surrenders to a Lone Woman': Frances Willard's Forgotten 1882 Texas Temperance Tour," *Southwestern Historical Quarterly* 102, no. 1 (1998): 44–61 (on which chapter 1 of Ivy's *No Saloon in the Valley* was based); and Judith N. McArthur, *Creating the New Woman: The Rise of Southern Women's Progressive Culture in Texas, 1893–1918* (Urbana: University of Illinois Press, 1998).

3. Gin Crow Begins: White Drys and Jim Crow

1. "HEFLIN DEFENDS HIS ACTION IN AFFRAY ON CAR," *Washington, DC, Times,* March 28, 1908, 1–2.

2. Douglas A. Blackmon, *Slavery by Another Name: The Re-Enslavement of Black Americans from the Civil War to World War II* (New York: Doubleday, 2008), 122.

3. Blackmon, *Slavery by Another Name,* 196, 222, 225, 230, 233–34; Elbert L. Watson, "J. Thomas Heflin," *Encyclopedia of Alabama,* www.encyclopediaofalabama.org/article/h-2952 (updated May 26, 2017).

4. Harris & Ewing, photographer, "HEFLIN, J. THOMAS. SENATOR," around 1920–28, Library of Congress LC-H25-80439-EW.

5. "House Stirred by the Affray on Mr. Heflin," *Washington, DC, Times,* March 28, 1908, 2.

6. "HEFLIN DEFENDS HIS ACTION IN AFFRAY ON CAR," 1–2.

7. Watson, "J. Thomas Heflin."

8. "Dry," *Prescott, AR, Daily News,* July 31, 1907, 1; Cherrington, ed., *Anti-Saloon League Year Book* (1908), 174.

9. Gerald H. Gaither, *Blacks and the Populist Movement: Ballots and Bigotry in the "New South"* (rev. ed., Tuscaloosa: University of Alabama Press, 2005), x. The same page provides names for representatives of the different schools: For the progressive view, see Alex Mathews Arnett, *The Populist Movement in Georgia: A View of the "Agrarian Crusade" in the Light of Solid-South Politics* (New York: AMS Press, 1967); John B. Clare, "Populism in Alabama: 1874–1896," PhD diss., New York University, 1926; and Roscoe C. Martin, "The Grange as a Political Factor in Texas," *Southwestern Political and Social Science Quarterly* 6, no. 4 (1926): 363–83.

10. Raleigh *Progressive Farmer,* September 9, 1887, quoted in Gaither, *Blacks and the Populist Movement,* 2; see also C. Vann Woodward, *Tom Watson: Agrarian Rebel* (1938; rpt. New York: Oxford University Press, 1963), 136; C. Vann. Woodward, *The Strange Career of Jim Crow* (2nd ed., New York: Oxford University Press, 1966).

11. Gaither, *Blacks and the Populist Movement,* 2–3.

12. Gaither, *Blacks and the Populist Movement,* 31–48.

13. Postel, *Populist Vision,* 186, 137–63.

14. Gaither, *Blacks and the Populist Movement,* 42–43.

15. Ronald A. Walter, "Robert R. Church Sr.," *Tennessee Encyclopedia,* tennesseeencyclopedia .net/entries/robert-r-church-sr/ (updated March 1, 2018).

16. Gaither, *Blacks and the Populist Movement,* 3.

17. Gaither, *Blacks and the Populist Movement,* 51; Postel, *Populist Vision,* 179–203.

18. Cantrell, *Feeding the Wolf,* viii, 73. For more accounts of the relationship between Populism and race, see Gaither, *Blacks and the Populist Movement;* Richard Hofstadter, *The Age of Reform: From Bryan to FDR* (New York: Random House, 1955), 83–84; Norman Pollack, *The Populist Response to Industrial America: Midwestern Populist Thought* (Cambridge, MA: Harvard

University Press, 1962); Lawrence Goodwyn, *Democratic Promise: The Populist Moment in America* (New York: Oxford University Press, 1976).

19. Postel, *Populist Vision,* 189; see also 157, 173–76, 188–95, 199–203, 255, 267, 274, 284–85, 323–30, 341–47.

20. The North Carolina Populists were Alonzo Craig Shuford, Harry Skinner, William Franklin Strowd, Charles Henry Martin, John Edgar Fowler, and John Wilbur Atwater; at the same time, several Republicans also represented North Carolina in Congress: Romulus Zachariah Linney, Richmond Pearson, and an African American, George Henry White. Caroline Jones Gibbons, "Albert Taylor Goodwyn," *Encyclopedia of Alabama,* www.encyclopediaofalabama.org /article/h-3953 (updated November 1, 2017); Caroline Gibbons, "Milford Wriarson Howard," *Encyclopedia of Alabama,* encyclopediaofalabama.org/article/h-3955 (updated November 7, 2017); Worth Robert Miller, "NUGENT, THOMAS LEWIS (1841–1895)," *Handbook of Texas Online,* www.tshaonline.org/handbook/entries/nugent-thomas-lewis (accessed August 30, 2020); James Sanders Day, "Truman Aldrich," *Encyclopedia of Alabama,* www.encyclopediaofalabama.org /article/h-3674 (updated October 10, 2018); Postel, *Populist Vision,* 188–99.

21. The North Carolina Populists in the US House were Alonzo Craig Shuford, Harry Skinner, William Franklin Strowd, Charles Henry Martin, John Edgar Fowler, and John Wilbur Atwater. At the same time, in addition to White, several other Republicans also represented North Carolina in Congress: Romulus Zachariah Linney and Richmond Pearson. Postel, *Populist Vision,* 198–200.

22. Ronnie W. Faulkner, "Furnifold McLendel Simmons (1854–1940)," *North Carolina History Project,* northcarolinahistory.org/encyclopedia/furnifold-mclendel-simmons-1854-1940 (accessed August 29, 2020).

23. Davidson, "AFRICAN AMERICANS AND POLITICS"; Cantrell, *Kenneth and John B. Rayner,* 200–233, 247–48; Cantrell, *Feeding the Wolf,* 32–82.

24. Gaither, *Blacks and the Populist Movement,* 50.

25. Postel, *Populist Vision,* 176, 200.

26. Howard N. Rabinowitz, *Race, Ethnicity, and Urbanization: Selected Essays* (Columbia: University of Missouri Press, 1993), 131.

27. Quote in Steven J. Hoffman, *Race, Class and Power in the Building of Richmond, 1870–1920* (Jefferson, NC: McFarland, 2004), 125. See also Hamm, *Murder, Honor, and Law,* 67; Frank Abbott Magruder, "Recent Administration in Virginia," PhD diss., Johns Hopkins University, 1911, 82.

28. Walter Edgar, *South Carolina: A History* (Columbia: University of South Carolina Press, 1998), 414; William Lewis Burke, *All for Civil Rights: African American Lawyers in South Carolina, 1868–1968* (Athens: University of Georgia Press, 2017), 119.

29. Abel A. Bartley, *Keeping the Faith: Race, Politics, and Social Development in Jacksonville, Florida, 1940–1970* (Westwood, CT: Greenwood Press, 2000), 8.

30. Catherine M. Lewis and J. Richard Lewis, eds., *Jim Crow America: A Documentary History* (Fayetteville: University of Arkansas Press, 2009), xi–xxi; Jerrold M. Packard, *American Nightmare: The History of Jim Crow* (New York: St. Martin's Press, 2002); Robert Hays, ed., *The Age of Segregation: Race Relations in the South, 1890–1945* (Jackson: University Press of Mississippi); Melissa Milewski, *Litigating Across the Color Line: Civil Cases Between Black and White Southerners from the End of Slavery to Civil Rights* (New York: Oxford University Press, 2018); I. A.

Newby, *Jim Crow's Defense: Anti-Negro Thought in America, 1900–1930* (Baton Rouge: Louisiana State University Press, 1965).

31. John William Graves, "Poll Tax," Central Arkansas Library System, *Encyclopedia of Arkansas,* encyclopediaofarkansas.net/entries/poll-tax-5045/ (updated December 3, 2018).

32. Brent Tarter, "Poll Tax," Library of Virginia, *Encyclopedia Virginia,* www.encyclopediaVirginia.org/Poll_Tax (July 2, 2014); Clarissa Myrick-Harris and Norman Harris, "Atlanta in the Civil Rights Movement," *Atlanta Regional Consortium for Higher Education,* (published 2004); Brent Tarter, "Disfranchisement," *Encyclopedia Virginia,* www.encyclopediavirginia.org /Disfranchisement (July 19, 2016).

33. Darryl Paulson, "Florida's History of Suppressing Blacks' Votes," (October 11, 2013); Connie L. Lester, "Disfranchising Laws," *Tennessee Encyclopedia,* tennesseeencyclopedia.net/entries /disfranchising-laws/ (updated March 1, 2018); Mississippi State Constitution of 1890, Article 12 § 243; Graves, "Poll Tax." See also Dewey W. Grantham, "Tennessee and Twentieth-Century American Politics," *Tennessee Historical Quarterly* 53 (1996): 210–12.

34. Josephus Daniels, Raleigh, NC, *News and Observer,* January 28, 1900, cited in W. Joseph Campbell, "'One of the Fine Figures of American Journalism': A Closer Look at Josephus Daniels of the Raleigh 'News and Observer,'" *American Journalism* 16 (Fall 1999): 37–55.

35. Tarter, "Poll Tax"; "Evelyn Butts Challenged the Poll Tax, 1966," Library of Virginia, *Education at Library of Virginia,* edu.lva.virginia.gov/online_classroom/shaping_the_constitution /doc/poll_tax (accessed March 30, 2020).

36. Tarter, "Disfranchisement."

37. Tarter, "Disfranchisement"; McGirr, *War on Alcohol,* 73–74.

38. Amanda Brown, "*Dixon v. Mississippi,*" Center for the Study of Southern Culture and the Mississippi Humanities Council, *Mississippi Encyclopedia,* mississippiencyclopedia.org/entries /dixon-v-mississippi/ (July 10, 2017); Amanda Brown, "*Williams v. Mississippi,*" *Mississippi Encyclopedia,* mississippiencyclopedia.org/entries/williams-v-mississippi (July 11, 2017).

39. Allen Caperton Braxton, "The Fifteenth Amendment," in *Oratory of the South from the Civil War to the Present Time,* ed. Edwin Du Bois Shurter (New York: Neale Publishing Co., 1908), 266–69.

40. Eaton J. Bowers, "The Negro Problem" (April 8, 1904), in *Oratory of the South,* ed. Shurter, 259–60. Dry stance in "Another Blow for Canteen," Sumter, SC, *Watchman and Southron,* May 20, 1908, 7.

41. Jennifer Lee, "Samuel Bowers, 82, Klan Leader Convicted in Fatal Bombing, Dies," *New York Times,* November 6, 2006, www.nytimes.com/2006/11/06/us/06bowers.html.

42. Edgar, *South Carolina,* 414; Burke, *All for Civil Rights,* 119; Leon F. Litwack, *Trouble in Mind: Black Southerners in the Age of Jim Crow* (New York: Vintage, 1999), 225. Barbara Bair, "Though Justice Sleeps: 1880–1900," *To Make Our World Anew: A History of African Americans,* ed. Robin E. G. Kelley and Earl Lewis (New York: Oxford University Press, 2000), 281–301.

43. Cantrell, *Kenneth and John B. Rayner,* 248, 327n10; Plocheck, "Prohibition Elections in Texas."

44. Coker, *Liquor in the Land of the Lost Cause,* 123–74.

45. Foster, *Moral Reconstruction,* 113–30.

46. Odegard, *Pressure Politics,* 18; 1911 quotes from *Houston Post,* April 26, 1911, cited in Watson, "Evangelical Protestants and the Prohibition Movement in Texas," 185–86; 1913 quotes from

Odegard, *Pressure Politics,* 24–25. See also Watson, "Evangelical Protestants and the Prohibition Movement in Texas," 185–86, 196.

47. Odegard, *Pressure Politics,* 18.

48. Atticus Webb, *Face the Facts Relating to the Wet and Dry Issues* (Dallas: Anti-Saloon League of Texas, 1927), 92. The Federal Council of Christian Churches was the forerunner of the National Council of Churches (NCC).

49. H. A. Ivy, *Rum on the Run in Texas: A Brief History of Prohibition in the Lone Star State,* introd. George C. Rankin (Dallas: Temperance Pub. Co., 1910), 68.

50. Webb, *Face the Facts,* 99–101; Dallas *Home and State,* November 15, 1915–January 31, 1916, esp. November 30, 1915, 2.

51. In 1890, Texas had the second-smallest percentage of Baptists and Methodists of all southern states, including African American believers, though that number grew rapidly in the early twentieth century. Mark A. Noll, *God and Race in American Politics: A Short History* (Princeton, NJ: Princeton University Press, 2010), 88–89.

52. Looney, ed., *Brewers and Texas Politics* 1: 237.

53. Looney, ed., *Brewers and Texas Politics* 1: 46.

54. *Austin,* TX, *Statesman,* June 29, 1911. See also Gould, *Alexander Watkins Terrell,* 163.

55. Plocheck, "Prohibition Elections in Texas."

56. Coker, *Liquor in the Land of the Lost Cause,* 124; see also 123–74.

57. Michael Lewis, *The Coming of Southern Prohibition: The Dispensary System and the Battle over Liquor in South Carolina, 1907-1915* (Baton Rouge: Louisiana State University Press, 2016), 3.

58. Dr. G. C. Rankin, "Progress of Reform: Mob Spirit in Texas," *Home and State,* September 1905, 13.

59. *Home and State,* September 15, 1916, 1.

60. *Home and State,* September 15, 1916, 1.

61. The description of the liquor bottle, at least, seems to be true. Apparently another drunk African American man convicted of rape in Birmingham actually was carrying Black Cock Liquor Gin in his pocket on his arrest. Okrent, *Last Call,* 45–46. Paul E. Isaac, *Prohibition and Politics: Turbulent decades in Tennessee, 1885-1920* (Knoxville: University of Tennessee Press, 1965), 148. Michael James Pfeifer, *Rough Justice: Lynching and American Society, 1874-1947* (Urbana: University of Illinois Press, 2004), 142–43. Various articles in *Collier's,* May 16 and August 15, 1908; May 2, 1925. *U.S. v. Lee Levy and Adolph S. Asher,* Eastern District of Missouri, 1908, Grand Jury indictment and sentence rendered.

62. "Decreased Lynchings Under Prohibition," *Home and State,* February 1928, 5.

63. Coker, *Liquor in the Land of the Lost Cause,* 124, 123–74.

64. While it was attempted murder, it did not meet the common definition of lynching: three or more people committing an extralegal killing. While lynchings are commonly associated with hanging and mostly targeted racial minorities, neither noose nor rope is a required part of a lynching, and people of every racial group can be lynched.

65. "Wounded Negro Has Bad Record in Police Court," *Washington,* DC, *Times,* March 28, 1908, 2.

66. "HEFLIN DEFENDS HIS ACTION IN AFFRAY ON CAR," *Washington,* DC, *Times,* March 28, 1908, 2.

67. Clayton implausibly claimed that Heflin "fired to prevent the negroes renewing their attack," and Ellerbe likewise stated that Heflin shot because "the attack on Mr. Heflin was renewed." While Ellerbe described in detail how one of Heflin's shots ricocheted off the ground into McCreary's leg, he mistakenly believed that both of Heflin's shots hit the ground and neither hit "the negro," when in fact Lundy was shot in the neck. This mistake is plausible only if Lundy was shot at while he was on the ground. "HEFLIN DEFENDS HIS ACTION IN AFFRAY ON CAR," *Washington, DC, Times,* March 28, 1908, 1–2.

68. Kenneth W. Goings, "Memphis Free Speech," *Tennessee Encyclopedia,* tennesseeencyclo pedia.net/entries/memphis-free-speech/ (updated October 7, 2019). See also James West Davidson, *"They Say": Ida B. Wells and the Reconstruction of Race* (New York: Oxford University Press, 2008).

69. O'Daniel, *Crusaders, Gangsters, and Whiskey,* 8–17.

70. Richmond Pearson Hobson, *The Great Destroyer: Speech of Hon. Richmond P. Hobson of Alabama in the House of Representatives, February 2, 1911* (Washington, DC: n.p., 1911), 7.

71. Richmond Pearson Hobson, *The Truth About Alcohol: Speech of Hon. Richmond P. Hobson of Alabama in the House of Representatives, December 22, 1914* (Washington, DC: n.p., 1914), 13.

72. Hobson, *Truth About Alcohol,* 15.

73. Hobson, *Truth About Alcohol,* 17.

74. Hobson, *Truth About Alcohol,* 17.

75. J. B. Gambrell and G. C. Rankin, "The Preacher and the Pending Issue," *Home and State,* June 29, 1912, 3.

76. S. M. Lesesne, "A Study of Our Mexican 'Citizens,'" *Home and State,* July 20, 1912, 1.

77. Noll, *History of Christianity,* 342–44. See also Robert J. Norrell, *Up from History: The Life of Booker T. Washington* (Cambridge, MA: Harvard University Press, 2009).

78. Wuthnow, *Rough Country,* 171.

79. Wuthnow, *Rough Country,* 171; see also "Communication from Negro Ministers," *Beaumont Journal,* June 26, 1911.

80. Unsigned editorial, "A Negro Preacher's View," *Home and State,* August 31, 1912, 3.

81. "A Negro Preacher's View," *Home and State,* August 31, 1912, 3.

82. Robert A. Hohner, *Prohibition and Politics: The Life of Bishop James Cannon, Jr.* (Columbia: University of South Carolina Press, 1999), 168.

83. Cherrington, ed., *Anti-Saloon League Year Book* (1909), 21; "Prohibition for Alabama Passes," *Prescott, AR, Daily News,* November 21, 1907, 1; "Alabama Prohibition," Newbery, SC, *Herald and News,* November 22, 1907, 3; "Prohibition in Mississippi," *Newport, VA, News,* February 8, 1908, 3.

84. The source incorrectly named the judge "Peter." "Prohibition in North Carolina," *Bluefield, WV, Daily Leader,* May 26, 1908, 5. The other states were Maine, North Dakota, Kansas, and Oklahoma, the last of which entered the union as a dry state in 1907.

85. Cherrington, ed., *Anti-Saloon League Year Book* (1910), 79.

86. *Alabama Official and Statistical Register, 1911,* comp. Thomas M. Owen (Montgomery, AL: Brown Printing Co., 1912), 318–19; Ernest Hurst Cherrington, *History of the Anti-Saloon League* (Westerville, OH: American Issue Publishing Co., 1913), 118, 134.

87. Willis, *Southern Prohibition,* 3.

88. Cherrington, ed., *Anti-Saloon League Year Book* (1911), 172–73.

89. Cherrington, ed., *Anti-Saloon League Year Book* (1917), 135.

4. "Fidelity to That Liberty": Defeat and Success for Gin Crow

1. NBC membership in 1906 bested the Southern Baptist Convention by 2.2 million to 1.9 million, while the Northern Baptists held only 0.9 million. In Texas, however, Southern Baptists outnumbered National Baptists almost two to one. Durand, ed., *Religious Bodies, 1906: Part I,* 30, 272.

2. *Twenty-Fifth Annual Session of the National Baptist Convention* (Nashville, TN: National Baptist Publishing Board, 1905), 156–57.

3. Oscar Branch Colquitt, "Opening Speech of Campaign of 1910," 9, Literary Productions folder, box 2E177, Oscar Branch Colquitt Papers.

4. Colquitt, "Opening Speech of Campaign of 1910," 14.

5. Colquitt, "Opening Speech of Campaign of 1910," 14–15.

6. Colquitt, "Opening Speech of Campaign of 1910," 17.

7. Shuler, *New Issue,* "The Antis and the Preachers" section.

8. Shuler, *New Issue.*

9. Oscar Branch Colquitt, "Speech at Palistine, July 13, 1911," first quote, 10; second and third quotes, 13, Literary Productions folder, box 2E177, Oscar Branch Colquitt Papers. Texas's US senators at the time were Charles Allen Culberson and Joseph Weldon Bailey Sr.

10. Joseph Locke, "Making the Bible Belt: Preachers, Prohibition, and the Politicization of Southern Religion, 1877–1918," PhD diss., Rice University, 2012, 308.

11. *Texas Christian Advocate,* January 11, 1912.

12. *Temple,* TX, *Daily Telegram,* October 31, 1912, 8, cited in Locke, "Making the Bible Belt," 308.

13. "DECLARATION OF PRINCIPLES," *Ocala,* FL, *Evening Star,* September 22, 1910, 1.

14. "DECLARATION OF PRINCIPLES," 1.

15. Cantrell, *Kenneth and John B. Rayner,* 188–92; Cantrell, *Feeding the Wolf,* 1–24; L. B. Scott, "Hon. J. B. Rayner," Dallas *Southwestern Christian Advocate,* September 1, 1898; for Rayner's writings, see J. B. Rayner, "The Worth of Character," Dallas *Southwestern Christian Advocate,* December 29, 1898; J. B. Rayner, "Does History Repeat Itself?" Dallas *Southwestern Christian Advocate,* May 8, 1902; *Twenty-Fifth Annual Session of the National Baptist Convention,* 156–57.

16. In 1916, the majority-Black Methodist denominations that had the most members, by state, were: AME (South Carolina, Georgia, Florida, Arkansas), MEC (Virginia, Tennessee, Mississippi, Louisiana, Texas), and AMEZ (North Carolina, Alabama). (While the northern-based MEC was majority-white nationally, it was majority-Black in the South, where most white Methodists were MECS.) National Baptists were by far the largest majority-Black denomination in every southern state, and in all states except North Carolina, Tennessee, Louisiana, and Texas, the National Baptists were the largest denomination of any kind. (SBC was the largest in North Carolina and Tennessee, and Catholics in Louisiana and Texas). William Chamberlin Hunt and Edwin Munsell Bliss, eds., *Religious Bodies, 1916* (Washington, DC: US Census Bureau, 1916), 110–12.

17. P. C. Hunt to Ormund Paget, December 21, 1910, in Looney, ed., *Brewers and Texas Politics* 1: 63. Hunt had served as a licensed AME preacher in Texas since 1883, had personally brought in more than 1,500 members into the denomination, some 1,250 of whom he baptized, had served over a dozen churches well by paying off their debt and organizing the construction of their church buildings, and was a politically engaged Republican. Richard R. Wright and John R. Hawkins, *Centennial Encyclopedia of the African Methodist Episcopal Church* (Philadelphia: Book Concern of the A.M.E. Church, 1916), vol. 1: 120.

18. John B. Rayner, "Political Ingratitude," 4, Literary Productions folder, J. B. Rayner Papers (one box), Dolph Briscoe Center for American History, University of Texas at Austin. The context and format of the paper, with frequent scratch marks, addendums, and typos, best fit the format of a speech manuscript used several times. While undated, it was undoubtedly given in the summer or fall of 1910 because it addressed Colquitt as a primary candidate who had not yet won the Democratic nomination against Cone Johnson.

19. Rayner, "Political Ingratitude," 8.

20. Rayner, "Political Ingratitude," 10.

21. Rayner, "Political Ingratitude," 10.

22. *Twenty-Eighth Annual Session of the National Baptist Convention, Eighth Annual Assembly of the Woman's Convention, Auxiliary to the National Baptist Convention,* 308. *Twenty-Ninth Annual Session of the National Baptist Convention,* 317.

23. "Bishop's Address," *Journal of the Sixth Annual Session of the West Texas Conference of the Protestant Episcopal Church,* 1910, 85–86. The bishop urged his Episcopal clergy to cooperate with other Christian denominations "in every good work that has for its purpose the betterment of social and civic conditions," though he failed to explicitly include prohibition in his purview (87).

24. "Bishop's Address," 82–87; *Journal of the Seventh Annual Session of the West Texas Conference of the Protestant Episcopal Church, South,* 1911, 29–31.

25. "George H. Kinsolving Says High License and Local Option Is the Remedy," Fort Worth *Star Telegram,* April 11, 1911, 7.

26. *Dallas Morning News,* July 5, 1911, 2.

27. *Dallas Morning News,* May 2, 1911, 7.

28. According to its own history, Trinity Episcopal was founded by eight women in 1907, had just finished building the church edifice in 1909, and had only eighteen communicants by 1912. The only priests listed for this period were the Rev. Dr. D. G. Gunn, a church planter who was there in 1909 and 1910, and the Rev. J. B. Finn, who joined in 1912. No mention is made of a "J. T. Smith" or any other priest in 1911, though it did mention the bishop's visit (in 1910?), which was described as "one of the most eloquent discourses ever delivered in Jacksonville." It seems likely the parish preferred their bishop to Father Smith, whom they omitted from the record. Trinity Episcopal Church, "Our History," www.trinityepiscopaljacksonville.org/about_us, published 2016 (accessed July 18, 2020).

29. Shuler, *New Issue,* "Tut! Tut! Bishop Tuttle!" section.

30. Colquitt, "Speech at Palistine," 13.

31. Looney, ed., *Brewers and Texas Politics* 1: 447; 2: 668.

32. Shuler, *New Issue.*

33. A. C. Flusche and Catholic Archives of Texas, *Sketch of the German Catholic Colonies in North Texas Founded by Flusche Brothers* (n.p., 1900), 5–6.

34. Flusche and Catholic Archives of Texas, *Sketch of the German Catholic Colonies in North Texas,* 6.

35. William H. Dunn, "KNIGHTS OF COLUMBUS," June 15, 2010, tshaonline.org/handbook /online/articles/vnk02.

36. John Ireland, "Patriotism" (1894), in Ireland, *The Church and Modern Society* (Chicago: Paulist Press, 1905), 161.

37. Ireland, "American Citizenship" (1895), in *Church and Modern Society,* 211. For more on Ultramontanism and Americanism from a contemporary anti-Catholic perspective, see I. K.

Funk and D. S. Gregory, eds., *Homiletic Review* (New York: Funk and Wagnalls), vol. 38 (July–December 1899): 97.

38. Ireland, "American Citizenship," in *Church and Modern Society,* 192.

39. Ireland, "American Citizenship," in *Church and Modern Society,* 206–7. Cf. John T. McGreevy, *Catholicism and American Freedom: A History* (New York: Norton, 2003), 121.

40. Ireland, "American Citizenship," in *Church and Modern Society,* 207.

41. *Catholic Citizen,* May 9, 1891, 1; *Congressional Record,* April 22, 1892, 3532; cf. Colman J. Barry, *The Catholic Church and German Americans* (Milwaukee, 1953), 131–82; Edward Claude Stibili, "The St. Paphael Society for the Protection of Italian Immigrants, 1887–1923," PhD diss., University of Notre Dame, 1977, 76–77, 81–89; Scalabrini to Archbishop Michael Corrigan, August 10, 1891, in *For the Love of Immigrants: Migration Writings and Letters of Bishop John Baptist Scalabrini (1839–1905),* ed. Archbishop Silvano M. Tomasi (New York, 2000), 276–78. All sources from McGreevy, *Catholicism and American Freedom,* 121. Noll, *History of Christianity,* argues that a lack of Italian clergy, among other factors, contributed to many Italian American immigrants leaving the faith.

42. Odegard, *Pressure Politics,* 5; Okrent, *Last Call,* 97–106.

43. 1911 quotes from *Houston Post,* April 26, 1911, cited in Watson, "Evangelical Protestants and the Prohibition Movement in Texas," 185–86; 1913 quotes from Odegard, *Pressure Politics,* 24–25. Watson, ""Evangelical Protestants and the Prohibition Movement in Texas," 185–86, 196.

44. *Log Cabin Democrat,* Conway, AR, August 26, 1912, 2.

45. Quote in Abdel Ross Wentz, *A Basic History of Lutheranism in America* (Philadelphia: Muhlenberg Press, 1964), 205; see also 352–53.

46. In 1917 the arrangement shifted from an association of autonomous synods to a single synod with various districts. In 1919 the synod changed its name to the Evangelical Lutheran Joint Synod of Wisconsin and Other States, or "Wisconsin Synod," and in 1959 was renamed the Wisconsin Evangelical Lutheran Synod, with the tidy acronym WELS. Erwin L. Lueker, Luther Poellot, and Paul Jackson, eds., "Wisconsin Evangelical Lutheran Synod," *Christian Cyclopedia* (Concordia Publishing House, 2000), cyclopedia.lcms.org/display.asp?t1=w&word=WISCONSIN EVANGELICALLUTHERANSYNOD. The Michigan group had joined the association in 1890 and experienced the split in 1896, but the rise of new leaders led to more friendly relations from 1904 on, culminating in the reunification in 1909.

47. Edward C. Fredrich, *The Wisconsin Synod Lutherans: A History of the Single Synod, Federation, and Merger* (Milwaukee: Northwestern Pub. House, 2000), 123.

48. Fredrich, *Wisconsin Synod Lutherans,* 124.

49. Fredrich, *Wisconsin Synod Lutherans,* 124.

50. "Saloon Not Real Issue," *Dallas Morning News,* April 22, 1911. See also Wuthnow, *Rough Country,* 106–7.

51. *Ocala,* FL, *Evening Star,* October 16, 1907, 1.

52. Colquitt, "Speech at Palistine," first quote, 10; second and third quotes, 13. Texas's two US senators at the time were Charles Allen Culberson and Joseph Weldon Bailey Sr.

53. *Washington,* DC, *Times,* January 26, 1920, 3.

54. "Entire Moslem World Showing Interest in U.S. Prohibition," *Brownsville,* TX, *Herald,* April 6, 1924, sec. 2, p. 3.

55. *Wheeling,* WV, *Intelligencer,* October 29, 1912, 10.

56. Erskine, *Prohibition and Christianity,* 17.

57. P. W. Wilson, "The Influence of the American Example," Westerville, OH, *American Issue,* April 8, 1921, 4.

58. William E. "Pussyfoot" Johnson, "And I Went Down into Egypt," Westerville, OH, *American Issue,* February 1, 1927, 6.

59. Erskine, *Prohibition and Christianity,* 17.

60. Erskine, *Prohibition and Christianity,* 17.

61. Erskine, *Prohibition and Christianity,* 18.

62. Erskine, *Prohibition and Christianity,* 19, emphasis in original.

63. Lamar Taney Beman, ed., *Selected Articles on Prohibition of the Liquor Traffic* (New York: H. W. Wilson, 1915), 121.

64. Elbert L. Watson, "Oscar Underwood," *Encyclopedia of Alabama,* www.encyclopediaofalabama.org/article/h-2961 (updated February 16, 2017).

65. Beman, ed., *Selected Articles on Prohibition,* 120.

66. Beman, ed., *Selected Articles on Prohibition,* 123.

67. Beman, ed., *Selected Articles on Prohibition,* 138.

68. *Home and State,* December 15, 1915, 4.

69. *Home and State,* December 15, 1915, 4.

70. Michael Meagher and Larry D. Gragg, *John F. Kennedy: A Biography* (Santa Barbara, CA: Greenwood, 2011), 2; O'Daniel, *Crusaders, Gangsters, and Whiskey,* 13; see also Lauterback, *Beale Street Dynasty.*

71. "Your friend" to Wahrmund, August 11, 1909, in Looney, ed., *Brewers and Texas Politics* 1: 71.

72. Lester, "Disfranchising Laws."

73. Looney, ed., *Brewers and Texas Politics* 1: 1; brewers' vigorous opposition to the poll tax provision in the Texas constitution is attested in 214–16.

74. Paget, letter to TBA, December 7, 1910, in Looney, ed., *Brewers and Texas Politics* 1: 296.

75. Looney, ed., *Brewers and Texas Politics* 1: 33–36. Adjutant General's Department Texas Volunteer Guard Military Rolls, 1880–1903, Archives and Information Services Division, *Texas State Library and Archives Commission.*

76. Looney, ed., *Brewers and Texas Politics* 1: 39, 42.

77. Looney, ed., *Brewers and Texas Politics* 1: 42.

78. Looney, ed., *Brewers and Texas Politics* 1: 296.

79. *Alabama Official and Statistical Register, 1911,* comp. Owen, 318–19; Cherrington, *History of the Anti-Saloon League,* 118, 134.

80. "DECLARATION OF PRINCIPLES," *Ocala,* FL, *Evening Star,* October 6, 1910, 2.

81. *Report of the Secretary of State of the State of Florida,* ed. H. Clay Crawford (Tallahassee: 1911), 16–22; *Report of the Secretary of State of the State of Florida* (Tallahassee: T. J. Appleyard, 1919).

82. Cherrington, ed., *Anti-Saloon League Year Book* (1914), 116; see also Cherrington, ed., *Anti-Saloon League Year Book* (1913), 60.

83. Plocheck, "Prohibition Elections in Texas." Statistics on some elections missing in Plocheck provided by Endersby, "Prohibition and Repeal," 506. When their numbers differ, I defer to Plocheck.

84. Van Craddock, "Bullets bedeviled Sinkiller's revival," Longview, TX, *New-Journal,* April 10, 2011, www.news-journal.com/opinion/columnists/van_craddock/bullets-bedeviled-sinkiller-s-revival/article_167eb552-7427-5700-8a9d-8c04a646e879.html (accessed March 24, 2014).

85. C. C. Garrett to Otto Koehler, November 26, 1910, in Looney, ed., *Brewers and Texas Politics* 1: 78.

86. Looney, ed., *Brewers and Texas Politics* 1: 78–79.

87. Looney, ed., *Brewers and Texas Politics* 1: 79.

88. P. C. Hunt to Ormund Paget, December 21, 1910, in Looney, ed., *Brewers and Texas Politics* 1: 63.

89. Looney, ed., *Brewers and Texas Politics* 1: 63; Wright and Hawkins, *Centennial Encyclopedia of the African Methodist Episcopal Church* 1: 120.

90. Hunt to Paget, December 21, 1910, in Looney, ed., *Brewers and Texas Politics* 1: 63.

91. Chana Kai Lee, *For Freedom's Sake: The Life of Fannie Lou Hamer* (Urbana: University of Illinois Press, 1999), 1–2.

92. Theodore Baughman to Lone Star Brewery, December 11, 1912, in Looney, ed., *Brewers and Texas Politics* 1: 310; Adoue to TBA, November 27, 1908, in Looney, ed., *Brewers and Texas Politics* 1: 264; S. T. Morgan, Dallas Brewery, to F. G. Cook, Texarkana, April 23, 1912, in Looney, ed., *Brewers and Texas Politics* 2: 622.

93. Looney, ed., *Brewers and Texas Politics* 1: 48.

94. Looney, ed., *Brewers and Texas Politics* 1: 48.

95. All quotes from Dallas *Texas Christian Advocate,* August 17, 1911, 1. When Blackshear reversed himself again and spoke out for prohibition in 1914, he lost his position as head of the school a year later due to pressure from another wet governor, Jim Ferguson. This pressure suggests that he might have lost his position in 1911 if he had not declared himself against Prohibition. Watson, "Evangelical Protestants and the Prohibition Movement in Texas," 141. For a critical take on Colquitt's stance as a wet, see Shuler, *New Issue.*

96. J.B.R. to B. H. Carroll, San Antonio *Daily Express,* July 27, 1887; Cantrell, *Kenneth and John B. Rayner,* 193.

97. Cantrell, *Feeding the Wolf,* 23–25.

98. Cantrell, *Feeding the Wolf,* 88–102.

99. Washington's dry position in Okrent, *Last Call,* 43, 74. For a favorable treatment of a similar kind of flexibility by Washington, see Norrell, *Up from History.* Cantrell, *Kenneth and John B. Rayner,* 188–92; Cantrell, *Feeding the Wolf,* 1–24; L. B. Scott, "Hon. J. B. Rayner," Dallas *Southwestern Christian Advocate,* September 1, 1898; for Rayner's writings, see J. B. Rayner, "The Worth of Character," Dallas *Southwestern Christian Advocate,* December 29, 1898; J. B. Rayner, "Does History Repeat Itself?" Dallas *Southwestern Christian Advocate,* May 8, 1902; *Twenty-Fifth Annual Session of the National Baptist Convention,* 156–57.

100. A small sampling of J. B. Rayner's writings is "The Worth of Character," *Southwestern Christian Advocate,* December 29, 1898, and "Does History Repeat Itself?" *Southwestern Christian Advocate,* May 8, 1902.

101. "J. B. Rayner is here helping us, and he is patriotic enough not to make any specific charges for his labors; he leaves his wages to us." Letter from L. R. Callaway, Corsicana, TX, to S. T. Morgan, Dallas Brewery, June 13, 1907, in Looney, ed., *Brewers and Texas Politics* 2 : 658.

102. Marian Jean Barber, "How the Irish, Germans, and Czechs Became Anglo: Race and Identity in the Texas-Mexico Borderlands," PhD diss., University of Texas at Austin, 2010; David R. Roediger, *Working Toward Whiteness: How America's Immigrants Became White* (New York: Basic Books, 2005).

103. *Legislative Reference Library of Texas,* "Constitutional amendment election dates"; Plocheck, "Prohibition Elections in Texas."

104. Sutton, "Ethnic Minorities," 57, 53.

105. Cherrington, ed., *Anti-Saloon League Year Book* (1912), 188. A "practically solid Mexican vote" and 85 percent of Black votes wet from *El Paso Herald,* July 24, 1911, 3; *Austin Statesman,* July 24, 1911, 2.

106. Rayner to Zane Cetti, November 14, 1908, in Looney, ed., *Brewers and Texas Politics* 1: 263; two weeks later an internal brewers' report admitted, "we need him in three counties holding elections this next year," but expressed no skepticism about his 50,000 estimate, in Looney, ed., *Brewers and Texas Politics* 1: 264.

107. Szymanski, *Pathways to Prohibition,* 15. The 40,000 number is the high-end estimate in Gould, *Progressives and Prohibitionists,* 48–49; Cantrell, *Kenneth and John B. Rayner,* 272. Alwyn Barr, *Black Texans: A History of African Americans in Texas, 1528–1995* (Norman: University of Oklahoma Press, 1996), 113. Locke cites Barr's assessment when stating that Black political activism was largely muted by 1908 in "Making the Bible Belt," 260–61.

108. Chicago *Day Book,* September 10, 1912, 28.

109. "COUNTY CONVENTION TO BE HELD," *Prescott,* AR, *Daily News,* May 6, 1912, 1.

110. *Sentinel-Record,* Hot Springs, AR, September 8, 1912, 10.

111. "W.C.T.U.," *Prescott,* AR, *Daily News,* August 15, 1912, 3.

112. Cherrington, ed., *Anti-Saloon League Year Book* (1913), 39; Cherrington, *History of the Anti-Saloon League,* 118, 134.

113. Cherrington, ed., *Anti-Saloon League Year Book* (1914), 116; Cherrington, ed., *Anti-Saloon League Year Book* (1913), 39.

114. "Your friend" to Wahrmund, August 5, 1909, in Looney, ed., *Brewers and Texas Politics* 1: 70.

115. "Your friend" to Wahrmund, August 11, 1909, in Looney, ed., *Brewers and Texas Politics* 1: 71.

116. Rayner to Wahrmund, July 9, 1912, in Looney, ed., *Brewers and Texas Politics* 1: 68–69.

117. Wahrmund to Rayner, July 12, 1912, in Looney, ed., *Brewers and Texas Politics* 1: 69. The only further evidence of Rayner's interaction with the brewers was a ninety-day loan for seventy-five dollars on March 26, 1914, years later. Looney, ed., *Brewers and Texas Politics* 1: 211.

118. *Houston Chronicle,* October 20, 1912. See also Cantrell, *Kenneth and John B. Rayner,* 271.

119. J. B. Gambrell and G. C. Rankin, "The Preacher and the Pending Issue," *Home and State,* June 29, 1912, 3; cartoon from *Home and State,* August 5, 1911, 3.

120. *Baptist Standard,* August 24 and October 19, 1911. See also Ivy, *No Saloon in the Valley,* 117–18.

121. H. C. Park, "Let the People Rule," *Home and State,* July 6, 1912, 5.

122. Cantrell, *Kenneth and John B. Rayner,* 248, 327n10; Plocheck, "Prohibition Elections in Texas." Since overall turnout—including whites—was about 23.7 percent in 1919, it is likely that Black turnout was much lower, likely in single digits.

123. *Abilene Daily Reporter,* January 10, 1915, 1.

124. In Looney's words, "This volume [*There were two volumes*] contains practically all of the evidence introduced." Looney, ed., *Brewers and Texas Politics,* vol. 1: 1–2. For further discussion of this and related lawsuits by Attorney General Looney, see Kevin C. Motl's delightfully titled "Under the Influence: The Texas Business Men's Association and the Campaign against Reform, 1906–1915," *Southwestern Historical Quarterly* 109 (April 2006): 494–529.

125. For percentages, see Cantrell, *Kenneth and John B. Rayner,* 248, 327n10; Plocheck, "Prohibition Elections in Texas." For absolute numbers, see Cantrell, *Kenneth and John B. Rayner,* 272; Gould, *Progressives and Prohibitionists,* 48–49; J. Morgan Kousser, *The Shaping of Southern*

Politics: Suffrage Restriction and the Establishment of the One-Party South (New Haven, CT: Yale University Press, 1974), 240–46.

126. Cherrington, ed., *Anti-Saloon League Year Book* (1915), 206–7; Cherrington, ed., *Anti-Saloon League Year Book* (1917), 221; Lewis, *Coming of Southern Prohibition.*

127. Cherrington, ed., *Anti-Saloon League Year Book* (1914), 101; O'Daniel, *Crusaders, Gangsters, and Whiskey,* 23; Cherrington, ed., *Anti-Saloon League Year Book* (1915), 206–7; Cherrington, ed., *Anti-Saloon League Year Book* (1917), 221; Cherrington, ed., *Anti-Saloon League Year Book* (1926), 151–52.

128. Hankins, *Jesus and Gin,* 187.

129. Plocheck, "Prohibition Elections in Texas."

5. Rebels against Rum and Romanism

1. Barry Hankins, *God's Rascal: J. Frank Norris & the Beginnings of Southern Fundamentalism* (Lexington: University Press of Kentucky, 1996), 188n35.

2. *Alabama Baptist,* February 15, 1894, cited in Wayne Flynt, *Cracker Messiah: Governor Sidney J. Catts of Florida* (Baton Rouge: Louisiana State University Press, 1977), 10.

3. Frank Norris, "The Conspiracy of Rum and Romanism to Rule This Government," *Searchlight,* Fort Worth, February 5, 1926, 6.

4. Schmidt, *Souls or the Social Order,* 199; Mark Noll, *The Old Religion in a New World: The History of North American Christianity* (Grand Rapids, MI: Eerdmans, 2002), 135. See also Odegard, *Pressure Politics,* 18; Okrent, *Last Call.*

5. Texas was about 18 percent Catholic in 1890. Hunt and Bliss, eds., *Religious Bodies, 1916,* 112.

6. Brian, "1887 Prohibition Crusade in Texas," 17–18, 25; Noll, *History of Christianity,* 295–99. See also Timberlake, *Prohibition and the Progressive Movement;* McGreevy, *Catholicism and American Freedom.*

7. Flynt, *Cracker Messiah,* 3–22; "Early Figures About Correct," *Birmingham,* AL, *Age-Herald,* April 14, 1904, 1.

8. Flynt, *Cracker Messiah,* 25–26.

9. "SIDNEY J. CATTS GELS [*sic*] IN RACE FOR GOVERNOR," *Orlando Evening Star,* October 27, 1914, 1; "Former Governor of Florida Dies," *Montgomery Advertiser,* March 10, 1936, 3.

10. Flynt, *Cracker Messiah,* 340, 76.

11. "Campaign Flier for Sidney J. Catts, 1916," *Florida Memory.*

12. "Campaign Flier for Sidney J. Catts, 1916."

13. "PUBLIC WARNED OF A SERIOUS SITUATION," *Pensacola Journal,* January 9, 1916, 4. chroniclingamerica.loc.gov/lccn/sn87062268/1916-01-09/ed-1/seq-4.

14. "SIDNEY J. CATTS GELS IN RACE FOR GOVERNOR," *Orlando Evening Star,* October 27, 1914, 1.

15. Flynt, *Cracker Messiah,* 79, 60–94.

16. Flynt, *Cracker Messiah,* 95.

17. Flynt, *Cracker Messiah,* 94–275.

18. Nicholas Graves, "Pat Neff and the Pat Neff Collection: Biography, History, and Interpretation," MA thesis, Baylor University, 2011.

19. Pat Neff, *The Battles of Peace* (Fort Worth: Pioneer Publishing Co., 1925), 275. This book represents a collection of Neff's speeches from various occasions compiled and sold shortly after the end of his second term as governor.

20. R. V. Nichols and L. C. Sutton, *The Dean Law and the Prohibition Amendment to the Texas Constitution: With Synopsis and Explanations* (Austin, TX: Nichols and Sutton, 1919), 3–5, 21–22; Norman D. Brown, *Hood, Bonnet, and Little Brown Jug: Texas Politics, 1921-1928* (College Station: Texas A&M University Press, 1984), 5–6.

21. Jeanne Bozzell McCarty, *The Struggle for Sobriety: Protestants and Prohibition in Texas: 1919-1935* (El Paso: Texas Western Press, 1980), 12–13.

22. Neff, *Battles of Peace,* 290. Note that the Texas Constitution omits the words "all of"; apparently Neff had added them for emphasis. *Texas Constitution,* Article 4, Section 10.

23. Neff, *Battles of Peace,* 290.

24. Neff, *Battles of Peace,* 305.

25. Neff, *Battles of Peace,* 306.

26. Neff, *Battles of Peace,* 307.

27. Westmoreland Davis, *Address of Governor Westmoreland Davis Delivered Before the General Assembly of Virginia, January 11, 1922* (Richmond, VA: Davis Bottom, Superintendent Public Printing, 1922), 24. Found in Pat Neff Collection, Baylor University Texas Collection.

28. Davis, *Address of Governor Westmoreland Davis,* 25.

29. McGirr, *War on Alcohol,* 71.

30. McGirr, *War on Alcohol,* 82, 73–85.

31. McGirr, *War on Alcohol,* 85–86.

32. McGirr, *War on Alcohol,* 88, 87; Lee, *For Freedom's Sake,* 1–2.

33. See also McGirr, *War on Alcohol,* 89–100; O'Daniel, *Crusaders, Gangsters, and Whiskey,* 6, 13–16, 34, 38–41, 45, 47, 86, 140, 171, 218, 241–42, esp. 93–95.

34. McGirr, *War on Alcohol,* 83, 88.

35. *Bolivar,* TN, *Bulletin,* October 14, 1887, 2; Thompson, *"A Most Stirring and Significant Episode,"* 206.

36. O'Daniel, *Crusaders, Gangsters, and Whiskey,* 8–17.

37. Adam Tamburin and Natalie Allison, "Protests in downtown Nashville: Arrests made for those out after curfew," *Nashville Tennessean,* www.tennessean.com/story/news/2020/05/30/george-floyd-death-nashville-tennessee-protest-may-john-cooper/5286837002 (May 30, 2020).

38. First two quotes from Atticus Webb to Pat Neff, February 7, 1921, last quotes Preston P. Reynolds to Neff, Pat M. Neff Papers, Texas Collection, Baylor University; see also Dallas *Home and State,* April 1, 1921 (clipping), Pat M. Neff Biographical File, Barker Texas History Center; Brown, *Hood, Bonnet, and Little Brown Jug,* 22, 441.

39. "The Liquor Crowd Showing Their Hand," *Home and State,* November 30, 1915, 4.

40. McGirr, *War on Alcohol,* xx.

41. O'Daniel, *Crusaders, Gangsters, and Whiskey,* 6, 107–14, 242; Christopher Long, "KU KLUX KLAN," *Handbook of Texas Online,* www.tshaonline.org/handbook/online/articles/vek02 (accessed November 20, 2016).

42. Christopher Long, "KU KLUX KLAN," *Handbook of Texas Online,* www.tshaonline.org/handbook/online/articles/vek02 (accessed November 23, 2013); Lisa C. Maxwell, "EVANS, HIRAM WESLEY," *Handbook of Texas Online,* www.tshaonline.org/handbook/online/articles/fev17 (accessed November 23, 2013); Brown, *Hood, Bonnet, and Little Brown Jug,* 66–87. For the ASL's reluctance to support a Klansman, see "'DRYS' AND KU KLUX COMBINE IN TEXAS: Both Backing

Mayfield Against Ferguson in Fight for Senatorial Nomination," *New York Times,* August 5, 1922, 6; the article mentions that the ASL's general counsel, Wayne B. Wheeler, admitted, "Yes, it is peculiar that in this campaign we happen to be linked with the klan [*sic*] behind Mayfield, but this is a circumstance over which we have no control." Contra traditional historiography associating drys with the Klan, see Hofstadter, *Age of Reform* 291–92.

43. Quotes from J. B. Cranfill to J. D. Sandefer, April 29, 1922, J. B. Cranfill Papers, University of Texas Archives; as cited in Brown, *Hood, Bonnet, and Little Brown Jug,* 55, 446n14; other data, 54–55.

44. Long, "KLAN"; Maxwell, "EVANS"; Adolphus Hotel, "Our Story," www.hoteladolphus.com /our-story (accessed November 29, 2012).

45. Frank H. Smyrl, "MAYFIELD, EARLE BRADFORD," *Handbook of Texas Online,* www.tsha online.org/handbook/online/articles/fma91 (accessed November 29, 2012).

46. "'DRYS' AND KU KLUX COMBINE IN TEXAS," 6. For traditional historiography associating drys with the Klan, see Hofstadter, *Age of Reform,* 291–92.

47. "WET DEMOCRATS NOMINATE DRY REPUBLICAN FOR THE UNITED STATES SENATE," unsigned editorial, *Home and State,* October 1922, 1.

48. *Home and State,* October 1922, 1.

49. Sarah Woolfolk Wiggins, ed., *From Civil War to Civil Rights–Alabama, 1860–1960* (Tuscaloosa: University of Alabama Press, 1987), 316.

50. "Profiles in Courage Episode List," www.imdb.com/title/tt0057780/episodes?year=1964& ref_=tt_eps_yr_1964 (accessed August 22, 2020).

51. Watson, "J. Thomas Heflin."

52. John D. Huddleston, "FERGUSON, MIRIAM AMANDA WALLACE [MA]," *Handbook of Texas Online,* www.tshaonline.org/handbook/online/articles/ffe06 (accessed November 20, 2016).

53. David M. Chalmers, *Hooded Americanism: The History of the Ku Klux Klan* (3rd ed., Durham, NC: Duke University Press, 1987) 46–48.

54. O'Daniel, *Crusaders, Gangsters, and Whiskey,* 242.

55. Hankins, *Jesus and Gin,* 187–211.

56. "For the Time Is Come That Judgment Must Begin at the House of God," *Fundamentalist,* November 16, 1928, 1, 8.

57. The Ohio paper had criticized Baptist minister John Roach Straton of New York for calling Al Smith the "deadliest foe in America of the forces of moral progress." *Home and State,* August 1928, 4.

58. *Home and State,* October 1928, 8.

59. *Home and State,* October 1928, 8. See also "Partisan Politics and the Churches," *Home and State,* October 1928, 4.

60. Quote from *Dallas Morning News,* July 4, 1928, as cited in Brown, *Hood, Bonnet, and Little Brown Jug,* 9, 440n15. Slayton, *Empire Statesman,* 257–58.

61. "UNDERWOOD LAUDS SMITH," *New York Times,* December 10, 1927, 4, www.encyclopediao-falabama.org/article/h-2961; Frederic William Wile, "DEMOCRATS FEEL CERTAIN OF SOUTH," *Evening Star,* Washington, DC, September 11, 1928, 5; Watson, "Oscar Underwood; Steve Suitts, "Hugo L. Black," *Encyclopedia of Alabama,* encyclopediaofalabama.org/article/h-1848 (updated January 31, 2017).

62. "Shall Roman Catholicism Rule Tarrant County?" *Searchlight,* July 21, 1922, 1–2.

63. Hankins, *Jesus and Gin,* 133–43.

64. Frank Norris, "Sermon Delivered Sunday Night to Audience of Ten Thousand," *Searchlight,* August 1, 1924, 1–4.

65. Frank Norris, "The Boy v. the Bootlegger," *Searchlight,* March 25, 1927, 1.

66. Frank Norris, "Robertson vs. Jim Ferguson: Rum, Romanism, Russianism, the Issue," *Searchlight,* August 1, 1924, 1.

67. Frank Norris, "The Conspiracy of Rum and Romanism to Rule This Government," *Searchlight,* February 5, 1926, 6.

68. Charles C. Marshall, "An Open Letter to the Honorable Alfred E. Smith," *Atlantic Monthly* 139 (April 1927): 540; McGreevy, *Catholicism and American Freedom,* 149, 355n128; Norris's reprint of Marshall's "Open Letter" in *Fundamentalist,* April 22, 1927, 4–6.

69. Hankins, *God's Rascal,* first quote 47, other quotes 47–51.

70. Norris to R. B. Craeger [*sic*], May 20, 1927, Norris Papers, Texas Collection, Baylor University.

71. "Six Thousand Dallasites Enthusiastically Cheer Name of Hoover Monday Night," *Fundamentalist,* August 24, 1928, 4.

72. L. R. Scarborough, "The Ground of My Opposition to Putting Governor Smith in the White House," *Fundamentalist,* October 5, 1928, 1–2, 7.

73. Slayton, *Empire Statesman,* 310.

74. *Home and State,* July 1928, 1.

75. Hohner, *Prohibition and Politics,* 218.

76. Hohner, *Prohibition and Politics,* 217–25.

77. Hohner, *Prohibition and Politics,* 229–34.

78. *Congressional Record,* January 28, 1928, 1st Session, 70th Congress, vol. 69, pt. 2: 1654–58; Watson, "J. Thomas Heflin."

79. Faulkner, "Furnifold McLendel Simmons"; Frederic William Wile, "DEMOCRATS FEEL CERTAIN OF SOUTH," *Evening Star,* Washington, DC, September 11, 1928, 5.

80. *Home and State,* September 1928, 1; July 1928, 1; January 1928, 5.

81. Hofstadter, *Age of Reform,* 298–301; Hankins, *Jesus and Gin,* 187–212; Hankins, *God's Rascal,* esp. 45–73. *Home and State,* September 1928, 1; July 1928, 1; January 1928, 5.

82. *Home and State,* December 1927, 4.

83. *Home and State,* November 1928, 2.

84. *Home and State,* September 1928, 5.

85. *Home and State,* July 1928, 1.

86. *Home and State,* September 1928, 5.

87. *Home and State,* October 1928, 1.

88. *Home and State,* October 1928, 5.

89. Hohner, *Prohibition and Politics,* 227.

90. Watson, "J. Thomas Heflin"; Faulkner, "Furnifold McLendel Simmons."

91. Editorial, "Kelly Miller on Prohibition," Boston *Christian Leader,* September 22, 1928. The quote is from Romans 14, which referred to individuals voluntarily giving up liberty, not forcing others to conform to their morality.

92. Joe Soss and Vesla Weaver, "Police Are Our Government: Politics, Political Science, and the Policing of Race–Class Subjugated Communities," *Annual Review of Political Science* 20 (May 2017): 575.

93. McCarty, *Struggle for Sobriety,* 18.

94. Hankins, *God's Rascal,* 51–65.

95. Faulkner, "Furnifold McLendel Simmons"; Frederic William Wile, "DEMOCRATS FEEL CERTAIN OF SOUTH," Boston *Evening Star,* September 11, 1928, 5.

96. Watson, "J. Thomas Heflin."

97. McCarty, *Struggle for Sobriety,* 20, citing Dallas *Baptist Standard,* November 22, 1928.

98. McCarty, *Struggle for Sobriety,* 21, citing Dallas *Christian Courier,* November 8, 1928.

99. McCarty, *Struggle for Sobriety,* 21, citing Dallas *Christian Courier,* November 15, 1928.

100. Hankins, *God's Rascal,* 66.

6. Lily-White Repeal: White Women and the Decline of Gin Crow

1. Mrs. S. J. Sweeny, "The Negro and Mexican vs. Woman," *Home and State,* September 13, 1911, 5.

2. Sinclair Moreland, "Woman Suffrage," *Home and State,* November 2, 1912, 1.

3. Moreland, "Woman Suffrage," 1.

4. Ida Husted Harper, ed., *The History of Woman Suffrage* (New York: J. J. Little and Ives, 1922), 2.

5. Harper, *History of Woman Suffrage,* 2–3; Valerie Pope Burnes, "Pattie Ruffner Jacobs," *Encyclopedia of Alabama,* www.encyclopediaofalabama.org/article/h-1107 (updated August 24, 2017).

6. Harper, *History of Woman Suffrage,* 3–7, 333, 492, 691; Burnes, "Pattie Ruffner Jacobs."

7. Harper, *History of Woman Suffrage,* 7–8.

8. Harper, *History of Woman Suffrage,* 8; Burnes, "Pattie Ruffner Jacobs."

9. Jennifer M. Murray, "Richmond Pearson Hobson," *Encyclopedia of Alabama,* www.encyclopediaofalabama.org/article/h-3235 (updated April 21, 2015); Richmond Pearson Hobson, *Alcohol and the Human Race* (New York: Fleming R. Revell Co., 1919).

10. Brown, *Hood, Bonnet, and Little Brown Jug,* 226.

11. *The Constitution of the United States of America Analysis and Interpretation Analysis of Cases Decided by the Supreme Court of the United States to July 1, 2014,* US Senate Document 108-17, 35n10 and 36n11.

12. A. Elizabeth Taylor, "WOMAN SUFFRAGE," *Handbook of Texas Online,* www.tshaonline.org/handbook/online/articles/viw01 (accessed November 20, 2016); Plocheck, "Prohibition Elections in Texas."

13. Odegard, *Pressure Politics;* "A Nation of Drunkards," *Prohibition,* produced by Burns and Novick.

14. "The Sheppard-Towner Maternity and Infancy Act," Historical Highlights, US House of Representatives, history.house.gov/Historical-Highlights/1901-1950/The-Sheppard%E2%80%93Towner-Maternity-and-Infancy-Act/ (accessed April 4, 2020).

15. Birmingham *Age-Herald,* September 30, 1898, 5; June 9 and 15, 1899, 6; January 9, 1901, 2; April 18 and 27, 1902, 6.

16. *Omaha Daily Bee,* June 13, 1920, 1.

17. *Evening Star,* Washington, DC, March 13, 1933, 19.

18. Neff, *Battles of Peace,* 275.

19. Neff, *Battles of Peace,* 293.

20. Carl Randall McQueary and May Nelson Paulissen, *Ma's in the Kitchen: You'll Know When It's Done! The Recipes and History of Governor Miriam A. Ferguson, First Woman Governor of Texas* (Austin: Eakin Press: 1994), 47. While the book was written for a popular audience and is evidently hagiographic, one of the authors holds a PhD and so carries some academic weight.

21. Huddleston, "FERGUSON, MIRIAM AMANDA WALLACE [MA]."

22. Grace C. Root, *Women and Repeal: The Story of the Women's Organization for National Prohibition Reform,* authorized by Mrs. Charles H. Sabin (New York: Harper and Brothers, 1934), 3–4.

23. Root, *Women and Repeal,* 4.

24. "Recognition of Representative De Priest by Hoovers Is Causing Stir in Washington," Springfield, OH[?], June 17, 1929, in Barbara De Priest Clipping Collection, White House Historical Association. See also Davis S. Day, "Herbert Hoover and Racial Politics: The De Priest Incident," *Journal of Negro History* 65 (Winter 1980): 6–17.

25. Quote in "STRANGE PARTY LINEUP DRAWN AGAINST RASKOB," *Indianapolis Times,* June 19, 1929, 7; "1,000 VIRGINIA 'HOOVERCRATS' IN OPEN SESSION," *Indianapolis Times,* June 18, 1929, 16.

26. "STRANGE PARTY LINEUP DRAWN AGAINST RASKOB," *Indianapolis Times,* June 19, 1929, 7; "1,000 VIRGINIA 'HOOVERCRATS' IN OPEN SESSION," *Indianapolis Times,* June 18, 1929, 16.

27. "MOODY CRITICIZES DE PRIEST INCIDENT," *Evening Star,* Washington, DC, June 23, 1929, 5.

28. "BLEASE POETRY IS EXPUNGED FROM RECORD," *Afro American,* June 22, 1929, 1.

29. "GOVERNORS OF SOUTH ASSAIL 'MOB JUSTICE,'" *Indianapolis Times,* July 22, 1930, 14.

30. Isaac Stanley-Becker, "Who's behind the law making undocumented immigrants criminals? An 'unrepentant white supremacist,'" *Washington Post,* June 27, 2019, www.washingtonpost .com/nation/2019/06/27/julian-castro-beto-orourke-section-immigration-illegal-coleman -livingstone-blease.

31. "TEXAS SENATE HITS MRS. HOOVER'S ACTION," *Evening Star,* Washington, DC, June 15, 1929, 6; "Texas Senate Flays Mrs. Hoover for Entertaining Mrs. Oscar De Priest," *Bismarck,* NC, *Tribune,* June 15, 1929, 1.

32. "MISSISSIPPI ACTS ON DE PRIEST AFFAIR," *Evening Star,* Washington, DC, June 26, 1929, 4.

33. "Recognition of Representative De Priest."

34. Root, *Women and Repeal,* 15.

35. Root, *Women and Repeal,* 40.

36. Root, *Women and Repeal,* 19. Root routinely quotes Sabin and other sources without full citation.

37. Root, *Women and Repeal,* 20–21.

38. Frederick Lewis Allen, *Only Yesterday* (1931; rpt. New York: Perennial Classics, 2000), 87; 76–105.

39. Paula Fass, *The Damned and the Beautiful: American Youth in the 1920's* (New York: Oxford University Press, 1977); Beth L. Bailey, *From Front Porch to Back Seat: Courtship in Twentieth-Century America* (Baltimore: Johns Hopkins University Press, 1989).

40. *New York Tribune,* June 18, 1930, cited in Root, *Women and Repeal,* 13.

41. Root, *Women and Repeal,* 13.

42. Irving Fisher, *Prohibition at Its Worst* (New York: Macmillan Co., 1926), 15. Though this book is written by a prohibitionist, it does report the rhetoric of the anti-prohibitionists.

43. Root, *Women and Repeal,* 162.

44. Root, *Women and Repeal,* 69.

45. Root, *Women and Repeal,* 26–27.

46. Root, *Women and Repeal,* 1.

47. Root, *Women and Repeal,* 3.

48. R.W.G., "From Our Western Correspondent," Boston *Christian Leader,* January 19, 1928, 71; "A Nation of Drunkards" and "A Nation of Hypocrites," *Prohibition,* produced by Burns and Novick.

49. Root, *Women and Repeal,* opposite title page.

50. WONPR numbers in Root, *Women and Repeal,* vii–ix; WCTU numbers in Ian Tyrrell, *Woman's World/Woman's Empire: The Woman's Christian Temperance Union in International Perspective, 1800–1930* (Chapel Hill: University of North Carolina Press, 1991), 2. Tyrrell also states, "The WCTU was not the largest organization of women in the United States over the period of the 1870s to the 1930s," a claim that seemingly confirms the WONPR's claim to have more members than the WCTU ever did. It must be noted, however, that WONPR members were not required to pay dues, whereas WCTU members were, indicating a greater degree of commitment among dry women. The WCTU also claimed a following of over a million, comparable to the WONPR at its height. Even if the WONPR number is inflated, it is still clear that the WCTU declined after 1927 and WONPR membership overtook that of the WCTU by early 1933, the crucial year in which sheer numbers of women's votes mattered most for determining state conventions on prohibition.

51. Root, *Women and Repeal,* 133.

52. Root, *Women and Repeal,* photo between 32 and 33.

53. Root, *Women and Repeal,* 136.

54. Priscilla Myers Benham, "MOORE, HELEN EDMUNDS," *Handbook of Texas Online,* www.tshaonline.org/handbook/online/articles/fm083 (accessed February 4, 2017); Nancy Baker Jones and Ruthe Winegarten, *Capitol Women: Texas Female Legislators, 1923–1999* (Austin: University of Texas Press, 2000), 89–91; Root, *Women and Repeal,* 89.

55. Harper, *History of Woman Suffrage,* 9; Burnes, "Pattie Ruffner Jacobs."

56. *Evening Star,* Washington, DC, March 13, 1933, 19, and April 4, 1933, A-2.

57. "WOMEN FIGHT PROHIBITION: Mobile School Women Lobby Against Bill in Alabama Senate," Newbery, SC, *Herald and News,* November 22, 1907, 3. On the United Daughters of the Confederacy, see Cynthia Mills and Pamela Hemenway Simpson, eds., *Monuments to the Lost Cause: Women, Art, and the Landscapes of Southern Memory.* Knoxville: University of Tennessee Press, 2003; John M. Murrin, et al., *Liberty, Equality, Power: A History of the American People,* vol. 1: *To 1877* (6th ed., Boston: Cengage, 2013), 425; Greg Huffman, "The group behind Confederate monuments also built a memorial to the Klan," *Facing South: The Online Magazine for the Institute of Southern Studies,* June 8, 2018, www.facingsouth.org/2018/06/group-behind-confederate-monuments-also-built-memorial-klan.

58. Root, *Women and Repeal,* 34.

59. Root, *Women and Repeal,* 161–62.

60. Fisher, *Prohibition at Its Worst,* 18.

61. Quoted in Hankins, *Jesus and Gin,* 38.

62. Okrent, *Last Call,* 182–92; Erskine, *Prohibition and Christianity,* 11–27.

63. Hankins, *Jesus and Gin,* 187–212.

64. Root, *Women and Repeal,* 39.

65. Kenneth D. Rose, *American Women and the Repeal of Prohibition* (New York: New York University Press, 1996), 4.

66. Root, *Women and Repeal,* 1.

67. Root, *Women and Repeal,* 15.

68. Root, *Women and Repeal,* 127.

69. Root, *Women and Repeal,* 69.

70. Root, *Women and Repeal,* 103–4.

71. Slayton, *Empire Statesman,* 237–328; Finan, *Alfred E. Smith,* 189–230; Kerr, "ANTI-SALOON LEAGUE OF TEXAS."

72. Root, *Women and Repeal,* 29.

73. Root, *Women and Repeal,* 58.

74. McQueary and Paulissen, *Ma's in the Kitchen,* quote on 56, 56–57.

75. Root, *Women and Repeal,* 57, 114.

76. R. G. Mood, ed., *Minutes of the Sixty-Sixth Annual Session of the North Texas Annual Conference of the Methodist Episcopal Church, South* (Gainesville, TX, 1932), 35.

77. *Evening Star,* Washington, DC, March 30, 1933, A-6.

78. The nineteen states of April 7 were: Arizona, California, Colorado, Delaware, Illinois, Indiana, Kentucky, Maryland, Minnesota, Missouri, Montana, Nevada, New Jersey, New York, Ohio, Oregon, Pennsylvania, Washington, and Wisconsin. *Evening Star,* Washington, DC, April 6, 1933, A-4.

79. *Evening Star,* Washington, DC, July 11, 1933, A-6.

80. The other state was Kansas. *Hendersonville,* NC, *Times-News,* August 25, 1933, 3; O'Daniel, *Crusaders, Gangsters, and Whiskey,* 203; *Evening Star,* Washington, DC, September 10, 1933, A-3; *Indianapolis Times,* December 18, 1934, 6.

81. J. E. Hays, comp., *Georgia's Official Register: 1933–1935–1937* (Atlanta: Georgia Department of Archives and History, 1938), 766–71.

82. "TENNESSEE IN 'WET' COLUMN BY SLIM VOTE," *Hendersonville,* NC, *Times-News,* July 21, 1933, 1; *Evening Star,* Washington, DC, October 4, 1933, A-3, and November 8, 1933, A-4; H. M. London, comp. and ed., *North Carolina Manual, 1935* (Raleigh, NC: Mitchell Printing Co., 1935), 113; *Key West,* FL, *Citizen,* October 11, 1933, 1.

83. Initial results from "VIRGINIA'S REPEAL VOTE NEARLY 2–1," *Evening Star,* Washington, DC, October 4, 1933, 3.

84. "5 STATES VOTE WET; KANSAS REMAINS DRY," *Indianapolis Times,* November 7, 1934, 22. R. A. Gray, *Report of the Secretary of State of the State of Florida: For the Period Beginning January 1, 1933, and Ending December 31, 1934* (Tallahassee: Rose Printing Co., 1935), between 302–3; *Hendersonville,* NC, *Times-News,* July 21, 1933, 1; February 26, 1935, 1. *Evening Star,* Washington, DC, October 4, 1933, A-3; November 8, 1933, A-4. *Key West,* FL, *Citizen,* October 11, 1933, 1. *Roanoke Rapids Herald,* August 30, 1934, 20.

85. Plocheck, "Prohibition Elections in Texas."

86. *Evening Star,* Washington, DC, December 2, 1935, A-7; *Alabama Official and Statistical Register, 1935,* comp. Marie B. Owen (Wetumpka, AL: Wetumpka Printing Co., 1935), 764–65;

Hays, comp., *Georgia's Official Register,* 766–71; "Georgia's Rural Voters Defeat Repeal," *Elizabeth City,* NC, *Daily Independent,* June 10, 1937, 1.

87. Dallas *Southwestern Advocate,* February 14, 1935, 4; February 21, 1935, 5.

88. Endersby, "Prohibition and Repeal," 503–12.

89. "BIRMINGHAM DRY BUT ONLY IN NAME," *Evening Star,* Washington, DC, November 10, 1936, 6; "PROHIBITION VOTED OUT BY ALABAMANS," *Bismarck,* NC, *Tribune,* March 11, 1937, 9; "North Carolina Bone Dry Law Is Scrapped," *Bismarck,* NC, *Tribune,* February 20, 1937, 7; "RIVERS SIGNS LIQUOR BILL," *New York Times,* February 5, 1938, 7.

90. O'Daniel, *Crusaders, Gangsters, and Whiskey,* 203, 236; "TENNESSEE IN 'WET' COLUMN BY SLIM VOTE," Hendersonville, NC, *Times-News,* July 21, 1933, 1; "TENNESSEE VOTES 4 TO 1 TO KEEP BANS ON WHISKEY SALES," *Hendersonville,* NC, *Times-News,* September 24, 1937, 1.

91. Ted Ownby, "Prohibition," *Mississippi Encyclopedia,* Center for Study of Southern Culture, mississippiencyclopedia.org/entries/prohibition (July 11, 2017).

92. J. Frank Norris, "The NRA and the Mark of the Beast," *Fundamentalist,* October 18, 1935, 2, 6, and 8. See also Hankins, *God's Rascal,* 71.

93. Root, *Women and Repeal,* 151.

94. Jones and Winegarten, *Capitol Women,* 89–91.

95. J. Frank Norris, "The NRA and the Mark of the Beast," *Fundamentalist,* October 18, 1935, 2, 6, and 8. See also Hankins, *God's Rascal,* 71.

96. Olin W. Nail, "Lest We Forget, Lest We Forget," Dallas *Southwestern Advocate,* August 22, 1935, 18, 31.

97. Dallas *Southwestern Advocate,* January 10, 1935, 2. The paper continued as the *Texas Christian Advocate* and *Oklahoma Methodist* and officially represented the views of the Methodist Episcopal Church, South, for the conferences of Texas, North Texas, Central Texas, West Texas, Northwest Texas, Oklahoma, and New Mexico.

Epilogue

1. The percentage of dry counties in Texas continues to shrink, having fallen from 128 in 1970 to just 35 in 2008. However, a few states such as Arkansas and Kansas have seen a significant increase over the same period, showing that prohibition's universal demise is by no means inevitable. John Frendreis and Raymond Tatalovich, "Secularization, Modernization, or Population Change: Explaining the Decline of Prohibition in the United States," *Social Science Quarterly* 94 (June 2013): 386.

2. Whitener, *Prohibition in North Carolina,* 71–72; J. D. Lewis, "Robert Heriot Clarkson," *Carolina,* www.carolana.com/NC/Courts/hclarkson.html (accessed July 30, 2010).

3. Jeff Davis, comp., *Drinking and Its Moral Lessons: A Scrap Book* (Dallas: United Texas Drys, 1938), 5.

4. Davis, *Drinking and Its Moral Lessons,* 3: "The weak point in our years of prohibition, was lack of, or our failure to keep up an aggressive educational program. As a result, we have one generation of young people of voting age, with thousands of younger men and women, boys and girls, who are absolutely ignorant of the evils of drink."

5. Frendreis and Tatalovich, "Secularization, Modernization, or Population Change," 386. For the 1953 number, see United Texas Drys, "Official Wet and Dry Map 1-1-'53," United Texas Drys Vertical File, Texas Collection, Baylor University.

6. K. Austin Kerr, "PROHIBITION," *Handbook of Texas Online,* www.tshaonline.org/handbook /online/articles/vap01 (accessed December 2, 2013).

7. Bryan Naylor, "'Black Votes Matter': African-Americans Propel Jones to Alabama Win," NPR, www.npr.org/2017/12/13/570531505/black-votes-matter-african-americans-propel-jones -to-alabama-win (December 13, 2017).

8. AP VoteCast, "2018 Voter Poll Results: Texas," *Washington Post.*

9. Tamburin and Allison, "Protests in downtown Nashville."

10. Steve Almasy, "NASCAR bans Confederate flags at all races, events," *CNN,* www.cnn .com/2020/06/10/us/nascar-bans-confederate-flag-spt-trnd/index.html (June 10, 2020).

11. Courtney Subramanian, Nicholas Wu, David Jackson, and John Fritze, "Trump Tulsa speech ends, president said he wanted to 'slow the testing down' on coronavirus," *USA Today,* www.usatoday.com/story/news/politics/elections/2020/06/20/trump-rally-tulsa-oklahoma -live-updates-coronavirus/3207784001 (June 20, 2020).

12. Geoff Pender, "'It's a moral issue:' Mississippi Baptist Convention calls for new state flag," *Mississippi Today,* www.tennessean.com/story/news/2020/05/30/george-floyd-death-nashville -tennessee-protest-may-john-cooper/5286837002 (June 23, 2020).

13. Seth Stevenson, "A Cold One with Donald," *Slate,* slate.com/news-and-politics/2016/02 /trump-is-winning-the-guy-youd-want-to-have-a-beer-with-election.html (February 11, 2016).

14. Hankins, *God's Rascal,* 123, 150–52.

15. Texas Secretary of State, *Elections and Voter Information,* "Presidential Election Results," www.sos.state.tx.us/elections/historical/presidential.shtml (accessed December 2, 2013).

16. Elena Kagan, a Jewish justice, succeeded the Protestant John Paul Stevens on August 7, 2010; the sixth Catholic on the court was Sonya Sotomayor, appointed in 2009. The court regained a single Protestant on April 10, 2017, with the appointment of Neil Gorsuch; he is Episcopalian. In 2012, the Democrats' vice presidential nominee was then–vice president Joe Biden, while the Republicans' nominee was Paul Ryan, both Catholics.

17. Just one of several popular books on that point is Matthew Vines, *God and the Gay Christian: The Biblical Case in Support of Same-Sex Relationships* (New York: Convergent Books, 2014). Vines's arguments are not original but popularize decades of scholarship on the issue, challenging the common assumption that the Bible can only be used to support the traditional position on marriage.

Bibliography

Primary Sources

BOOKS AND PAMPHLETS

Andreae, Percy. *The Prohibition Movement in Its Broader Bearings upon Our Social, Commercial and Religious Liberties: Addresses and Writings of Percy Andreae.* Chicago: Felix Mendelsohn, 1915.

Andrew, John A. *The Errors of Prohibition: An Argument Delivered in the Representatives' Hall, Boston, April 3, 1867, before a Joint Special Committee of the General Court of Massachusetts.* Boston: Ticknor and Fields, 1867.

Ansley, Lula Barnes. *History of the Georgia Woman's Christian Temperance Union from Its Organization, 1883–1907.* Columbus, OH: Gilbert Printing Co., 1914.

Bailey, Thomas Jefferson. *Prohibition in Mississippi: or Anti-Liquor Legislation from Territorial Days, with Its Results in the Counties.* Jackson, MS: Hederman Bros., 1917.

Beman, Lamar Taney, ed. *Selected Articles on Prohibition of the Liquor Traffic.* New York: H. W. Wilson, 1915.

"Campaign Flier for Sidney J. Catts, 1916." *Florida Memory.* www.floridamemory.com/items /show/212322.

Carroll, B. H. *Prohibition: Dr. B. H. Carroll's Reply to Senator Coke.* Austin, TX: J. B. Link, 1885.

Carroll, J. M. *A History of Texas Baptists, Comprising a Detailed Account of their Activities, Their Progress and their Achievements.* Dallas: Baptist Standard Book Pub. Co., 1923.

Cherrington, Ernest H., ed. *Anti-Saloon League Year Book: An Encyclopedia of Facts and Figures Dealing with the Liquor Traffic and the Temperance Reform.* Westerville, OH: American Issue Press Co., 1908–30.

——. *The Evolution of Prohibition in the United States of America: A Chronological History of the Liquor Problem and the Temperance Reform in the United States from the Earliest Settlements to the Consummation of National Prohibition.* Westerville, OH: American Issue Press, 1920.

——. *History of the Anti-Saloon League.* Westerville, OH: American Issue Publishing Co., 1913.

Connor, Robert Digges Wimberly, ed. *A Manual of North Carolina Issued by the North Carolina Historical Commission for the Use of Members of the General Assembly Session 1913.* Raleigh: E. M. Uzzell and Co., 1913.

Cuney-Hare, Maud. *Norris Wright Cuney: A Tribune of the Black People.* New York: n.p., 1913.

Davis, Jeff, comp. *Drinking and Its Moral Lessons: A Scrap Book.* Dallas: United Texas Drys, 1938.

Davis, Westmoreland. *Address of Governor Westmoreland Davis Delivered Before the General Assembly of Virginia, January 11, 1922.* Richmond, VA: Davis Bottom, Superintendent Public Printing, 1922.

Drink and the Drink Question: A Discriminating License the True Policy; Prohibition a Fraud and Failure. Dallas: [Texas] Anti-Prohibition State Convention, 1887.

Du Bois, William Edward Burghardt. "An Open Letter to the Southern People," 1887. W. E. B. Du Bois Papers, ser. 3: Articles. University of Massachusetts, Amherst. credo.library.umass.edu/view/full/mums312-b211-i093.

Dunn, James B., ed. *Moody's Talks on Temperance with Anecdotes and Incidents in Connection with the Tabernacle Temperance Work in Boston.* New York: National Temperance Society and Publication House, 1877.

Durand, E. Dana, ed. *Religious Bodies, 1906: Part 1–Summary and General Tables.* Washington, DC: US Bureau of the Census, 1910.

Emerson, Edward R. *A Lay Thesis on Bible Wines.* New York: Merrill & Baker, 1902.

Erskine, John. *Prohibition and Christianity: And Other Paradoxes of the American Spirit.* Indianapolis: Bobbs-Merrill Co., 1927.

Fisher, Irving. *Prohibition at Its Worst.* New York: Macmillan Co., 1926.

Forstall, Richard L., comp. and ed. *Population of States and Counties of the United States: 1790–1990.* Washington, DC: Department of Commerce, Bureau of the Census Population Division, 1996.

Gibbs, Joseph C. *History of the Catholic Total Abstinence Union of America.* Philadelphia: Penn Printing House, 1907.

Harper, Ida Husted, ed. *The History of Woman Suffrage.* New York: J. J. Little and Ives, 1922.

Hays, J. E., comp. *Georgia's Official Register: 1933–1935–1937.* Atlanta: Georgia Department of Archives and History, 1938.

Hobson, Richmond Pearson. *Alcohol and the Human Race.* New York: Fleming R. Revell Co., 1919.

——. *The Great Destroyer: Speech of Hon. Richmond P. Hobson of Alabama in the House of Representatives, February 2, 1911.* Washington, DC: n.p., 1911. catalog.hathitrust.org/Record/007123395.

——. *The Truth About Alcohol: Speech of Hon. Richmond P. Hobson of Alabama in the House of Representatives, December 22, 1914.* Washington, DC: n.p., 1914. catalog.hathitrust.org/Record/002874657.

Hunt, William Chamberlin, and Edwin Munsell Bliss, eds. *Religious Bodies, 1916.* Washington, DC: US Census Bureau, 1916.

Iglehart, Ferdinand Cowle. *King Alcohol Dethroned.* Westerville, OH: American Issue Publishing Co., 1919.

Ireland, John. *The Church and Modern Society.* Chicago: Paulist Press, 1905.

Ivy, H. A. *Rum on the Run in Texas: A Brief History of Prohibition in the Lone Star State.* Dallas: Temperance Pub. Co., 1910.

Jefferson, Ray. *B. H. Carroll.* Nashville: Sunday School Board Press, 1927.

Jewett, Edward H. *The Two-Wine Theory Discussed by Two Hundred and Eighty-Six Clergymen on the Basis of "Communion Wine."* New York: E. Steiger & Co., 1888.

Knight, Kevin. *New Advent.* "Frequent Communion." www.newadvent.org/cathen/06278a.htm.

Legislative Reference Library of Texas. "Constitutional amendment election dates." lrl.texas.gov /legis/ConstAmends/electiondates.cfm.

Looney, B. F. ed. *The Brewers and Texas Politics.* 2 vols. San Antonio: B. F. Looney, 1916.

McPherson, Edward, ed. *The Political History of the United States of America, During the Period of Reconstruction (from April 15, 1865, to July 15, 1870,) Including a Classified Summary of the Legislation of the Thirty-ninth, Fortieth, and Forty-first Congresses, With the Votes Thereon; Together with the Action, Congressional and State, on the Fourteenth and Fifteenth Amendments to the Constitution of the United States, and the Other Important Executive, Legislative, Politico-military, and Judicial Facts of that Period.* Washington, DC: Philp and Solomons, 1871.

Methodist Episcopal Church. *Doctrines and Disciplines of the Methodist Episcopal Church.* New York: Carlton & Porter, 1864.

———. *A Reprint of the Discipline of the Methodist Episcopal Church for 1787.* Cleveland: W. A. Ingham, 1900.

Methodist Episcopal Church, South. *The Doctrines and Disciplines of the Methodist Episcopal Church, South.* Nashville: Southern Methodist Publishing House, 1878, 1886.

Neff, Pat. *The Battles of Peace.* Fort Worth: Pioneer Publishing Co., 1925.

Nichols, R. V., and L. C. Sutton. *The Dean Law and the Prohibition Amendment to the Texas Constitution: With Synopsis and Explanations, Including an Opinion of the Attorney General Construing Said Law and Amendment.* Austin, TX: Nichols & Sutton, 1919.

Odegard, Peter H. *Pressure Politics: The Story of the Anti-Saloon League.* 1928. Rpt. New York: Octagon Books, 1966.

Pickett, Deets. *Alcohol and the New Age: An Elective Course for Young People.* New York: Methodist Book Concern, 1926.

Root, Grace C. *Women and Repeal: The Story of the Women's Organization for National Prohibition Reform.* New York: Harper and Brothers, 1934.

Scannell, Thomas. "Frequent Communion." *Catholic Encyclopedia,* vol. 6. New York: Robert Appleton Co., 1909.

A Series of Temperance Sermons, Delivered in the City Hall, Lowell, by the Several Clergymen of the City. Lowell, MA: Leonard Huntress, E. A. Rice & Co., 1841.

Shuler, Robert Pierce. *The New Issue, or, Local Booze Government: Being a Collection of Articles on "Prohibition."* Temple, TX: Temple Printing and Office Appliance Co., 1911.

Shurter, Edwin Du Bois, ed. *Oratory of the South from the Civil War to the Present Time.* New York: Neal Publishing Co., 1908.

Smith, Joseph. "History—1839." In *The Papers of Joseph Smith, vol. 1: Autobiographical and Historical Writings.* Ed. Dean C. Jesse. Salt Lake City: Deseret Book, 1989.

Stelzle, Charles. *Why Prohibition!* New York: George H. Doran Co., 1918.

Walker, Francis A. and Chas. W. Seaton. *1880 Census,* vol. 1: *Statistics of the Population of the United States.* Washington, DC: US Department of the Interior, Census Office, 1883.

Webb, Atticus. *Face the Facts Relating to the Wet and Dry Issues.* Dallas: Anti-Saloon League of Texas, 1927.

Wesleyan Methodist Association. *The Constitution of Wesleyan Methodism as Settled in 1795 and 1797.* London: Egerton Smith and Co., 1835.

Willard, Frances. *Glimpses of Fifty Years: The Autobiography of an American Woman.* Toronto: Rose Publishing Co., 1889.

———. *The Ideal of "The New Woman" According to the Woman's Christian Temperance Union.* Ed. Carolyn De Swarte Gifford. New York: Garland, 1987.

———. *Woman and Temperance, or, The Work and Workers of the Woman's Christian Temperance Union.* Hartford, CT: Park Publishing Co., 1883.

Wright, Richard R., and John R. Hawkins. *Centennial Encyclopedia of the African Methodist Episcopal Church,* vol. 1. Philadelphia: Book Concern of the A.M.E. Church, 1916.

MINUTES, JOURNALS, LAWS, AND COLLECTIONS

1740 South Carolina Slave Code. Acts of the South Carolina General Assembly, 1740 #670. Columbia: South Carolina Department of Archives and History.

Actas del . . . Periodo de Sessiones de la Mision Mexicana del Occidente. 1921.

Adjutant General's Department. Texas Volunteer Guard Military Rolls, 1880–1903. Archives and Information Services Division, Texas State Library and Archives Commission. www.lib.utexas.edu/taro/tslac/30079/30079-P.html.

Alabama Official and Statistical Register, 1911. Comp. Thomas M. Owen. Montgomery, AL: Brown Printing Co., 1912.

Alabama Official and Statistical Register, 1935. Comp. Marie B. Owen. Wetumpka, AL: Wetumpka Printing Co., 1935.

Annual Session of the National Baptist Convention. 1905–10.

Barbara DePriest Clipping Collection. White House Historical Association. www.whitehousehistory.org/photos/photo-3-46.

Benajah Harvey Carroll Collection. Southern Baptist Historical Library and Archives, Nashville, TN.

Congressional Record. 1917–28.

The Constitution of the United States of America Analysis and Interpretation Analysis of Cases Decided by the Supreme Court of the United States to July 1, 2014. US Senate doc. no. 108–17. www.govinfo.gov/app/details/CDOC-108sdoc17/context.

Florida Baptist Convention. *Minutes.* 1872, 1895.

Georgia Baptist Convention. *Minutes.* 1873.

Journal of the . . . Annual Session of the West Texas Conference of the Protestant Episcopal Church. 1910–11.

Mood, R. G., ed. *Minutes of the Sixty-Sixth Annual Session of the North Texas Annual Conference of the Methodist Episcopal Church, South.* Gainesville, TX, 1932.

Oscar Branch Colquitt Papers. Dolph Briscoe Center for American History, University of Texas at Austin.

Proceedings of the . . . Annual Session of the Baptist General Convention of Texas. 1892–96.

Proceedings of the Conventions of the . . . Anti-Saloon League Convention, 1913.

Southern Baptist Convention. *Proceedings.* 1986.

Woman's Christian Temperance Union of Texas. *Twenty-Seventh Annual Report.* Marlin, TX: n.p., 1909.

NEWSPAPERS

Abilene, TX, *Daily Reporter.* 1915.

Afro American. Baltimore, 1929.

Alabama Baptist. Selma, 1885.

American Issue. Westerville, OH, 1927.

Austin, TX, *Daily Statesman.* 1885.

The Baptist. Memphis, 1888.

Baptist Record. Meridian, MS, 1884–86.

Baptist Standard. 1892–1935.

Beaumont, TX, *Journal.* 1911.

Biblical Recorder. Raleigh, NC, 1876.

Birmingham, AL, *Age-Herald.* 1898–1904.

Bismarck, NC, *Tribune.* 1929.

Bismarck, ND, *Tribune.* 1937.

Bluefield, WV, *Daily Leader.* 1908.

Bolivar, TN, *Bulletin.* 1887.

Brownsville, TX, *Herald.* 1924.

Carolina Watchman. Salisbury, NC, 1908.

Christian Courier. Dallas, 1928.

Christian Index. Atlanta, 1866–83.

Christian Leader. Boston, 1928.

Congregationalist and Advance. Boston, 1919.

County Paper. Oregon, MO, 1881.

Daily Express. San Antonio, 1887.

Daily Independent. Elizabeth City, NC, 1937.

Daily News. Prescott, AR, 1907.

Dallas Daily Herald. 1881.

Dallas Morning News. 1911.

Day Book. Chicago, 1912.

El Paso Herald. 1911.

Evening Star. Washington, DC, 1929–33.

Express. San Antonio, 1917.

Fair Play. Ste. Genevieve, MO, 1881.

Fundamentalist. Fort Worth, 1928–35.

Galveston, TX, *Daily News.* 1885–87.

Goldsboro, NC, *Star.* 1881.

Herald and News. Newbery, SC, 1907.

Home and State. Dallas, 1904–30.

Houston Chronicle. 1912.

Houston Post. 1911–18.

Indianapolis Times. 1929–34.

Key West, FL, *Citizen.* 1933.

Knoxville, TN, *Daily Chronicle.* 1881.

Log Cabin Democrat. Conway, AR, 1912.

Montgomery, AL, *Advertiser.* 1936.

Morning News. El Paso, TX, 1918.

Newberry, SC, *Herald.* 1881.

New-Journal. Longview, TX, 2011.

New York Times. 1881–1938.

Ocala, FL, *Evening Star.* 1907–10.

Omaha Daily Bee. 1920.

Orangeburg, SC, *Times.* 1881.

Orange County Observer. Hillsborough, NC, 1881.

Orlando Evening Star. 1914.

Panama City, FL, *Pilot.* 1908.

Pensacola Journal. 1916.

Prescott, AR, *Daily News.* 1907.

Religious Herald. Richmond, VA, 1872–88.

Roanoke Rapids Herald. 1934.

Salt Lake Herald. 1881.

Searchlight. Fort Worth, 1922–27.

Sentinel-Record. Hot Springs, AR, 1912.

Southern Mercury. Dallas, 1902.

Southern Standard. McMinnville, TN, 1887.

Southwestern Advocate. Dallas, 1935.

Southwestern Christian Advocate. Dallas, 1898–1902.

Star of Zion. Salisbury, NC, 1887–96.

Star Telegram. Fort Worth, 1911–17.

Sunday Gazetteer. Denison, TX, 1887.

Temple, TX, *Daily Telegram.* 1912.

Texas Baptist and Herald. 1887.

Texas Christian Advocate. 1866–1908, 1911–12.

Times-News. Hendersonville, NC, 1933–37.

True Blue. Waco, 1887.

Universalist Leader. Boston, 1919.

Washington, DC, *Times.* 1908–20.

Watchman and Southron. Sumter, SC, 1881.

Waterbury, CT, *Evening Democrat.* 1888.

Western Recorder. Louisville, KY, 1884.

Wheeling, WV, *Intelligencer.* 1912.

Wisconsin Tobacco Reporter. Edgerton, 1910.

Working Christian. Columbia, SC, 1877.

Newport, VA, *News.* 1908.

Waco, TX, *Daily Examiner.* 1887.

Secondary Sources

BOOKS, CHAPTERS, ARTICLES, AND VIDEOS

Abramowitz, Jack. "John B. Rayner—A Grass-Roots Leader." *Journal of Negro History* 36, no. 2 (April 1951): 160–93.

Alexander, Charles C. *Crusade for Conformity: The Ku Klux Klan in Texas, 1920–1930.* Houston: Texas Gulf Coast Historical Association, 1962.

Anders, Evan. *Boss Rule in South Texas: The Progressive Era.* Austin: University of Texas Press, 1982.

Angell, Stephen Ward. *Bishop Henry McNeal Turner and African American Religion in the South.* Knoxville: University of Tennessee Press, 1992.

Arnett, Alex Mathews. *The Populist Movement in Georgia: A View of the "Agrarian Crusade" in the Light of Solid-South Politics.* New York: AMS Press, 1967.

Bailey, Beth L. *From Front Porch to Back Seat: Courtship in Twentieth-Century America.* Baltimore: Johns Hopkins University Press, 1989.

Bair, Barbara. "Though Justice Sleeps: 1880–1900." In *To Make Our World Anew: A History of African Americans,* ed. Robin E. G. Kelley and Earl Lewis. New York: Oxford University Press, 2000.

Baker, Jean H. *Sisters: The Lives of America's Suffragists.* New York: Hill and Wang, 2005.

Barr, Alwyn. *Black Texans: A History of African Americans in Texas, 1528–1995.* Norman: University of Oklahoma Press, 1996.

Bartley, Abel A. *Keeping the Faith: Race, Politics, and Social Development in Jacksonville, Florida, 1940–1970.* Westwood, CT: Greenwood Press, 2000.

Barton, Paul. *Hispanic Methodists, Presbyterians, and Baptists in Texas.* Austin: University of Texas Press, 2006.

Beezley, William H. *Judas at the Jockey Club: and Other Episodes of Porfirian Mexico.* 2nd ed. Lincoln: University of Nebraska Press, 2004.

Blackmon, Douglas A. *Slavery by Another Name: The Re-Enslavement of Black Americans from the Civil War to World War II.* New York: Doubleday, 2008.

Bland, Sister Joan. *Hibernian Crusade: The Story of the Catholic Total Abstinence Union of America.* Washington, DC: Catholic University of America Press, 1951.

Blocker Jr., Jack S. *American Temperance Movements: Cycles of Reform.* Boston: Twayne Publishers, 1989.

———. *Retreat from Reform: the Prohibition Movement in the United States, 1890–1913.* Westport, CT: Greenwood Press, 1976.

Blom, Philipp. *Fracture: Life and Culture in the West, 1918–1938.* New York: Basic Books, 2015.

Brown, Norman D. *Hood, Bonnet, and Little Brown Jug: Texas Politics, 1921–1928.* College Station: Texas A&M University Press, 1984.

Buenger, Walter Louis. *The Path to a Modern South: Northeast Texas Between Reconstruction and the Great Depression.* Austin: University of Texas Press, 2001.

Burke, William Lewis. *All for Civil Rights: African American Lawyers in South Carolina, 1868–1968.* Athens: University of Georgia Press, 2017.

Campbell, W. Joseph. "'One of the Fine Figures of American Journalism': A Closer Look at Josephus Daniels of the Raleigh 'News and Observer.'" *American Journalism* 16 (Fall 1999): 37–55. doi.org/10.1080/08821127.1999.10739206.

Cantrell, Gregg. "'Dark Tactics': Black Politics in the 1887 Texas Prohibition Campaign." *Journal of American Studies* 25 (April 1991): 85–93.

———. *Feeding the Wolf: John B. Rayner and the Politics of Race, 1850–1918.* Wheeling, IL: Harlan Davidson, 2001.

———. *Kenneth and John B. Rayner and the Limits of Southern Dissent.* Urbana: University of Illinois Press, 1993.

Chalmers, David M. *Hooded Americanism: The History of the Ku Klux Klan.* 3rd ed. Durham, NC: Duke University Press, 1987.

Chappell, David L. *A Stone of Hope: Prophetic Religion and the Death of Jim Crow.* Chapel Hill: University of North Carolina Press, 2004.

Clark, Norman H. *Deliver Us from Evil: An Interpretation of American Prohibition.* New York: W. W. Norton and Co., 1976.

———. *The Dry Years: Prohibition and Social Change in Washington.* Seattle: University of Washington Press, 1965.

Coker, Joe L. *Liquor in the Land of the Lost Cause: Southern White Evangelicals and the Prohibition Movement.* Lexington: University of Kentucky Press, 2007.

Crowgey, Henry G. *Kentucky Bourbon: The Early Years of Whiskey-Making.* Lexington: University of Kentucky Press, 1971.

Davidson, James West. *"They Say": Ida B. Wells and the Reconstruction of Race.* New York: Oxford University Press, 2008.

Davis, Marni. *Jews and Booze: Becoming American in the Age of Prohibition.* New York: New York University Press, 2012.

Day, Davis S. "Herbert Hoover and Racial Politics: The De Priest Incident." *Journal of Negro History* 65 (Winter 1980): 6–17. doi.org/10.2307/3031544.

Deweese, Charles W. *Baptist Church Covenants.* Nashville: Broadman Press, 1990.

Dochuk, Darren. *Bible Belt to Sunbelt: Plain-Folk Religion, Grassroots Politics, and the Rise of Evangelical Conservatism.* New York: Norton, 2010.

Du Mez, Kristin Kobes. *Jesus and John Wayne: How White Evangelicals Corrupted a Faith and Fractured a Nation.* New York: Liveright, 2020.

Edgar, Walter. *South Carolina: A History.* Columbia: University of South Carolina Press, 1998.

Endersby, James W. "Prohibition and Repeal: Voting on Statewide Liquor Referenda in Texas." *Social Science Journal* 49 (December 2012): 503–12. doi.org/10.1016/j.soscij.2012.09.004.

Fahey, David N. *Temperance and Racism: John Bull, Johnny Reb, and the Good Templars.* Lexington: University Press of Kentucky, 1996.

Farish, Hunter Dickinson. *The Circuit Rider Dismounts: A Social History of Southern Methodism 1865–1900.* Richmond, VA: Dietz Press, 1938.

Fass, Paula. *The Damned and the Beautiful: American Youth in the 1920's.* New York: Oxford University Press, 1977.

Finan, Christopher M. *Alfred E. Smith: The Happy Warrior.* New York: Hill and Wang, 2002.

Flannery, John B. *The Irish Texans*. San Antonio: University of Texas, Institute of Texan Cultures, 1980.

Flusche, A. C., and Catholic Archives of Texas. *Sketch of the German Catholic Colonies in North Texas Founded by Flusche Brothers*. N.p., 1900.

Flynt, Wayne. *Cracker Messiah: Governor Sidney J. Catts of Florida*. Baton Rouge: Louisiana State University Press, 1977.

Foster, Gaines M. *Ghosts of the Confederacy: Defeat, the Lost Cause, and the Emergence of the New South, 1865–1913*. New York: Oxford University Press, 1987.

———. *Moral Reconstruction: Christian Lobbyists and the Federal Legislation of Morality, 1865–1920*. Chapel Hill: University of North Carolina Press, 2002.

Franklin, Jimmie Lewis. *Born Sober: Prohibition in Oklahoma, 1907–1959*. Norman: University of Oklahoma Press, 1971.

Fredrich, Edward C. *The Wisconsin Synod Lutherans: A History of the Single Synod, Federation, and Merger*. Milwaukee: Northwestern Pub. House, 2000.

Frendreis, John, and Raymond Tatalovich. "Secularization, Modernization, or Population Change: Explaining the Decline of Prohibition in the United States." *Social Science Quarterly* 94 (June 2013): 379–94. doi.org/10.1111/j.1540-6237.2012.00878.x.

Gaither, Gerald H. *Blacks and the Populist Movement: Ballots and Bigotry in the "New South."* Rev. ed. Tuscaloosa: University of Alabama Press, 2005.

Gaustad, Edwin S., ed. *Religion in America*. New York: Arno Press, 1972.

Giggie, John. *After Redemption: Jim Crow and the Transformation of African American Religion in the Delta, 1875–1915*. New York: Oxford University Press, 2008.

Gilliam, George Harrison. "Making Virginia Progressive: Courts and Parties, Railroads and Regulators, 1890–1910." *Virginia Magazine of History and Biography* 107 (Spring 1999): 189–222. www.jstor.org/stable/4249768.

Gilmore, Glenda Elizabeth. *Gender and Jim Crow: Women and the Politics of White Supremacy in North Carolina, 1896–1920*. Chapel Hill: University of North Carolina Press, 1996.

Goodwyn, Lawrence. *Democratic Promise: The Populist Moment in America*. New York: Oxford University Press, 1976.

Gould, Lewis L. *Alexander Watkins Terrell: Civil War Soldier, Texas Lawmaker, American Diplomat*. Austin: University of Texas Press, 2004.

———. *Progressives and Prohibitionists: Texas Democrats in the Wilson Era*. Austin: University of Texas Press, 1973.

Grantham, Dewey W. *Southern Progressivism: The Reconciliation of Progress and Tradition*. Knoxville: University of Tennessee Press, 1983.

Griffith, Aaron. *God's Law and Order: The Politics of Punishment in Evangelical America*. Cambridge, MA: Harvard University Press, 2020.

Grijalva, Joshua. *A History of Mexican Baptists in Texas 1881–1981: Comprising an Account of the Genesis, the Progress, and the Accomplishments of the People Called "Los Bautistas de Texas."* Dallas: Office of Language Missions, Baptist General Convention of Texas, 1982.

Gusfield, Joseph R. *Symbolic Crusade: Status Politics and the American Temperance Movement*. Champaign: University of Illinois Press, 1963.

Hamm, Richard F. *Murder, Honor, and Law: Four Virginia Homicides from Reconstruction to the Great Depression*. Charlottesville: University of Virginia Press, 1995.

——. *Shaping the Eighteenth Amendment: Temperance Reform, Legal Culture, and the Polity, 1880–1920*. Chapel Hill: University of North Carolina Press, 1995.

Hankins, Barry. *God's Rascal: J. Frank Norris & the Beginnings of Southern Fundamentalism*. Lexington: University Press of Kentucky, 1996.

——. *Jesus and Gin: Evangelicalism, the Roaring Twenties, and Today's Culture Wars*. New York: Palgrave Macmillan, 2010.

Harvey, Paul. *Redeeming the South: Religious Cultures and Racial Identities Among Southern Baptists, 1865–1925*. Chapel Hill: University of North Carolina Press, 1997.

——. "Southern Baptists and the Social Gospel: White Religious Progressivism in the South, 1900–1925." *Fides et Historia* 27 (Summer–Fall 1995): 59–77.

——. *Through the Storm, through the Night: A History of African American Christianity*. Lanham, MD: Rowman & Littlefield, 2011.

Hatch, Nathan O. *The Democratization of American Christianity*. New Haven, CT: Yale University Press, 1989.

Hays, Robert, ed. *The Age of Segregation: Race Relations in the South, 1890–1945*. Jackson: University Press of Mississippi.

Hennech, Mike. *Encyclopedia of Texas Breweries: Pre-Prohibition: 1836–1918*. Irving, TX: Ale Pub. Co., 1990.

Heyrman, Christine Leigh. *Southern Cross: The Beginnings of the Bible Belt*. New York: Knopf, 1997.

Hill, Larry D. "Texas Progressivism: A Search for Definition." In Walter L. Buenger and Robert A. Calvert, eds., *Texas through Time: Evolving Interpretations*. College Station: Texas A&M University Press, 1991, 229–50.

Hoffman, Steven J. *Race, Class and Power in the Building of Richmond, 1870–1920*. Jefferson, NC: McFarland, 2004.

Hofstadter, Richard. *The Age of Reform: From Bryan to FDR*. New York: Random House, 1955.

Hohner, Robert A. *Prohibition and Politics: The Life of Bishop James Cannon, Jr.* Columbia: University of South Carolina Press, 1999.

Isaac, Paul E. Prohibition and Politics: Turbulent Decades in Tennessee, 1885–1920. Knoxville: University of Tennessee Press, 1965.

Ivey, Darren L. *The Texas Rangers: A Registry and History*. Jefferson, NC: McFarland & Co., 2010.

Ivy, James D. "'The Lone Star State Surrenders to a Lone Woman': Frances Willard's Forgotten 1882 Texas Temperance Tour." *Southwestern Historical Quarterly* 102 (1998): 44–61. www .jstor.org/stable/30239154.

——. *No Saloon in the Valley: The Southern Strategy of Texas Prohibitionists in the 1880s*. Waco, TX: Baylor University Press, 2003.

Jackson, Joy. "Prohibition in New Orleans: The Unlikeliest Crusade." *Louisiana History* 19 (Summer 1978): 261–84. www.jstor.org/stable/4231785.

Johnson, Andre E. *The Forgotten Prophet: Bishop Henry McNeal Turner and the African American Prophetic Tradition*. Lanham, MD: Lexington Books, 2012.

Johnson, Benjamin Heber. *Revolution in Texas: How a Forgotten Rebellion and Its Bloody Suppression Turned Mexicans into Americans*. New Haven, CT: Yale University Press, 2003.

Jones, Nancy Baker, and Ruthe Winegarten. *Capitol Women: Texas Female Legislators, 1923–1999*. Austin: University of Texas Press, 2000.

Jordan, Terry G. "A Century and a Half of Ethnic Change in Texas, 1836–1986." *Southwestern Historical Quarterly* 89 (April 1986): 390–411. www.jstor.org/stable/30239930.

Katz, Friedrich. *The Secret War in Mexico: Europe, the United States, and the Mexican Revolution.* Chicago: University of Chicago Press, 1981.

Kern, Kathi. *Mrs. Stanton's Bible.* Ithaca, NY: Cornell University Press, 2001.

Kerr, K. Austin. *Organized for Prohibition: A New History of the Anti-Saloon League.* New Haven, CT: Yale University Press, 1985.

Kousser, J. Morgan. *The Shaping of Southern Politics: Suffrage Restriction and the Establishment of the One-Party South.* New Haven, CT: Yale University Press, 1974.

Kleber, John E., ed. *The Kentucky Encyclopedia.* Lexington: University Press of Kentucky, 1992.

Kruse, Kevin M. *One Nation Under God: How Corporate America Invented Christian America.* New York: Basic, 2015.

Lack, Paul D. "Occupied Texas: Bexar and Goliad, 1835–1836." In *Mexican Americans in Texas History,* ed. Emilio Zamora, Cythia Orozco, and Rodolfo Rocha. Austin: Texas State Historical Association, 2000.

Lacy, Eric Russell. "Tennessee Teetotalism: Social Forces and the Politics or Progressivism." *Tennessee Historical Quarterly* 24 (Fall 1965): 219–40. www-jstor-org.ngu.idm.oclc.org/stable /42622823.

Lauterback, Preston. *Beale Street Dynasty: Sex, Song, and the Struggle for the Soul of Memphis.* New York: Norton, 2015.

Leab, Grace. "Tennessee Temperance Activities, 1870–1899." *East Tennessee Historical Society's Publications* 21 (1949): 52–68.

Lee, Chana Kai. *For Freedom's Sake: The Life of Fannie Lou Hamer.* Urbana: University of Illinois Press, 1999.

Lefever, Alan J. *Fighting the Good Fight: The Life and Work of Benajah Harvey Carroll.* Austin, TX: Eakin Press, 1994.

León, Arnoldo De. *They Called Them Greasers: Anglo Attitudes Toward Mexicans in Texas, 1821–1900.* Austin: University of Texas Press, 1983.

———. *War Along the Border: The Mexican Revolution and Tejano Communities.* College Station: Texas A&M University Press, 2011.

Lerner, Michael A. *Dry Manhattan: Prohibition in New York City.* New York: Cambridge University Press, 2008.

Levario, Miguel Antonio. *Militarizing the Border: When Mexicans Became the Enemy.* College Station: Texas A&M University Press, 2012.

Lewis, Catherine M., and J. Richard Lewis, eds. *Jim Crow America: A Documentary History.* Fayetteville: University of Arkansas Press, 2009.

Lewis, J. D. "North Carolina State House of Representatives, 1872–1874." *Carolina,* www.carolana .com/NC/1800s/nc_1800s_house_1872-1874.html (accessed July 24, 2020).

Lewis, Michael. *The Coming of Southern Prohibition: The Dispensary System and the Battle over Liquor in South Carolina, 1907–1915.* Baton Rouge: Louisiana State University Press, 2016.

Lich, Glen E. *The German Texans.* San Antonio: University of Texas Institute of Texan Cultures, 1981.

Link, William A. *The Paradox of Southern Progressivism, 1880–1930.* Chapel Hill: University of North Carolina Press, 1992.

Litwack, Leon F. *Trouble in Mind: Black Southerners in the Age of Jim Crow.* New York: Vintage, 1999.

Locke, Joseph. *Making the Bible Belt: Texas Prohibitionists and the Politicization of Southern Religion.* New York: Oxford University Press, 2017.

London, H. M., comp. and ed. *North Carolina Manual, 1935.* Raleigh, NC: Mitchell Printing Co., 1935.

Marsh, Charles. *God's Long Summer: Stories of Faith and Civil Rights.* Princeton, NJ: Princeton University Press, 1997.

McArthur, Judith N. *Creating the New Woman: The Rise of Southern Women's Progressive Culture in Texas, 1893–1918.* Urbana: University of Illinois Press, 1998.

McCarty, Jeanne Bozzel. *The Struggle for Sobriety: Protestants and Prohibition in Texas, 1919–1935.* El Paso: Texas Western Press, 1980.

McGirr, Lisa. *The War on Alcohol: Prohibition and the Rise of the American State.* New York: Norton, 2015.

McGreevy, John T. *Catholicism and American Freedom: A History.* New York: Norton, 2003.

McQueary, Carl Randall, and May Nelson Paulissen. *Ma's in the Kitchen: You'll Know When It's Done! The Recipes and History of Governor Miriam A. Ferguson, First Woman Governor of Texas.* Austin: Eakin Press: 1994.

Meagher, Michael, and Larry D. Gragg. *John F. Kennedy: A Biography.* Santa Barbara, CA: Greenwood, 2011.

Meyer, Michael C. *Huerta: A Political Portrait.* Lincoln: University of Nebraska Press, 1972.

———. "The Mexican-German Conspiracy of 1915." *Americas* 23 (July 1966): 76–89. doi.org /10.2307/980141.

———. *Mexican Rebel: Pasccual Orozco and the Mexican Revolution, 1910–1915.* Lincoln: University of Nebraska Press, 1967.

Meyer, Sabine N. *We Are What We Drink: The Temperance Battle in Minnesota.* Urbana: University of Illinois Press, 2015.

Milewski, Melissa. *Litigating Across the Color Line: Civil Cases Between Black and White Southerners from the End of Slavery to Civil Rights.* New York: Oxford University Press, 2018.

Motl, Kevin C. "Under the Influence: The Texas Business Men's Association and the Campaign against Reform, 1906–1915." *Southwestern Historical Quarterly* 109 (April 2006): 494–529.

Myrick-Harris, Clarissa, and Norman Harris. "Atlanta in the Civil Rights Movement." Atlanta Regional Consortium for Higher Education. web.archive.org/web/20040622202115/http:/ www.atlantahighered.org/civilrights/essay_detail.asp?phase=1 (published 2004).

Naylor, Bryan. "'Black Votes Matter': African-Americans Propel Jones to Alabama Win." *NPR.* www.npr.org/2017/12/13/570531505/black-votes-matter-african-americans-propel-jones -to-alabama-win (December 13, 2017).

Newby, I. A. *Jim Crow's Defense: Anti-Negro Thought in America, 1900–1930.* Baton Rouge: Louisiana State University Press, 1965.

Noll, Mark A. *America's God: From Jonathan Edwards to Abraham Lincoln.* New York: Oxford University Press, 2002.

———. *The Civil War as a Theological Crisis.* Chapel Hill: University of North Carolina Press, 2006.

———. *God and Race in American Politics: A Short History.* Princeton, NJ: Princeton University Press, 2010.

———. *A History of Christianity in the United States and Canada.* Grand Rapids, MI: Eerdmans, 1992.

———. *The Old Religion in a New World: The History of North American Christianity* Grand Rapids, MI: Eerdmans, 2002.

————. *One Nation Under God? Christian Faith and Political Action in America*. San Francisco: Harper and Row, 1988.

Norrell, Robert J. *Up from History: The Life of Booker T. Washington*. Cambridge, MA: Harvard University Press, 2009.

O'Daniel, Patrick. *Crusaders, Gangsters, and Whiskey: Prohibition in Memphis*. Jackson: University Press of Mississippi, 2018.

Okrent, Daniel. *Last Call: The Rise and Fall of Prohibition*. New York: Scribner, 2010.

Packard, Jerrold M. *American Nightmare: The History of Jim Crow*. New York: St. Martin's Press, 2002.

Payne, Brendan J. "Protecting Black Suffrage: Poll Taxes, Preachers, and Anti-Prohibition in Texas, 1887–1916." *Journal of Southern History* 83 (November 2017): 815–52. doi.org/10.1353/soh.2017.0243.

————. "Southern White Protestant Men, Church-State Relations, and Prohibition in Texas, 1865–1920." *Social History of Alcohol and Drugs* 29 (Winter 2015), 92–111. doi.org/10.1086/SHAD29010092.

Pegram, Thomas R. "'Temperance Politics and Regional Political Culture: The Anti-Saloon League in Maryland and the South, 1907–1915." *Journal of Southern History* 63 (February 1997): 57–90.

Pollack, Norman. *The Populist Response to Industrial America: Midwestern Populist Thought*. Cambridge, MA: Harvard University Press, 1962.

Postel, Charles. *The Populist Vision*. New York: Oxford University Press, 2007.

Prohibition. Produced by Ken Burns and Lynn Novick. 6 hours. 3 DVDs. PBS Video. 2011.

Quinn, John F. "Father Mathew's Disciples: American Catholic Support for Temperance, 1840–1920." *Church History* 65 (December 1996): 624–40. www.jstor.org/stable/3170390.

Rabinowitz, Howard N. *Race, Ethnicity, and Urbanization: Selected Essays*. Columbia: University of Missouri Press, 1993.

————. *Race Relations in the Urban South, 1865–1890*. New York: Oxford University Press, 1978.

Ramírez, José A. *To the Line of Fire: Mexican Texans and World War I*. College Station: Texas A&M University Press, 2009.

Roediger, David R. *Working Toward Whiteness: How America's Immigrants Became White: The Strange Journey from Ellis Island to the Suburbs*. New York: Basic Books, 2005.

Rorabaugh, W. J. *The Alcohol Republic: An American Tradition*. New York: Oxford University Press, 1979.

Rose, Kenneth D. *American Women and the Repeal of Prohibition*. New York: New York University Press, 1996.

Rosenbaum, Robert J. *Mexicano Resistance in the Southwest: "The Sacred Right of Self-Preservation."* Austin: University of Texas Press, 1981.

Rosenzweig, Roy. *Eight Hours for What We Will: Workers and Leisure in an Industrial City, 1870–1920*. New York: Cambridge University Press, 1983.

Sáenz, Andrés. *Early Tejano Ranching: Daily Life at Ranchos San José and El Fresnillo*, ed. Andrés Tijerina. College Station: Texas A&M Press, 2001.

Sandos, James A. *Rebellion in the Borderlands: Anarchism and the Plan of San Diego, 1904–1923*. Norman: University of Oklahoma Press, 1992.

Schmidt, Jeanette Miller. *Souls or the Social Order: The Two-Party System in American Protestantism* Brooklyn, NY: Carlson Publishing, 1991.

Sellers, James Benson. *The Prohibition Movement in Alabama, 1702 to 1943*. Chapel Hill: University of North Carolina Press, 1943.

Slayton, Robert A. *Empire Statesman: The Rise and Redemption of Al Smith*. New York: Free Press, 2001.

Smith, Timothy L. *Revivalism and Social Reform: American Protestantism on the eve of the Civil War*. New York: Abingdon, 1957.

Soss, Joe, and Vesla Weaver. "Police Are Our Government: Politics, Political Science, and the Policing of Race-Class Subjugated Communities." *Annual Review of Political Science* 20 (May 2017): 565–91. doi.org/10.1146/annurev-polisci-060415-093825.

Spain, Rufus B. *At Ease in Zion: Social History of Southern Baptists*. 1967. Rpt. Tuscaloosa: University of Alabama Press: 2003.

Sutton, Matthew Avery. *Aimee Semple McPherson and the Resurrection of Christian America*. Cambridge, MA: Harvard University Press, 2009.

Szymanski, Ann-Marie E. "Beyond Parochialism: Southern Progressivism, Prohibition, and State-Building." *Journal of Southern History* 69 (February 2003): 107–36. doi.org/10.2307/30039842.

———. *Pathways to Prohibition: Radicals, Moderates, and Social Movement Outcomes*. Durham, NC: Duke University Press, 2003.

Tait, Jennifer Lynn Woodruff. *The Poisoned Chalice: Eucharistic Grape Juice and Common-Sense Realism in Victorian Methodism*. Tuscaloosa: University of Alabama Press, 2011.

Thompson Jr., H. Paul. *"A Most Stirring and Significant Episode": Religion and the Rise and Fall of Prohibition in Black Atlanta, 1865–1887*. DeKalb: Northern Illinois University Press, 2013.

———. "Temperance and Prohibition." *The Oxford Encyclopedia of American Urban History*, vol. 1, ed. Timothy J. Gilfoyle. New York: Oxford University Press, 2019, 406–30.

Timberlake, James H. *Prohibition and the Progressive Movement, 1900–1920*. Cambridge, MA: Harvard University Press, 1963.

Treviño, Roberto R. *The Church in the Barrio: Mexican American Ethno-Catholicism in Houston*. Chapel Hill: University of North Carolina Press, 2006.

Tuchmann, Barbara. *The Zimmerman Telegram*. New York: Ballantine Books, 1979.

Tucker, Karen B. Westerfield. *American Methodist Worship*. New York: Oxford University Press, 2001.

Turner, Nicole Meyers. *Soul Liberty: The Evolution of Black Religious Politics in Postemancipation Virginia*. Chapel Hill: University of North Carolina Press, 2020.

Tyrrell, Ian. *Woman's World/Woman's Empire: The Woman's Christian Temperance Union in International Perspective, 1800–1930*. Chapel Hill: University of North Carolina Press, 1991.

US Census Bureau. "2010 Census Regions and Divisions of the United States." www.census.gov/geographies/reference-maps/2010/geo/2010-census-regions-and-divisions-of-the-united-states.html (rev. August 20, 2018).

Vanderwood, Paul J. and Frank N. Samponaro. *Border Fury: A Picture Postcard Record of Mexico's Revolution and U.S. War Preparedness, 1910–1917*. Albuquerque: University of New Mexico Press, 1988.

Veach, Michael R. *Kentucky Bourbon Whiskey: An American Heritage*. Lexington: University of Kentucky Press, 2013.

Wentz, Abdel Ross. *A Basic History of Lutheranism in America*. Philadelphia: Muhlenberg Press, 1964.

West, Stephen A. "'A Hot Municipal Contest': Prohibition and Black Politics in Greenville, South Carolina, after Reconstruction." *Journal of the Gilded Age and Progressive Era* 11 (October 2012): 519–51. doi.org/10.1017/S1537781412000382.

Whitener, Daniel Jay. *Prohibition in North Carolina, 1715–1945.* Chapel Hill: University of North Carolina Press, 1945.

Wiggins, Sarah Woolfolk, ed. *From Civil War to Civil Rights—Alabama, 1860–1960.* Tuscaloosa: University of Alabama Press, 1987.

Willis, Lee L. *Southern Prohibition: Race, Reform, and Public Life in Middle Florida, 1821–1920.* Athens: University of Georgia Press, 2011.

Woodward, C. Vann. *The Strange Career of Jim Crow.* 2nd ed. New York: Oxford University Press, 1966.

———. *Tom Watson: Agrarian Rebel.* 1938. Rpt. New York: Oxford University Press, 1963.

Wuthnow, Robert. *Rough Country: How Texas Became America's Most Powerful Bible-Belt State.* Princeton, NJ: Princeton University Press, 2014.

Young, Darius J. *Robert R. Church Jr. and the African American Political Struggle.* Gainesville: University of Florida Press, 2019.

ENCYCLOPEDIAS AND MISCELLANEOUS

AP VoteCast. "2018 Voter Poll Results: Texas." *Washington Post.* www.washingtonpost.com /graphics/2018/politics/voter-polls/texas.html?noredirect=on&utm_term=.d12240126b59.

Arlington [VA] Public Library. "If You Don't Vote, You Don't Count." library.arlingtonva.us/2019 /08/15/if-you-dont-vote-you-dont-count (updated August 15, 2019*).

Center for the Study of Southern Culture and the Mississippi Humanities Council. *Mississippi Encyclopedia.* mississippiencyclopedia.org.

Central Arkansas Library System. *Encyclopedia of Arkansas.* encyclopediaofarkansas.net.

Encyclopedia of Alabama. Alabama Humanities Foundation and Auburn University. www.encyclopediaofalabama.org.

Faulkner, Ronnie W. "Furnifold McLendel Simmons (1854–1940)." *North Carolina History Project.* northcarolinahistory.org/encyclopedia/furnifold-mclendel-simmons-1854-1940 (accessed August 29, 2020).

Library of Virginia. *Education at Library of Virginia.* edu.lva.virginia.gov.

———. *Encyclopedia Virginia.* www.EncyclopediaVirginia.org.

The New Encyclopedia of Southern Culture. Chapel Hill: University of North Carolina Press, 2007.

Paulson, Darryl. "Florida's History of Suppressing Blacks' Votes." *Tampa Bay Times.* www.tampabay.com/news/perspective/floridas-history-of-suppressing-blacks-votes/2146546 (October 11, 2013).

Plocheck, Robert. "Prohibition Elections in Texas." *Texas Almanac,* www.texasalmanac.com/topics /elections/prohibition-elections-texas (accessed November 28, 2012). Texas State Historical Association.

Tennessee Encyclopedia. Tennessee Historical Society and University of Tennessee Press. tennesseeencyclopedia.net.

Texas State Historical Association. Handbook of Texas Online. www.tshaonline.org/handbook /online.

————. Texas Almanac. www.texasalmanac.com.

Watson, Elbert L. "J. Thomas Heflin." *Encyclopedia of Alabama.* www.encyclopediaofalabama .org/article/h-2952 (updated May 26, 2017).

Watson, Elwood. "Robert Reed Church, Sr. (1839–1912)." *Black Past.* www.blackpast.org/african -american-history/robert-reed-church-sr-1839-1912 (November 19, 2007).

THESES AND DISSERTATIONS

Barber, Marian Jean. "How the Irish, Germans, and Czechs Became Anglo: Race and Identity in the Texas-Mexico Borderlands." PhD diss., University of Texas at Austin, 2010.

Brian, Thomas J. "The 1887 Prohibition Crusade in Texas." MA thesis, Baylor University, 1972.

Cannon, Tina N. "Bordering on Trouble: Conflict between Tejanos and Anglos in South Texas, 1880–1920." MA thesis, Baylor University, 2001.

Carlson, Douglas Wiley. "Temperance Reform in the Cotton Kingdom." PhD diss., University of Illinois at Urbana-Champaign, 1982.

Davis, William Graham. "Attacking 'the Matchless Evil': Temperance and Prohibition in Mississippi, 1817–1908." PhD diss., Mississippi State University, 1975.

Garay, Maria Aurea Toxqui. "'El Recreo de los Amigos,' Mexico City's Pulquerias During the Liberal Republic (1856–1911)." PhD diss., University of Arizona, 2008.

Graves, Nicholas. "Pat Neff and the Pat Neff Collection: Biography, History, and Interpretation." MA thesis, Baylor University, 2011.

Jones, Christopher C. "'We Latter-day Saints Are Methodists': The Influence of Methodism on Early Mormon Religiosity." MA thesis, Brigham Young University, 2009.

Lancaster, Dennis R. "Dixie Wine." MA thesis, Brigham Young University, 1972.

Langston, Edward Lonnie. "The Impact of Prohibition on the Mexican–United States Border: The El Paso-Ciudad Juarez Case." MA thesis, Texas Tech University, 1974.

León, Arnoldo De. "Cuando vino la mexicanada: Authority, Race, and Conflict in West Texas, 1895–1924." PhD diss., University of Texas at Austin, 2007.

Locke, Joseph. "Making the Bible Belt: Preachers, Prohibition, and the Politicization of Southern Religion, 1877–1918." PhD diss., Rice University, 2012.

Magruder, Frank Abbott. "Recent Administration in Virginia." PhD diss., Johns Hopkins University, 1911.

Robinson, Robin Espy. "Monte Carlo of the Southwest: A Reinterpretation of U.S. Prohibition's Impact on Ciudad Juárez." MA thesis: University of Texas at Arlington, 1997.

Schneider, H. William. "Dr. James B. Cranfill's Prohibition Activities, 1882–1887." MA thesis, Baylor University, 1971.

Strickland, Michael Richard. "'Rum, Rebellion, Racketeers, and Rascals': Alexander Copeland Millar and the Fight to Preserve Prohibition in Arkansas, 1927–1933." MA thesis, University of Arkansas, 1993.

Sutton, Jared Paul. "Ethnic Minorities and Prohibition in Texas, 1887–1919." MA thesis, University of North Texas, 2006.

Watson, Larry Jerome. "Evangelical Protestants and the Prohibition Movement in Texas, 1887–1919." PhD diss., Texas A&M University, 1993.

Index

Mather, Increase, 17

Mayfield, Earle Bradford, 152–54, 158, 164, 239. *See also* Ku Klux Klan

McAdoo, William Gibbs, 155, 171

McKimil, Jim H., 130–31

Memphis, 56, 100, 127, 190

Mencken, H. L., 182

Methodist Board of Temperance, 180

Methodist Book of Discipline, 21, 205

Methodist Episcopal Church (MEC), 49, 115, 132, 216, 231

Methodist Episcopal Church South (MECS), 21, 49, 114, 159, 188, 231; General Conference, 34, 188

Mexican Americans, 89, 103, 129, 133, 203. *See also* Latinos; Tejanos

Mexico, 119, 159, 183

Michigan, 122, 188, 222, 233

Michigan Synod, 122, 233

Miller, Kelly, 163

Mills, Roger Quarles, 34–35

ministers, 1–2, 7–8, 15, 28–30, 33, 38, 45, 54–55, 63, 67, 103, 112–13, 115–19, 123, 126, 130, 132, 138, 142–43, 149, 152, 155–56, 159–60, 195. *See also* preachers; priests

Minnesota, 244

Mississippi, 4, 11, 34, 40, 48, 56, 83, 90, 94–96, 105–6, 156, 160, 164, 171–72, 184, 190–91, 194, 205

Missouri, 53, 83, 118, 122, 156, 171, 213–14

Missouri, Episcopal Diocese of, 118

Missouri Synod, 122

Mitchell, Arthur, 202

modernism: of prohibition, 16, 29, 110, 122–23, 199; of theology, 8, 16, 25, 29, 110, 122–23

Molly Pitcher Club, 180

Monk, Alonzo, 152

Moody, Dan, 154, 175, 177

Moore, Helen Edmunds, 183–84, 186, 194

Moore, Lillian V. D., 184

morality, 7, 16, 30, 33, 37, 47, 54, 110, 163, 187, 191, 193, 205

moral suasion, 10, 18, 32, 34–35

Moreland, Sinclair, 169–70

morphine, 116

Motlow Tunnel, 150

Mouzon, Edwin DuBose, 104, 113, 160,

Muenster, Texas, 112, 118–19

Muroch, W. L., 184

Murphy, Patrick J., 120–21

Nashville, TN, xii, 58, 75, 101, 150, 190

National American Woman Suffrage Association (NAWSA), 170–71, 174

National Association for the Advancement of Colored Peoples (NAACP), 178

National Baptist Convention (NBC), 28, 31, 109, 115–17, 132–33, 231

National Collegiate Athletic Association (NCAA), 205

National Council of Churches (NCC), 205, 229

National Temperance Society, 41

Native Americans. *See* Amerindians

Neal, Margie K., 178, 184

Neff, Pat, 146–48, 150, 152, 154, 174–75

New Deal, 9, 164, 186, 188, 198–99, 202

New Orleans, LA, 64, 105, 133, 214

Nineteenth Amendment, 80, 140, 167, 171–73, 184, 201

Nixon, T. J., 114

Norris, J. Frank, 8, 56, 142, 155–59, 161–62, 164, 166, 194, 206. *See also* First Baptist Church of Fort Worth

North Carolina, 9, 11, 36, 38, 44, 46–48, 50–54, 57–59, 64, 86–87, 89, 94, 96, 105, 107, 115, 127, 132, 142, 161, 163–64, 171–72, 177–78, 184, 189, 191–92, 196, 201, 203

Norwood, Hal L., 189

Oklahoma, 105, 156, 160, 214, 230

Oliver, William B., 171

ordinance, 27. *See also* sacrament

Overman, Lee Slater, 177

Overman Committee, 177

Paget, Ormund, 127–28, 131

Park, H. C., 138

CPSIA information can be obtained
at www.ICGtesting.com
Printed in the USA
LVHW110817070922
727759LV00003B/83